Roman History

An Enthralling Guide to the Republic, Empire, and Legacy of Ancient Rome and Byzantium

© Copyright 2025 - All rights reserved.

The content contained within this book may not be reproduced, duplicated, or transmitted without direct written permission from the author or the publisher.

Under no circumstances will any blame or legal responsibility be held against the publisher, or author, for any damages, reparation, or monetary loss due to the information contained within this book, either directly or indirectly.

Legal Notice:

This book is copyright protected. It is only for personal use. You cannot amend, distribute, sell, use, quote, or paraphrase any part, or the content within this book, without the consent of the author or publisher.

Disclaimer Notice:

Please note the information contained within this document is for educational and entertainment purposes only. All effort has been executed to present accurate, up-to-date, reliable, and complete information. No warranties of any kind are declared or implied. Readers acknowledge that the author is not engaging in the rendering of legal, financial, medical, or professional advice. The content within this book has been derived from various sources. Please consult a licensed professional before attempting any techniques outlined in this book.

By reading this document, the reader agrees that under no circumstances is the author responsible for any losses, direct or indirect, that are incurred as a result of the use of the information contained within this document, including, but not limited to, errors, omissions, or inaccuracies.

Free limited time bonus

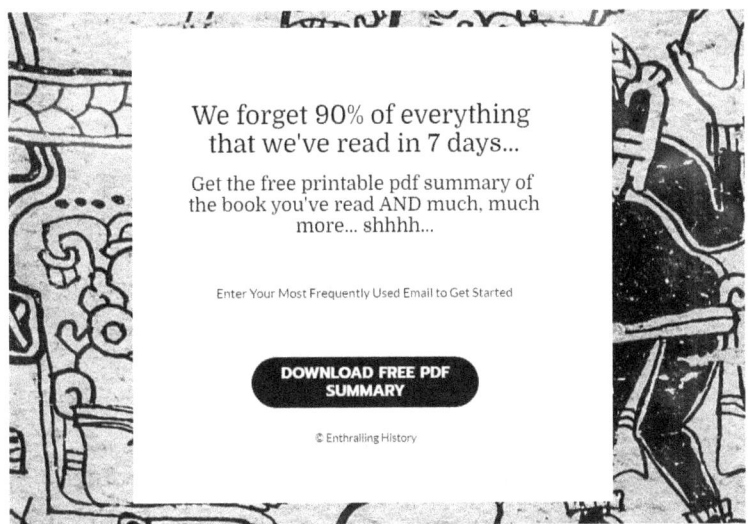

Stop for a moment. We have a free bonus set up for you. The problem is this: we forget 90% of everything that we read after 7 days. Crazy fact, right? Here's the solution: we've created a printable, 1-page pdf summary for this book that you're reading now. All you have to do to get your free pdf summary is to go to the following website: https://livetolearn.lpages.co/enthrallinghistory/

Or, Scan the QR code!

Once you do, it will be intuitive. Enjoy, and thank you!

Table of Contents

PART 1: ROMAN REPUBLIC 1
    INTRODUCTION 3
    SECTION ONE: LIFE AND TIMES OF THE EARLY REPUBLIC
    (500 BCE) 7
        CHAPTER 1: THE EARLY REPUBLIC 9
        CHAPTER 2: POLITICS AND POLITICAL INFLUENCE 18
        CHAPTER 3: SOCIETAL ROLES AND CULTURE 26
        CHAPTER 4: LITERATURE, ART, AND RELIGION 35
    SECTION TWO: WARFARE AND EXPANSION (350–200 BCE) 45
        CHAPTER 5: THE ROMAN ARMY 47
        CHAPTER 6: GREEK AND ROMAN RELATIONS 55
        CHAPTER 7: MEDITERRANEAN CONQUEST: THE PUNIC
        WARS 63
        CHAPTER 8: THE THIRD PUNIC WAR AND THE FALL OF
        CARTHAGE 71
    SECTION THREE: CONSEQUENCE AND LEGACY (120–40
    BCE) 79
        CHAPTER 9: THE GALLIC WARS 81
        CHAPTER 10: CAESAR AND POMPEY: TRIUMVIRATES
        AND CIVIL WAR 88
        CHAPTER 11: CAUSES AND CONSEQUENCES OF THE
        FALLEN REPUBLIC 96
        CHAPTER 12: INFLUENCE AND LEGACY OF THE ROMAN
        REPUBLIC 103
        CONCLUSION 112

PART 2: ROMAN EMPIRE 117
    INTRODUCTION 119
    CHAPTER 1 – AUGUSTUS AND THE CLAUDIANS 121
    CHAPTER 2 – THE PAX ROMANA 133
    CHAPTER 3 – THE FIVE GOOD EMPERORS 139
    CHAPTER 4 – THE THIRD CENTURY CRISIS 148
    CHAPTER 5 – FROM THE TETRARCHY TO THE FALL OF THE WEST 156
    CHAPTER 6 – TRADE AND TRANSPORTATION 165
    CHAPTER 7 – CENTRAL AND PROVINCIAL GOVERNING 174
    CHAPTER 8 – IMPERIAL ARMY AND WARFARE 182
    CHAPTER 9 – SOCIAL STRUCTURE AND STATUS 191
    CHAPTER 10 – ARTS AND ARCHITECTURE 199
    CHAPTER 11 – DAILY LIFE AND CUSTOMS 208
    CHAPTER 12 – RELIGION AND EDUCATION 218
    CONCLUSION 227
PART 3: THE BYZANTINE EMPIRE 229
    INTRODUCTION 231
    SECTION ONE: THE EARLY YEARS (330–565 CE) 233
        CHAPTER 1: FROM ROME TO CONSTANTINOPLE 235
        CHAPTER 2: THE EMPIRE OF CHRIST 248
        CHAPTER 3: SEPARATION FROM THE WEST 258
        CHAPTER 4: JUSTINIAN'S DREAM OF RESTORATION 267
    SECTION TWO: FROM LATIN TO GREEK EMPIRES (565–867 CE) 279
        CHAPTER 5: NEW ENEMIES AT THE GATES 281
        CHAPTER 6: THE ARAB INVASION 290
        CHAPTER 7: ICONOCLASM 302
    SECTION THREE: BYZANTIUM'S HEYDAY (867–1025 CE) 313
        CHAPTER 8: CHRISTIANIZATION OF THE SLAVS 315
        CHAPTER 9: THE BULGAR WARS 323
        CHAPTER 10: BASIL II: THE BULGARS' DEMISE 332
        CHAPTER 11: SIGNS OF DESTABILIZATION 346
        CHAPTER 12: THE GREAT SCHISM 358
    SECTION FOUR: DECLINE AND FALL (1081–1453 CE) 369
        CHAPTER 13: THE KOMNENIAN DYNASTY AND THE CRUSADES 371

CHAPTER 14: THE FOURTH CRUSADE AND RECOVERY 388
CHAPTER 15: THE PALAIOLOGOI: THE LAST STAND 398
BONUS CHAPTER: BYZANTINE ART, ARCHITECTURE, AND SOCIETY 409
CONCLUSION 417
HERE'S ANOTHER BOOK BY ENTHRALLING HISTORY THAT YOU MIGHT LIKE 419
FREE LIMITED TIME BONUS 420
REFERENCES 421
IMAGE SOURCES 430

Part 1: Roman Republic

An Enthralling Overview of the Rise and Fall

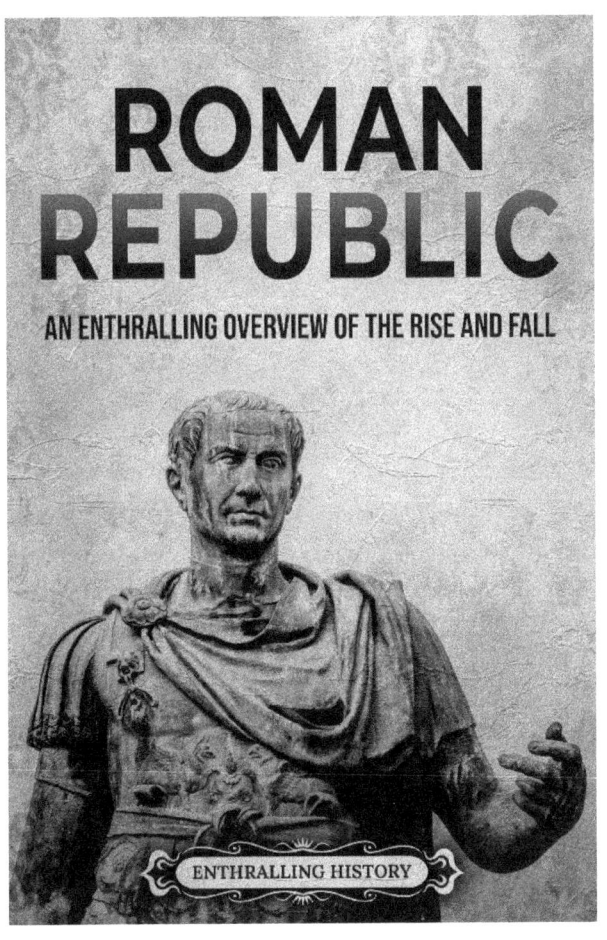

Introduction

In the dead of night, Prince Tarquin crept through the house, silently stepping over the bodyguard sleeping at Lucretia's door. He gently opened the door and slipped in. There! In the moonlight shining through the window, he saw the exquisite woman deep in sleep. He had met her earlier when he was a guest of her husband Collatinus, who often expressed pride in his cherished wife's stunning looks and exemplary character. One look and Tarquin was desperate to have her.

Stealthily, he approached her bed and placed his hand over her mouth as Lucretia awoke with a start. "Shh! It's me, Prince Tarquin. Oh, beautiful Lucretia! I have thought of nothing else since I first saw you. I want you for my own! Marry me, and be my queen. We will rule Rome together!"

Lucretia desperately struggled to push Tarquin away, but pressing his sword to her belly, he hissed, "Give in! Otherwise, I'll kill you and your bodyguard. I'll say I found him sleeping with you! What will your husband think of your virtue then?"

In the morning, Lucretia dressed in black and messaged her father and husband, who were with the army, laying siege on Ardea. "Come at once! Bring two witnesses with you."

Lucretia told her husband, father, and their two friends what Tarquin had done to her. The men comforted and reassured her, saying, "You did not consent, so you have no guilt; you have not sinned!"

But the distraught Lucretia cried out, "Give me your oath! Avenge my rape!"

She slipped a dagger from under her pillow and plunged it into her heart as Collatinus screamed in horror. Sobbing and shattered, he clasped her to him, kissing her and stroking her hair. "Lucretia! My darling wife! Oh, my poor Lucretia."

Her father and the other men collapsed to the floor, wailing. But then Brutus, one of the witnesses, suddenly stood up, jerked the dagger out of Lucretia's breast, and held it up, her blood dripping down his arm. "By Mars and all the gods, I will overthrow the power of the evil Tarquinii clan! We've had enough of tyrants ruling over us! We cannot tolerate this any longer. With Lucretia's blood, I swear my oath! Who is with me?"

Each man reached for the dagger, swearing, "By Lucretia's pure blood, we shall avenge this outrage by the king's son. The gods are our witnesses! We will drive out King Lucius Tarquinius Superbus, his accursed wife, and all his family! By fire, sword, and every means possible, we will eradicate the reign of kings over Rome!"[i]

Thus ended the Roman monarchy. It would soon be replaced by the Roman Republic. After tyrannical kings abused their power, the Romans boldly established a form of government never seen before, one that would influence new governments two millennia later. In its metamorphosis from a modest city-state, Rome conquered and ruled vast territories around the Mediterranean. The Romans were master assimilators, putting new knowledge and techniques into play in their evolving political system. And yet, social unrest, economic crises, and political instability rocked the republic until it eventually crumbled after five centuries.

We have much to learn from the sensational rise and cataclysmic fall of the Roman Republic. This book will bring the remarkable men and women who formed the republic to life as we examine how their brilliant triumphs and asinine misjudgments unfolded. What were the distinctive pillars of the republic's nascent government? How did the Romans ascend to power over central Italy only to be crushed by the Celts? Like a phoenix rising from the ashes, how did they bounce back, more competent and cunning, to confront Pyrrhus's war elephants in the Pyrrhic Wars and crush Carthage in the Punic Wars? As Rome warred with Greece, what factors led to supremacy over the Achaean League and Macedonia?

---

[i] Titus Livius, *The History of Rome, Vol. 1*, trans. George Baker (New York: Peter A. Mesier et al., 10). https://oll.libertyfund.org/title/baker-the-history-of-rome-vol-1.

And how did it all come crashing down? What social inequalities led to Rome's civil wars and internal storms? How did Spartacus's great slave revolt unfold? Why did the republican government unravel so much that Caesar, Pompey, and Crassus sidestepped the constitutional checks and balances, forming the First Triumvirate? How did Julius Caesar manipulate events to become Rome's dictator for life, and why did a mob of senators stab him to death?

Many books have been written about Rome, but this overview of the Roman Republic is not simply a chronological assortment of dry facts. It explores the enthralling stories of real people in all their pride and passion: the foresighted fathers of Rome's constitution, the ingenious military leaders, the disenfranchised lower classes, and the nefarious plotters. They all made Rome what it was for an astounding five centuries of empire-building, intrigue, and brutal feuds.

Exploring history is incredibly advantageous, as it helps us understand how our world got to where we are. In the past five centuries, over a hundred countries have abandoned monarchies or empires to form a government modeled on the founding principles of the Roman Republic. Understanding the past in all its glory and chaotic destruction inspires, instructs, and cautions us. What can Rome's experience teach us about today's social, economic, and political struggles? Let's step back twenty-seven centuries and find out.

Section One:
Life and Times of the Early Republic (500 BCE)

Chapter 1: The Early Republic

How was Rome ruled before it became a republic? For over two centuries, kings ruled Rome, some exemplary and some inept. The last king, Tarquinius Superbus (known as Tarquin), was evil personified. To comprehend his diabolical depths, we must step back a generation to Servius Tullius, the previous king. Tullius was the son of a slave-woman, and no one was sure who his father was, but whispers swirled that he was King Tarquinius Priscus's illegitimate son.

One night, screams rang out from the palace as assassins snuck in and murdered King Tarquinius. His sons were too young to rule, and Queen Tanaquil knew the Senate would elect another man to the throne. She had to make a quick decision to hold on to power so one of her sons could have a chance to rule. So, she plotted with Tullius.

Hurrying out to the balcony, she called down to the crowd assembled below, "The king is alive! He is seriously injured, but he is recovering from the attack. In the meantime, he has assigned Tullius to take care of his affairs."

For several weeks, Tullius pretended to be acting on orders from the king as the royal guard hunted down the assassins and executed some, while others fled the country. Then, Tanaquil walked out on the balcony again. "My dearest people, I bring sad news. My husband has died of his wounds. He assigned Tullius as his regent until our sons are old enough to rule."[i]

---

[i] Cassius Dio, *Roman History*, trans. H. B. Foster (Vol. I, Loeb Classical Library edition, New

Tullius became the de facto king while the boys were growing up, but even when they came of age, he kept the throne. Through those years, he cultivated popularity with the working-class plebeians by giving them land. Only landowners could vote, and, of course, they would vote for him. He even initiated a plan to emancipate the enslaved people and grant them citizenship. He infuriated the patrician aristocrats, who didn't want to lose their slaves.

Tullius assured Tanaquil's sons he would relinquish the throne when the time was right and gave his two daughters in marriage to the two princes. But the oldest son, Tarquin, knew he would never be king as long as Tullius lived. After his younger brother Arruns refused to join him in a coup, Tarquin angrily conspired with his brother's wife, Tullia Minor, and they poisoned Arruns. When Tarquin's wife criticized his devilry, he poisoned her, then married her sister, Tullia Minor.

Tarquin had been stirring up the senators and patricians, who disliked the king's support of the oppressed commoners and slaves. Hearing that Tarquin was in the Senate denouncing his kingship, King Tullius rushed to the building. But Tarquin grabbed him by his toga and pushed him out of the building, sending him tumbling down the steps. Tullius sat, bruised and confused, on the pavement, wondering why no one came to his aid. And where did his bodyguards get off to?

As Tullius limped away to be murdered by Tarquin's henchmen, the Senate elected Tarquin as Rome's new king. Hearing the news, his wife Tullia (Tullius's daughter) rushed to the Senate to congratulate her husband, then jumped back into her chariot. Charging full speed down the cobblestones, she ran over her father's body. The new king (and the last) protected himself against assassins by keeping a wall of bodyguards around him. He eliminated all the senators who might challenge him by executing or banishing most on trumped-up charges and clandestinely murdering others.[i]

York: Macmillan Publishers, 1914).
https://penelope.uchicago.edu/Thayer/E/Roman/Texts/Cassius_Dio/1*.html.
[i] Livius, *The History of Rome, Vol. 1.*

Tullia drove over her father's body. Painting by Jean Bardin. [1]

Tarquin didn't even trust his close friends who had supported his coup d'état. Instead of appointing them as senators, he suppressed the Senate's power. He ruled with only his sons, paranoid that anyone else would kill or displace him. He even killed family members he considered a threat, including his sister's son and husband. Her other son, Brutus, pretended to be mentally impaired, so Tarquin left him alone.

Brutus spearheaded the revolution after Lucretia's rape, toppling his uncle's throne and ending the monarchy begun by the wolf-child Romulus, Rome's mythical founder. A crowd gathered as the men carried Lucretia's body into the Forum. Brutus explained that he wasn't really mentally disabled; it was a ruse to survive King Tarquin's purges. Now he called out, "Act like men and Romans! Take up arms against our shameless enemies!"

One look at Lucretia's bloodstained corpse convinced most of the crowd. The senators knew a change was necessary for their survival. King Tarquin and his sons had ruled through fear and coercion and were hated by most Romans. With the crowd's approval, the senators voted to end the monarchy, eject the Tarquin family, and establish a different type of government. The royal family slipped out of Rome, away from the angry citizens, to drum up support from a few Etruscan and Latin cities.

In 509 BCE, Rome's citizens created a new government: the republic. They annually elected magistrates, established assemblies representing the people, and instituted the separation of powers. The stronger constitution required checks and balances to keep politicians in line. Politics now included novel concepts like filibusters, impeachments, quorum requirements, regular elections, term limits, and vetoes. The constitution was fluid, driven by Rome's expanding borders and tensions between the plebeian workers and the patrician aristocrats.

Instead of a king, the new republic established two heads of state called consuls, who ruled jointly for a one-year term. The first two consuls were Lucius Junius Brutus, the ringleader of the revolution, and Lucius Tarquinius Collatinus, Lucretia's husband. They immediately appointed new senators, bringing the number back to three hundred. Oddly, the consuls were both members of the Tarquin family that had been forced into exile. Brutus was King Tarquinius Superbus's nephew and King Tarquinius Priscus's grandson. Collatinus was King Tarquinius Priscus's nephew and a first cousin of his wife's rapist, Prince Tarquin.

Within weeks, the Tarquinian conspiracy arose: the exiled king's attempt to recapture his throne. He still had insiders among Rome's elite stirring up dissent. Brutus was unaware that his two sons and his wife's brothers were the chief conspirators. A slave named Vindicius came upon a gruesome scene. The plotters were gathered around the corpse of a man they'd killed, swearing an oath by pouring out his blood and touching his intestines. Unnoticed, Vindicius slipped away to tell the consuls that the conspirators had sworn to kill them. Soldiers arrested the rebels and discovered letters to King Tarquin in their possession.

Brutus sentenced his own sons to death for conspiracy.[3]

Brutus sentenced his sons, Titus and Tiberius, to death, grimly watching their execution. After the rest of the conspirators were executed, the Romans were uneasy about Collatinus; after all, he was a Tarquin. Collatinus resigned as consul and went into exile. Brutus's execution of his sons spared his removal.[i] Yet before his one-year term was up, he died in battle against the former royal family. He and his first cousin, Prince Arruns, impaled each other in a cavalry charge.

The center of the new republic was the Forum: Rome's political, religious, and social hub. Initially a rectangular open-air gathering place, it soon housed elegant arches, basilicas, monuments, statues, and temples. People assembled in the Forum for business affairs, criminal trials, elections, gladiator matches, public meetings, religious ceremonies, speeches, and trade. The Senate met in the Forum to debate proposed laws and vote.

From its inception, constant warfare defined the Roman Republic. For the first two hundred years, Rome warred against other Italian tribes and the invading Celts. The Romans displayed incredible tenacity in heroic battles and sprang back from catastrophic losses. From 483 to 476 BCE, Rome fended off the Etruscan city of Veii, just ten miles north of Rome. The Etruscans allied with the Sabines, an Apennine Mountain tribe. After joining the nearby Latins, their kinsmen, the Romans finally defeated the Veientes and Sabines, forcing them to pay tribute.

In 458 BCE, another Apennine Mountain tribe called the Aequi attacked while Rome was dealing with a slave revolt, the death of a consul, and friction between the plebeians and patricians. Rome defeated the Aequi, but the following year, the Aequi appeared again, to the Romans' great annoyance. In a time of great peril, the Roman constitution permitted the Romans to nominate a temporary dictator to deal with the crisis, and they chose Cincinnatus. The brilliant leader defeated the Aequi in sixteen days with hardly any bloodshed. He then resigned from his dictatorship and returned to his farm.

Suddenly, a new enemy exploded onto the scene: the Celts from eastern Gaul (France). The Gallic Senones had surged over the Alps, wreaking havoc in northern Italy and then settling down and building Mediolanum (today's Milan). Hearing of central Italy's rich farmland that

---

[i] Plutarch, *The Parallel Lives*. (Volume I: Loeb Classical Library edition, 1914).
https://penelope.uchicago.edu/Thayer/E/Roman/Texts/Plutarch/Lives/Publicola*.html

produced olives, figs, and grapes for fine wines, the Senones sent their warriors to invade the Etruscan city of Clusium. When the Etruscans appealed to Rome for help, the Romans sent three ambassadors, who informed the Celts that if they attacked Clusium, they would have to fight Rome.

The tense standoff ended in a brawl, and one of the ambassadors killed a Senone war chief, a grave breach of the ancient law shared by the nations. Rome was unprepared for the consequences. With lightning speed, the Senones, led by their chieftain Brennus, marched out to confront Rome. The Romans quickly mustered their army and met the Senones at the Tiber River, several miles north of Rome.

In the 390 BCE Battle of the Allia, the Senone chief Brennus charged through the Romans' middle line, cutting its army in two. In terror, Rome's left flank plunged into the river, where many drowned, weighed down by their armor in the swift current. The ones who managed to swim to the other side escaped to Veii. Meanwhile, the right flank desperately made a break for Rome; over half the Roman army fell in battle or drowned that day.

The Senones couldn't believe they had so easily trounced Rome. They set about pillaging the Roman camp for two days, then arrived at Rome at sunset. Oddly, the city gates were open, and no one appeared to be defending the city. Was it a trap? The Celts decided to wait until morning, unwilling to walk into an ambush at night. The gates were, in fact, undefended. Most of the Romans had fled to the hills. The army and the city leaders had fenced off the steep Capitoline Hill inside Rome and were bunkered down at the top. Some elderly priests and former consuls arrayed themselves in their finest robes and sat in their ivory chairs in the Forum.

In the morning, the Celts hesitantly entered Rome, expecting an attack at any moment. But no one challenged them. It was a ghost town! Making their way to the Forum, they found the elders stoically seated in majestic splendor. Were they gods? One Celt reached out to touch an ancient patrician's beard and received a rap on the head with the elder's staff. They were men! The invaders hewed down the elders and anyone else foolish enough to stay in the city, but the men on the steep Capitoline Hill behind the barricades managed to hold them off.

The death of the Consul Papirius by Philipp Friedrich Hetsch. [a]

The rest of Rome was wide open for the Celts to plunder and burn, which they did so for the next seven months, destroying relics and records of Rome's ancient history. The military on Capitoline Hill had stockpiled food, but the Senones were scavenging the surrounding farms and villages. The one-time Roman dictator Camillus, who had been exiled by political enemies, lived in the town of Ardea. He and the men of Ardea observed that the Celts got drunk at night, so they launched a night raid, wiping out the raiding party. This victory motivated the Roman soldiers in Veii to ask Camillus to lead them in retaking Rome.

Camillus agreed but insisted that Rome's leadership had to reverse his exile and officially endorse his new dictatorship. For that to happen, someone had to communicate with the Roman leaders bunkered down at Capitoline Hill. A young man knew of a secret path up the hill, so he snuck into Rome by night, climbing up the steep cliffside. He met with the senators, who appointed Camillus as dictator. Camillus put together an army of twelve thousand men, including Etruscan allies. At this point, the men on Capitoline Hill were starving. How long would it be before Camillus's force could rescue them?[i]

---

[i] Livius, *The History of Rome, Vol. 3*.

The Celts were likewise suffering from dysentery in a city reeking of rotting, unburied corpses in the summer heat. The Senones were hill people with no acquired immunity to malaria, which devastated their numbers. Chief Brennus met with Rome's tribune Sulpicius to mediate an end to the siege. The Celts agreed to leave Rome in exchange for one thousand pounds of gold. But the Romans felt the scale was faulty. As the Senones and Romans were contesting the scale's integrity, Camillus suddenly marched in with his twelve thousand soldiers. Pointing his sword at the Celts, he snarled, "Leave now, Senones! Iron will deliver Rome, not gold!"[i]

The Senones only retreated eight miles from Rome, which proved to be fatal. Camillus attacked the next day, annihilating the entire Celtic army. Rome spent the next fifty years rebuilding the city and consolidating authority over the central and southern Italian tribes. By 295 BCE, Rome ruled over all of central Italy and most of the southern peninsula. Now, it was time to conquer the Mediterranean.

The Pyrrhic War, which lasted from 280 to 275 BCE, involved Epirus "aiding" the Greek city-states of southern Italy in their struggle against Rome. Sicily, Carthage, and Italy's Samnite and Etruscan tribes all got involved in battles, which ultimately brought southern Italy under the Roman fold. Then, Rome and Carthage clashed in the legendary Punic Wars, which lasted from 264 to 146 BCE, while Rome simultaneously fought against the Macedonian Kingdom, the Achaean League in Corinth, and the Seleucid Empire.

Rome's most lethal war was its toxic conflict between the working-class plebeians and the aristocratic patricians. The plebeians lost their ancestral farmland to huge slave-operated plantations owned by the patricians, who grew fabulously wealthy as the plebeians sunk deeper into debt. A group of prisoner-of-war slaves led a revolt, amassing an army of thousands. They were able to hold off the Roman forces at Mount Vesuvius.

Rome's internal unrest led to the First Triumvirate, led by Crassus, Rome's richest man, and two brilliant war heroes: Pompey and Caesar. This leadership change spelled the beginning of the end for the Roman Republic. It opened the door to the Roman Empire, which would be led by emperors instead of consuls. Throughout the five centuries of the republic, the Romans had to adapt to several challenges. They evolved

---

[i] Plutarch, *The Parallel Lives, Vol. 2.*

from a city-state into a republic that spanned three continents, stretching from the Middle East to Britain and south to North Africa.

How would the conquered territories be ruled, though? The elite Romans had to deal with the plebeian commoners, who demanded equal representation in the government, and the question of freeing the slaves. No sooner was one predicament addressed than another emerged. But they weathered the crises for five centuries while conquering 750,000 square miles of territory and spreading their language, culture, and political system throughout the known world.

Chapter 2: Politics and Political Influence

What did this new government of the Roman Republic look like? Its official title was *Senatus Populusque Romanus*: the Senate and People of Rome. After perceiving that rule by hereditary kingship was rife with problems, the Romans established a government that endured until 27 BCE, when emperors began ruling Rome. Up to this point, most nations were monarchies, except for Greece, where Athens was developing a democracy. A republic was a completely new system. It did not have a king, but it was not quite a democracy either, especially not in the beginning. Athenian democracy was a government where all classes had a vote, while the elite patricians initially held power in the Roman Republic.

When Rome was a city-state, its legal system applied only to Roman citizens: male descendants of Rome's founding tribes. As it began to conquer neighboring regions, the new territories' courts decided on legal disputes based on their own laws. However, as Rome expanded and conquered other nations, they used the *jus gentium* or "law of nations" for non-Romans living within new Roman territory. These were basic "natural" laws and legal traditions that most nations of the day considered universal.

As for Rome itself, the republic started with unwritten laws based on customs and precedents. The Twelve Tables, which stood in the Forum, was Rome's first written legislation, passed in 450 BCE to provide a standard code for all citizens. Before this, the plebeian working class often had no idea what the laws were, leaving them vulnerable to abuse by the patrician upper class. The Twelve Tables consolidated earlier unwritten laws on legal procedures, family laws, property laws, personal injury laws, and sacred laws.

Rome's constitution was a work in process. Its earliest rules were unwritten, such as laws dealing with elections, assemblies, and Senate functions. Later, new legislation inscribed in bronze was placed at eye level in public areas where all could read them. Of course, not everyone could read, but they were available so literate individuals could explain them to the masses. The Senate issued new decrees by recommending a course of action for the magistrates to enforce.[i] An innovation of the Romans was the power of *intercessio* or veto. A consul could veto his co-consul's actions, and tribunes could protect the plebeians by vetoing senatorial decrees.

Each year, two men were elected to serve as consuls. In Rome, the consuls were the chief administrators of all aspects of life, with all other leaders subordinate to them except for the tribunes. They decided what business the Senate would discuss and enforced the Senate's mandates. They also were the commanders in chief of the military.[ii] Rome often had two forces fighting on different fronts, so the consuls would split up. For instance, one might be fighting in Greece, while the other would be in Carthage.

Why two commanders in chief? Some city-states already had two kings, such as in Sparta, where one headed the military and the other the political arena. But the kings usually served for life, while Rome's consuls served for one year. For the Romans, it was a matter of checks and balances; if one consul made idiotic decisions, the other could veto him. If a consul abused his powers, he faced prosecution at the end of his term. One consul led the Centuriate Assembly, which was comprised of military centuries (one hundred soldiers); each century's collective vote was counted rather than individual votes. The other consul led the Assembly of Tribes, a non-military assembly where each "tribe" represented a geographical division.

---

[i] Andrew Lintott, *The Constitution of the Roman Republic* (Oxford: Oxford University Press, 2003), 1-4.

[ii] Lintott, *The Constitution*, 17.

The Roman monarchy had senators whose chief function was to elect kings and advise them. The senators' role changed in the Roman Republic. They instead gave "recommendations" to the magistrates, who essentially considered them new laws. In the monarchy, the Senate had focused on internal affairs; in the republic, the senators concentrated on foreign policy for all the new regions Rome was conquering. They controlled the budget, giving them power over the military. Senatorial power over all aspects of the Roman Republic grew over time.

In the early republic, the consuls appointed senators from the elite patrician class. After about two centuries, new senators were appointed for a life term out of a pool of magistrates, including plebeians and freed slaves. The republic started out with one hundred senators but grew to three hundred by 312 BCE. Some consuls liked to "pack" the Senate with appointees who were likely to support them, so by the end of the Roman Republic, the number of senators grew to one thousand.

If Rome was embroiled in a crisis, the Senate could recommend a temporary dictator. One of the consuls would nominate him to the *Comitia Curiata* (the Curiate Assembly) for approval. The dictator only served for the length of the crisis, which would last anywhere from several weeks to a few months. After the first three centuries of the republic, the plebeians' power over the position of dictator drastically weakened it.

Censors and praetors served under the consuls. The censors administered the census and "censored" what they considered public immorality or a breach of ethics. They had the power to strip a person of citizenship if he committed unworthy actions.[i] The praetors served dual roles as army generals and judges. When Rome's borders extended out of Italy, the praetors became governors of the provinces. If both consuls were away at war, the *praetor urbanus* led Rome.

Living in Rome didn't automatically make a person a citizen. Only non-enslaved males aged sixteen and up who descended from Rome's original tribes could be full citizens. Women could have limited citizenship through their fathers or husbands but could not vote, hold political office, or attend assemblies. To flaunt their status, citizens wore white togas, the symbol of full legal rights, including voting rights. Citizens belonged to the Curate Assembly (*Comitia Curiata*), where they cast their votes on legislative matters. The Curate Assembly was later split into the

---

[i] Livius, *The History of Rome*, Vol. 4.

Assembly of Tribes and the Centuriate Assembly. A third assembly, the Plebeian Assembly, was added in 494 BCE to represent the working class.

Two other political roles were tribunes and magistrates. With up to ten elected tribunes, the *tribunus plebis* led the Plebeian Assembly for the working class. They proposed legislation for the assembly's vote and vetoed senatorial legislation that favored the aristocrats over the ordinary people. The military tribunes held a high rank in the army and served at least five years. Each legion, which consisted of about five thousand men, had two commanders serving from a rotation of six tribunes. The *tribuni aerarii* administered the treasury and tax collection. The tribuni militum consulari potestate (military tribunes with consular authority) occasionally served instead of consuls in the early republic. A plebeian could be a military tribune with consular authority but not a consul.

Magistrates had authority over a specific geographical area or a particular duty. The patricians and eventually the plebeians elected them for one-year terms. After their year was up, they couldn't stand for election for another decade. The two top magistrates were the consuls, and if the times called for a dictator, he would be a magistrate. Other magistrates served as military commanders, censors, praetors, and tribunes.

At the top of Rome's society and politics were the patricians: wealthy, aristocratic citizens from fifty leading families (*gens*) with large farms. Among the most prominent ancient families were the Cornelii, Claudii, Fabii, Valerii, and Aemilii. Most of the population was in the middle and formed the plebeian working class. The enslaved people were at the bottom of society; these people were prisoners of war or people enslaved due to their debts. The enslaved population comprised up to 20 percent of Rome's population and had virtually no rights.

Initially, the patricians held almost absolute power over the government, religious affairs, and the military. They served as patrons for "clients," usually plebeians and freed slaves (freedmen) considered part of the extended *gens* (family clan). The patrons negotiated marriages and provided food, legal assistance, protection, financial loans, and assistance with business transactions. The clients would greet their patron at dawn with their needs, and after assisting them, the patron would walk to the Forum, accompanied by his clients. The more clients he had, the higher his prestige!

The plebeians (plebs) were the working class. They were the bakers, builders, craftsmen, farmers, and small business owners, to name a few. In the early republic, they held minimal political clout, but that quickly changed, as they realized the patricians depended on them for life's basic needs. In the Conflict of the Orders—the struggle of the plebeians against patrician discrimination—they exercised *secessio plebis*: "plebeian withdrawal" or going on strike. They left their shops, farms, and even the army for a short time. The patricians had to fend for themselves. The strike reminded them how much they depended on the plebeians and forced them to listen to the plebeians' grievances.

The plebeian soldiers refused to fight due to injustices. Artist: B. Barloccini. '

One injustice at the top of the plebeians' list was the senators failing to inform the plebeians of new laws, which resulted in the magistrates arresting them for breaking them. The plebeians were fined or imprisoned for laws they didn't even know existed. Another grievance for the plebeians was losing the lands where they had been tenant farmers, as the aristocratic landowners began using more slave labor due to all the prisoners of war.

All the plebeians could do was head to the towns and cities and try to find work. They would endure beatings and imprisonment if they couldn't pay their debts. Gradually, the plebeians began to win political leverage with their strikes. In 494 BCE, the plebeian soldiers went on strike when Rome clashed with the Aequi, Sabines, and Volsci. Their refusal to fight the enemy won them the Plebeian Council, the plebeian tribune, and the right to vote for their officials.

After Rome conquered the Hernici tribe south of Rome in 486 BCE, the consul Spurius Cassius Vecellinus proposed giving one-third of the Hernici lands to the plebeians. Another one-third would go to their Latin allies who had helped win the war, and the Hernici would keep one-third of their farms. The patricians hated this idea because they wouldn't get any land. They saw Cassius as a traitor. He was tried for treason and executed at the end of his one-year term.

When the Senone Gauls sacked Rome, the plebeians suffered devastating losses to their shops and farms. The military also suffered, as the men weren't paid for their services and had no income from their destroyed shops, farms, or trades. Marcus Manlius Capitolinus, a former consul and war hero, saw a centurion he knew who had defended Rome. The centurion was now poverty-stricken, unable to pay his debts. When Manlius saw him marched to prison, he jumped in and paid his debt on the spot.

After this experience, Manlius became increasingly aware of the crushing debt looming over most of the plebeians and did what he could to help them. He sold his land to pay off debts and advocated on their behalf against the Senate, which was misusing funds that could ease the plebeians' suffering. His efforts at swaying the Senate did not go well; the patricians pushed him off the eighty-foot-high Tarpeian Rock, killing him.

However, Camillus, who had earlier obliterated the Senones, was appointed dictator again to fight another Celtic onslaught. He surprisingly came to the plebeians' aid after initially siding with the patricians. The plebeians demanded one of the consuls be plebeian, and Camillus negotiated an agreement with the Senate. He built the Temple of Concord next to the Forum to celebrate the new co-rule of plebeians and patricians.

Soon, the plebeians began filling the offices of censor and dictator, but as they progressed in political status, some became nouveau-riche social climbers. The new elites were excited about their surge to the top while ignoring the needs of the working poor. However, the brothers Tiberius and Gaius Gracchus, who both served as plebeian tribunes, championed social reform yet paid a bitter price.

The Gracchi brothers advocated for land redistribution.⁵

As Rome conquered additional territory, the aristocratic patricians grabbed most of the newly acquired farmland. After Tiberius's election in 133 BCE, he proposed that the maximum property one person could hold should be about 325 acres. The rest of the land would be redistributed to the war veterans and homeless poor in plots of about twenty acres. The senators hated the idea because they would have to give up a lot of lands, which were their source of wealth.

Tiberius's term was running out, and the matter was still unsettled, so he ran for reelection. But running for a consecutive term went against precedent. His political enemies accused him of aspiring to be a tyrant (an absolute ruler who comes into power outside the usual channels). On election day, the senators and other patricians led a mob that surrounded Tiberius and three hundred supporters, beating them to death with wooden chairs and clubs.

Tiberius's brother Gaius was elected as tribune ten years later. He supported his brother's land redistribution reform and insisted on the government funding basic armor and weapons for the soldiers. Many poor citizens were drafted into the military but went into debt paying for their equipment. His political opponents stirred up a riot, and one of the rioters died in the fray, stirring the Senate to declare Gaius an enemy of the state without a jury trial. Gaius committed suicide before he could be executed, but the Senate rounded up three thousand of his supporters and executed them.

The plebeian tribune Drusus continued to fight for land redistribution and for everyone living in Italy to become citizens. His assassination sparked the Social War (91-87 BCE), as the Italian tribes revolted, demanding the right to vote in Rome's elections and to be protected by Roman law. The Senate appointed Gaius Marius, a plebeian tribune and uncle to Julius Caesar, to subdue the rebels. As the war dragged on, Marius killed or captured thirteen thousand rebels but then became ill and had to end the campaign. Despite technically winning the brutal war, Rome finally gave citizenship rights and the right to vote to all free males on Italy's mainland.

Chapter 3: Societal Roles and Culture

Rome's extraordinary military conquests are enthralling to read about, as are its political intrigues, but what about the lives of the ordinary people? How did they live? What sort of jobs did they have? What did they eat, and what were their living conditions? What were their gender roles and expectations? And how did slavery impact Roman society? Let's explore

What sort of housing did the Romans have? It depended on the family's economic status. About 80 percent of the urban population lived in tiny apartments in buildings known as *insulae*. These multi-family dwellings could house up to fifty people and were three to five stories high. Some were higher, but after fires and earthquakes killed many citizens, laws limited the height of new buildings.

The first floor usually had shops, and the upper floors contained two-room apartments for families, although some *insulae* had larger apartments on the lower floors. The *insulae* surrounded a city block, with a row of connected rowhouses running along the street and a central courtyard in the middle. Most *insulae* were constructed of shoddy materials, such as wood and mudbrick, making them susceptible to fire and collapse.

This 3rd-century BCE insula is west of Rome in Ostia.⁶

Wealthy aristocrats usually had two homes: a single-family *domus* in the city and a large private villa in the suburbs or the countryside. The *domus* had an exquisitely decorated entryway leading to the atrium, a grand hall where the hosts welcomed their guests. A large rectangular opening in the atrium's roof let in sunlight, and directly underneath was a shallow pool that collected rainwater with pipes leading to an underground cistern. The family left offerings to the household gods and their ancestral spirits at a household shrine in the atrium.

Rooms leading out of the atrium included the *tablinum* or the master's office, where the men received their clients' appeals and conducted business. The dining room was spectacularly decorated, with murals on the walls and tile mosaics on the floor to dazzle the family's frequent dinner-party guests. Instead of chairs, the dining room had several couches, where the family and guests reclined to eat from small tables. A garden often graced the rear of the home.

The villas of upper-class families didn't have the noise, offensive odors, and crime of the city and were a pleasant weekend retreat. Often, this was where the wife and children spent most of their time, as it was comfortable and offered more space for the children to play. Like the *domus*, they usually had a central, open-air atrium or courtyard surrounded by living areas, bedrooms, and servant quarters.

Exquisite frescoes like this one in Pompeii decorated Roman villas. [7]

Close to the time the Roman Republic was established, the Etruscans built Rome's first sewers. The Cloaca Maxima, which still operates today, was an open channel that drained the marshy areas, reducing the malaria-causing mosquitoes. It was later covered and used to drain rainwater from the streets and sewage from the public latrines into the Tiber River.[i] The *insulae* had running water on the lower floors but no indoor toilets. Everyone had to use a public latrine or chamber pots.

Daily life for people in the Roman Republic depended on one's social class and level of wealth. Rome's population wasn't just Roman. It never was just Roman, even in their mythological beginnings. When Romulus founded Rome, there weren't enough women for all the men, so they abducted young women from the Sabine tribe to marry. Further back in time, Romulus's ancestors were refugees from Troy who intermarried with the Latin tribe. Rome's founding families were a blend of several ethnicities.

---

[i] Emily Gowers, "The Anatomy of Rome from Capitol to Cloaca," *The Journal of Roman Studies* Vol.85 (1995): 23-32.

Rome was a cosmopolitan mixture of Italian tribes and merchant traders from around the Mediterranean: Egyptians and Carthaginians from North Africa, Syrians and Jews from the Levant, and seafaring Greeks. As the republic conquered and expanded, Rome drew in people from present-day Spain, France, and Great Britain. The Roman military and merchants traveled and lived on three continents. That meant many Romans were multi-lingual and adopted some of the food, apparel, and customs from other parts of the world.

For all its grandeur, the streets of Rome could be unpleasant. Before indoor plumbing became widely available, chamber pots of feces and urine were emptied from windows and balconies to the street below, leaving a smelly, slippery, unhygienic mess for pedestrians to gingerly tread through. Rome was rife with crime, especially at night. And its population of at least a million was noisy.

What sort of medical assistance was available in a crowded, unsanitary city with the looming threat of malaria? Tomb art shows a woman giving birth in a unique reclining chair with an opening in the seat for the newborn to pass through. Artifacts show Roman doctors had steel forceps, probes, scalpels, and wound retractors. Most doctors in Rome were Greek and believed the Greek god Apollo and other Greek deities had healing powers. When a plague swept through Italy in 431 BCE, they built a temple to Apollo Medicus in Rome. Romans who didn't use Greek doctors depended on the family head to dispense traditional medicine.

What did the Romans eat? It depended on their economic level, but most Romans ate three meals daily. Ancient murals give glimpses of what was served in upper-class homes, and archaeologists have examined ancient food stores, garbage piles, and human feces for more clues. The mainstays of the lower classes were dried legumes and millet porridge. All classes enjoyed fermented fish sauces made from salted and dried fish guts.

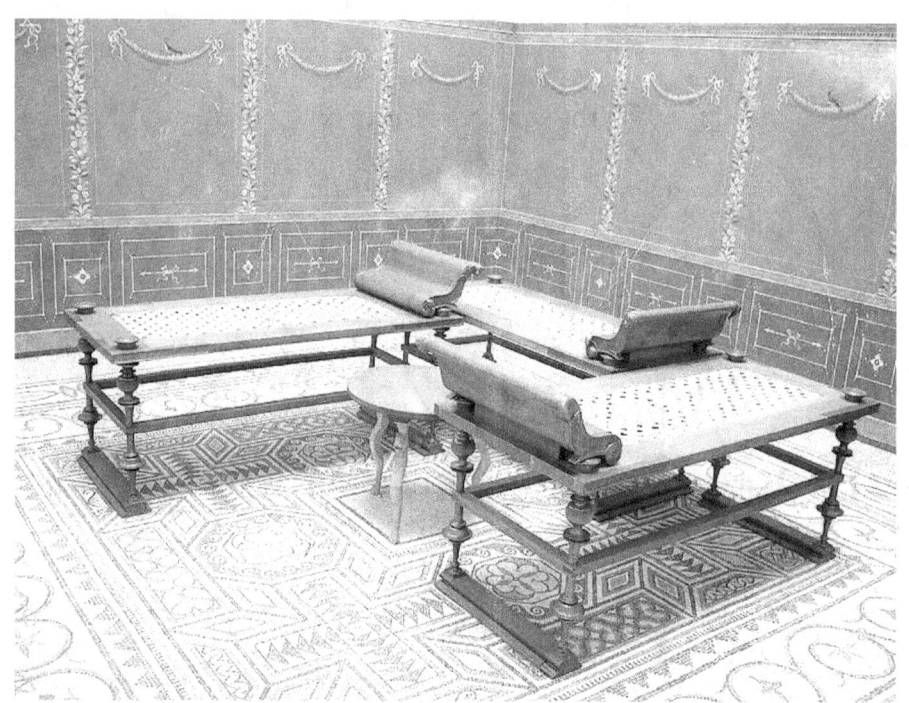

The triclinium (dining room) of elite Roman homes had couches and small tables.*

Upper-class Romans ate a diet similar to today's Mediterranean diet; it featured fish, shellfish, cheese, eggs, chickens, pheasants, and other birds for protein. They ate legumes, bread, and a wide array of vegetables and fruits, such as apples, beans, grapes, onions, pears, and olives. They cherished cabbage as a source of good health. They had no tomatoes, as those originated in South America and weren't introduced until much later. With no ovens in the home for baking, they purchased bread from bakeries.

Rome was established as an agricultural community, where most men served dual roles as farmers and soldiers. By the time of the Roman Republic, these were still the two primary occupations. They also had more specialized careers, primarily employing plebeians, such as accountants, architects, artists, bankers, construction workers, craftsmen, doctors, engineers, entertainers, fishermen, government officials, jewelers, merchants, shopkeepers, sailors, teachers, tax collectors, and smiths.

Roman tradition held that senators should be farmers who occasionally served the state. Senators who commanded military legions often became the governors of new provinces they brought into the republic. The governmental changes in the republic required the senators to spend more time dealing with administrative tasks and financial and military decisions, as well as organizing diplomatic missions. The senators still owned their farms; in fact, as Rome conquered new lands, the senators and other patricians acquired huge plantations. But they usually had a land manager and dozens or hundreds of enslaved people working the fields.

At the beginning of the Roman Republic, the senators were all from the patrician class and felt that work in trade and commerce was déclassé, fit only for the plebeians. Furthermore, engaging in business could present a conflict of interest in politics. They even had laws restricting senators' engagement in commodities; for instance, they couldn't own a merchant ship.[i] But they found ways around the law, becoming silent partners and investors in business ventures, as they were unwilling to let the plebeians reap all the vast riches available in commerce. Once plebeians became part of the Senate, class lines began to blur.

A huge issue during the republic was unemployment, which was primarily due to previous tenant farmers being displaced by slave labor on the plantations. Toward the end of the republic, more than 300,000 people had gravitated toward Rome in hopes of finding work, to no avail. Sometimes, Rome sent these unemployed farmers and other unemployed workers to new colonies it established around the Mediterranean.

Freedmen (freed slaves) competed with these displaced farmers; they sometimes had more advanced skills, depending on their previous occupation or education before becoming enslaved. They also had the patronage of their former owners, which could open doors of opportunity.[ii] Freedmen often worked as bakers, carpenters, and in the fish trade, while their wives worked as midwives, hairdressers, or seamstresses.

What gender roles did men and women have in the Roman Republic? Rome was clearly male-dominated. The husband and/or father was the undisputed master of the home. Husbands openly had mistresses, visited prostitutes, and had sexual relationships with adolescent boys who were

---

[i] Lionel Casson, *Everyday Life in Ancient Rome*, (Baltimore: Johns Hopkins University Press, 1998), 48-56.

[ii] Cory R DiBacco, "The Position of Freedmen in Roman Society," *MAD-RUSH Undergraduate Research Conference*, (Spring 2017), JMU Scholarly Commons. https://commons.lib.jmu.edu/cgi/viewcontent.cgi?article=1069&context=madrush.

usually slaves or freed slaves. Male same-sex relationships were socially acceptable as long as the older man was the dominant partner with a male of lower social status.

A woman's primary role was the caretaker of the home and raising children. She was expected to be a virgin before marriage and chaste afterward. Fathers arranged marriages for their daughters, and a woman could use either her husband's surname or her father's surname after marriage.

Upper-class girls went to school but not as long as boys did. They could read and write and were knowledgeable in literature and philosophy. Girls from poor families did not attend school, although their brothers might. Plebeian women were out in public much more than aristocratic women because many had jobs. They could be shopkeepers, hairdressers, midwives, and craftworkers.

If a woman had legal or financial affairs that needed attention, even with inherited property, she usually had to have a male relative take care of it. However, widows had more freedom to manage their business affairs. By Roman law, a woman's property could not be comingled with her husband's, and if they divorced, she got it back. Unfortunately, she did not get custody of her children if she divorced.

Slavery in Rome and its territories experienced exponential growth during the republican era, as Rome conquered massive territories and brought back enslaved prisoners of war. Enslaved people in Rome came from many races; some had been highly educated or skilled in specific crafts in their home country. Aside from prisoners of war, some enslaved people were sailors captured at sea by pirates and sold in the slave market. Slaves could also be Roman; sometimes, impoverished parents sold their children to pay debts or because they could not feed them.

Slave labor included field workers, household servants, skilled craftsmen, architects, engineers, teachers, and scribes; it all depended on their skills and education. Rome had no laws protecting enslaved people from abuse or even murder by their masters. However, some slave owners allowed their slaves to buy their freedom or even set them free with no strings attached and assisted them in adapting to life as freedmen.

Some slaves became gladiators, like those depicted in the Zliten mosaic.⁹

Spartacus, a captured soldier from Thrace, became a gladiator, which often happened to prisoners of war with military experience. Romans flocked to the Forum (the Colosseum wasn't built until the early imperial era) to watch the gory matches. While being a gladiator had its glamorous moments, the combatants weren't enthusiastic about their short lifespan. So, one night in 73 BCE, Spartacus and seventy-eight fellow gladiators grabbed their chance to escape, arming themselves with knives from the kitchen.

They made their way to Mount Vesuvius, which had been dormant for centuries but would explode 152 years later and bury Pompeii. Other enslaved people joined them on their journey, and the escapees plundered fields and villages, accumulating weapons and food. The Roman praetor Claudius Glaber marched to Vesuvius with a force of three thousand, intending to trap the runaways at the top of the mountain and starve them out.

But the intrepid slaves made rope ladders from vines and escaped down the cliff to the valley below. They traipsed through Italy, freeing enslaved people from plantations, storming Roman units by surprise, and building their weapons supply as their numbers escalated to seventy thousand. The vagabonds split up when two consuls leading separate legions pursued them. Part of them stayed in southern Italy and fell to the Roman army, but the rest hiked into northern Italy with Spartacus. The plan was to cross the Alps out of Italy, and then everyone could return to their home countries. (There are many different theories as to why Spartacus chose to go south and why the slaves split into two groups, but these are the most popular theories.)

When they got to the Alps, most runaways lost heart at the sight of the ten-thousand-foot peaks. It was spring, and the snow cap hadn't melted enough to cross over. They worried that if they stayed, they might get trapped against the mountains. They decided to march south, cross the straits to Sicily, and stir up the enslaved people there, who had revolted a couple of decades earlier. They were confident they could take Sicily and hold it against the Romans. They reached the straits and paid pirates to take them across, but the pirates sailed off with their money, leaving them behind.

The Roman commander Crassus thought he had Spartacus trapped in the toe of Italy's boot. He built a thirty-seven-mile canal across the peninsula and a wall behind the channel to keep the slaves from escaping. But Spartacus's followers dammed the canal, crossed over, and scaled the wall. At this point, the escapees were at odds regarding their next step. They split up, leaving Spartacus with a much smaller group. Their overconfidence after winning one battle against the Roman legion spelled their death, as they succumbed to the Romans in the next fight. The Romans crucified the six thousand who survived the battle; their gory crosses spread one hundred miles along the Appian Way from Capua to Rome.

Chapter 4: Literature, Art, and Religion

In the heel of Italy's boot lay Tarentum, a Greek city, one of the largest in the world in its day. It had the most powerful naval fleet and ground forces in southern Italy, and with its lucrative trade, it was unimaginably wealthy. But in 209 BCE, it fell to Rome. The Romans slaughtered thousands and pillaged the city's priceless artwork, carrying the treasures off to Rome along with thirty thousand enslaved people.

Among those thirty thousand was Andronicus, a scholarly and cultured young man. Realizing his value, a Roman general named Marcus Livius Salinator purchased him to tutor his children. Taking his master's family name, Livius Andronicus translated Greek masterpieces like Homer's *Odyssey* into Latin to instruct Salinator's children. Salinator later set Andronicus free, and Andronicus established his own school and wrote tragedies and comedies for the stage. He became the first known writer of epic poetry and dramatic works in the Latin language.

This Pompeii mosaic depicts Livius Andronicus, Rome's first Latin writer. [10]

The Roman Republic's early writers were often educated Greek slaves, freedmen like Andronicus, or the Roman students they taught. Many educated Romans spoke Greek and studied Greek philosophy and satire. The Golden Age of Latin literature during the republic's last seventy years was a time of intense cultural advancement in Rome, despite civil wars and political collapse. Distinctive Roman styles marked Rome's remarkable literary accomplishments during the Golden Age.

Rome's Golden Age writers included Cicero, a political philosopher desperate to solve Rome's multiple crises. He wrote many treatises that supported the old patrician aristocracy, tried to repair the constitution, and defended peace and order. He asserted that preserving life and property united the people, enabling them to achieve their maximum potential. Cooperation was the key to achieving goals and fulfilling duties, which he said was the highest good.

Publius Vergilius Maro, better known as Virgil, grew up in a farming community in northern Italy. His first collection of poems, *Eclogues* (or *Bucolics*), explored the agony of his pastoral neighbors who lost their ancestral lands in Rome's shifting political scene. Three centuries later, Emperor Constantine interpreted some lines in his fourth *Eclogues* as a prophecy of Jesus Christ: "The Virgin returns bringing the beloved King." Saint Augustine agreed with Constantine but said Virgil didn't understand his own prophecy.[i]

Virgil's final and most famous work was the *Aeneid*, which is about the travels of Rome's mythical ancestor Aeneas as he escapes from the flames of Troy to finally settle in central Italy. Virgil never finished the *Aeneid*; he died while still editing it. Nevertheless, it

Virgil's epic poetry covered current issues and Roman myths.[ii]

served to rally hope in Rome's chaotic times. It has endured through the millennia as a pillar of classical education and influenced later literary works like *Beowulf*, *Paradise Lost*, and the *Divine Comedy*. The story is retold in Enthralling History's *Ancient Rome*.[ii]

Publius Ovidius Naso, better known as Ovid, opted for a poet's life rather than following his patrician father into public service. His humorous poems advising on love amused the Roman population, who raved about his three-book series, *The Art of Love*. In the first book, he told men how to find a woman: "She won't fall out of thin air; you have to look for her." He suggested specific places to find a girl, like the races or the circus, where the crowded seating meant you could "press your thigh to hers." He instructed the men to pay gentlemanly attention to the young lady while perhaps catching "a glimpse of her legs." He told young men to get a decent haircut, wear a clean toga, and ensure they had no dirt under their nails, no hair sprouting from their nostrils, and no bad breath! In the

---

[i] Ella Bourne, "The Messianic Prophecy in Vergil's Fourth Eclogue," *The Classical Journal* Vol. 11, No. 7, (April 1916), 390-400. https://www.jstor.org/stable/pdf/3287925.pdf.

[ii] Enthralling History, *Ancient Rome: An Enthralling Overview of Roman History, Starting from the Romulus and Remus Myth through the Republic to the Fall of the Roman Empire* (2021), 10-24.

second book, he told men how to keep a woman once they got one, and the third book advised women on how to find and keep a man.[i]

Ovid's most prominent work was *Metamorphosis*, a collection of fifteen books dealing with mythology and the transformations the protagonists experienced. He discusses the world's creation and the Golden Age when humans had no laws or punishments and were pure and good. Then came the Silver Age, when Saturn was banished from heaven. Humans had to work hard to plow the land and sheltered in crude houses from the cold. Because of the humans' violence, Jupiter decided to destroy all people with a great flood, but he chose one family to survive. Ovid also describes other Roman myths and the relationship between the gods and humanity in *Metamorphosis*.[ii]

Art in the Roman Republic encompassed various disciplines, including marble sculptures, buildings, murals, mosaics, and silver and bronze metalworking. The republic's early artwork was not much different than during the monarchy, nor was it prolific; the Romans were utilitarian, so they were more concerned with function than aesthetics. But Rome's clashes with Greece led to a new appreciation of art.

When Rome conquered Greek cities like Corinth, the soldiers plundered priceless sculptures and other artwork to carry back to Rome. Tragically, they often damaged the pieces in transit, but the Romans copied the Greek statues and other artwork, absorbing their innovative techniques. Rome's adaptation of the Greek culture led to the Greco-Roman style, which has graced architecture and art to the present age. In the republic's last century, artists and architects began producing uniquely Roman creations, such as realistic portraits and stunning buildings.

Roman buildings were initially constructed from wood, stone, or mudbrick, but by the 2nd century BCE, Roman concrete enabled gigantic columns and free-flowing building styles to be created. Roman concrete incorporated volcanic ash, making it durable and free of cracks. Architecture generally followed Greek design, but the Romans borrowed Etruscan technology to build aqueducts. The Etruscan aqueducts were mainly in-ground uncovered channels (like a paved ditch) that drained the swampy areas or moved water from rivers for irrigation.

---

[i] Ovid, *The Art of Love (Ars Amatoria)*, trans. A. S. Kline. Poetry in Translation. https://www.poetryintranslation.com/PITBR/Latin/ArtofLoveBkII.php.

[ii] Ovid, *Metamorphoses*, trans. Sir Samuel Garth, John Dryden, et al. http://classics.mit.edu/Ovid/metam.1.first.html

This Roman aqueduct in Spain used three levels of arches to span the ravine, keeping the water pipe through the top section level. [12]

The Romans also borrowed the arch from the Etruscans. Middle Eastern countries had used the arch for centuries, but the Romans refined the above-ground arch, incorporating it into breathtaking buildings, bridges, and above-ground aqueducts. They literally took the arch to new heights! And they took the multi-arched aqueduct everywhere, as far as Spain, France, and Germany.[i] In the late republic, the Romans built the earliest monumental dome and the world's largest dome up to that point. Located close to Naples, the "Temple of Mercury" (not actually a temple) was seventy-one feet in diameter. It covered one of the public baths in the resort town of Baia and is the oldest surviving concrete dome.

The Temple of Mercury was in the resort town of Baiae. [18]

---

[i] Bono, P. and C. Boni, "Water Supply of Rome in Antiquity and Today," *Geo* 27, (1996), 126-134. https://doi.org/10.1007/BF01061685.

In the Roman Republic, only elected magistrates could commission new public buildings. Because they only had one-year terms, they could build smaller projects like temples, but grand projects were not feasible. It wasn't until the last century of the Roman Republic that politicians commissioned self-aggrandizing and extravagant architectural projects like the Forum of Caesar and the Portico of Pompey.[i]

The Temple of Portunus, built in the 1st century BCE, exemplifies Roman Republican architecture. It was constructed of limestone and porous volcanic tuff with a plaster covering meant to resemble Greek marble. The frieze decorations on the upper pillars and roof feature garlands and an ox-skull motif. The temple dedicated to the water god Portunus was converted into a church in the 9th century CE, preserving it from the destruction of temples and fine buildings that occurred during the Dark Ages.

Elegant carvings graced the "capital" (top) of the pillars in the Temple to Portunus.[ii]

Romans carved exquisite columns and sculptures from translucent white marble. They enjoyed adding color to their designs with colored marble and other semi-precious materials. Artists decorated the faces of

---

[i] Penelope E. Davies, *Architecture and Politics in Republican Rome* (Cambridge: Cambridge University Press, 2017), 2-4.

sculptures with paint and gilding and sometimes painted the entire statue. Color was as essential to Roman sculpture as the fluid form.[i]

Sculptures of this era had a marked Hellenistic (Greek) influence and were usually lifelike portrayals of Roman leaders carved in marble and bronze. These sculptures featured incredible realism. They included people's imperfections, such as warts, wrinkles, sagging jowls, scowls, and huge, hooked noses. It seemed to reflect the Romans' intent to sensibly observe reality and the understanding that the leaders democratically representing the people *were* people, with all their frailties.

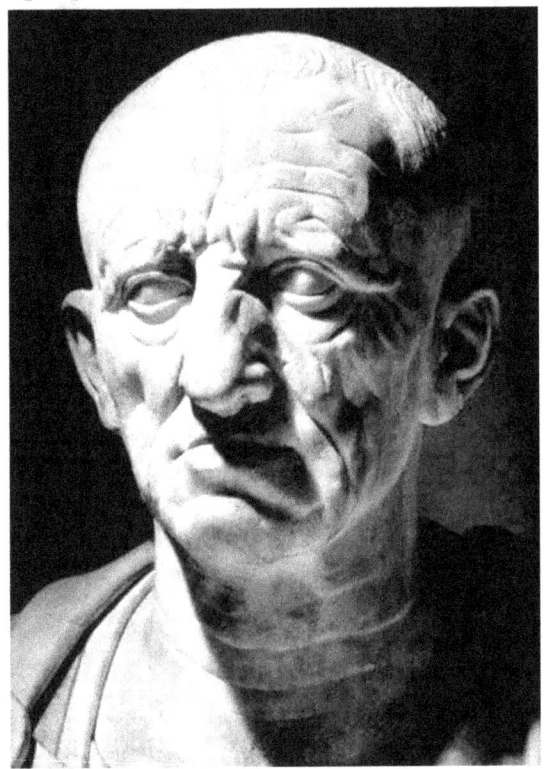

This marble bust reveals Cato the Elder in stark realism. [15]

When Mount Vesuvius erupted in 79 CE, it killed thousands of people and buried Pompeii and nearby cities under twenty feet of volcanic ash and pumice. This covering preserved the city for two millennia, so recent excavations have revealed breathtaking paintings and

---

[i] Mark B. Abbe, "Polychromy of Roman Marble Sculpture," in *Heilbrunn Timeline of Art History* (New York: The Metropolitan Museum of Art, 2007) http://www.metmuseum.org/toah/hd/prms/hd_prms.htm.

mosaics from the late republic and early imperial ages. Many Greek painters relocated to Italy in the late republic; they were hired by aristocratic families to decorate their dining rooms and atriums with wall frescoes. Some of these paintings were copies of original Greek works from a century or more prior. Mosaic tile art emerged in Rome and its colonies in the 3rd century BCE. First used as a practical yet decorative floor covering, mosaics later covered walls with intricate and realistic scenes.

This 2nd-century BCE Pompeii mosaic warned, "Cave Canem" ("Beware the dog"). [16]

Virgil's *Aeneid* records that Rome's ancestors worshiped two household gods called the Penates. They were lifelike male images and small enough for Aeneas's father to cling to while he was carried on Aeneas's back in the escape from Troy. The Penates guided Aeneas in his wanderings, redirecting him to Italy when he made a wrong turn to Crete. Dionysius reported that after settling in Lavinium (nineteen miles south of what would be Rome), Aeneas constructed a shrine for the Penates at the top of the city's hill. They were no longer household gods but deities and guardians for all the refugees, an embodiment of their Trojan past.

This republican era denarius struck in 106 BCE shows the two Penates (left); on the other side is a scene from the Aeneid where Aeneas finds the prophesied white sow.[17]

Curiously, Virgil said that after Aeneas's son Ascanius built Alba Longa and moved most of his population there, he made a shrine for the Penates at Alba Longa, but they didn't want to stay there. He woke up in the morning to find them gone, and someone reported they had returned to Lavinium. How the Penates got there was a mystery. Finally, Ascanius gave up and let them stay in Lavinium in his father's shrine. Lavinium persisted as a sacred city through the Roman Republic; newly elected consuls and praetors traveled there from Rome to bring sacrifices to the Penates.

From Rome's inception, it was polytheistic, adopting gods from Greece and other countries. Aeneas brought the worship of Vesta, the virgin goddess of the family and hearth, from Troy, and her worship continued throughout the republic. The sacred temple fire tended by the Vestal Virgins represented her rather than images. Unlike the typical Roman and Greek deities, Vesta had few myths and did not engage in feuds with other gods. Other chief gods were Jupiter (the Greek Zeus), king of the gods; his wife Juno (the Greek Hera), goddess of the moon and fertility; the sea-god Neptune (the Greek Poseidon); and Mars (the Greek Ares), the god of war.

The Romans practiced animal sacrifice. They preferred to sacrifice pigs but also offered sheep and oxen. Human sacrifice was rare, but in the struggle against Hannibal in 216 BCE, Livy recorded the sacrifice of human victims, probably enslaved people, from France and Greece:

"By the direction of the Books of Fate, some unusual sacrifices were offered; amongst others a Gaulish man and woman and a Greek man and woman were buried alive in the Cattle Market, in a place walled in with stone, which even before this time had been defiled with human victims, a sacrifice wholly alien to the Roman spirit."[i]

During the monarchy, the king held priestly duties, but during the Roman Republic, a patrician took on those religious responsibilities in a lifelong position called *rex sacrorum* ("king of the priests"). Rome also had an elected chief priest over the state clergy (the College of Pontiffs) called *pontifex maximus*, the pope's title today. Different religions had their own *flamines* (high priests of a cult). The rest of the priests were part-time positions held by men and women of high social standing.

During the republican era, the Romans did not interfere with the religions of conquered countries; they sometimes even assimilated them. What they believed was not as crucial as their active involvement in religious rites. The Romans believed their divine right to rule over much of the known world came from their dedication to religion and the understanding that the gods control everything.

---

[i] Livius, *History of Rome, Vol. V.*

Section Two: Warfare and Expansion (350–200 BCE)

Chapter 5: The Roman Army

How did the Romans manage to conquer lands stretching from the Middle East to North Africa and into western Europe? How did they accomplish incredible success without initially being tactically and technologically unremarkable? Part of their phenomenal triumph flowed from their indomitable, dogged nature. They refused to accept defeat, even in the face of military catastrophes. Sheer unwavering determination enabled the Romans to achieve victories, despite the odds stacked against them.

Throughout the centuries of the Roman Republic, the Roman military retained its tenacity but matured and evolved into an insurmountable military machine. To what do we credit Rome's inconceivable achievements on land and at sea? Military organization, rigid discipline, rewards for bravery, siege warfare technology, ingenious tactics, and formidable weaponry all played a decisive part.

How were soldiers recruited into the army? Who could serve, and for how long? In the early republic, soldiers were conscripts, mostly from Rome, although an additional one thousand soldiers were provided from the Etruscan, Latin, and Sabine tribes. To serve in the army, a Roman citizen had to be a landowner. Most soldiers were also farmers, so their deployments were only for a brief period, usually between spring planting and fall harvest—the traditional war season. Although they might spend time training in the winter or when no wars were going on, they were generally only called up for specific conflicts. The troops disbanded whenever a military campaign ended; the early republic had no standing army.

When General Marius ran for consul in 107 BCE, his campaign promise was a swift and victorious end to the war dragging out with Numidia in North Africa. When he won, he realized Rome didn't have enough soldiers because there weren't enough property owners. Marius received the Senate's permission to recruit plebeian men who didn't own property. Rather than drafting military personnel, he felt that volunteer soldiers were more willing to fight. He especially preferred to recruit veterans with fighting experience.[i]

Marius's military reforms also included the government paying for soldiers' basic armor and weapons. This was the beginning of Rome's standing army. Two decades later, Rome was still short of soldiers, so it recruited from other tribes in Italy, rewarding them with citizenship at the end of their service. With Romans and non-Romans serving together for months, a new culture emerged in the military, one that was loyal to Rome rather than their home cities and tribes.

One hundred Roman soldiers (later eighty) formed a group called a century. Six centuries formed a cohort. Ten cohorts made up a legion, which would consist of 4,800 to 6,000 men depending on the size of the century. Livius said that in 362 BCE, Rome had two legions, each led by one of the consuls. By 311 BCE, the number grew to four legions, enabling Rome to defeat the Samnites after decades of war. More legions empowered Rome to fight on multiple fronts in the ensuing Pyrrhic and Punic Wars.

As Rome began to fight outside of Italy, in lands thousands of miles away, it needed soldiers who could commit to long-term deployments. Thus, the part-time, mostly volunteer army morphed into a standing army with legions positioned around the Mediterranean. By the end of the Roman Republic, Rome had more than twenty legions stationed at permanent bases. Each legion usually had a 120-horse cavalry, which was used more for scouting and carrying messages than fighting.

The Jewish historian and military commander Josephus described the Roman army as highly skillful in war, well organized, and fighting with elegant unity. Impeccably armed, they unhesitatingly followed their leaders' clear-headed orders. Josephus said their rigid discipline enabled even a smaller force to prevail over larger, more disorganized units.

---

[i] Andrew Lintott, "Political History, 146–95 BC," in *The Cambridge Ancient History*, ed. by John Crook, Andrew Lintott, and Elizabeth Rawson (Cambridge: Cambridge University Press, 1992), 92.

Lastly, the Romans were tireless in battle, stoically pressing on until they achieved their objective.[i]

The Romans used a variety of siege engines to break down city gates, thick high walls, and other fortifications. Some siege towers and catapults were on wheels and could be rolled up to the city walls. Siege ladders enabled soldiers to scale the walls. Engineers built trenches and defensive walls to protect the soldiers from arrows launched from the city and dug tunnels under the walls.

As commander of the Jewish forces when Rome besieged Lower Galilee, Josephus gave a firsthand account of the devastation wrought by the Roman siege engines. Most of the Jewish army had holed up in the city of Jotapata (Yodfat), which sat on the top of a precipice encircled by a heavy wall. The Romans began their assault by cutting down hundreds of trees and gathering stones and earth to build a bank against the city wall. They worked in the "tortoise formation," with a shield wall protecting them from arrows shot from atop the city walls.

Rome ballista of 1 talent caliber

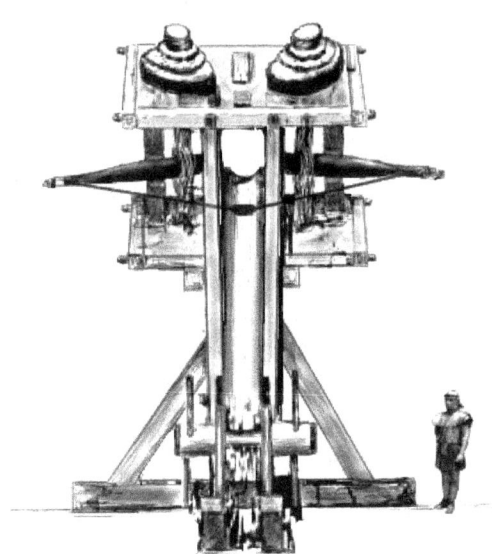

The ballista's levers with torsion springs launched stones five hundred yards. [18]

---

[i] Flavius Josephus, *The Jewish War*, Book III, Chapter 1.
http://penelope.uchicago.edu/josephus/war-3.html.

The bank enabled the Romans to get their 160 catapults high enough to fire huge rocks into the city, along with arrows shot by their allied Arabian forces. Vespasian then brought his battering ram into play, a massive wooden beam with an iron ram's head at the end, slung through the air by ropes. Many men pulled the ram backward, then flung it forward, smashing the wall with the iron head.

The Galileans screamed as the walls around them shook. But the Jews fended off the battering ram by dropping bags of chaff on ropes on the part of the wall being attacked by the ram, softening the blows. Other Jews snuck out by night and set fire to the siege engines. Yet the Romans maintained order, rebuilt their equipment, and continued the siege. The battering ram and rocks thrown by the catapults began crumbling the walls and striking the people inside.

The Galileans blunted the battering ram's swing propulsion with bags of chaff. [19]

One massive rock hit a pregnant woman in the belly, expelling the fetus from her body. Another boulder hit a man standing next to Josephus, decapitating him and flinging his head far away. The streets were slippery with blood as the dead bodies piled up. The Romans rushed the wall's breaches with a resounding trumpet blast and a loud shout. But the Jews poured scalding oil on them, and the Romans fell away, screaming as the hot oil seeped into their helmets and armor.

Yet, the indefatigable Romans behind them pressed in, calling anyone who faltered a coward. Vespasian had his men erect three fifty-foot towers covered with iron plates and filled them with archers. He rolled these up the embankment against the wall, along with the catapults. The Galileans abandoned the city walls as the Roman arrows darkened the sky. The city finally fell. Forty thousand Jews died in battle or by suicide, and the Romans enslaved twelve hundred women and children.[i]

What were the expectations for a Roman soldier? They needed immense physical strength and the ability to endure hardship, such as long marches while carrying all their gear. They had to obey any commands their superiors gave them instantly. Insubordinate or cowardly soldiers were mercilessly punished, often by death. The generals recognized the soldiers who displayed unusual courage on the battlefield or performed exemplary feats. Polybius said the general would give a speech lauding the soldiers who stood out in battle and then hand out rewards. Anyone who wounded the enemy got a spear. The first soldier to scale the wall of a city under siege got a gold crown.

> "For the recipients of such gifts, quite apart from becoming famous in the army and famous too for the time at their homes, are especially distinguished in religious processions after their return, as no one is allowed to wear decorations except those on whom the consul has conferred these honors for bravery; and in their houses they hang up the spoils they won in the most conspicuous places, looking upon them as tokens and evidence of their courage. Considering all this attention given to the matter of punishments and rewards in the army and the importance attached to both, no wonder that the wars in which the Romans engage end so successfully and brilliantly."[ii]

The standard weapons for a Roman soldier were a spear, a sword, and a dagger. The *pilum* was a six-and-a-half-foot spear weighing between two to five pounds with a wooden shaft and an iron shank. The *pilum* was hurled at the enemy rather than being used in hand-to-hand combat and was famous for piercing through armor. After fighting on the Iberian Peninsula in the Punic Wars, the Romans adopted the iron *gladius*

---

[i] Josephus, *The Jewish War*, Book III, Chapter 7.
[ii] Polybius, *The Histories*, Vol. 6, Sect. 6.
http://penelope.uchicago.edu/Thayer/E/Roman/Texts/Polybius/home.html.

Hispaniensis, or Spanish sword, in the 2ⁿᵈ century BCE. This sword was ideal for hand-to-hand combat on a packed battlefield, as its twenty-five-inch blade was shorter and easier to use for stabbing and slashing.

The *pugio* dagger was a sidearm commonly carried both on the battlefield and by officials going about their tasks in Rome. It was a handy defensive tool in battle if the soldier lost his sword and spear. In civilian life, it was a weapon of assassination and suicide. Officials often concealed it in their toga in case they needed to kill a rival or defend themselves from attack.

During the Roman Republic, soldiers carried a round *scutum* shield, which was later replaced by a large rectangular shield in the imperial age. The middle of the shield had a boss, a rounded or conical-shaped protrusion of bronze or iron. This type of shield would effectively deflect blows when the soldier used a punching motion; he could also use it as an offensive weapon to smash an opponent.

A soldier usually had chainmail armor in the republican era; the armor was formed by tiny rings of iron linked together to form a flexible and breathable cover. Some soldiers wore scale armor with iron or bronze scales sewn into the cloth so the scales overlapped. The typical helmet for most soldiers at this time was the Montefortino, adopted from the Celts, which resembled a metal baseball cap worn backward.

The Montefortino helmet was popular in the Roman Republic. [20]

Roman commanders had multiple tactics in their repertoire. In the earlier republic, the soldiers lined up in a formation similar to a Greek phalanx. Rows of soldiers stood shoulder to shoulder, with their shields slightly overlapping, forming a shield wall. This formation protected the front line from enemy projectiles. The multiple rows of soldiers pushed those in front of them with their shields, turning the whole mass into a human bulldozer that could trample an opposing army.

The Romans later implemented their twist of the Macedonian phalanx, which was developed by Philip II, the father of Alexander the Great. By 315 BCE, the Romans used a manipular formation composed of multiple groups or maniples of 120 men. Rather than a solid line, each smaller unit operated independently. The front lines had fifteen maniples or groups, followed by another fifteen maniples, and then finally fifteen *principes*, groups of older military veterans. Each section had a junior commander who could direct the troops according to the moment's need rather than waiting for the general's order.

Plutarch told the story of one battle in the Pyrrhic Wars where the Romans faced a Macedonian phalanx that seemed impenetrable. But the Roman junior commander grabbed his company's standard and threw it into the middle of the adversary's phalanx. The standard had a bronze eagle or some other similar figure atop a long pole. The soldiers rallied around their standard and protected it at all costs. When they saw it flung among the enemy, they immediately surged forward to rescue it, breaking the enemy's phalanx. Both sides suffered horrendous casualties.

Romans began using carrier pigeons in the Roman Republic to send messages. Spies in Mark Antony's camp sent messages to Brutus via pigeon that helped him devise a successful strategy based on his inside information about the enemy. The Romans also sometimes set booby traps for their adversaries. In one battle, a commander named Quintus Sertorius faced a cavalry much larger than his. That night, he dug trenches all over, then faced off against the enemy. His men moved their horses to the side when they charged, letting the enemy surge through right into the ditches!

In the First Punic War, the Romans realized that prevailing over Carthage in North Africa required a navy. The Greeks, Egyptians, and ancient Phoenicians of Carthage and Lebanon had ruled the waves for over a millennium. Rome had merchant ships but no navy and no master shipbuilders. But that didn't stop the irrepressible Romans. They inspected a Carthaginian quinquereme that had washed ashore in a storm. Using it as a model, they built one hundred warships in only two months!

Rome celebrated military victories with a triumph, a dazzling parade and ceremony that lasted an entire day. It began with the conquering commander, dressed in purple and wearing a laurel crown, giving speeches and distributing rewards and money to his men. Then, a grand procession would proceed through the city accompanied by flag-wavers and musicians. The people cheered at the sight of the commander in his chariot, as well as the plundered treasures and royal captives led in gold chains.

The Romans seemed unrefined by the standards of the Greeks and other ancient civilizations. Yet, the unsophisticated "barbarians" possessed a dynamic spirit that developed a well-oiled military machine that soon ruled the Mediterranean. Rome's conquests during the Roman Republic brought tremendous political power and astounding wealth to Italy. By the end of the republic, it had spawned the Pax Romana: domestic peace around the Mediterranean that permitted a flourishing trade and an enriching exchange of cultures.

Chapter 6: Greek and Roman Relations

For over a century, Rome squared off with the remnants of Alexander the Great's empire in a fierce quest for dominance over the Mediterranean. First, Pyrrhus of Epirus came to "assist" southern Italy's Greek cities as they wrestled with Rome. Next, Rome inserted itself into the Greek world's convoluted politics while simultaneously struggling with Hannibal and other Carthaginians in the Punic Wars.

King Pyrrhus became famous for his costly "pyrrhic victories" against Rome. After his second technical win, he groaned, "If we are victorious in one more battle with the Romans, we shall be utterly ruined."[1]

The Pyrrhic Wars entangled Rome with the Greek city-states of southern Italy, their allied Italian tribes, and the Macedonian-Greek world to the east. In 282 BCE, Roman ships sailed into the Gulf of Taranto in southernmost Italy, which was off-limits to Rome based on a treaty with the massive city of Tarentum. Why were the Romans in the forbidden bay? They were transporting troops to a Roman garrison in Thurii, a Greek city allied with Rome.

The indignant Tarentines considered this intrusion an act of war, so they attacked and sunk four transport ships and captured one. They then sailed to Thurii and incited a democratic revolution, influencing the population to eject the Roman garrison. Rome responded by declaring

---

[1] Plutarch, *The Parallel Lives*, Volume IX, "The Life of Pyrrhus."

war on Tarentum, so the Tarentines called on King Pyrrhus of Epirus (Albania) across the Adriatic Sea.

King Pyrrhus of Epirus had empire-building ambitions.[21]

King Pyrrhus had delusions of grandeur; he imagined reigning over an empire like his cousin Alexander the Great. He came to Tarentum's aid, thinking he could gain a foothold in Italy, despite his insufficient resources for a military campaign. He borrowed ships from King Antigonus of Macedonia and funding from Antiochus of the Seleucid Empire. Pharoah Ptolemy of Egypt loaned him soldiers, horses, and twenty war elephants.[i]

Overly eager, Pyrrhus crossed the Adriatic before spring, but a fierce winter storm decimated part of his forces. Then, Pyrrhus realized the Tarentines wanted him to fight their battles while they enjoyed drinking bouts and festivities. Pyrrhus outlawed revelry and drunkenness and drafted the men for military service. Some left town, unwilling to fight and disgruntled at losing their freedom.

The Romans mobilized thirty thousand men and marched south to attack Pyrrhus. Pyrrhus met them at the Siris River with thirty-five thousand troops, three thousand cavalry, and twenty elephants. He viewed the Roman camp from a high bluff and admired their discipline and order. At first light, the Romans charged across the river, and Pyrrhus met the most ferocious army he'd ever encountered.

---

[i] N. G. L. Hammond, "Which Ptolemy Gave Troops and Stood as Protector of Pyrrhus' Kingdom?" *Historia: Zeitschrift Für Alte Geschichte* 37, no. 4 (1988): 405. http://www.jstor.org/stable/4436071.

In a panic, he exchanged his armor with his lieutenant, fearing the Romans would target him. He was right: they killed the hapless lieutenant wearing the king's battle gear. Pyrrhus swung the battle by sending his elephants charging toward the Romans, who had never seen such enormous animals. Their frenzied horses raced off the field, and Pyrrhus's cavalry quickly scattered the petrified Roman soldiers.

Pyrrhus won the battle but not before a wounded elephant stampeded his own troops, leaving mangled bodies in its wake. Up to fifteen thousand Romans and thirteen thousand Macedonian and Greeks perished that day. However, Rome still had tens of thousands of troops in southern Italy. Pyrrhus was relieved when some of the Italian tribes and Italy's Greek city-states replenished his forces.

While both sides regrouped, Pyrrhus's physician Nicias sent a letter to the Romans, offering to poison Pyrrhus in exchange for a reward. The outraged Consul Fabricius sputtered that Rome would win through tenacity, tactics, and toughness, not poison! He alerted Pyrrhus of Nicias's plot, who thanked Fabricius by releasing his Roman prisoners of war. Pyrrhus killed and flayed Nicias, using his skin to form the straps of a chair.

Pyrrhus met Rome's army with forty thousand men in the gruesome Battle of Asculum, which raged for two days. The rough, forested terrain hindered elephant and cavalry charges. Rome had created three hundred anti-elephant wagons pulled by oxen. Spears projected out from iron beams, and the wagons carried catapults that launched fire missiles and rocks at the Greeks and their elephants.

Pyrrhus's elephants circumnavigated the wagons on the second day and chased Rome's panicked horses off the field. The battle ended with at least 6,000 dead Romans and 3,500 Greek casualties. However, Pyrrhus had a spear wound, and the Romans looted his camp and killed most of his commanders. It was indeed a pyrrhic victory, as it was hardly worth the hollow win.

Part of Pyrrhus's long-term empire-building plan was to conquer Sicily, using it to launch a campaign against Carthage in North Africa. He leaped at an offer from Sicily's Greek city of Syracuse: "Protect us from Carthage, rid us of tyrants, and you can be our king."

The Tarentines seethed when Pyrrhus abandoned the Roman war. "Finish what you started here, or put our city back the way you found it and leave permanently!"

The Romans chuckled; now, they could subdue the Samnites, Bruttians, and Lucanians (all of which were ancient Italic tribes) who had fought on Pyrrhus's side. Rome used this interlude to conquer all the Greek city-states in southern Italy except for Tarentum and Regi. Meanwhile, Pyrrhus's plot to rule Sicily was a dismal failure. The Carthaginians outnumbered and outpowered him and drove him off the island.

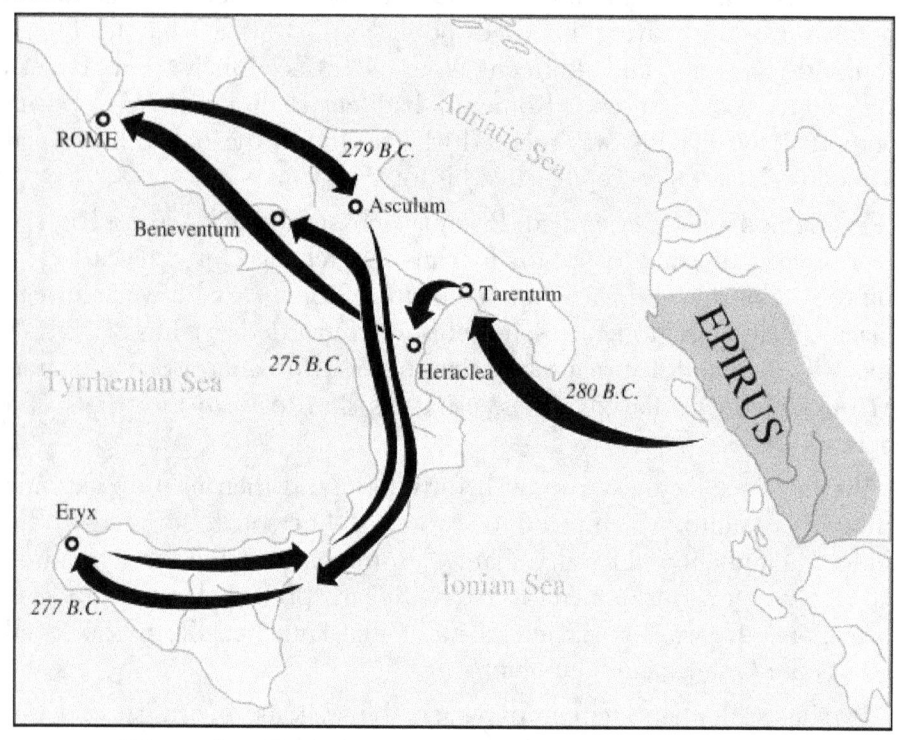

This map shows Pyrrhus's route from Epirus to Italy to Sicily and back. [22]

Pyrrhus returned to Italy in 276 BCE with only twenty thousand men. Despite having lost his Italian and Greek allies' support, he confidently marched toward the Roman encampment at Maleventum. Maleventum meant "bad omen" or "unfortunate arrival," which struck true for Pyrrhus's bungled arrival and the ensuing debacle. Planning a surprise attack, Pyrrhus marched his men at night through the woods, but they wandered off the trail in the dark.

At sunrise, they emerged from the woods on a high bluff in full view of the Roman camp, losing the element of surprise. They were exhausted and dehydrated, and the elephants were irritable. Before they could rest and regroup, the Romans charged up the hill. Many of Pyrrhus's men chose that moment to flee. Pyrrhus's war elephants forced the Romans back, but the Romans had learned to spear the elephants in the side. The panicked and pain-crazed elephants reversed course, charging straight toward Pyrrhus and trampling the troops.

Pyrrhus couldn't even score a pyrrhic victory this time. He escaped to Tarentum, then sailed home, leaving behind the chair made from Nicias's skin. He died three years later when an old woman threw a tile at him from a rooftop. When the news reached Italy, Tarentum and Regi surrendered to Rome, giving the Romans complete control of all of Italy except for the far northern border, which was held by the Gauls.

Six decades later, Rome fought in Greece for the first time. Alexander the Great's empire had split into the Egyptian, Macedonian, and Seleucid Empires. As Egypt faltered, the Macedonians and Seleucids made a power grab. King Philip V of Macedonia didn't like Rome's involvement with Epirus and Illyria (today's Albania, Montenegro, Bosnia, and Croatia); he planned to incorporate them into Macedonia.

This map shows the regions involved in the Macedonian Wars.[28]

The conflict between Philip V and Rome led to the First Macedonian War (214-205 BCE) when Philip attacked Apollonia, located in Illyria. The Romans chased him off, but Philip was back a year later, capturing two important fortresses. Rome allied with central Greece's Aetolian League and King Attalus of Pergamum (today's western Turkey). The joint forces captured the cities of Nasus, Oeniadae, Zakynthos, and Anticyra on Greece's mainland.

Philip allied with Bithynia (northern Turkey on the Black Sea) to drive the Aetolian League out of northern Greece. Philip won this conflict, but Rome's fleet sailed in just as they were negotiating the terms of surrender. However, Philip prevailed over Rome before leaving to deal with a Dardanian invasion of Macedonia. Rome moved its ships into the Adriatic Sea, focusing on protecting its trade allies by stationing ten thousand infantry and a thousand cavalry in Illyria.

Philip returned to attack the Aetolian League, driving them out of Ionia and Thessaly. After hearing that Rome was beating Carthage in the Second Punic War, Philip decided to end his war in Greece before Rome had more resources to use in the fight against him. The Aetolian League, Macedonia, and Rome agreed to the Peace of Phoenice in 205. Philip now held part of mainland Greece and inland Illyria, but Rome was confident that coastal Illyria was safe.

The Second Macedonian War (200-197 BCE) began with a plot to grab Egypt. Ptolemy IV had died, leaving his six-year-old son, Ptolemy V, as pharaoh, and the royal family was squabbling over who would be regent. Philip V of Macedonia and Antiochus the Great of the Seleucid Empire conspired to take advantage of the chaos and divide the Egyptian territory between themselves. Antiochus would get Egypt and Cyprus, while Philip would get Cyrene and Egypt's territories in the Aegean Sea.

First, Philip needed to secure the Greek colonies near the Dardanelles Strait, which were critical to shipping traffic between the Aegean and Black Seas. Meanwhile, Antiochus conquered Sidon, Damascus, and Samaria. Philip began his Aegean Sea campaign by defeating Miletus and attacking Egypt's naval base at Samos in 201 BCE. Antiochus drove the Egyptians out of Judea, and the jubilant Jews hailed him as their conquering hero. Their joy turned to horror three decades later when Antiochus's son, Epiphanes, installed an image of Zeus in Jerusalem's temple and sacrificed a pig, sparking the Maccabean Revolt.

Rome finally triumphed over Carthage in 201 BCE and now had time to focus on Greece and Macedonia. Rome warned Philip V to withdraw his troops from Greece, leave Egypt alone, and stop aggressive actions in other regions. Philip ignored this stipulation by attacking Abydos in the Dardanelles. When all hope was lost, the men of Abydos killed their families, threw the city's treasures into the sea, and fought to the last man. Rome did not want Philip to control the Dardanelle Strait, so it declared war.

The newly elected consul, Sulpicius, sailed east with his exhausted troops, who had just returned from a lengthy deployment against Carthage. He confronted Philip in 200 BCE, but after two inconclusive battles, Philip left in the middle of the night to defend Macedonia against a Dardanian invasion. Sulpicius chased after him initially but then decided to attack the Macedonian naval bases.

In 199 BCE, Rome elected the twenty-nine-year-old Titus Quinctius Flamininus as consul, despite the age requirement of forty-one. Flamininus replaced Sulpicius and proved to be a stellar leader. He quickly freed the territory Philip had taken in Greece. He faced off with Philip at a pass in Albania. After a shepherd revealed an alternative route through the mountains, Flamininus attacked Philip's rearguard in a surprise attack, killing two thousand Macedonians.

The Senate was so pleased with Flaminius that they told him to keep fighting, even though his term as consul was about to end. Flamininus had twenty war elephants in the 197 BCE Battle of Cynoscephalae in Thessaly, which was fought in a valley covered with deep fog. His elephants won the day, with the Romans inflicting eight thousand Macedonian casualties. Philip finally surrendered, agreeing to give up any claim to Greece and stay in Macedonia.

Rome told Antiochus he could keep his empire and Egypt but to leave Thrace (today's Bulgaria) and stay clear of the Dardanelles. But Antiochus felt he had a hereditary claim to Thrace. Greece's Aetolian League abandoned its alliance with Rome for Antiochus, making him their commander in chief. He sailed to southern Greece's Peloponnese Peninsula to attack the Aetolian League's rival and Rome's ally, the Achaean League. But Rome sent them packing with two legions. The war segued to a naval battle in the Aegean Sea, where Antiochus lost half his ships. The final land battle in Thessaly in 197 BCE cost him half his land army. Antiochus surrendered his conquered cities and paid a war debt to

Rome and Pergamum but continued ruling the colossal Seleucid Empire.

The Third Macedonian War began in 171 BCE, shortly after Philip V's son Perseus ascended Macedonia's throne. Perseus promised the Greeks he could restore their ancient power and wealth. But Pergamon's king, Eumenes II, sailed to Rome to warn it of Perseus's ambitions, strategic alliances, and his massive arms stockpile. The Romans declared war, allying with Pergamon.[i]

Perseus won the first round in Thessaly, losing only four hundred men to Rome's two thousand in 171 BCE. He then attacked the Roman camp while most of the soldiers were away stealing grain from the nearby farmlands. The Romans hurried back and trapped Perseus in a ravine, killing eight thousand Macedonians while suffering four thousand casualties of their own. In the final 168 BCE Battle of Pydna, the Romans killed twenty thousand Macedonians and captured eleven thousand.

The Romans collected so much booty that Rome gave its citizens a huge tax break. The city celebrated the astounding victory over Macedonia with Rome's most spectacular triumph. The crowds went wild at the sight of Perseus led in chains, high-spirited soldiers wearing laurel wreaths, and Macedonia's treasures. Macedonia came under Rome's control and was divided into four republics.

In 146 BCE, Rome fought against the Achaean League, their former allies who now wanted to expand, despite Rome's wishes. Rome quickly squelched the league; in the last battle in Corinth, Rome captured or killed most of the Achaean soldiers and enslaved the women and children. The Romans pillaged Corinth's priceless artwork, hauling it back to Rome and damaging many pieces in transit. Rome usurped Greece's place as a world power, but Hellenistic influences would continue to impact Roman literature, philosophy, art, and religion for centuries.

---

[i] Titus Livius, *The History of Rome*, Vol. VII.

Chapter 7: Mediterranean Conquest: The Punic Wars

"If you leave, I'll kill myself!"

Distraught, Queen Dido watched Aeneas prepare his ships for departure. After Aeneas, the ancestor of the Romans, had fled burning Troy, the gods directed him to Italy to build a new city. But as he was sailing toward Italy's mainland, a fierce storm forced his fleet southwest, driving the ships ashore in North Africa. Aeneas walked down the beach the following morning and encountered men building a city.

Aeneas learned they were Phoenicians from Tyre, led by their queen, Dido, and that the new city's name was Carthage. When Aeneas met Queen Dido, they were mutually attracted to each other and became lovers. Aeneas forgot his foreordained destiny until Jupiter sent Mercury to remind him: "Why are you wasting time in Libya? This is not why the gods rescued you from the Greeks! You are destined to rule Italy and give birth to an empire!"

Aeneas knew he couldn't disobey the gods, but Dido raged when she saw Aeneas resolutely preparing to leave. She told him, "There will be no love or treaties between your people and mine. Your descendants will have unending strife with Carthage! After I'm dead, I'll follow you with dark fires. You'll be punished, and I'll hear of it from the depths of Hades."

As Aeneas's ships sailed away during the night, Queen Dido sank into madness, unsheathing Aeneas's sword he'd left behind and plunging it into her chest.[i]

Queen Dido of Carthage cursed Aeneas before her suicide. ³⁴

Almost a millennium later, Dido's prophecy came to pass, as Rome and Carthage fought three legendary wars against each other for nearly eight decades. In the contest for Mediterranean sovereignty, both sides performed fantastic feats. Rome built a navy in two months, Hannibal's army scaled the thirteen-thousand-foot Alps, and Rome learned how to turn war elephants around to pulverize their masters.

The name "Punic Wars" comes from the Latin word *Punicus*, meaning Phoenician, a Semitic-speaking, seafaring people from Lebanon's coast. The Phoenicians colonized Carthage in today's Tunisia in North Africa. Carthage grew incredibly prosperous through its sea trade and ruled an empire that skirted the lower Mediterranean for centuries. But in the mid-200s BCE, it grappled with Rome in a lethal struggle for dominance.

It all began with pirates. Nefarious mercenaries invaded Messana (today's Messina) in Sicily, six miles across the Strait of Messina from southern Italy. The Mamertines plundered ships passing through the

---

[i] Virgil, *The Aeneid, Book IV*, trans. A. S. Kline (Poetry in Translation, 2002). https://www.poetryintranslation.com/PITBR/Latin/VirgilAeneidIV.php.

strait and raided the fields and cities of eastern Sicily for two decades. Finally, Hiero II, the ruler of Syracuse, decided to end their pillaging. He marched one hundred miles north to Messana, but the Mamertines allied with Carthage, which had a nearby fleet, and Hiero backed off.

To the pirates' dismay, Carthage stationed troops at Messana, cracking down on their plundering. The Mamertines decided to seek Rome's protection from Syracuse and kick out Carthage's garrison. Although hesitant to get involved with buccaneers, Rome was eager to impede Carthage's expanding control over Sicily. So, in 264 BCE, the Romans allied with the Mamertines and sent two legions to Sicily in their first military campaign off Italy's shores.

Apprehensive at this turn of events, Hiero turned to Carthage for help with Rome and the pirates. The first order of business for the Carthaginian commander Hanno was to crucify the garrison captain who had abandoned Messana without orders. Hanno then sailed his fleet to Messana before the Roman legions crossed the strait. The Roman legions sailed over at night, catching the Carthaginians and Syracusans by surprise and defeating their dual forces. The Romans then sailed down the channel to Syracuse, but Hiero immediately surrendered, brokering a deal where he allied with Rome to keep his position as Syracuse's ruler.

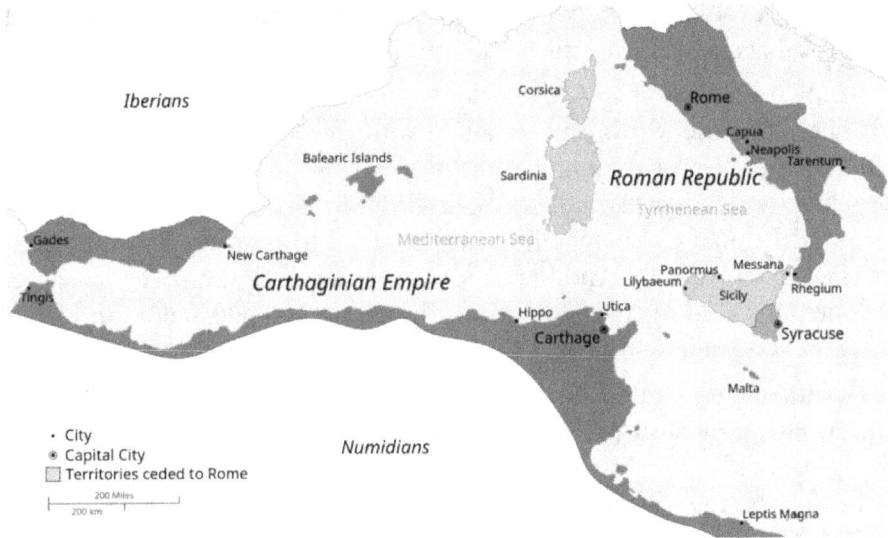

At the beginning of the First Punic War, Rome's only territory was Italy, while Carthage's empire covered Africa's northern coast and southern Spain. [35]

In 262 BCE, the Roman forces in Sicily swelled to four legions led by both consuls. They conquered Carthage's ally Akragas on Sicily's southeastern coast and enslaved the citizens, prompting other Sicilian cities to defect to Rome rather than face its wrath. At this point, Rome realized that taking on Carthage, the world's supreme naval power, required warships, which it built at breakneck speed.

    While the crews built one hundred quinqueremes and twenty smaller triremes, the future sailors practiced rowing in unison. The Romans knew their inexperience would put them at a disadvantage with Carthage's seasoned naval maneuvers. To put their close-contact combat skills into play, the Romans developed thirty-six-foot-long gangplanks to hook on the adversaries' ships so they could board and fight man to man. They also carried their catapults on board to shoot flaming missiles.

    To Carthage's shock, Rome's neophyte navy won stunning victories in the Battle of Mylae and the Battle of Sulci. The Romans built over a hundred more ships and a naval force of fourteen thousand marines within two years. In what some consider history's largest naval battle—the Battle of Cape Ecnomus—they fought Carthage's navy off Sicily's coast. There were 680 ships and 300,000 men between the two navies. After a prolonged, bizarre day of fighting, Rome triumphed over Carthage, sinking or capturing ninety-four ships compared to twenty-four of their own. Carthage lost at least thirty thousand men.

    Rome took the war to Africa, winning a land battle only ten miles from Carthage. But the Carthaginians allied with the Spartans and launched a counterattack, overwhelming the Romans with one hundred war elephants and a cavalry unit of four thousand. They butchered twelve thousand Romans; only two thousand escaped to be picked up by a fleet arriving from Rome. Another apocalypse awaited them, as a savage cyclone sunk 320 of their 400 ships, drowning 100,000 sailors in one of the world's deadliest shipwrecks of all time.

    But the unstoppable Romans regrouped in Sicily, conquering Palermo and enslaving most of the population. They triumphed over Carthage in two more battles in 251 and 250 BCE, sending their captured elephants to Rome for the citizens' amusement. However, another brutal storm sunk 150 ships on the way back from the war in Africa. Then, the Romans suffered a degrading loss when Carthage captured ninety-three more vessels.

That last fiasco was all Consul Pulcher's fault. He consulted his sacred chickens for an omen regarding his planned surprise attack on Carthage. But the chickens refused to eat, implying his plans were doomed. Unwilling to accept the omen, Pulcher thundered, "If you won't eat, you'll drink!"

He tossed the chickens, squawking and flapping, into the sea. After his ignominious naval disaster, Rome recalled him, where he stood trial on charges of impiety for drowning the sacred chickens. A sudden rainstorm interrupted the proceedings, and the magistrates never rescheduled. Yet, the Fates had their way, as Pulcher died soon after.[i]

Carthage's new admiral, Hamilcar Barca ("lightning"), plundered Italy's coastal towns and launched guerrilla attacks on Sicily. But Rome quickly built more ships and crushed Carthage's naval force. Carthage finally surrendered in 241 BCE, paying thirty-two hundred silver talents and turning Sicily over to Rome—its first offshore territory. The Romans quickly acquired the island of Sardinia, which threw off its Carthaginian overlords at the end of the First Punic War.

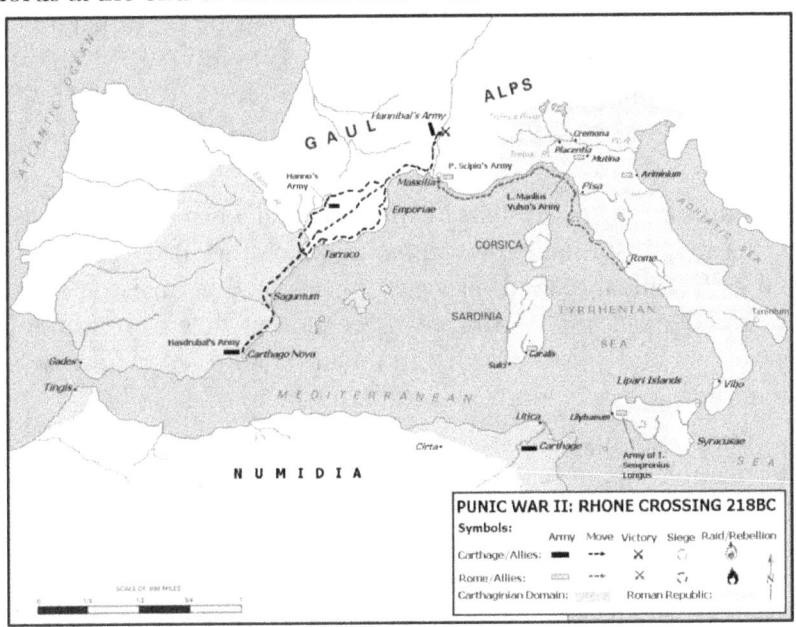

When the Second Punic War began, Carthage controlled part of North Africa's coast and most of Spain. Rome controlled Italy and the islands of Sicily, Sardinia, and Corsica.[26]

---

[i] Paul Sheridan, "The Sacred Chickens of Rome," *Anecdotes from Antiquity* (November 8th, 2015). http://www.anecdotesfromantiquity.net/the-sacred-chickens-of-rome.

The Second Punic War began in Iberia (Spain), where Carthage had colonies for centuries. After the First Punic War, Hamilcar Barca expanded Carthage's control from the coastal region to most of modern-day Spain. This enriched Carthage, helping it recover economically and renew its military resources. In 221 BCE, Carthage's army appointed Hamilcar's son, Hannibal, as their commander in chief, seeing his father's fire in his eyes.

Some Spanish cities resisted Carthage, including Saguntum, a trade ally with Rome. They had been messaging Rome about Hannibal's growing power, but Rome was distracted by the Macedonians. Hannibal attacked Saguntum in 219 BCE, taking the city and killing every adult. This atrocity triggered Rome's declaration of war on Carthage, beginning the Second Punic War. General Scipio Africanus sailed to Spain with sixty warships, but Hannibal had disappeared!

Leading ninety thousand soldiers, twelve thousand horsemen, and thirty-seven war elephants, Hannibal had marched up Spain's coast and scaled the 11,000-foot Pyrenees Mountains. After doing that, he was in Gaul (France) and headed toward the Alps. Receiving word that the Gauls were planning an attack on the opposite side of the Rhone River, Hannibal's lieutenant, Hanno, led a contingent of troops twenty-five miles upstream. They crossed the river and stealthily crept toward the Gauls' camp.

The Gauls were utterly fixated on Hannibal's army on the opposite side of the river, especially the elephants, which they'd never seen. They watched as Hannibal loaded his army, horses, and animals on boats and rafts, ready to attack the Carthaginians as soon as they were within range of their arrows and spears. At that moment, Hanno led a surprise attack from their rear, overwhelming and scattering them to the hills.

The thirteen-thousand-foot Isère Alps lay between France and Italy, and the Carthaginians had to get across before the December snows. They clawed their way up the steep pass with their horses and elephants, dodging boulders thrown from above by the menacing mountain people. They left their assailants behind on their downward trek, but the terrain was terrifying, with constricted, ice-slick paths and deep snow. Occasionally, someone would lose their footing and freefall a mile to the jagged stones below.

Then, the Carthaginians turned a bend to find a landslide covering the path; the deep snow prevented them from moving further. The soldiers laboriously removed the rocks so the horses, mules, and elephants could cross. The horses and mules clambered over first, trotting down to the tree line, where they finally found grass. But the famished elephants had to wait three more days before the path was safe enough for them to maneuver.

Hannibal's brutal trek over the Alps gave him the element of surprise.⁷⁷

Hannibal lost two-thirds of his army, half his cavalry, and an unknown number of elephants in the confrontations with the Gauls and in the dangerous passage over the Alps.[i] But as he descended into Italy, the Gauls there, who had immigrated centuries earlier and sacked Rome in 390 BCE, quickly joined forces with him. The Romans thought Hannibal was somewhere in Spain or France; he caught them off-guard when he suddenly showed up at their northern border.

Hannibal wreaked havoc, pursuing a scorched-earth strategy through Italy, destroying crops and other resources. In the 217 BCE Battle at Lake Trasimene in central Italy, he killed or captured twenty-five thousand men. Rome had the numerical advantage, but Hannibal had ingenious tactics and an indomitable spirit. In the 216 BCE Battle of Cannae in southern Italy, he killed 50,000 Romans, losing only 5,700 of his own. While central Italy staunchly supported Rome, Italy's southern city-states defected to Carthage.

Rome finally rallied, cutting off the Carthaginians' supplies and manpower that were coming into Italy. General Scipio was still in Iberia

---

[i] Polybius, *Histories, Book III.*

and racked up an astounding triumph in 209 BCE by taking control of Carthage's supply network and treasury. The ecstatic Romans elected Scipio as their new consul. Africa became his next target. With 440 ships, he sailed to Carthage and attacked in the middle of the night, dividing his forces and pouncing on the Carthaginians from both sides.

After Carthage's loss, its Numidian Berber allies switched sides to Rome. Scipio's cavalry had outmaneuvered the Numidians' expert horsemen, and they wanted to be on the winning side. In the concluding Battle of Zama, Hannibal rushed back to Africa in 202 BCE to defend Carthage from Scipio. The Romans outnumbered the Carthaginians, although they still put up a ferocious defense.

Eighty war elephants decided the battle. Hannibal sent them in an onslaught toward the Romans, but Scipio was experienced with elephants by this time. He ordered his men to step aside, allowing the elephants to charge through to the back of the Roman lines. The Romans surrounded the creatures with their spears and sent them toward the Carthaginians in a counterstrike. While the Carthaginians were busy getting out of the elephants' way, the Roman and Berber cavalry swooped around to Hannibal's rearguard. They trapped his forces against the Roman infantry, with the elephants creating chaos in the middle.

The day ended with a spectacular victory for Rome, with Carthage losing twenty thousand men to Rome's five thousand. Carthage surrendered, ending the Second Punic War by disbanding its navy and agreeing not to fight anyone without Rome's permission. Carthage kept their North African territories, except for Numidia, but lost Spain and other offshore holdings. It paid two hundred gold talents for Rome's war expenses and annual tribute for the next fifty years.

Hannibal remained in Carthage as chief magistrate and attempted to reform the city's political system. He established direct elections of officials and term limits and eliminated the misuse of state funds. But Hannibal's reform efforts earned him enemies in Carthage. When Rome became suspicious that Hannibal was colluding with the Seleucid Empire, Hannibal decided to leave town and spent the rest of his life in Asia. For the next five decades, Carthage kept its treaty and paid tribute to Rome. Carthage provided barley and grain and even allied with Rome on occasional military expeditions. But trouble loomed ahead for the two great cities.

Chapter 8: The Third Punic War and the Fall of Carthage

"It's not fair! We can't defend ourselves!" the Carthaginians wailed in desperation.

Numidia (today's Algeria and western Libya) surrounded Carthage to the west and south and was an ally of Rome. Numidia's King Masinissa took advantage of this alliance to invade Carthage's territory, steadily chipping away until Carthage's lands decreased by half. Carthage was frustratingly helpless to do anything. The treaty with Rome stipulated it couldn't fight anyone without Rome's permission. But Rome, which was secretly pleased that their one-time greatest rival was rapidly losing territory, wouldn't permit Cartage to fight a Roman ally.

Finally, the desperate Carthaginians could no longer restrain themselves. If they didn't do something, they would lose everything! When King Masinissa brazenly attacked the Carthaginian city of Oroscopa, Carthage mustered thirty-one thousand troops to defend their territory. But after fifty years, Carthage had fallen out of practice in the art of war. They underestimated their enemy, assuming the Numidians were an undisciplined desert tribe when Masinissa had formed a regimented force with sensational tactics and logistics.

Masinissa slyly moved the battle to rugged desert terrain, where there was little water or food. Eventually, the starving, dehydrated Carthaginian army surrendered. But the Numidians ignored their surrender and massacred them. Carthage's warriors never left their borders; they were only defending themselves against Numidia. Even then, they failed wretchedly. But they didn't ask or receive permission from Rome. So, technically, they had broken their treaty.

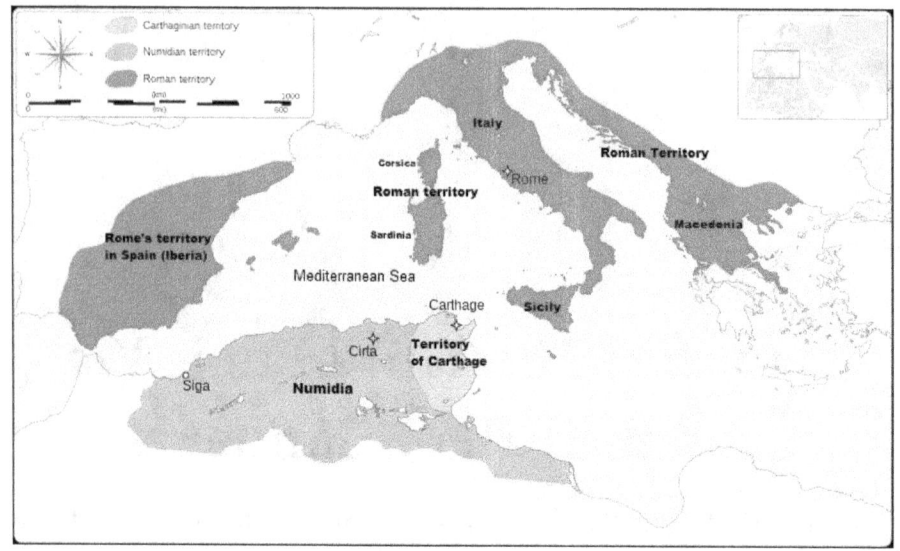

Rome controlled most of the upper Mediterranean, and Numidia surrounded Carthage at the beginning of the Third Punic War. *

"Carthago delendam est!" Cato cried out. "Carthage must be destroyed!"

Two years earlier, the ancient Cato the Elder had visited Carthage with some fellow senators to sort out the problems with Numidia. Cato was astounded at Carthage's staggering wealth. Carthage had always been a vital trade center. Now that it no longer funded a navy and wasn't spending a fortune on military campaigns, it had recouped its former splendor. To Cato, Carthage's conspicuous prosperity presented a tremendous threat to Rome.

It wasn't that Carthage had done anything terrible. Rome received its annual tribute like clockwork, and Carthage had shown nothing but respect to Rome. It wasn't what Carthage had done; it was what it could do with such vast wealth, like build or buy a naval fleet and hire a legion of mercenary warriors. And so, the octogenarian Cato ended every speech in the Senate with "Carthago delenda est! Carthage must be destroyed!"

The younger senators, those born after the Second Punic War had ended, smirked and rolled their eyes when the veteran of the Second Punic War ranted. Carthage had no navy, and its army was a joke. It presented no threat to Rome. And anyway, a little fear was good for the republic: it kept everyone on their toes. The younger senators nodded vigorously when Corculum, Scipio Africanus's son-in-law, responded to Cato by ending his speeches with "Carthago servanda est! Carthage must be saved!"

But Cato's fear-mongering began stirring the Roman concept of a "just war." For the Romans, justification for war included more than defending the republic against attack. It could also include perceived slights to Roman prestige. Since Carthage's surrender during the Second Punic War, it had not posed a threat to Rome or anyone else. But Cato regularly stirred up fear in the Romans' minds, despite all the evidence to the contrary. Rumors circulated that Carthage was cutting timber to build a new naval fleet. The Carthaginians were cutting trees but for building merchant ships, not war vessels.[i]

And now, it seemed like Cato's dire predictions were coming true. Carthage had dared to go to war without permission! They breached the treaty and attacked an ally! It did not matter that they had acted in self-defense and suffered a horrendous loss. Their insubordination and military action against a Roman ally insulted Rome's honor and prestige. Something had to be done.

Carthage sent its ambassadors to Rome to explain what happened: they'd only fought in self-defense and lost most of their army in the debacle. But Rome had already decided it had cause for a just war. They shot back at the Carthaginians, "Send us three hundred children from your nobility as hostages, and maybe then we'll consider peace terms."

The ambassadors took the news home to the distraught people, who moaned, "How could we give up three hundred of our children? Who knows what the Romans would do to them!"

But in anguish, they surrendered three hundred of their sons to Rome. Would they ever see them again? And would it even help? The Romans' stipulations only grew. In 149 BCE, Rome sent eighty thousand soldiers and four thousand cavalry units to Africa, demanding Carthage's unconditional surrender. "You must shut down your army, recall your military, and turn over all your weapons."

---

[i] Robert J. Kane, "The Third Punic War: An Intelligence Failure from Antiquity," *American Intelligence Journal* 36, no. 1 (2019): 162-63. https://www.jstor.org/stable/27066349.

The Carthaginians fumed, "They can't seriously think we'll give up our army and disarm! How would we protect ourselves?"

But just as they had handed over their children, they relinquished their weapons. They turned over 200,000 sets of chainmail armor and 2,000 catapults. Then came the Romans' final ultimatum: "Oh, one more thing: leave Carthage. You can resettle inland, but you must be at least ten miles from the coast."

When the envoys brought the news back to Carthage, the citizens raged. "Leave Carthage? This has been our home for a thousand years! We'd lose our harbor; how would we pursue trade? We'd end up poverty-stricken! Our walls protect us here. Would we settle inland? In the desert? With no protection from the Berbers? How could we possibly survive?"

The Carthaginians refused, and Rome's legions headed to Carthage, starting the Third Punic War. The city of Carthage lay on a piece of land that jutted out into the Gulf of Tunis, protected to the south by the Lake of Tunis. A twenty-three-mile wall encircled the city. The three miles of the brick wall facing the mainland was forty-two feet high and thirty feet thick. In front of the wall was a seventy-foot-wide ditch. No army ever penetrated that stretch of wall. The Romans tried but gave up at the beginning of the Third Punic War. Instead, they focused on cutting off the supply lines between Carthage and its allies.

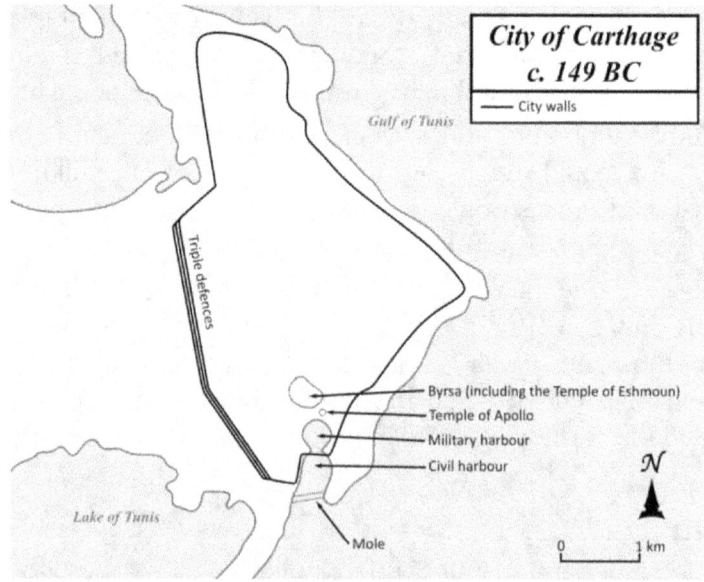

Carthage was on an isthmus with impenetrable triple walls facing the mainland.[29]

Most of our information on the Third Punic War comes from the Greek historian Polybius. He was also a hostage, among about a thousand that Rome demanded from the recently conquered Achaean League. He arrived in Italy from Greece at the same time as the child hostages from Carthage.[i] Polybius became friends with Scipio Aemilianus, the adopted grandson of Scipio Africanus, the hero of the Second Punic War. After being released from his captivity, Polybius accompanied Scipio to Africa, interviewing both the Romans and Carthaginians as he recorded the war's history.

The siege of Carthage lasted almost three years. Carthage released any slaves willing to fight for the city and amassed a twenty-thousand-man army. To the Romans' surprise, the Carthaginians had either not relinquished all their weapons or reaccumulated some of them. Led by General Hasdrubal, the Carthaginians disrupted the Roman supply lines and attacked smaller bands of Romans foraging in the agricultural regions around the city.

The Roman army was divided into two contingents, each with a specific assignment. One legion was to fill the ditch in front of the great wall so that they could scale it. The other group was to approach the smaller wall facing the lake and put ladders up from their ships to scale the walls. Both attempts failed. The next plan was to fill in Lake Tunis's shoreline just next to the walls so they could roll their siege engines close to them. They constructed two battering rams and managed to break down part of the wall facing the Lake of Tunis, but the Carthaginians fought fiercely, driving the Romans away from the breach. That night, they snuck out of the city and burned many of the Roman siege engines.

The Carthaginians received a welcome lull when the roman contingent at the Lake of Tunis fell ill due to the mosquito-ridden swampland, the July heat, and inadequate clean drinking water. The commander decided to move his men away from the marsh to the gulf side, where there was more fresh air and fewer insects. Once the men had recovered, they began focusing on Carthage's harbor. Carthage had a protected port for its merchant ships. Its warships passed through the first harbor to a second, more secure circular harbor.

---

[i] Polybius, *Histories, Book 36*.

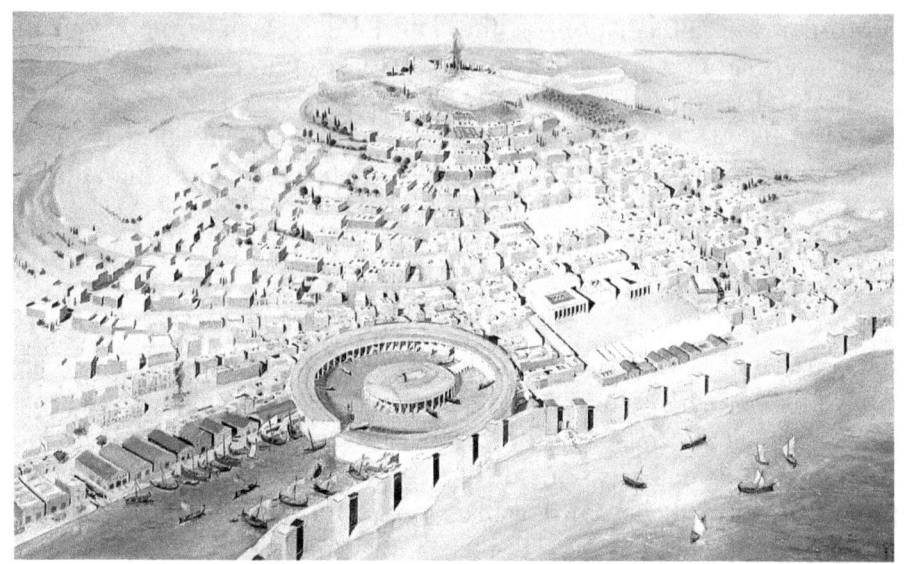

Carthage had a harbor for merchant ships (lower left) and a round interior port for military ships accessed through the first harbor.[30]

Despite the Romans' vigilance, supply ships from Carthage's Phoenician allies continually managed to elude the blockade. The Phoenicians had been seafaring people for almost two millennia; they were perhaps the world's first long-distance seafarers. Their ships were faster than the Romans' and could maneuver more easily. With their superior marine skills, Carthage still received regular shipments of food, weapons, and other necessities.

Moving the Roman camp placed them closer to Carthage's harbor, which they first considered an advantage because they could monitor any ships trying to enter or leave. But the intrepid Carthaginians used fireships against them. These were older ships near the end of their lifespan, which they would fill with brush and cover with tar. They would sail out into the harbor, set the ships on fire, and quickly jump off. They launched the fireships in coordination with the wind and tide so that they would sail straight toward the Roman fleet, crashing into their ships and setting them on fire. The Carthaginians swiftly decimated the Roman fleet by using this tactic.

What Rome had expected to be a swift victory was morphing into a prolonged siege in which they could not seem to gain any advantage. What's worse, the other Phoenician cities on Africa's coast, except for Utica, refused to submit, as did the smaller towns in Carthage's territory. To top it off, one of the Numidian tribes, led by its king, Bithyas, defected to Carthage, sending eight hundred cavalry units to fight the Romans. By this point, King Masinissa of Numidia had died. His two sons assured Rome they'd send money and weapons, but they did not follow through. They seemed to be waiting to see how events played out in the struggle between Rome and Carthage.[i]

Back in Rome, the senators were livid that affairs were still dragging out in Carthage. It was time for the elections of new consuls for the typical one-year term. The public demanded Scipio Aemilianus be elected, even though he was younger than the age requirement of forty-one. He was the grandson of Scipio Africanus, who many considered to be the most stellar military commander in history. After all, he was the general who defeated Hannibal and ended the Second Punic War.

After being elected and dispatched to Carthage, Scipio Aemilianus wasted no time dealing with the issues that had stymied his predecessors. He built a causeway across the entrance to Carthage's harbor, preventing any ships from coming or going. Out of sight in the military port, the Carthaginians were surreptitiously building fifty new ships. When they finished construction, they broke through their own wall to open a new harbor entrance. The fifty vessels sailed out to confront the Roman fleet. Due to the Carthaginians' advantage of surprise, the battle was in their favor until they tried to reenter their new narrow harbor entrance at the end of the day. They quickly clogged the small entrance, and the prevailing current pushed many of them against the sea wall, damaging the ships beyond repair or leaving them vulnerable to the Romans.

Scipio Aemilianus's catapults flung boulders against the walls, and the battering ramps slammed them, but the walls did not budge. He focused on the walls along the harbor, which weren't as thick as those facing the mainland. The Carthaginians snuck out at night, swimming across the harbor to set fire to the siege engines, but the Romans would quickly repair or rebuild them. The Romans also controlled the new entrance into the port, preventing supplies and food from coming in.

In the spring of 146 BCE, the Romans finally got inside the city. In a nighttime attack, some younger soldiers climbed a brick tower that the Romans had spent months building near the wall. They threw a long

---

[i] Appian. *Punic Wars.*
http://www.perseus.tufts.edu/hopper/text?doc=Perseus%3Atext%3A1999.01.0230%3Atext%3D Pun.%3Achapter%3D16%3Asection%3D111.

gangplank over to the walls. Once inside the city, they opened the gates for the Roman army, and four thousand soldiers poured in. The people inside were disoriented and panicked at the soldiers' loud shouts, but they spilled into the streets with whatever weapons they had to defend their city.

The Romans worked their way through Carthage for six days and nights, taking each street and house until all the citizens had either escaped, been hewed down, or perished in the buildings as they burned. Exhausted, Scipio Aemilianus climbed up a high bluff to watch the ancient city reduced to ashes. He wept as he remembered Carthage's vast empire, astounding wealth, massive fleets, and elephants. He honored the bravery with which the Carthaginians had defended their city for three years, only for it to end in the city's total destruction. He reflected on the rise and fall of his ancestral Troy and wept again as he prophesied Rome's fall in the future. Carthage's destruction was complete. Never again would the Carthaginians thrive and rule the waves from their glittering city. With all competition obliterated, Rome now had total power over the western Mediterranean.

Section Three:
Consequence and Legacy
(120–40 BCE)

Chapter 9: The Gallic Wars

"Sir! We have news! The Helvetii are on the move!"

Julius Caesar swung around. "The Helvetii? I thought they abandoned their plan to migrate. Where are they heading?"

"Straight toward us, sir! They plan to cross the bridge at Geneva."

"Well then, we'll have to assemble the troops and march on the double to Geneva!"

"Yes, sir. And I'm sorry this is happening just after you got here."

"Oh, don't be sorry." Caesar grinned. "This fits my agenda perfectly."

Julius Caesar, the descendent of an ancient aristocratic Roman family, was a statesman, a warrior, and a writer. While fighting in Gaul (France and parts of Belgium, western Germany, and northern Italy), he wrote an eight-volume account of his experiences in the Gallic Wars.[i] As he finished each book, he sent it back to Italy, keeping Rome abreast of his campaign with a coherent narrative of his victories over the immense territory.[ii]

Pliny reported that Caesar was an avid multitasker, with at least one slave always by his side as his secretary who quickly transcribed Caesar's rapid-fire dictations. As Caesar heard or read reports from the battlefield

---

[i] Julius Caesar, *The Gallic Wars*, trans. W. A. McDevitte and W. S. Bohn (The Internet Classics Archive). http://classics.mit.edu/Caesar/gallic.1.1.html.

[ii] Josiah Osgood, "The Pen and the Sword: Writing and Conquest in Caesar's Gaul," *Classical Antiquity* 28, no. 2 (2009): 328. https://doi.org/10.1525/ca.2009.28.2.328.

or letters from Rome, he would dictate several letters at once to various recipients. He would travel around in his sedan chair to inspect camps, garrisons, and cities, with his slave always by his side, taking dictation.

In 59 BCE, Caesar became one of Rome's two consuls, with Bibulus as the other. Bibulus was literally the victim of dirty politics, as Caesar organized his cronies to fling him to the ground and pour excrement over him when he attempted to block a bill. Humiliated, Bibulus remained at home for the rest of the year as a puppet consul while Caesar swung the senators' votes. At the end of his one-year consulship, the Senate appointed Caesar to a five-year term as proconsul and governor of Cisalpine Gaul and Transalpine Gaul.

Sculpture of Julius Caesar by Andrea di Pietro di Marco Ferrucci, circa 1512. [81]

Cisalpine Gaul was the northernmost region of Italy. Cisalpine means "this side of the Alps." Centuries earlier, the Celts crossed the Alps into Italy and sacked Rome in 390 BCE, but the Italians eventually forced them back into northern Italy. Transalpine Gaul, on the other side of the Alps in today's southeastern France, became a Roman province in 118 BCE. By this point, the Celts of Gaul were building cities and becoming affluent through trade with Rome. But they were still ferocious and powerful warriors with sharp fighting skills and towering physiques.

At the end of a consul's term, he could face prosecution for abusing the powers of his office. Caesar had bent a few rules and abused his co-consul, so finagling a governorship abroad kept him immune from prosecution. Victorious military campaigns would ramp up his prestige and build his political power, not to mention enriching him through the plunders of war. Caesar headed to Gaul with four legions, veterans he had already led into battle as the governor of Hispania three years earlier.

In his *Gallic Wars*, Caesar describes three main tribal confederations in Gaul: the northern Belgae, the southwestern Aquitani, and the Celtic Gauls in central Transalpine Gaul. He said each tribal group had its own language and distinctive culture. In Caesar's opinion, the Belgae were the bravest of the three because they were remote from civilization and things that "tend to effeminate the mind." They were also in constant warfare with the Germans, which kept them in excellent fighting shape. A fourth group was the Celtic Helvetii, who had been forced out of southern Germany by the Teutonic Germans into today's northern Switzerland.

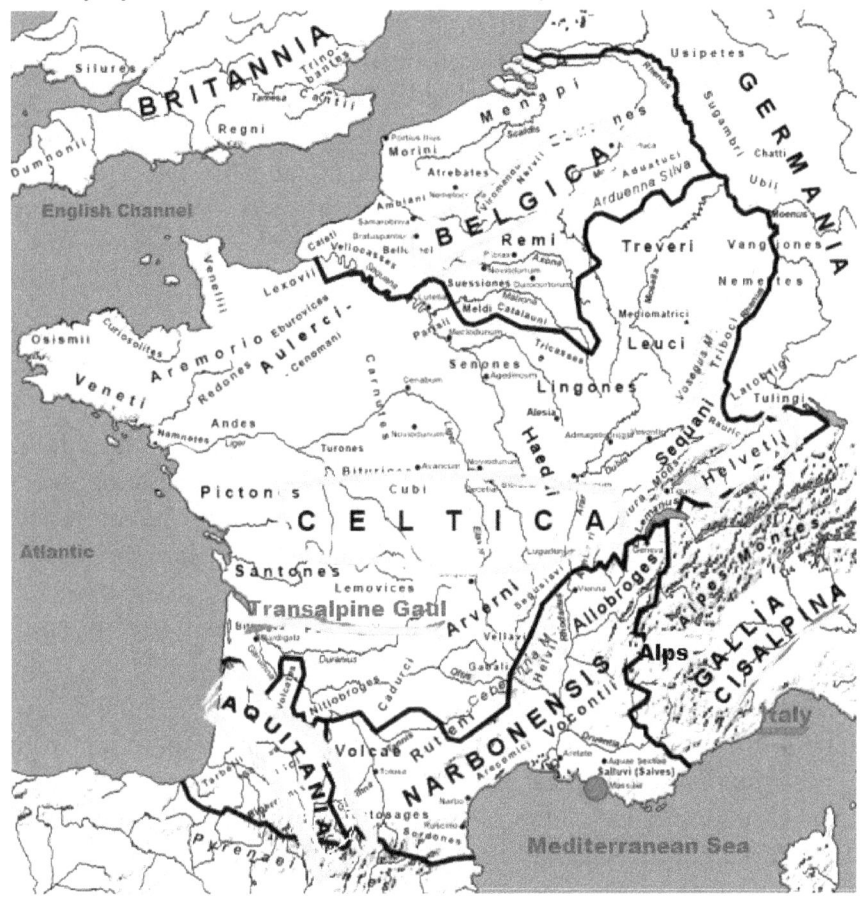

The regions of Gaul in Julius Caesar's day.[32]

The Greek historian Posidonius described the Helvetii as peaceable people who became affluent through prospecting for gold in the rivers. Several years earlier, one of their noblemen, Orgetorix, convinced many of the Helvetii that they should migrate into Gaul and establish a kingdom on the coast. At that point, the Helvetii were a confederation ruled by local leaders, but Orgetorix wanted to unite all the tribes with himself as king. The tribal magistrates squelched the idea, and Orgetorix died, apparently of suicide.

When the Romans heard this news, they thought the situation was resolved. However, in March 58 BCE, just as Julius Caesar assumed the governorship of Gaul, the Helvetii burned down their homes and farmlands in about twelve towns and four hundred villages. Caesar said that 368,000 Helvetii began trekking west, carrying provisions for three months. Several neighboring tribes joined them, also destroying their homes before leaving.

The best route for their trek toward the Atlantic coast was right through the Roman section of Gaul. They headed for the town of Geneva, where a bridge covered the Rhone River. The Allobroges people of Geneva had no strong ties to the Romans, and the Helvetii thought they might let them cross. If not, they would force their way over the bridge. But Caesar's legion got there first and ordered the Genevans to break down the bridge.

The Helvetii sent their ambassadors to Caesar. They told him, "Sir, we intend to march through your province without harming it in any way. This is the only way to our destination. Please give your consent."

But Caesar remembered an incident five decades earlier when he was just a child. The Tigurini tribe, part of the Helvetii confederation, was on a raiding spree through Gaul. The consul at the time, Lucius Cassius Longinus, had chased them to the Atlantic Ocean, but the Tigurini ambushed and killed him and ten thousand of his legionaries. The Tigurini forced the surviving Romans to "pass under the yoke" of spears, a ritual humiliation.[i]

Caesar leaned back and rubbed his chin. He doubted the Helvetii would pass through his province without stirring up trouble and didn't intend to grant their request. But he needed time for the rest of his soldiers to arrive. "I need a few days to consider your request. Come back on the Ides of April, and I'll give you my answer then."

In the next two weeks, Caesar put his men to work building a sixteen-foot high and eighteen-mile-long wall along Lake Geneva. He appointed garrisons and guard stations all along the Rhone River to prevent the Helvetii from crossing. When the Helvetii returned for his answer, he told them they could not cross. They tried to pass over by boat or by fording a shallow part of the river, but the Romans were alert and stymied their attempts.

---

[i] Caesar, *The Gallic Wars*, Book 1, Chapter 7.

The Helvetii negotiated an alternative route through the Sequani tribe's territory. The Helvetii and Sequani exchanged hostages, pledging that the Helvetii would have safe passage if they respected the Sequani territory. Caesar caught up with them just as they were crossing the slow-flowing Saône River. All but about one-fourth had crossed, and Caesar massacred the ones left behind, then built a pontoon bridge and crossed over. He hunted down the Helvetii and fought them in the horrendous Battle of Bibracte, reportedly killing two-thirds of the Helvetii.

Caesar's next challenge was the Germanic Suebi tribe, which was pouring across the Rhine River into Gaul. By this point, Caesar had returned briefly to Italy to round up two more legions, giving him six legions in Gaul. He met the Suebi army and put them to flight, killing most of their soldiers and chasing the remnants back across the river; they would never challenge Rome again. Caesar's victories against the Helvetii and Suebi prompted many Gallic tribes to ally with Rome. He dealt with Belgae raiders (from today's Belgium) by circumnavigating them and attacking their primary city. The Belgae snuck back into their town by night but were unprepared for a Roman siege and quickly surrendered.

An embarrassing setback faced Caesar in the Battle of the Sabis with the Nervii, another Belgic tribe. With sixty thousand men, the Nervii launched a surprise attack on the Romans as they set up camp. Two of Caesar's legions were still nine miles away. The Romans put their military discipline into play against the more disorganized Nervii, driving part of the Nervii back across the river. But the remaining Nervii outflanked the Romans' right wing and captured the unguarded Roman camp. Caesar jumped into the front lines himself to fight the onslaught. Caesar's two remaining legions showed up just in the nick of time to turn the tide of the battle and send the remaining Nervii packing.

In 56 BCE, the Roman forces collided with the seafaring Veneti of the northern Brittany peninsula when the Veneti imprisoned the Roman officers who came to collect grain requisitions. The Romans had little experience in the rough Atlantic Ocean, but Caesar set his men to work building ships to take on the Veneti in a naval battle. That did not go well for the Romans, as the Veneti had superior seamanship skills and could easily outmaneuver them.

Rome finally prevailed in the Battle of Morbihan, as better weather enabled them to employ the naval skills they'd perfected in the Punic Wars. They used grappling hooks to destroy the Venetis' sails and rigging and pull their ships close enough to slap their gangplank on the enemy's ships to board them. Then, the Romans exercised their superior combat skills, fighting man to man, and destroyed the Veneti fleet.

While Caesar was fighting at sea, his generals, Crassus and Sabinus, confronted Normandy and Aquitania. Sabinus easily defeated the coalition tribes of Normandy by forcing them to approach his army on a grueling uphill climb. They were too tired to fight when they reached the top. Crassus faced more difficulties in Aquitania, as these tribes had previously allied with the Romans and knew their strategies and tricks. Crassus finally launched a surprise rear attack on their camp, which was only fortified at the front. The ensuing victory brought southwest Gaul to the Roman Republic. At the end of 56 BCE, the Senate awarded Caesar another five years of governing Gaul.

In 55 BCE, Caesar pulled two attention-getting feats to build prestige back in Rome: crossing the Rhine and crossing the English Channel to Britain. The Rhine divided Germany from Gaul, and once again, the Germanic tribes were forcing the Celts out of Germany and into Gaul. The initial battle ended with the Celts defeating the Roman Gallic allies, despite being outnumbered five to one. Embarrassed, Caesar attacked their undefended base camp and massacred thousands of women and children, compelling Rome's Senate to prosecute him for war crimes. Prosecution was futile, given that Caesar was immune as long as he served as Gaul's governor. Caesar then launched an eighteen-day raid in Germany, building a timber bridge over the Rhine and burning the bridge behind him on his return.

Caesar crossed the English Channel to Britain in August with two legions, but the Britons were lined up on the shore awaiting him. He tried sailing up the coast, but they followed. Finally, the standard-bearer led the way by jumping in the sea and wading ashore to plant the Roman standard on Britain's shore. The Roman soldiers quickly waded after him to protect the standard. After a short, indecisive battle, the Romans returned to Gaul for the winter.

Caesar spent the winter devising a more organized assault on Britain, crossing the channel in 54 BCE with five legions and two thousand cavalry units. Rather than facing the Romans in open battle, the Britons launched guerilla raids with their chariots and horses, skillfully outmaneuvering the Roman cavalry. They attacked a small Roman contingent, expecting an easy win. But to their surprise, the Romans formed ranks and soundly defeated them, taking the wind out of the Britons' sails. Although the Briton tribes had previously fought each other, they united under the warlord Cassivellaunus, Caesar defeated Cassivellaunus, and the Briton tribes surrendered, agreeing to pay an annual tribute.

At this point, Caesar received news of mayhem in Gaul. Many tribes had revolted against Rome and ambushed General Sabine, killing most of his army. Caesar immediately sailed back from Britain with two legions to rescue General Cicero but not before Cicero lost 90 percent of his legion. Unrest continued among the conquered tribes until war finally exploded in 52 BCE. The conflict had been instigated by druid priests, and the people were united under King Vercingetorix of the Arverni tribe.

The revolt culminated with the Romans laying siege to the town of Alesia in Burgundy, where Vercingetorix had amassed a hundred thousand troops. The Celtic king planned to trap Caesar's forces between Alesia's walls and another Celtic army that was on its way to the region. But he never expected the extent of Caesar's siegeworks: twenty-five miles of trenches, towers, and hidden snares. And yes, Caesar *did* anticipate the Gauls launching a rear attack and was well prepared, pulverizing the rebellion. Vercingetorix and most of the Gallic tribes surrendered, except for holdouts in southwestern Gaul positioned in the hill fort of Uxellodunum. The Romans dug tunnels to the spring supplying water to the citadel, cutting off their water supply. When the rebels surrendered, Caesar cut off their hands.

By 50 BCE, Rome held control over all of Gaul only eight years after Caesar assumed its governorship. Rome would rule Gaul for almost five centuries, and the Old French language would rise out of Roman Latin. Caesar had grown in political prestige and wealth through the process. He was poised to turn Roman politics upside down, becoming Rome's first long-term dictator, which was the beginning of the end for the republic.

Chapter 10: Caesar and Pompey: Triumvirates and Civil War

"It's absolutely absurd, Caesar!" Pompey growled. "My men have been fighting nonstop in Asia! We've conquered nine hundred cities, captured eight hundred pirate ships, and won massive provinces for Rome! All I'm asking is a small plot of farmland for each of my soldiers so that they can support their families. And I need the Senate to honor the treaties I made with the new provinces. Can you believe those idiots in the Senate are opposing the bill? They all own vast estates but are refusing my men a patch of land in the eastern regions they've conquered!"

"I know, I know, my friend," Caesar soothed. "The senators are incompetent fools only interested in retaining their wealth and power."

The two men sipped their wine silently for a few minutes as Caesar looked speculatively at Pompey. "You know," he said softly, "there's a way around your impasse."

Pompey's eyebrow lifted. "Keep talking!"

"A triumvirate. You're a popular war hero. I've got influential connections in the Senate, and I'm the high priest of the College of Pontiffs. You get me elected as consul, and I'll pass your land bill!"

Pompey frowned. "But you said a triumvirate. Who's the third person?"

Caesar chose his words carefully. "Well, we need money to sway the votes. And I haven't any; I'm deep in debt."

Pompey nodded. "I haven't that kind of money either. So, who's going to be our financier? Oh, you can't possibly mean Crassus? I loathe the man!"

Caesar leaned forward. "You don't have to like Crassus or have much to do with him. You're manipulating things behind the scenes. I champion your bill, and Crassus swings the votes with his money. What do you say?"

Pompey smiled. "I say I need a wife!"

Caesar looked confused for a moment. "Ah! You mean Julia! You want to marry Julia?"

Pompey reddened. "I do. I know I'm much older, but I'm ready to settle down now. Your daughter is beautiful, kind, and conscientious. Quite frankly, I'm infatuated with her!"

Caesar grinned. "All right, my friend. Julia shall be your bride!"

And so, the "Gang of Three," which would upend Roman politics, was formed.

Crassus, Pompey, and Caesar, the three men who formed the First Triumvirate, were all previously connected to a civil war between the consul Lucius Sulla and his former military commander Gaius Marius. Marius, who was married to Julius Caesar's aunt Julia, had the distinction of serving as Rome's consul seven times, but between his sixth and seventh consulship, Sulla was elected consul. The former comrades-in-arms became bitter rivals.

After his election, Sulla immediately headed to Pontus to fight King Mithridates VI. No sooner had he left than his political enemies convinced the Senate to recall Sulla and send Marius to command the campaign instead. Receiving this news, an enraged Sulla marched back to Rome with five legions, reconsolidated his power, declared Marius a *hostis publicus* ("public enemy"), then returned to Pontus. Marius fled to Africa, but after Sulla left Rome, Marius slipped back to Italy with his army while Rome was in the throes of a civil war between the patricians and plebeians. He usurped control of Rome, murderously purging his political foes. In late 85 BCE, he was elected to his seventh term as consul. He took office on January 1st, 86 BCE, but suddenly died two weeks later.

Sulla wrapped up his campaign in Pontus and sailed back to Rome, retaking the city. The Senate appointed him dictator, which was customary during an emergency, but it was only meant to last a few months. Instead, Sulla ruled as dictator until shortly before his death, turning Rome into a bloodbath by executing everyone he considered a potential threat. He killed dozens each day, sometimes hundreds. In the power play between Marius and Sulla, Crassus's and Pompey's families supported Sulla, while Caesar's family supported Marius.

The slave trade, extortion, and land speculation made Crassus Rome's richest man.[38]

Marcus Licinius Crassus came from a respected plebeian family. Before Sulla regained control of Rome, Consul Cinna was executing or exiling Sulla's supporters, so Crassus had to get out of town quickly. He joined up with Sulla in Greece, where he fought alongside Pompey. Crassus won special distinction in a battle against the Marian forces, where he annihilated his foes and then asked Sulla if he needed help. Sulla was in trouble; his center forces were giving way before the enemy, so Crassus jumped in and saved the day.

Marius confiscated Crassus's family's property, so when the tables turned, Crassus gained back his fortune and more. He bought property expropriated from Sulla's enemies at scandalously low prices. Plutarch said he built his fabulous riches by "making the public calamities his greatest source of revenue." He established Rome's first fire brigade with five hundred firemen but only put out the fires if the owners agreed to sell the properties to him at rock bottom prices.[i] Estimates by Plutarch and Pliny place his wealth around what would be $13.7 billion today.

Despite Crassus's successful military career and enormous fortune, he couldn't compete with Pompey, who was building up a stellar reputation with his campaign in Hispania. Crassus's chance to gain fame came when

---

[i] Plutarch, *The Parallel Lives*, Volume III.

Spartacus led the great slave revolt. Crassus offered to fund, train, and provide weapons for an army to defeat the slaves since Rome's legions were tied up in Hispania and Pontus.

The war against the runaway slaves dragged on for two years. In the meantime, Pompey returned from Hispania with his legions, flushed with victory. Rome appointed Pompey to deal with the slave crisis, but Crassus didn't want to share his glory. Propelled to end the revolt in a grand show of force before Pompey arrived in southern Italy, Crassus relentlessly chased down the escaped slaves. He killed most of them in battle or by crucifixion.

The renowned war hero Pompey joined forces with Caesar and Crassus.

When Pompey was nominated to become Rome's consul in 70 BCE, Crassus swallowed his pride and asked for his support for his own nomination as co-consul. Pompey agreed, figuring that Crassus's immense prosperity made him a better friend than an enemy. Both men won the election; however, neither man trusted the other, and "their contentiousness rendered their consulship barren politically and without achievement."[i]

Gnaeus Pompeius Magnus (better known as Pompey) came from the Picentes tribe on the far side of the Apennine Mountains from Rome. Pompey's father, Strabo, had risen through the ranks to become Rome's consul in 89 BCE but was struck by lightning two years later while defending Rome from Marius. When Sulla marched back to Rome to retake it in 84 BCE, Pompey raised three legions of his father's men to help defeat the Marians. Sulla persuaded Pompey to divorce his first wife and marry Sulla's stepdaughter, Aemilia. As it turned out, she was already pregnant with another man's child and died in childbirth soon after.

Pompey spent the next decade chasing down the remnants of the Marian rebels who had escaped and were attempting to establish

---

[i] Plutarch, *The Parallel Lives*, Volume III.

strongholds in Sicily, North Africa, and Hispania. He crushed the rebellion of Rome's one-time general Sertorius, who had fallen in with pirates and led the Spanish tribes in fighting Roman forces in Hispania. After Pompey's skillful conquest, he marched over the Pyrenees into Gaul and then over the Alps into Italy, conquering 876 towns for Rome along the way.

In 66 BCE, Rome sent Pompey and eight legions east to deal with King Mithridates VI in Pontus, who once again attempted to overthrow Roman power in the Black Sea region. Overwhelmed and outnumbered, Mithridates fled his kingdom, unsuccessfully seeking asylum in Armenia with his son-in-law King Tigranes. He then hid out in the Crimean Peninsula in today's Ukraine, where he eventually committed suicide. Once Mithridates no longer presented a threat, Pompey organized Rome's new frontiers in eastern Europe and western Asia into provinces.

Next, Pompey marched to Syria, which had destabilized when the Seleucid Empire, which had once ruled most of the Middle East, had collapsed. Pompey conquered the major Syrian cities and turned Syria into a Roman province. He then headed south to Judea, which had been semi-autonomous since the 163 BCE Maccabean Revolt. Judea's two princes were immersed in a civil war after Aristobulus II stole his brother Hyrcanus II's throne and priesthood. In this era, the Jewish high priest was also the king. Antipater the Idumean, Hyrcanus's advisor, convinced Hyrcanus to ally with the Arabian king Aretas III and overthrow Aristobulus.

Pompey arrived just as the Arabians were laying siege to Jerusalem. He chased off the Arabs and attacked the heavily fortified temple where Aristobulus was hiding. Pompey broke down the temple walls but left the temple treasures in place, telling the priests to purify the temple and resume their sacrifices. He took Aristobulus back to Rome as a prisoner and restored Hyrcanus II as the high priest but not as king. Judea was now a Roman province, and Julius Caesar later appointed Antipater as the Roman procurator there. After Antipater's death, the Roman Senate appointed his son, Herod the Great, as Judea's vassal king. Herod was a bloodthirsty ruler and is remembered for his atrocities against his citizens and his own family.

Julius Caesar united Pompey and Crassus in the First Triumvirate. [85]

Julius Caesar was born into the ancient Jules family, said to be descended from Rome's mythical ancestor Aeneus. Julius Caesar came of age during the chaotic conflict between Marius and Sulla. Marius was married to Caesar's aunt. When Sulla regained control, one of his targets was Caesar, who had just married Cornelia, the daughter of the former Consul Cinna, one of Sulla's enemies. Sulla ordered the teenage couple to divorce, which Caesar refused to do. He left town in disguise and joined the military.

Cilician pirates kidnapped Caesar while he was abroad, and his family had to pay a ransom for his freedom. He eventually reaped his revenge on the pirates by seizing and crucifying them. In 67 BCE, Pompey systematically eliminated the Cilician pirate threat, which was impeding sea commerce, by capturing and rehabilitating them into farm work in areas with small populations but fertile land.[1] Caesar returned to Rome after Sulla's death and pursued a career in politics. Soon after his young wife Cornelia died, Caesar headed to Hispania as governor.

---

[1] Plutarch, "The Life of Pompey," *Parallel Lives*, Vol. V.

Caesar was deeply in debt because Sulla had seized his inheritance and his wife's dowry, which compelled him to link up with Crassus. In exchange for Caesar's political support, Crassus assisted Caesar in repaying some of his debt. After completing his term in Hispania with distinction, Caesar ran for consul. But he needed more political clout to win, so he reached out to Pompey. The two worked out a quasi-reconciliation between Crassus and Pompey and formed the First Triumvirate.

The Triumvirate initially worked behind the scenes, using their political influence and financing to promote their political agenda, beginning with getting Caesar elected as consul in 59 BCE. Despite Caesar's heroic promotion of the land bill, he faced fierce opposition, most notably from his co-consul Bibulus. The secret Gang of Three became public knowledge when Caesar advocated for the oppressed lower classes and land redistribution. While facing Bibulus's opposition, Caesar called Pompey up to the speaker's platform.

"Pompey! Do you approve this bill?"

"I certainly do," Pompey replied.

"Will you come to the aid of the people?" Caesar asked.

Pompey bellowed, "I certainly will. If necessary, I will provide swords and shields."

Pompey's soldiers filled Rome and cleared the Forum of Caesar's opponents. The bill for land redistribution passed, and the now docile Senate quietly approved all of Caesar's bills for the rest of the year.

At the end of Caesar's consulship, the Senate appointed him as Gaul's new governor, and in 55 BCE, Pompey and Crassus once again served as co-consuls. At the end of that year, Pompey became Hispania's governor, and Crassus finally got his wish to command. However, he died in the Battle of Carrhae in present-day Turkey, and his severed head was used as a prop in Parthian performances. The relationship between Caesar and Pompey had already become strained when Caesar's daughter and Pompey's beloved wife Julia died in childbirth. After Crassus died in 53 BCE, the Triumvirate fell apart. Rome's power would ultimately go to one of the two survivors.

After eight years of stellar military conquests in Gaul, Caesar was powerful and renowned, with an army in peak condition. He was also rich, having paid off his debts and building wealth through war booty. His old friend Pompey was now a bitter rival for power. During Caesar's absence, Rome's political scene dissolved into chaos. Plutarch said bribery was so shameless that corrupt politicians publicly counted out bribe money. He said decisions weren't made by voting but by the force of weapons in the Forum, with blood staining the floor. Rome was like a ship adrift at sea, and the citizens began to think their only salvation was a return to a monarchy. Many thought Pompey was an excellent candidate.[i]

Caesar was returning to Rome from Gaul, but the Senate insisted that he disband his legions, which was customary for commanders returning from military campaigns. Marching toward Rome with an army could be considered an act of war against the city. But Caesar daringly crossed the Rubicon River, located between Cisalpine Gaul and Italy, with one legion of five thousand men in 49 BCE. Many senators scampered off to southern Italy, and Pompey fled to Macedonia.

Caesar entered Rome peacefully, politely addressing the senators who remained. He helped himself to the state reserve funds, using it to fund his next exploit: an astounding twenty-seven-day march back over the Alps into Gaul and down to Hispania, where Pompey's army encamped. "I shall fight an army without a leader so I can fight the leader without his army."

Pompey's army was caught off-guard and quickly fell. But Pompey had a network of allies throughout Asia and assembled a new army and a three-hundred-ship navy. Caesar did not have a large enough fleet to take him on, but an overconfident Pompey met him for a land battle in Thessaly, in which Caesar's battle-hardened army routed Pompey's forces. Pompey sailed to Egypt, hoping to find sanctuary, but the Egyptian pharaoh, Ptolemy XIII, had him killed and gave his head to Caesar when he arrived shortly after.

Caesar wept at the unexpected murder of his one-time friend and co-conspirator and vowed to avenge Pompey. He killed the two men who stabbed Pompey to death and the pharaoh's advisor who had suggested the murder. Caesar was now the last man standing in the Gang of Three, and for the next five years, he would be Rome's dictator. The Roman Republic was gasping its final breaths.

---

[i] Plutarch, *Fall of the Roman Republic* (London: Penguin Classics, April 25th, 2006), 242-250. Internet Archives:
https://archive.org/stream/FallOfTheRomanRepublicPlutarch.rOpts/Fall%20Of%20TheRomanRepublic%20Plutarch.r-opts_djvu.txt.

Chapter 11: Causes and Consequences of the Fallen Republic

What led to the fall of the Roman Republic? How did foreign and civil war impact Rome's instability? What role did Caesar play in its downfall? Could it be possible that a lack of war destroyed the republic since revenue slowed down? In this chapter, we will explore what happened in the final few years of the Roman Republic and analyze several factors that contributed to its fall.

Caesar got sidelined in Egypt when he met Cleopatra VII, the sister, wife, and co-pharaoh of thirteen-year-old Ptolemy XIII. Charmed by her beauty and wit, Caesar became her lover and got involved in Egypt's convoluted royal family politics. Cleopatra's brother-husband had forced her off the throne, making himself the sole ruler of Egypt. She left the country, put together her own army, and returned to fight for her throne close to the time Caesar arrived. Caesar got embroiled in the war between the two, and Ptolemy drowned in the conflict. Caesar arranged for a nominal marriage between Cleopatra and her twelve-year-old brother Ptolemy XIV while she was pregnant with Caesar's child. She gave birth to Caesarion in 47 BCE; he was Caesar's only biological son, although some argue that Caesarion was not his son.

From 49 to 44 BCE, Caesar alternated between consul, proconsul, and dictator but was always in control of Rome. Months before his assassination, he was appointed *dictator perpetuo*, or dictator for life. Caesar finally had the time and power to carry out his reforms, such as addressing the unemployment and debt of the plebeian masses and initiating further land reassignments. He modified the calendar and launched extensive construction projects that transformed Rome; he was greatly inspired by the beauty of Alexandria in Egypt.

Despite liking some of his reforms, Rome's senators feared Caesar would turn the republic back into a monarchy and plotted his murder. On March 15th, 44 BCE, just as Caesar walked into the Senate, a mob of senators reportedly stabbed him twenty-three times. Caesar's murderers' hopes to restore the republic to its former glory were dashed when Rome's citizens turned against them and rioted at his funeral. The conspirators escaped to foreign lands.

Octavian (Augustus) became Rome's first emperor, ending the Roman Republic. [86]

Caesar's heir was his eighteen-year-old grand-nephew Octavian, who was not the war hero or canny politician Caesar had been. He was a weak and sickly teenager with an overprotective mother. When news reached

Octavian's family of Caesar's assassination, they were in Apollonia (modern-day Albania). The household was in turmoil, fearing the assassins would come after them next, but they knew Caesar's murder must be avenged. His friends advised Octavian to join the army in Macedonia, as the soldiers there were loyal to Caesar and would protect him. But Octavian had no military experience. He decided to head to Rome and find out what the situation was.

When Octavian arrived in Italy, he discovered that Caesar's will had named him Caesar's adoptive son and left him three-fourths of his estate. Caesar's assassins who were still in Rome were promising freedom to Rome's slaves in exchange for protecting them. Hordes of people from the tribes around Italy who had benefited from Caesar's legislation were pouring into Rome and forming an ad hoc army.[i]

Caesar's well-known general and relative Mark Antony became Rome's next consul. Another leader was Marcus Lepidus, who became *pontifex maximus*, or high priest. When Octavian arrived in Rome, Mark Antony refused to release Caesar's estate to him. Public opinion turned against Antony in favor of Octavian. The Senate assigned Antony the governorship of Macedonia at the end of his consulship, but he demanded Cisalpine Gaul instead, marching north to claim the province. The Senate declared Antony an outlaw and sent Octavian to rein him in, but Antony escaped over the Alps into Transalpine Gaul, where Lepidus was governor.

Octavian returned to Rome to discover the senators were plotting to regain political power and eliminate him, giving Caesar's murderer Brutus command of Rome's legions. But some of the legions had fought under Caesar and refused Brutus's command. Octavian marched to Rome with Caesar's loyal legions, announced himself as the new consul, and tried and convicted Caesar's murderers in absentia.

Realizing he needed the support of Antony and Lepidus, Octavian formed the Second Triumvirate in 43 BCE, a three-person military dictatorship. They split up the western provinces: Antony became Gaul's governor, Lepidus took Hispania, and Octavian ruled North Africa. The opposition leaders— Pompey's son Sextus and two of Caesar's assassins, Brutus and Cassius—held the eastern provinces.

---

[i] Nicolaus of Damascus, *Life of Augustus*, trans. Clayton M. Hall. https://web.archive.org/web/20070714144802/http://www.csun.edu/~hcfll004/nicolaus.html.

The Second Triumvirate's first order of business was executing all of Caesar's assassins in Rome and replenishing Rome's nearly empty treasury with their fortunes. Next on the agenda was retaking the eastern Mediterranean. When Antony and Octavian prevailed over Brutus and Cassius, the two assassins committed suicide, leaving only Sextus Pompey, whose fleet was blocking grain from coming into Italy. Octavian negotiated a deal with Sextus, giving him control of some of Rome's territories in exchange for lifting the blockade.

Lepidus got kicked out of the Second Triumvirate when he and Octavian quarreled about control over Sicily. Antony became romantically involved with Caesar's former lover Cleopatra. Then, Octavian discovered Antony's will hidden in the Vestal Virgins' temple, in which Antony declared Cleopatra's son Caesarion as Caesar's biological son and heir. This threatened Octavian's legitimacy as Caesar's heir, which led to Antony's ejection from the Triumvirate in 32 BCE and the Senate declaring war on Cleopatra.

In 31 BCE, Octavian (now called Caesar Augustus) fought the Battle of Actium in the Ionian Sea, conquering Antony and Cleopatra, both of whom fled to Egypt. A year later, Augustus attacked Egypt, and Antony and Cleopatra committed suicide. Augustus killed Caesar's teenage son Caesarion but spared Cleopatra's young children by Antony, giving them to his sister (Antony's widow) to raise. With Antony's death, Caesar Augustus was now the sole ruler of Rome, and the government segued from a republic to an empire.

The contribution of foreign wars to the republic's downfall cannot be underestimated. Foreign conquests stimulated Rome's economy when they were successful, and most of them were. The Second Punic War brought 140,000 gold pieces, 600,000 silver pieces, and over 137,000 pounds of raw silver into Rome. One campaign in Hispania brought in forty thousand pounds of raw silver. The once-austere Romans began buying luxuries like fine jewelry and tapestries. This paradigm shift in values led Cato the Elder to warn, "We have crossed into Greece and Asia, places filled with all the allurements of vice, and we are handling the treasures of kings ... I fear these things will capture us rather than we them."[i]

---

[i] Michael Duncan, *The Storm Before the Storm: The Beginning of the End of the Roman Republic* (New York: PublicAffairs, 2017), 19.

Most of the spoils of war went to the upper classes, while the conscripted plebeian soldiers came home to overgrown and neglected farmlands. Sometimes the task of restoring the fields was overwhelming, and the patricians grabbed up the plebeians' farms at below-market prices. The patrician farms grew into enormous plantations farmed by enslaved people from abroad. Meanwhile, the landless plebeians had to look for work in the towns and cities.

> "The triumph of the Republic was also its tragedy. The very forces that drove the expansion of Rome, and the rewards that expansion brought, led to social, economic, and political crises and plunged the Republic into a descending spiral of civil war. The institutions of Republican government failed under the pressure of maintaining Rome's empire, and sole power finally passed into the hands of Augustus, the first Roman emperor."[i]

Callous abuse by the patricians led to escalating civil wars with the disenfranchised former soldiers and other plebeians. Furthermore, Rome faced the question of citizenship for the rest of Italy. Civil wars also raged between politicians in the quest for ultimate power, such as between Sulla and Marius and later between Pompey and Caesar. The civil wars reduced Rome's male citizens to only 150,000 by the end of Caesar's reign.[ii] These multiple issues causing social breakdown crumbled the democratic pillars upon which the republic had been established.

The Romans exploited the fighting skills and tax revenues from the tribes around Italy. About two-thirds of Rome's fighting force during the wars with Carthage were non-Roman Italians. Yet, Rome did not grant these soldiers any spoils of war or plots of land in the conquered regions. Furthermore, underlying prejudice kept Rome from extending citizenship to the rest of Italy, which the disgruntled Italian allies felt was their due, considering how much they contributed to defending and expanding the Republic.

Because of unrest, the Senate evicted all non-citizens from Rome in 95 BCE. When the Plebeian Tribune Drusus pushed for land redistribution and citizenship for all Italians, he was assassinated in 91 BCE, leading to the Social War between Rome and the Italian tribes. Marius and Sulla

---

[i] David M. Gwynn, *The Roman Republic: A Very Short Introduction* (Oxford: Oxford University Press, 2012), 1-2.
[ii] Plutarch, *Fall of the Roman Republic*, 263.

fought together against the rebel tribes (this was before they fell out), killing six thousand and capturing seven thousand. But finally, Rome granted citizenship and voting rights to all of Italy's men, almost doubling the number of male citizens.

Another factor contributing to the collapse of the Roman Republic was the eventual lack of war, leading to a slowdown in revenue. While Rome was conquering and expanding, the massive wealth pouring in created a system of corrupt officials who used their new wealth to bribe their way to greater power. The plebeian masses already had little faith in the senators, and the depraved behavior among the ruling class eroded the remnant of trust that remained. As Rome's foreign conquests grounded to a halt, so did the massive influx of income. Rome now had to raise taxes to support its infrastructure, which increased the population's resentment.

Julius Caesar's lifestyle and mode of governing contributed to the Roman Republic's demise, but his assassination arguably factored in more. After Caesar returned from Gaul and was reelected as consul, his reign grew increasingly autocratic. His passion for becoming king became apparent. His image was stamped on coins, royal diadems appeared on his statues, and Caesar enveloped himself in a purple toga.

The conspirators who stabbed Caesar twenty-three times believed they were preserving the republic but instead plunged Rome into another civil war. The lower and middle classes had lost their champion who had legislated on their behalf, and Caesar's murder left a power vacuum. By this point, political norms had broken down, and the people were so weary of rigged elections that they were ready to welcome an autocrat.

The republic functioned relatively well for its first three centuries, adjusting to new challenges while maintaining political standards. But violence reared its ugly head in 133 BCE when Rome's senators beat Tribune Tiberius Gracchus and his supporters to death with wooden chairs. Fifty years later, the war between Marius and Sulla led to the execution and confiscation of property of political opponents.

Senators began using absurd tactics against proposed legislation they didn't want to be passed. They simply found excuses not to meet for the vote, and there were all sorts of procedural delays. One consul declared every day of the year a religious holiday so no votes could be held. With rampant bribery and violence, the political norms of the republic had irretrievably fractured even before Julius Caesar's assassination. But Octavian, renamed Caesar Augustus, put the final nail in the coffin.

Rome was ready for a change, and Augustus seemed to provide a way forward.[97]

By the time the senators assassinated Caesar, most Romans had no memory of what a functioning republic should look like. All they knew was political dysfunction and violence. Caesar Augustus gallantly stepped into the power vacuum and promised a return to law and order. By this point, most Romans were willing to exchange the democratic ideals of the republic, which had not been in operation anyway, for an emperor. Even though elections were no longer "free" and no one could run for office without Augustus's approval, they welcomed the end of the chaos.

The fall of the Roman Republic wasn't due to a single factor but multiple causes. Violent, corrupt, and dysfunctional politics disillusioned the people. The astounding wealth pouring in from conquered countries corrupted the ruling class, who ignored the needs of the despairing working-class citizens. Lethal civil wars tore Rome apart and decimated the population. Caesar's heavy-handed politics dismayed the senators, but his legislation for the downtrodden pleased the masses. Most Romans perceived Augustus as the golden child who would rescue them from anarchy and lead Rome to new heights of civilization.

Chapter 12: Influence and Legacy of the Roman Republic

The shift from a republic to an empire was not as abrupt and complete as it might seem. Rome certainly experienced a shift in senior leadership, but many political and social institutions remained fundamentally unchanged. The complex legacy of the republic continued to influence the Roman Empire through its philosophy, political system, social structure, military organization, and other factors. The Roman Republic was ahead of its time in numerous aspects. It not only influenced the empire that followed it but left its mark on the Western world for two millennia.

One of the most enduring legacies of the republican era was its philosophy. Cicero, Lucretius, Seneca the Younger, and other Roman Republic philosophers promoted political and social ideas that impacted the Roman Empire and the Western world. Although it's easy to dwell on the republic's frailties and failures, it created a fluid constitutional system that accommodated change through the centuries. The Romans found novel ways to address unprecedented challenges as a society, and politics evolved. The Roman Republic had the world's first large-scale constitutional government, which eventually ruled over three continents and endured for centuries into the imperial era.

Cicero championed the republic's traditional political system, and he and like-minded statesmen strove to maintain its principles as the government crumbled. Although Rome borrowed some political ideas from the Greeks, Cicero felt that Rome had shown the Greeks how to do politics properly. He maintained that the Greeks were indebted to the Romans for developing a system that persisted through the centuries and the challenges of unimaginable expansion. The republic's underlying political philosophy was the foundation of its governmental system. Students and politicians studied these earlier philosophical treatises during the imperial age as they coped with the rapidly changing scenarios that rocked the empire.

The word "republic" comes from the Latin phrase *res publica*, meaning "the people's affair" or "the public's property." The Roman Republic was the affair of all the people rather than a single monarch or ruling group of elders. Its distinguishing feature was *libertas*, or freedom, but not unlimited freedom or license to trample on others' rights and freedoms. Cicero wrote, "Law is liberty's foundation, and we are all slaves of the law that we might be free."[i]

The "rule of law" protected liberty by preventing anyone from being above the law. Although not all citizens were socially equal, they were equal in the sense that the law applied to everyone. Cicero believed that a universal and unchanging natural law was intrinsic to human nature. He taught that immoral behavior and false ideology could suppress this innate law. He thought that this natural law was the bedrock of justice. This concept of natural law was reflected in Saint Paul's epistle to the Romans:

> "For when Gentiles, who do not have the law, by nature do what the law requires, they are a law to themselves, even though they do not have the law. They show that the work of the law is written on their hearts, while their conscience also bears witness, and their conflicting thoughts accuse or even excuse them."[ii]

Consequential elements of the republic's political system persisted into the empire. From its early days, the republic had the tradition of electing a short-term dictator to deal with crises, such as an invasion or a civil war. Once the crisis was over, the dictator resigned from his position. But this position opened the door for an emperor when the Senate appointed Julius Caesar "dictator for life" shortly before his assassination.

---

[i] Cicero, *Pro Cluentio*, http://www.thelatinlibrary.com/cicero/cluentio.shtml.
[ii] Rom 2:14-15, English Standard Version.

When Caesar Augustus (Octavian) became Rome's first "emperor," the power shifted from elected representatives to a monarch. Augustus could introduce laws and veto laws introduced by others. He also had to give consent to those running for political offices. This power shift made the political assemblies primarily ceremonial. Nevertheless, Augustus had to tread carefully.

The Romans had overthrown their despotic king five centuries earlier, and their abhorrence of anything resembling a monarchy persisted. The senators killed Julius Caesar because he seemed hellbent on making himself king. Even though Octavian cherished the same ambition, he engineered his ascension to power with great finesse. He was careful to acknowledge the Senate's authority and ostensibly restored its full power.

Octavian outwardly championed the republican traditions and constitution and was diligent not to *call* himself king or emperor. Instead, he humbly accepted the titles the Senate gave him, such as "Princeps" (first or chief of the Senate) and the religious title of "Augustus" (illustrious one). He also called himself "Imperator" (commander) but was careful not to wear a crown or purple toga and not to carry a scepter. Rather than declaring himself Rome's supreme ruler, he astutely gave outward respect to the Senate while quietly appointing new senators who supported him, gradually building his power base.

The Senate survived the leadership change because Augustus needed to legitimize his rule. His authority came from the Senate, and as Rome's leading citizens, the senators influenced the people's perception of their leader. Rome's emperors acquired the position in diverse ways. For example, some were the previous emperors' biological or adopted sons or grandsons. Others snatched the throne with the assistance of the military. But the Senate had to legitimize an emperor's rule, and the emperor had to keep the military's loyalty. Thus, the Senate played a decisive role in kingmaking, as it granted power to the emperor when he started his reign but stripped him of power if he displeased the senators.

Citizenship was an honor that progressively included more groups of people throughout the five centuries of the Roman Republic. At the founding of the republic, all men sixteen and older from the tribes of Rome were citizens. To flaunt their status, Roman citizens wore white togas on formal occasions. Citizenship gave men the right to vote and engage in trade. Eventually, all adult Italian freeborn males could become Roman citizens. Toward the end of the republic, "freedmen" or formerly enslaved people could receive citizenship.

Emperor Claudius extended Roman citizenship to the men of Gaul.[38]

Citizenship became even more inclusive during the empire. The Senate initially fought against people from Rome's foreign provinces receiving citizenship. But Emperor Claudius, who ruled from 41 to 54 CE, pushed for extending citizenship to the men of Gaul (France) and even admitting them into the Senate. The senators combatted this proposal, fearing that the Britons, Gauls, Greeks, and Spaniards would all be wearing togas, but Claudius prevailed. By 212 CE, the Edict of Caracalla granted citizenship to all free males in the Roman provinces.

From its earliest years, the republic experienced ongoing tension between the patrician aristocrats and the plebeian working class. Only fourteen years into the republic, the plebeians staged their first secession, where they went on strike, abandoning the Roman army in the midst of a war with the neighboring Italic tribes. Gradually, over time, the plebeians gained more and more power. By 287 BCE, they enjoyed the same rights and access to political positions that the patricians had. Lines between the patricians and plebeians had blurred by the time the empire began. Yet, there was still a distinct wealthy ruling class, which now included some nouveau-riche plebeians. As always, there were the poorer working classes and enslaved people.

The patriarchal family system also continued into the empire, which meant the men controlled politics and business while women were expected to run the household. Girls and women were under their father's authority, even after they married and started their own families. Their fathers arranged their marriages when they were as young as twelve, and they had little input into who they would marry. Women would lose their children to their husbands in the event of a divorce.

When Rome transitioned from a republic to an empire, Caesar Augustus implemented changes to the army, such as how long a man would serve. As Rome encountered new cultures and enemies, the military developed innovative strategies and troop formations to fight more effectively. The Roman army used its cavalry more often and improved the technology of its siege engines to launch artillery more competently.

The military also gained more political clout in the transition to an empire. In the Roman Republic, military commanders were often the consuls, and military generals who fought with distinction often won the election to the consulship. This close relationship between the military and top political power continued into the empire. However, the army was occasionally responsible for making a favorite general the new emperor. The military and the Praetorian Guard (the emperor's bodyguards) also assassinated some unpopular emperors.

Rome's remarkable road system began in the early republic with the 450 BCE Law of the Twelve Tables, which stipulated roads had to be at least eight Roman feet wide (a Roman foot is estimated to be 11.65 inches). As the Romans conquered the tribes around Italy, they built roads connecting Rome to their new territories. The central government financed the building costs of these arteries, but the provinces they passed through were responsible for maintaining the roads.

When Augustus came to power, he found the road maintenance system inefficient. He took personal charge of it, as did the emperors who followed him. Although merchants and ordinary people used the roads, their primary purpose was military transport. As the republic grew, the Romans built roads in the new provinces outside Italy. That road system increased to nearly seventy-five thousand miles during the empire.

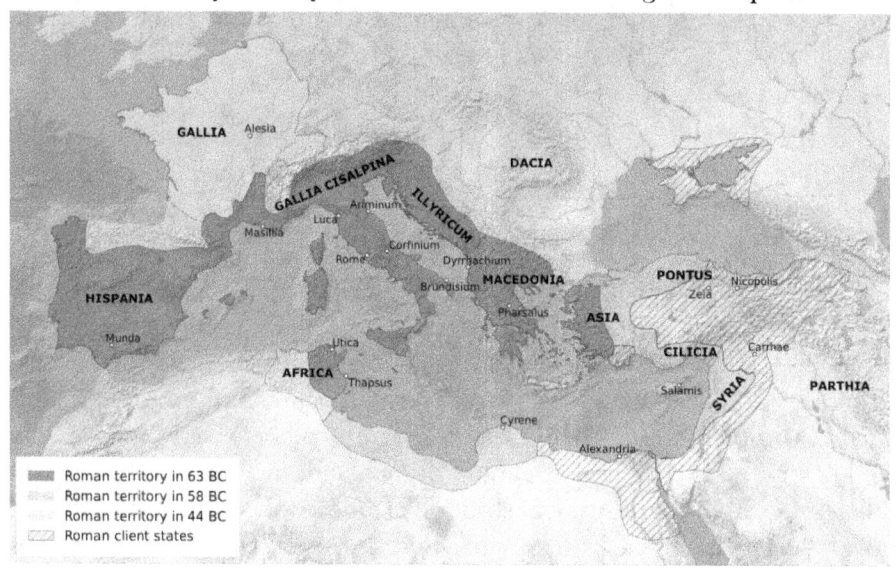

This map depicts Roman territory at the end of the republic. [89]

Over its five centuries, the Roman Republic grew from a modest city-state in central Italy to encompass the Italian Peninsula by 200 BCE. Over the next two hundred years, the republic conquered North Africa's coastal region, most of Hispania (Spain and Portugal), Gaul (France), part of Britain, and Greece. Toward the end of the republic, Rome conquered today's Macedonia, Bulgaria, Albania, Montenegro, Croatia, western Turkey, Syria, Lebanon, and Israel.

This avid quest for conquering territory continued during the Roman Empire. At its peak under Emperor Trajan, the empire contained about one-quarter of the global population. By this time, the Roman Empire included the North African coast, stretching from Egypt to Morocco, all of Spain and France, Belgium, part of Germany, all of England, most of Wales, Switzerland, Austria, the entire Balkan Peninsula, Turkey, Armenia, Iraq, Syria, Lebanon, and Israel.

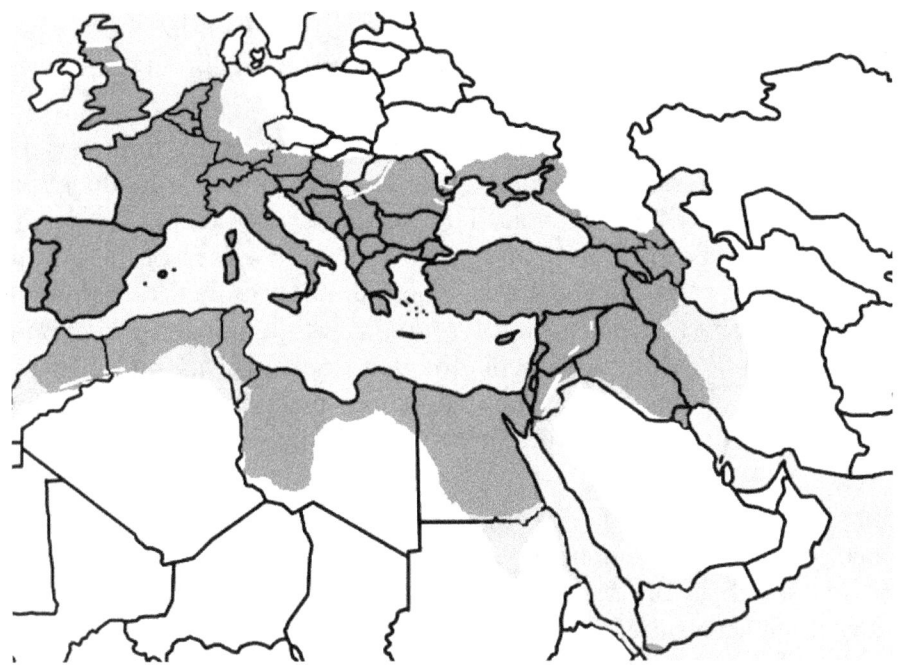
Rome's expansion began in the republic and continued into the imperial era. [40]

As the republic and then the empire grew to cover parts of three continents, it became increasingly diverse, absorbing the religions, art styles, architecture, and other elements of culture. The incredible size of the republic and empire brought inconceivable wealth to Rome. It also brought the burden and cost of maintaining roads, bridges, aqueducts, and other infrastructure across a considerable section of the world.

The Roman Republic was ahead of its time in multiple ways, one of which was its structured government. Rome's political institutions stood the test of time by being flexible enough to adapt to change. Many of today's democratic governments have implemented aspects of the Roman Republic's political system, such as checks and balances, representation of the people, term limits, separate executive and legislative branches, and the veto.

Enlightenment philosophers of the 18th century, such as Montesquieu and Rousseau, proposed that a serious study of politics required an examination of the Roman Republic. Montesquieu's analysis of the Roman Republic's government led him to propose the separation of powers: executive, legislative, and judicial. Rousseau's *The Social Contract* went into great detail on the Roman Republic's institutional workings, which he considered a model of virtue. Rousseau idealized the

Roman Republic as a place where absolute power lay with the people, while the republic's administration was the responsibility of an elected government.

Another way the Roman Republic was ahead of its time was by adopting the Forum as a meeting place for government, something that would be replicated for millennia. The Forum was the heart of Rome, the center of commerce, religion, and politics. A vital element of the Forum was the public nature of the Curia, where the Senate met. Government decisions weren't made in a throne room, as with a monarchy, nor were they made by a small group behind closed doors, as with an oligarchy. They were in a public venue where just about anybody could listen in on the proposals, debates, and votes, although only the senators could speak.

The Roman Republic was ahead of its time with progressive technology and brilliant engineering. The construction of its road system, which spanned three continents, involved tunneling through mountains and building high bridges over ravines and rivers. The Pons Fabricius bridge, built across the Tiber River in Rome in 62 BCE, is still in use in its original state, a testament to the extraordinary excellence of Roman engineering. Modern road construction still uses the road-building techniques developed by the Romans.

The Pons Fabricius bridge has stood for over two thousand years. [41]

The Romans had one of the world's first sewage systems, which was built about 2,500 years ago, around the same time as the republic's inception. Although the Mesopotamians had developed primitive aqueducts, the Romans took the technology of running water to new heights. Eleven aqueducts carried water into Rome. The water was held in large holding tanks and then piped throughout the city for drinking, cooking, bathing, and latrines. Public latrines were often connected to the public baths, and the bath water would be flushed through the toilets. The Romans used ingenious technology to construct the aqueducts so the water continued moving by force of gravity as it passed over mountains and deep ravines. When necessary, inverted siphons moved water uphill. They were in a U-shape, so the power of the water running downhill pushed it back up the other side.

The Romans of the republic were genuinely ahead of their time with their political philosophy and governmental institutions, which continued to influence the empire. Their political thought impacted Enlightenment philosophers in the Age of Reason and guided new democratic governments in recent centuries. Their roads, aqueducts, sewers, and military technology continued to be used and developed throughout the empire and beyond.

Conclusion

The Roman Republic's worldview, culture, military, government, legal system, language, and technology left an indelible imprint on the world for the next two millennia. The republic's legacy survived through the imperial era and beyond. It influenced the underlying philosophy of developing Western nations, impacted the literature and art of the Renaissance period, and has affected engineering and architecture to the present day.

The Roman Republic's ongoing struggle for dominance over Carthage and the Hellenistic powers ultimately changed the center of power in North Africa, Europe, and western Asia. But it also changed Rome. Carthage's Phoenician heritage, ship-building, navigational skills, and extensive trade networks left their mark on Rome. Rome appropriated Carthaginian achievements and knowledge, copied their ships, and eventually took over their empire.

Rome likewise assimilated Greek culture and innovations through military interactions, sometimes as allies and other times as conquerors. The combining of cultures led to the Greco-Roman blend of architecture, engineering, literature, medicine, philosophy, politics, religion, and sculpture, which still shapes today's worldview and aesthetics. Greco-Roman writers like Cicero, Plato, Varro, and Virgil influenced Saint Augustine's writings, which laid the foundation of Christian thought. The Renaissance awakened interest in Greco-Roman philosophers like Aristotle, Marcus Aurelius, and Seneca the Younger, influencing political opinion.

The Roman Republic's internal struggles between the plebeians and patricians and the issues of citizenship and slavery challenged and changed the republic over its five centuries. As Rome conquered much of the known world, the astounding profits of war corrupted its recipients while widening the gap between the aristocratic politicians and the common people. Economic stagnation accompanied a slowdown in expansion, and political infighting gradually descended into corruption, allowing violence to open the door to imperial rule.

As Rome grew from a city-state into an empire, its military inevitably changed. Rather than soldiers fighting for a few months of the year, young men were drafted to spend up to two decades in Rome's foreign provinces. These full-time soldiers were highly disciplined and impeccably trained. The Roman army and navy developed into an unusually advanced fighting force with phenomenal siege engines and strategies. Rome's structured and efficient military led to its unimaginable expansion.

The Romans were prodigious assimilators and replicated some of their military foes' strategies, armor, and weapons. Their war with Carthage compelled them to build their own navy by using a wrecked Phoenician ship as a model. As they honed their naval skills, the Romans proved to be a formidable and almost indomitable marine force against Carthage, which had previously ruled the seas. Rome's naval expertise drove Hannibal to fight Rome in land battles rather than at sea.

When confronted with Rome's intimidating military, many cities and tribes simply surrendered rather than fight a war they'd probably lose with enormous losses. Rome was surprisingly benign toward such cities, states, and tribal confederations. They usually allowed them to keep their own leadership as long as they acknowledged Rome's ultimate authority, paid tribute, and provided men for Rome's military machine. Any state that did not surrender immediately faced Rome's brutal wrath, which could mean completely leveling a city or wiping out most of the population, including women and children.

The Roman military left a remarkable legacy. Often, when one thinks of Rome, the image of a Roman soldier comes to mind, and for good reason. Rome's military discipline, strategies, engineering, and command have been studied and imitated throughout the centuries. Many modern military schools analyze the Roman military and the models of famous generals like Julius Caesar and Pompey.

Throughout history, Rome's legal system served as a foundation for law codes and practices in the Western world. Rome's codified law system began in 450 BCE with the Law of the Twelve Tables inscribed on twelve bronze tablets. In the republic, the citizens' assembly passed laws that were then sent to the Senate for ratification, a model still followed in many democratic governments today. The Roman legal system presumed innocence until proven guilty and held trials by jury.

The Latin language the Romans spoke became the lingua franca (common language) in its territories, which spanned three continents. It gave birth to the Romance languages, such as French, Italian, Portuguese, Romanian, and Spanish. About one-third of English words have Latin roots, and another one-third come from Romance languages descended from Latin. Latin is still used today in medicine, science, and law. The written Roman alphabet, a legacy of the Etruscans, also looks surprisingly similar to our letters today, except the Romans only had capital letters.

The road network of the Roman Republic led to the saying, "All roads lead to Rome." The roads were built so that they traveled in virtually straight lines from Rome to its conquered cities. A few small sections of Roman roads still have their original cobblestones today, and others were repaved into today's highways of Europe. The astonishingly resilient Roman roads used layers of dirt, gravel, brick, and paving stones. A slight decline from the center to the sides drained rainwater off the road. Rome's legions could march about twenty miles a day on these well-built roads.

The Roman Republic was an incredible era in time, as Rome changed both for the better and the worse. It still influences many aspects of our lives, perhaps more than we know. The calendar we use today is based on Julius Caesar's revision in 45 BCE, with a leap year every 4 years adding an extra day to the usual 365 days. His calendar assigned January 1st as the first day of the year. The names of the months we use today are all Roman; they are named after some of the gods, Roman numbers, Roman festivals, and Julius Caesar and Augustus.

The Roman Republic, in all its glory and tumultuous collapse, inspires and cautions us. The Roman Republic instructs us on the factors that make a society flourish and the elements that can quickly plunge it into a disastrous tailspin. When the Romans followed political norms, when they included all citizens in the political process, and when they promoted justice, the republic prospered. When they allowed wealth to corrupt, when they became violent and disorganized, when they ignored the needs of the masses, and when they trampled on political ethics, they descended into chaos. *Caveat lector!* Let the reader beware.

Part 2: Roman Empire

An Enthralling Overview of Imperial Rome

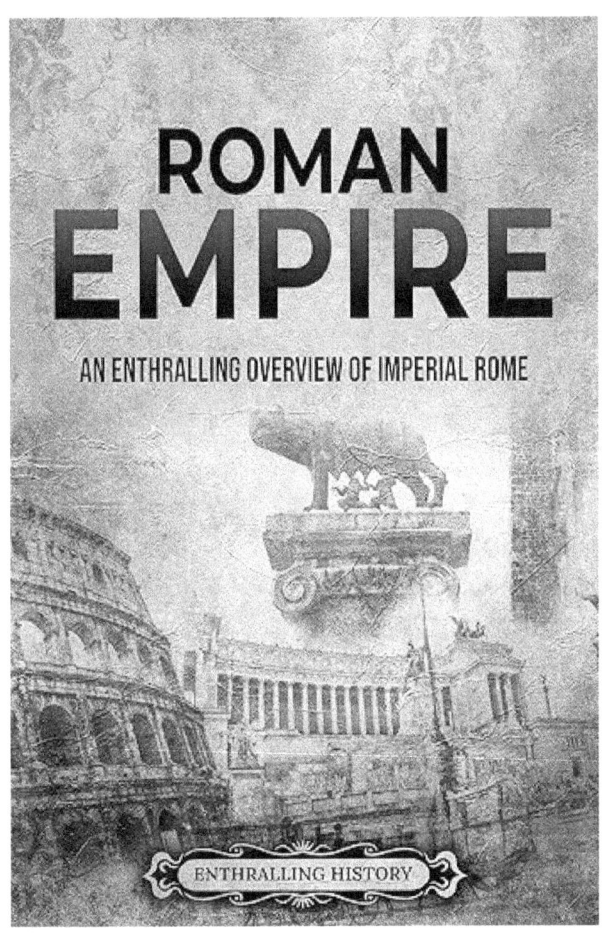

Introduction

The first civilization sprang to life sometime around 3500 BCE in Mesopotamia. A couple of centuries later, the Nile began to witness the first signs of settlers on its riverbanks. Later on, the Greeks were born and quickly rose as one of the most influential civilizations to ever exist. Fast forward to over a thousand years later, and the earth saw the emergence of yet another civilization. This time around, it was somewhere around the region of Yangtze, China. It was not until the mid-8th century BCE that the world finally welcomed the Roman civilization, which was believed to have been founded near the Tiber River.

Despite the Romans' late arrival compared, their ancient civilization managed to thrive. Starting with only a small, humble kingdom, the Romans then entered a long yet harsh period of a republic before finally transforming into one of the most powerful empires in the whole world. It encompassed the majority of the European continent, the Mediterranean islands, North Africa, and most parts of West Asia.

Rome, sometimes known as the Eternal City, was the empire's nucleus. In this very city, one could find the emperor's palace. It was also the heart of Rome, as senators would converge there to discuss pressing matters of the state. The Roman Forum, Circus Maximus, and, of course, the well-known Colosseum were all located within the glorious Eternal City. In fact, Rome is widely considered by historians as one of the greatest cities to ever exist in ancient history. Its many surviving structures and records are a constant reminder of how advanced the Roman civilization was back then.

As an empire that never ceased to see the expansion of its frontiers every few years, the Romans were no doubt proud of their military prowess. They experienced more than a dozen defeats throughout the years—Pyrrhus, Hannibal, and Mithridates VI of Pontus were some of ancient Rome's most formidable foes—but the Roman military was known for its strong resilience. Their training would only get harder, as did the punishments, which ensured the soldiers were always ready for another battle. To put it simply, the Romans had absolutely zero knowledge of how to lose, which eventually became the main key to the empire's success.

However, conquest campaigns and battles were not Rome's only pressing matters, as Rome was constantly entangled with its own political issues. The empire was governed by weak and selfish emperors multiple times, which often resulted in chaos. Economic crises, famine, and deadly plagues were also familiar to the Romans; these were some of the factors that nearly crushed the empire to the ground in the 3rd century CE. However, the Roman Empire prevailed and overcame each of the obstacles thrown at them, but the bloody skirmishes and conflicts would never fully end.

This book aims to provide readers with not only an enthralling journey into the events that took place in the Roman Empire but also an interesting overview of how the Romans lived their daily lives within the safe walls of the Eternal City. Discover how Augustus became the Father of Rome, the different social classes and their traditions, the spread of Christianity, and the terrible fall of the Western Roman Empire.

Chapter 1 – Augustus and the Claudians

Julius Caesar is remembered for being one of Rome's greatest generals. It is sometimes hard to remember that he was also human. When a blade stabbed the fifty-five-year-old dictator, he bled. All it took for the dictator to stumble and drop helplessly to the floor was a stab to the neck. After twenty-three stabs gifted by his fellow senators, Julius Caesar finally succumbed to his wounds. His purple toga was drenched in a pool of his blood, and his body was left unattended for a few hours at the base of the Curia of Pompey, as none dared to approach the once glorious dictator for life.

The assassination of Julius Caesar.[48]

Words about Caesar's terrible assassination reached nineteen-year-old Gaius Octavius (better known as Octavian), Caesar's grand-nephew, who was undergoing his military studies in Apollonia with his childhood friend, Marcus Vipsanius Agrippa. Some claimed that Octavian was initially hesitant to return to Rome after hearing the news, as he suspected the conspirators might hunt him next, especially since Caesar had no legitimate children by Roman law. However, he later changed his mind after listening to Agrippa's advice.

Octavian set sail to Italy, where he learned the contents of Caesar's will. Aside from leaving two-thirds of his fortune to Octavian, the late dictator had officially adopted Octavian, thus making him his heir. After officially accepting the adoption, Octavian assumed the name Gaius Julius Caesar, which led most of the public to welcome his return warmly. However, one influential figure was not on the same page as the others. His name was Mark Antony. He had been Caesar's closest ally and one of his best generals.

From the very beginning, Octavian never saw eye to eye with Antony. Although Octavian expressed his gratitude to Antony for arranging Caesar's funeral, he also criticized him for pardoning the conspirators. Antony, who consistently underestimated Octavian, fueled the rivalry between them by denying the future emperor's rights to Caesar's fortune—one of the signs that showed Antony's abuse of power.

Some of the senators, especially Marcus Tullius Cicero, Rome's greatest orator and statesman, began to withdraw their support for Antony, as they saw him as yet another power-hungry tyrant. Most of them shifted their focus to Octavian, whom they thought was the lesser evil. Seeing that the growing tension between the two rivals could be put to good use, Cicero composed the *Philippics*, a series of hate speeches condemning Antony in an effort to rally the senators against him. It was successful, as Mark Antony was declared a public enemy soon after.

Octavian, along with two other consuls, Hirtius and Pansa, were dispatched by the Senate to suppress Antony, who was laying siege on Decimus in Cisalpine Gaul. The two consuls, however, lost their lives during the battle, thus giving Octavian an opportunity to showcase his impressive command. Antony's forces were defeated in 43 BCE by Octavian. However, the Senate had no intention of rewarding the future emperor since his growing influence was considered a threat. The command of Rome's legions was granted to Decimus instead of Octavian, while Caesar's main assassins, Cassius and Brutus, were given governorships of Macedonia and Syria.

Seeing that there was no other way to bring Rome back to its glory with the Senate's treacherous decisions, Octavian resorted to an unlikely alliance with Antony and Marcus Aemilius Lepidus, another one of Caesar's close allies and generals. Together, they formed the Second Triumvirate and established the Lex Pedia, a law that punished all of those who were involved in Caesar's assassination. They hunted down every senator who was thought to be involved in the murder and confiscated their fortune—even Cicero, who did not participate in the murder directly, met his fate. The Second Triumvirate soon accomplished their mission when they emerged victorious at the Battle of Philippi, where they put an end to the main conspirators, Cassius and Brutus.

An illustration of the Battle of Actium in 31 BCE.[48]

With Caesar's murderers gone, the Second Triumvirate retained their power over the Roman Republic for years to come. However, Antony's decision to divorce Octavia (Octavian's sister) in favor of the Egyptian queen Cleopatra caused a horrendous stir in Rome. The Senate stripped Antony of his powers and declared war on Cleopatra, which led to the Battle of Actium—the last civil war of the Roman Republic, which eventually resulted in the rise of Octavian as Rome's first emperor.

Learning from his adoptive father's mistake, Octavian was careful not to flaunt his power over Rome, although he was already hailed as a hero after emerging victorious against Antony and Cleopatra. In 27 BCE, Octavian announced his retirement from the political world, to which the Senate disagreed and begged him to take the lead. He was granted the title of Augustus, which translates as the "Revered One." This marks the beginning of the Roman Empire. Although Octavian now held the title of Augustus, he made sure to never address himself with his honorable title, instead using the title of "first citizen."

Under Emperor Augustus's reign, Rome was rewarded with peace, and nearly every aspect of Roman life was changed for the better. Soon, a new taxation system was introduced, along with a census. New laws were passed to ensure both moral and marital stability among the citizens of Rome. According to the ancient Roman historian Cassius Dio, Augustus once banished his only daughter, Julia, to the small island of Pandateria upon discovering her scandalous behavior.

Map of the Roman Empire"

Augustus's brilliant strategies and commanding skills greatly helped the empire expand its borders. The Roman empire successfully annexed not only Egypt but also a part of Spain and Central Europe, along with regions of the Middle East, including Judaea, which eventually came under direct Roman rule by 6 CE. With more regions and territories in his grasp, the emperor expanded the network of Roman roads and founded Rome's first postal service to ensure better communication over long distances. Police and fire brigades were established during Augustus's reign, as was the Praetorian Guard, an elite force responsible for protecting both the imperial family and Rome.

The empire's economy and arts flourished. Rome saw the birth of the famous Roman Baths; the emperor's closest friend and chief deputy, Marcus Vipsanius Agrippa, designed the empire's first-ever bath. The emperor even renewed various religious practices in Rome and restored a great number of temples, including the Temple of Jupiter Feretrius, Rome's first-ever temple (now destroyed) was believed to have been built on the Capitoline Hill. In 28 BCE alone, the emperor restored at least eighty-two temples in the city.

Augustus was known for kickstarting the Pax Romana, the golden age of Rome. To honor his great success, the emperor was again bestowed another honorable title in 2 BCE: Pater Patriae or Father of the Country. Augustus faced several assassination plots, although none ever succeeded. He managed to rule the empire until he finally died of natural causes in August 14 CE. The mantle was then passed to his adopted son, Tiberius.

Tiberius Augustus Caesar, the Reluctant Emperor

Tiberius was not Augustus's first option. In fact, the emperor had previously chosen three other heirs to continue his legacy. They were his two grandsons, Lucius and Gaius Caesar, and his nephew, Marcellus. But when the three heirs took turns dying mysteriously—some claimed it was Tiberius's mother, Livia, who pulled the strings and eliminated them from the political arena, though it was never confirmed—Augustus was left with no choice but to shift his focus to his estranged stepson, Tiberius.

Statues of Tiberius and his mother, Livia.⁴⁵

Tiberius might have been known for his military prowess. After all, he was a successful general who had led the Roman forces to victory in both Armenia and Germany. But as much as he enjoyed commanding his legions, Tiberius had no intention of being in the spotlight of the political world. Nevertheless, he was crowned the empire's second emperor as soon as Augustus gasped his last breath. A year after Tiberius's succession, he became rather absent. Projects were abruptly put on hold, and his relationship with the Senate deteriorated. Few were fond of his rule, something the emperor was aware of.

The paranoia of being overthrown started to cloud Tiberius's judgment. He set his eyes on Germanicus, a brilliant general and the next emperor in line (Tiberius had adopted him per the request of the late Augustus). However, in 18 BCE, Germanicus died suddenly, leaving his wife alone with his six children.

Believing that it was a planned assassination, Germanicus's widow, Agrippina the Elder, accused Tiberius of staging the murder. As a result, Agrippina and her two older sons were killed. Her remaining younger children, Caligula and his sisters, were spared since they posed no real threat to Tiberius. After this incident, Tiberius grew increasingly cruel and would condemn those whom he thought to be against him to death. Treason trials became the norm, and the Romans lived in fear.

In 26 BCE, Tiberius was completely absent from the political arena. He left Rome and moved to Capri, an island off the coast of Italy. While he indulged himself in luxury and scandalous private affairs, the empire's official matters were left entirely to Sejanus, the head of the Praetorian Guard and a ruthless man who sought to take the throne. Eventually, word reached Tiberius, claiming that Sejanus was plotting to eliminate him—after all, Sejanus played a part in the death of Tiberius's favored son, Drusus.

With haste, Tiberius and another Praetorian Guard named Naevius Sutorius Macro (better known as Macro) lured and arrested Sejanus for treason. He was condemned to death right then and there. The ambitious guard was strangled, his limbs torn into pieces and fed to the dogs. The same fate befell his family and loyal followers.

Macro was appointed the new head of the Praetorian Guard, while Caligula was adopted by Tiberius and made his primary heir. But even with the death of Sejanus, the emperor was still not at ease. Treason trials continued to plague the empire, and many Romans died only because of his empty suspicions. Tiberius remained in his villa away from state matters until he died in 37 CE. Some sources claimed his death was orchestrated by Caligula and was killed by Macro, who smothered him to death with a pillow. Tiberius's death was celebrated by many, but peace would not linger in Rome for long.

Caligula, the Mad Emperor

Caligula had no experience in government, diplomacy, or even war when he was named the emperor of Rome. Still, his actions during the first few months of his succession caused the Romans to take a liking to him. To erase the horrors of his predecessor, Caligula stopped the vicious treason trials, recalled the exiles, and freed those whom Tiberius had unjustly captured. Unnecessary tax systems were abolished to the Roman citizens' delight, and long overdue bonuses were awarded to the Praetorian Guard. Most of Tiberius's abandoned projects were revived, with many dilapidated temples successfully restored and new, impressive structures erected all over Rome. To lift the gloomy mood in Rome, Caligula staged a great number of lavish events, such as chariot races, gladiator shows, luxurious banquets, and parties, to entertain his people. At this point, Caligula became the most admired emperor in Rome since the death of Augustus.

However, things took a different turn when the young emperor suffered from a mysterious sickness that almost took his life. Caligula's personality completely changed for the worst; he became almost like his predecessor. Paranoia soon took over the emperor, which led him to reestablish the cruel treason trials. Those whom he suspected to be his enemies were eliminated without question, and he confiscated their fortunes to cover up the deteriorating imperial coffers. Those who were spared from his assassination spree were constantly humiliated and tormented. Even his uncle and co-consul, Claudius, became a laughing stock and relentlessly insulted in front of the Senate. Caligula's extreme madness knew no limits. Not only did he once wage war with the Jewish population in Judea, but he also attempted to appoint Incitatus, his beloved horse, as consul.

The assassination of Caligula.[46]

Just like the emperors before him, Caligula had issues with providing a legitimate heir to the throne. Based on certain sources, the mad emperor was desperate for an heir until he resorted to having sexual relations with all three of his sisters; however, this claim remains disputed. Nevertheless, his reign only lasted for four years. In January 41 CE, the Praetorian Guard, spearheaded by Cassius Chaerea, who was one of the many victims of Caligula's ridiculous insults, murdered the emperor in cold blood. To rid Rome of his bloodline, they killed both his wife and his only daughter. Just like that, the empire was free from a bloodthirsty emperor. The next ruler, however, surprised many: it was none other than Caligula's fifty-year-old uncle, Claudius.

Claudius, the Unexpected Emperor

Claudius's ascension to the throne was unlike any of his predecessors. Instead of having his name written in the will of the previous emperor, Claudius was proclaimed emperor by the Praetorian Guard, who stumbled upon him cowering and quivering behind a set of curtains after witnessing Caligula's death. In his early life, Claudius was described by his own blood relatives, including his mother, as a fool. Despite being the grandson of Augustus, Claudius was thought by many to be dimwitted. That was, however, until he admitted that it was all an act for him to remain alive while Caligula was on the throne.

The Praetorian Guard proclaiming the terrified Claudius as the next emperor. ⁴⁷

Claudius was an unpopular candidate in the eyes of the Senate, so his efficiency was doubted. However, he began to shine when he took action against Caligula's murderers. Cassius Chaerea and a few of the conspirators were executed. Not wasting any time, the emperor moved to restore the peace in Rome. He reestablished the law, abolished the treason trials, built a handful of new structures, including a harbor in Ostia, and held gladiatorial games to entertain the people. When a riot broke out due to the extreme food shortage after a long drought, Claudius took the initiative to import grains and feed his subjects.

The empire also went through a major expansion. Several provinces were put under direct Roman rule. His biggest triumph was the conquest of Britannia, which had long been a target of Rome due to its wealth. To prove himself as a highly capable ruler, Claudius left Rome and led his army into Britain.

But, of course, like the emperors before him, Claudius had a dark side. When he was forced to face a revolt led by the governor of Upper Illyricum, the emperor grew paranoid. Although the revolt was easily stopped—with many of the participants executed—Claudius grew uneasy with those around him. Those whom he suspected of holding ill intentions toward him were killed or forced to commit suicide.

Other than his unfortunate luck in political matters during the last few years of his reign, the emperor was also unlucky with his marriages. Claudius was said to have married four times, but it was his marriage to Agrippina the Younger that cost him his life. Agrippina, who was also his niece, was hell-bent on seeing her son, Nero, ascend the imperial throne. While some suggest that Claudius died of old age in 54 CE, others believe his wife poisoned him. With Claudius no longer in the picture, the mantle was passed to Nero, just as his mother had dreamed.

Nero, the Emperor Who Entertains

Nero, the last of the Julio-Claudian emperors, was put on the throne at the age of sixteen and ruled over the vast empire for fourteen miserable years. During his first years as emperor, his people often described him as a generous and kind-hearted man who genuinely cared for his subjects. In an effort to remove the footsteps left by his adoptive father, Nero abolished a majority of Claudius's edicts and reduced the taxes. Games, concerts, plays, and chariot races were frequently held, as the emperor was fond of entertainment. He restored the power and importance of the

Senate, not only to strengthen his power but also so he could diverge from his responsibilities and pursue his private interests: singing and playing the lyre. It was said that whenever the emperor was performing, none of the audience was permitted to leave, no matter how bad it was.

As time passed, the emperor began to participate in things other than musical performances. When he grew restless with his mother, who claimed to be the true force behind the throne, Nero was quick to plan her murder. Two murder attempts were made, but Agrippina survived each time. However, the third attempt was a success; Agrippina was killed by her own son. His mother was not the only victim; Nero also got his hands dirty by killing his wives and unborn child.

Later on, another set of events caused Nero's life to go into turmoil. An unsuccessful coup, combined with a failed revolt in Britain, led the emperor into paranoia—just like the emperors before him. The biggest cause of Nero's downfall was the Great Fire of Rome, which engulfed 70 percent of the city. While hundreds of people succumbed to the fire, were left homeless, and were sent into chaos, the emperor was said to have watched from the safety of his palace while playing his lyre. The blame was put on the shoulders of the Christians.

The Great Fire of Rome, 64 CE. [48]

Although Rome was rebuilt soon after, Nero had seriously drained the treasury. Seeing the disasters that fell upon the city under his watch, the Senate declared him a public enemy, which led to his suicide at the ripe age of thirty. With Nero gone, the Romans trampled out of their homes, celebrating. Nero's death marked the end of the Julio-Claudian dynasty.

Chapter 2 – The Pax Romana

Many are familiar with or at least have heard of the main ancient Roman gods and goddesses, which included Jupiter, Neptune, Minerva, and Mars. Janus, on the other hand, is a rather mysterious Roman deity due to the lack of surviving information. Historians have tried to discover the god's origins, but unfortunately, only more mysteries and questions surfaced. Janus's depiction on Rome's oldest coin clearly indicates that he was one of the oldest gods in the Roman pantheon. The first month of the year, January, is said to have been derived from the ancient god's name. Janus was invoked at the start of every religious ceremony, and the first portion of a sacrifice had to be dedicated to him before the others. Yet, only a few shrines and statues were ever erected to honor him.

A part of a sculpture of the two-headed god Janus. [49]

The only well-known building dedicated to the obscure deity was the Temple of Janus. Commissioned by Rome's second king, Numa Pompilius, the temple, more accurately classified as a shrine, stood at the center of the Eternal City. The shrine was built to house only a bronze statue of the two-headed Janus. Its most prominent feature was the double doors, which the Romans often referred to as the Gates of War. The gates were left open when Rome was plagued with continuous warfare and would only be closed if peace was achieved—a rare occasion, according to the philosopher and biographer Plutarch, as the Eternal City was almost always in the midst of violent battles and bloodshed due to its constant expansion.

While the reason behind the closing and opening of the gates vary (some sources believe that leaving the gates open during active conflicts allowed the deity to watch over them), historians and experts are sure the gates were only closed twice since the foundation of Rome. Numa first closed it upon reaching peace during his reign, followed by the Roman commander Aulus Manlius Torquatus Atticus after gaining victory during the First Punic War. The gates were opened when the Gauls invaded northern Italy, and they would remain open for four hundred years until Augustus came along.

Before the arrival of Augustus, the Roman Republic had never experienced long-term peace. War raged without rest, worrying its people day and night. Later on, a series of never-ending civil wars broke out among influential figures who craved ultimate power. Marius, Sulla, Caesar, Crassus, Pompey, and Mark Antony were some of the most notable Roman figures who wished to seize power over the already chaotic republic. By this point in history, it is safe to assume that peace was far from the Romans' reach. However, the arrival of the late dictator's adopted son changed things. A sigh of relief could be had for the first time in four centuries, as peace was finally possible.

Despite his young age, Augustus had his heart set on continuing Julius Caesar's legacy. Witnessing all of the threats and catastrophes that befell the republic, the future emperor was left with no choice but to introduce new political reforms. This was not a simple task; achieving peace and restoring Rome to its glory would no doubt be time-consuming. The young emperor was also well aware that he had gained a great number of enemies, but he was ready to face anyone who dared to step in his way, including Mark Antony.

Despite having to battle a mysterious illness that sometimes forced him to remain in bed and away from ongoing wars, Augustus managed to showcase his exceptional skills and abilities to lead, thus earning him the support of many. When Mark Antony and his beloved Egyptian queen went a step too far, Augustus led his army against them without hesitation. The battle went down in history as one of the most important events in the ancient world, as it not only took the life of both Mark Antony and Cleopatra but also marked the end of the Roman Republic and the beginning of a new era.

Upon returning to the Eternal City, Augustus ordered the closing of the Gates of Janus in 29 BCE to signify peace. The long series of unrest and civil wars were finally brought to an end with the death of Mark Antony, one of Rome's greatest generals. The crowds cheered as Rome was ushered into its golden era, known as the Pax Romana (the "Roman Peace").

For the first time in history, ancient Rome enjoyed a period of relative peace for more than a few decades. The Pax Romana was believed to have lasted for nearly two centuries, starting from the reign of the first emperor, Augustus, until the death of Marcus Aurelius, the last of the Five Good Emperors, in 180 CE. During this time, Rome was at its peak. The empire underwent a massive territorial expansion alongside the rapid growth of its population; under the reign of Augustus alone, the empire consisted of about sixty million people.

However, not everyone was happy with the sudden peace. During the early years of the Pax Romana, many Romans were said to have struggled to adapt. Ever since the early foundation of Rome back in the 8th century BCE, the city was always intertwined with warfare to the point where its people began to see it as a form of might and power. The absence of constant battles and conquests somehow worried the Romans. To them, warfare was a good thing; they gained wealth by winning wars, and their reputation grew every time their enemies lay dead on the battlefield. This was one of the many issues that Augustus had to deal with the moment he accepted the responsibility of leading the people. In an effort to persuade his people to accept the Pax Romana with open arms, the young emperor came up with a series of propaganda campaigns. He assured the Romans that peace was the best way to achieve prosperity.

The Pax Romana was a relative peace; the empire was not entirely free from wars and battles. To put it in simple words, the Pax Romana was an era where the Romans had to face little to no internal skirmishes. Its people, especially those in power, were no longer at each other's throats, and large-scale civil wars were a thing of the past. Fewer soldiers were stationed at the heart of the empire, with most of the legions being sent to places that were likely to be in danger, such as the imperial frontier.

Wars and foreign forces at the empire's borders continued to exist during the Roman Peace. The Pax Romana did not mean the Romans completely sheathed their weapons. Military missions and campaigns were still launched; Augustus even went on several conquests to capture new regions in an effort to further expand the empire. Under his reign, captured provinces were allowed to exercise their local customs, traditions, and religious practices as long as they did not violate Roman law and as long as they chose to comply with Roman taxation and military control. Augustus even kept his eyes open for corrupt provincial governors; those who were caught exploiting their power for their own benefit were quickly punished.

Just as Augustus had promised his people, the empire's economy and trade skyrocketed during this era of peace. Long-distance trade flourished, especially when the Mediterranean was free of threats. The emperor ordered the Roman navy to launch an attack against pirates, making the sea safer for traders to enter and exit the harbors. Since Roman traders and merchants could sail farther east without having to fear for their safety, they were able to bring back precious gems and exquisite silks. Apart from jewelry, the Romans, typically the nobles and the rich, were very fond of silk; Emperor Heliogabalus, who ruled in 218 CE, was believed to have refused to wear clothing unless they were made out of silk. Export activities also boomed during this period of history, as the Romans could find more markets for their goods, which included wines, textiles, pottery, glass, and other construction materials.

With economic stability, the imperial government was able to invest in many major construction projects. The Romans are well known for their road networks, and Augustus commissioned the expansion of road systems throughout the empire, which no doubt benefited the movement of the legions. Information and mail could also arrive in a shorter amount of time. By the end of Emperor Augustus's reign, over eighty kilometers (fifty miles) of new roads had been constructed. Bridges, harbors, and aqueducts were also often built by the emperors who ruled during the golden age.

Apart from architecture and the economy, the Pax Romana witnessed the birth of many Roman poets and writers. Horace, Virgil, Tibullus, and Ovid are some of the most memorable Roman writers that thrived during this era. Despite being renowned for his exceptional works of poetry, the latter was sentenced to exile by Augustus due to the production of erotic poetry and opinions of the emperor's private life and marriage. However, the poet did not stop writing even after his exile; he wrote two more collections of poetry that told the stories of his sadness and desolation. Exiled for life, Ovid died in 17 CE, but his influence on poetry has lived on; Shakespeare was among the many modern authors to have been influenced by the exiled poet.

Ovid banished from Rome.[50]

"I found Rome of bricks; I leave to you one of marble."

These were the words of Augustus Caesar during the last years of his life. Rome had indeed been near shambles when it passed into his hands, but the emperor successfully brought it back to its glory. One might even say he turned it into one of the most prosperous empires of all time.

From a broken republic filled with nothing but a series of civil wars, Rome transformed itself into an empire that stretched as far as Britannia and Egypt. The death of Rome's first emperor caused a stir, as several problems arose during the reigns of the next few emperors. However, the Pax Romana was not broken, and the Eternal City continued to experience relative peace.

During Nero's reign, the people of Rome began to sense another catastrophe heading toward them. After the end of the Julio-Claudian dynasty, the city faced a few pressing matters that put a crack in the Roman Peace, but the era of the Five Good Emperors successfully reversed the damages and made the empire prosper again. The peace in the Eternal City was extended for a few more decades before it finally cracked and crumbled to pieces in 180 CE.

Chapter 3 – The Five Good Emperors

The last emperor of the Julio-Claudian dynasty, Nero, contributed to the many pressing issues that had taken over the Roman Empire. His death was celebrated by not only the Senate but also the suffering commoners of different social classes. With the throne now empty, the empire was put under the care of an emperor who founded a whole new dynasty. It was known as the Flavian dynasty, and it consisted of only three emperors: Vespasian, Titus, and Domitian.

The most popular among those three was Domitian. Early in his reign, the emperor portrayed great potential to lead the empire out of its troubles. He did not ignore the welfare of his people and rebuilt the city, which had been destroyed after the Great Fire. Unlike his brother, Titus, Domitian was not known for his military skills, but he spearheaded a few successful campaigns during his reign. Unfortunately, just like many of Rome's great emperors, Domitian succumbed to extreme paranoia. In 96 CE, the emperor was brutally killed at the hands of a group of conspirators. Instead of mourning the loss of their emperor, the Senate was overjoyed. Once again, Rome was free from the grasp of yet another insanely paranoid leader. Without wasting time, they announced a new emperor to the throne. His name was Nerva, and he was the first of Rome's Five Good Emperors.

Nerva (r. 96–98 CE)

The new emperor was rather old when he was put in charge of the vast empire; he was almost sixty-six. No one would have expected Nerva to take the mantle; he was not very popular among the Romans. Although he had spent the majority of his life serving the empire during the reigns of both the Julio-Claudian and Flavian dynasties, achieving great success, Nerva never gained any prominence. The Senate did not even plan to bestow him the power permanently; he was only hailed as emperor to fill the vacancy until the Senate could decide on someone with greater influence and potential.

After years of serving the empire behind the scenes, Nerva began to shine and eventually earned a spot among the public after voicing his promise to return liberty to the Romans. He ended the treason trials that had left the Romans cowering in fear, returned the properties confiscated by Domitian back to the senators, showered the common people with generous gifts, and lowered the taxes. He earned the support of many, but his generosity also depleted the imperial coffers to the point where the empire was almost on the verge of bankruptcy.

Another challenge that Nerva had to face was the military's rage, as the soldiers and officers preferred his predecessor. Upon learning that Nerva had no plans to prosecute the conspirators who took Domitian's life, the Praetorian Guard launched a siege on the imperial palace and demanded the assassins be held accountable. Instead of complying with the violent request, Nerva offered his own neck to slit—an action completely ignored by the Praetorian Guard, who chose to spare the emperor and slaughter the conspirators.

After the siege, Nerva was left shaken to his core—he even thought of stepping down from the throne at one point. He was well aware that his authority was beginning to decline, especially without the support of the military. Knowing that he could lose his life to anyone around him, the emperor began to think of a possible heir to succeed him.

Since he had no child of his own—some say he never even married—Nerva adopted the governor of Upper Germany, Marcus Ulpius Traianus, as his son. In January 98 CE, a day after Nerva died of natural causes, his adopted son rose as the next emperor of the Nerva-Antonine dynasty.

Trajan (r. 98–117 CE)

Marcus Ulpius Traianus was the second emperor of Rome not to be born in Italy; he was born in Hispania. After receiving news that his adoptive father had passed away and that the mantle would be passed to him, Traianus did not return to Rome straightaway. Instead, he stayed with his legions in Germany in case the barbarians invaded. It was only in early 99 CE that he journeyed back to Rome and participated in an official ceremony that declared him the next emperor.

A bust of Trajan.[51]

Now known by the name Trajan, the emperor received a warm welcome from nearly everyone in Rome, especially the military, given his strong influence on the battlefield. Some might even claim that Trajan was one of the few emperors who mimicked the rule of the great Augustus Caesar. Generous gifts were distributed to the people regardless of their status, and he sponsored multiple public games to keep the citizens entertained. However, he did not spend too much on the military. In fact, he only gave them half of what previous emperors before him had given. Since Trajan was already favored in the army due to his long service as a military officer before stepping on the throne, he did not receive backlash from his decision to tone down their payments. Trajan maintained a great relationship with the Senate by bestowing a certain amount of authority over the empire upon them, although his power was still considered supreme.

Even before he took the reins, Trajan had wished to expand the empire. So, when he finally had the opportunity to rule, the emperor decided to fulfill his ambition by launching two wars against Dacia (modern-day Romania and Moldova). Peace between Dacia and Rome was first bought about by Domitian, who had agreed to pay tribute to the king of Dacia, Decebalus. Trajan, however, was completely against this treaty. In the aftermath of the two wars, the capital of Dacia was destroyed. Despite his efforts to defend his kingdom, Decebalus committed suicide. With the victory, the empire expanded. Dacia was made into a Roman province, providing the Romans with valuable supplies of gold and metal, which they used to mint coins.

Trajan also oversaw the construction of a long bridge across the Danube River and into Dacia, which ensured easier access for his army. The solid stone bridge was not the only massive construction project launched during his reign. After acquiring resources from Dacia, the emperor commissioned the construction of various structures, roads, and highways in Rome and its surrounding cities. The *alimenta*, a welfare program founded by Nerva to assist orphans and poor children in the empire, was also carried on by Trajan.

In 113, Trajan yet again showed his mighty potential by strategizing the conquest of Parthia. After assembling the strongest soldiers, Trajan deployed them to invade Parthia, which was in the midst of a civil war. He managed to get his hands on Mesopotamia in 117, but his objective to conquer Parthia failed. In the same year, the sixty-three-year-old emperor fell terribly sick while defending the empire's borders and died.

Hadrian (r. 117–138 CE)

The third emperor of the Nerva-Antonine dynasty was Publius Aelius Hadrianus. Better known as Hadrian, he was a remarkable military officer who began to rise through the ranks in 91 CE. He served as tribune during the reign of Emperor Nerva and was handpicked to travel to Gaul by the end of 97 CE to relay the news of Trajan's adoption and his possible ascension to the throne.

Hadrian's rise to the throne, like his predecessor, was welcomed by the Romans. He was seen as a charismatic, honest, and peaceful leader by the public.

Despite Hadrian's long tenure in the military, he was not keen on conquests; instead, he wanted to consolidate the empire's defenses. He put a stop to Trajan's campaign in Parthia and planned peace negotiations. To achieve peace, the Romans withdrew from Armenia, leaving it a neutral state. Although this decision was not liked by many, especially those who had loyally served under Trajan, it saved the empire from further damage and made it even stronger than before.

Image: The remains of Hadrian's Wall.⁵³

Hadrian believed that the empire had reached its maximum extent and that the most crucial thing to focus on was its border security. He wished for the empire's stability and prosperity. So, instead of staying in Rome and planning strategy after strategy for a new conquest, Hadrian chose to leave the imperial palace and travel throughout the provinces to oversee the provincial administration. The emperor was said to have visited every single province in the empire by the year 133 and recognized where he needed to eliminate corruption. He also commissioned multiple construction projects. His greatest contribution was the great Hadrian's Wall in Britain, which was built for defensive purposes. The borders near Germany were also strengthened under his rule.

Hadrian was also a man of culture. During his travels across the provinces, he promoted the importance of culture to his people. Some sources claim that the emperor was fond of Greece and that he visited the province more than once during his reign. Unlike the other Roman emperors who preferred clean-shaven faces, Hadrian sported a Greek-style beard. Hadrian sponsored many poetry contests in Rome and was known for founding the city of Antinoöpolis on the banks of the Nile to honor his deceased lover, Antinous. Although Hadrian claimed that Antinous's death was accidental—he had drowned in the Nile—other scholars, including Cassius Dio, believed the young boy had performed a sacrificial ceremony to cure Hadrian's mysterious illness.

Hadrian's grief did not stop him from running the empire. He grew short-tempered as time passed, but he soon projected his anger on the Jews who had started a revolt in Judea. His solution to the revolt was to annihilate the Jews in the region. A thousand towns and villages were burned in the process, and nearly sixty thousand Jews were slaughtered, while others were banished. Afterward, Hadrian renamed Judea Syria Palaestina and turned it into a Roman city, further suppressing Jewish beliefs.

During his last few years, Hadrian remained in his luxurious villa away from Rome. He spent most of his time writing poetry while overseeing the empire's administration. His health declined, and in 138, Hadrian died due to a heart attack.

Antoninus Pius (r. 138–161 CE)

Having no child of his own, Hadrian resorted to adoption. He initially had his eyes on the consul Lucius Ceionius Commodus, but things quickly went south as soon as Lucius was appointed governor and sent to Pannonia. He suffered from tuberculosis and died in January 138. Thus, Hadrian was forced to search for another heir. This time around, he had his eyes on Marcus Aurelius. He somehow could see Aurelius's capabilities, but unfortunately, he was only sixteen at the time, which was too young to hold such power over the empire. Running out of time, Hadrian, who was already on his deathbed, finally announced Antoninus Pius, his most trusted advisor, as his successor.

Many thought Antoninus would rule for only a short amount of time, at least until Aurelius could reach an age fit to rule, especially after he agreed to adopt both Marcus Aurelius and Lucius Verus as his successors. Plus, he was already reaching the age of fifty, so most thought that it would not be too long before he passed the throne to his adoptive sons. Much to everyone's surprise, the emperor lived a long life. Although Antoninus was not as popular as his predecessor, the Romans began to show their support when they saw his unexpected efficiency and drive.

Emperor Antoninus in his military garb.⁵⁸

The new emperor took the reins when the empire was at its peak. The economy was blossoming. No political unrest or civil wars could be seen. The borders were well secured, and famine was a thing of the past. Liberty had been achieved, with the people of all classes living without fear. To ensure his position was never challenged, Antoninus maintained his relationship with almost everyone, be it the Senate, the military, nobles, and even the commoners. He even passed legislation that protected the rights of slaves and increased the chances of them obtaining their freedom.

Continuing Hadrian's legacy, Antoninus focused on upgrading Rome's infrastructure. He issued orders to complete Hadrian's many construction projects, although he had his own projects as well. The Temple of the Deified Hadrian and the Temple of the Deified Faustina were some of the impressive structures commissioned by Antoninus. The Colosseum was also restored during his rule. Following Hadrian's footsteps, the emperor issued the construction of the Antonine Wall, which took nearly twelve years to complete.

Antoninus was described as an even-tempered emperor. The empire was indeed at peace, as little to zero wars and conflicts took place during Antoninus's reign. After ruling for over twenty years, the emperor finally passed away at the age of seventy-four due to a fever. His remains were laid in Hadrian's Mausoleum, right next to his beloved wife and sons.

Marcus Aurelius (r. 161–180 CE)

Antoninus Pius was said to have properly groomed Marcus Aurelius to prepare him as his successor. So, when Marcus Aurelius's adoptive father passed away in 161, he was hailed as the new emperor, just as Hadrian intended a few decades prior. However, Aurelius, now at the age of forty, had to share his power with Lucius Verus, whom the Senate had announced as his co-emperor; this was the first time Rome had ever recognized two ruling emperors at the same time. But since Marcus was older than his adoptive brother, he held more power.

By the time they both rose to power, trouble had begun to brew across the empire. The Parthians decided to invade Armenia as soon as they learned of Antoninus's death. At the same time, the empire was faced with possible threats by people living in what is today Britain and Germany after decades of peace. Ever since he was young, Marcus had been groomed to be an efficient leader; however, he was never given any military experience. He was more fond of philosophy—his writings called *Meditations* can still be read today.

Nevertheless, he devoted himself to military studies to prepare for the upcoming threats. Lucius was supposed to soothe the ongoing war with the Parthians but instead stayed behind the city walls, which ultimately led the campaign into a stalemate. Thanks to his subordinate, Avidius Cassius, Rome eventually emerged victorious.

In 166, Marcus had to put everything he learned from his military studies on the battlefield when he was faced with multiple Germanic tribes that managed to pierce through the Roman frontiers and destroy several villages. Although their raids were devastating, the Roman army successfully put a stop to their advance. Warfare and invasions were not the worst events to happen during Marcus's reign, as the Antonine Plague terrorized the empire. Millions were killed in this catastrophe, including Lucius Verus.

Now the sole emperor of Rome, Marcus Aurelius put all of his efforts into seeing the empire flourish again. Some even claimed the emperor always placed the needs of his people before anything else. Despite not liking military life, he continued to defend the empire against threats. He nearly ended the continuous war with the Germanic tribes, but in 180, Marcus Aurelius perished in his military quarters due to unknown reasons.

His death marked the end of the era of the Five Good Emperors. Although great stability and peace had been restored by the five emperors of the Nerva-Antonine dynasty, Rome was forced to face many wars and political unrest in the decades to come.

Chapter 4 – The Third Century Crisis

The Romans knew the days of the Five Good Emperors were gone when they received the news of the devastating death of fifty-eight-year-old Marcus Aurelius. The Eternal City was entrusted in the hands of Commodus, who had already served the empire as joint emperor alongside Aurelius. Despite being the only son of the great Marcus Aurelius, Commodus was not a favorite among his subjects. He had endured many assassination attempts, and when his associate succumbed to one of the murderous plots, Commodus became paranoid. Many perished due to his suspicions—he even had a list of those he'd execute next—but in 192, Commodus was successfully murdered, strangled by a wrestler hired by the conspirators.

Commodus strangled by the Roman wrestler Narcissus.[54]

The death of Commodus did not solve the political unrest in the empire. In 193, Rome was yet again plunged into a period of civil war when five rulers fought for a chance to be crowned the next Caesar. The paranoid Commodus was succeeded by Pertinax, who portrayed far better qualities compared to his predecessor. However, his disagreements with the Praetorian Guard led to his death eighty-six days after his ascension. Afterward, three more men took turns claiming the throne before Septimius Severus finally took the mantle and ended the Year of the Five Emperors. With Severus as emperor, another dynasty was born: the Severan dynasty, which would rule the empire for over forty-two years and saw the beginning of the Third Century Crisis.

Taking a lesson from Pertinax, who the Praetorian Guard assassinated after refusing to come to terms with them, Severus quenched the military's possible disobedience by awarding them increased pay. Each soldier was paid at least five hundred denarii—a major increase from their previous salary of three hundred denarii annually. This decision was not a problem until the empire was enlarged even more; Severus successfully launched a campaign in Africa and Britain. More armed forces were required to defend the borders from foreign invasions, which meant more payments must be made to secure their service. To curb the issue, Severus debased the currency by decreasing the percentage of silver in the coinage, a method that was practiced by future emperors and extended the economic crisis.

While fulfilling the military demands played a part in keeping Severus in power, his dependence on the soldiers' loyalty proved to be a dangerous game. The military's role increased tenfold and shook not only the Senate but also the supreme standing of the emperor.

In 231, the Sassanid Empire, led by Ardashir I, invaded the Roman provinces of the east after successfully bringing down already-weakened Parthia a few years back. This threat left Severus Alexander, the last emperor of the Severan dynasty, with no other choice but to plan a retaliation. There are a few contradicting accounts that tell the story of the battle, but many suggest that despite experiencing heavy casualties and terrible setbacks, the Roman Empire's borders were secured and Ardashir's conquest was stopped. However, Severus Alexander was beginning to lose the support of his troops, especially during the invasion of Germanic tribes in 235.

Some claimed that Severus Alexander was only a puppet while his mother, Julia Mamaea, was the real power. Instead of fighting off the invaders on the battlefield, Severus Alexander made a fatal mistake by following his mother's advice. Julia had advised him to buy the peace, an action considered unacceptable and highly dishonorable to his legions. Severus Alexander and his mother were assassinated by his commanders, marking the beginning of the Third Century Crisis, a fifty-year period where the Roman Empire almost collapsed.

The economic crisis remained one of the empire's biggest concerns, and the military became the real source of power after the murder of Severus Alexander. The Roman Empire saw the succession of more than twenty-five barrack emperors over the span of almost five decades. Instead of rising to the throne through traditional adoptions by previous emperors or having their names written in wills, these barrack emperors were chosen based on their popularity within a military troop. Maximinus Thrax, who was the commander of a legion raised by Severus Alexander, was chosen as the next emperor, though he would be killed by his own troops three years later after failing to prove himself as an effective leader amidst the constant warfare, economic unrest, and famine.

The empire was also in the middle of battling a number of invasions by foreign enemies. The provinces along the Rhine-Danube frontiers were facing heavy threats imposed by the Germanic tribes: the Goths, Vandals, and Alemanni. Seeing that the empire was overwhelmed by the Germanic tribes, the Sassanid Empire—now led by Shapur I, the son of Ardashir—set its eyes on exploiting the Roman Empire's weakness and asserting control over the Levant in the east. In 252, Shapur I gained power over Nisibis and successfully seized Antioch the next year after defeating the Roman army.

With the eastern border in shambles, the barrack emperor Valerian left his son and co-emperor, Gallienus, in control of the west while he marched against the ruthless Sassanid Empire. Personally leading his troops, Valerian arrived in Asia Minor in 259 but was thrown into another battle when he came face to face with the Gothic tribes that were busy invading the region. Little is known about the battle, but historians suggest that the emperor managed to continue his march against Shapur I. Valerian's seventy thousand men soon clashed swords with Shapur's forty thousand men in Edessa. The Roman emperor was utterly defeated and made prisoner; Valerian was the first-ever Roman emperor to get captured and imprisoned by an enemy. He perished the following year.

Foreign attacks were not the only pressing matter terrorizing the empire. When Gallienus rose as the next emperor following his father's death, a rebellion erupted, although he managed to extinguish it in 260. Another obstacle arose when the Germanic tribes invaded northern Italy. With only 60,000 troops at his command, the emperor successfully defeated the 300,000 barbarians; it was said the victory was achieved thanks to his exceptional cavalry troops. Despite the triumph, the emperor was forced to face yet another rebellion. At the same time, Postumus, a well-respected administrator who had defended Germania from several invasions, declared his independence. Modeled after the central government of the Roman Empire, he formed the Gallic Empire, which was made up of Gaul, Britannia, and eventually Hispania.

The eastern provinces of the Roman Empire were secured by Septimius Odaenathus, an aristocrat from the Roman colony Palmyra. He laid an attack on Shapur's army in 260 and emerged victorious. The foreign forces were pushed back to their capital, and by 263, the lands that had once been lost to the Sassanid Empire were safely returned to the Romans. Gallienus appreciated Odaenathus's remarkable success in securing the eastern borders and awarded him with the title of *corrector totius Orientis* or governor of all the east. Odaenathus preferred another title: King of Kings. While remaining a loyal Roman vassal, Odaenathus continued to drive away the foreign invaders who dared to set foot in the eastern provinces. That was, however, until late 267 CE when he and his son were mysteriously assassinated. His widow soon took control and became regent to their underage son.

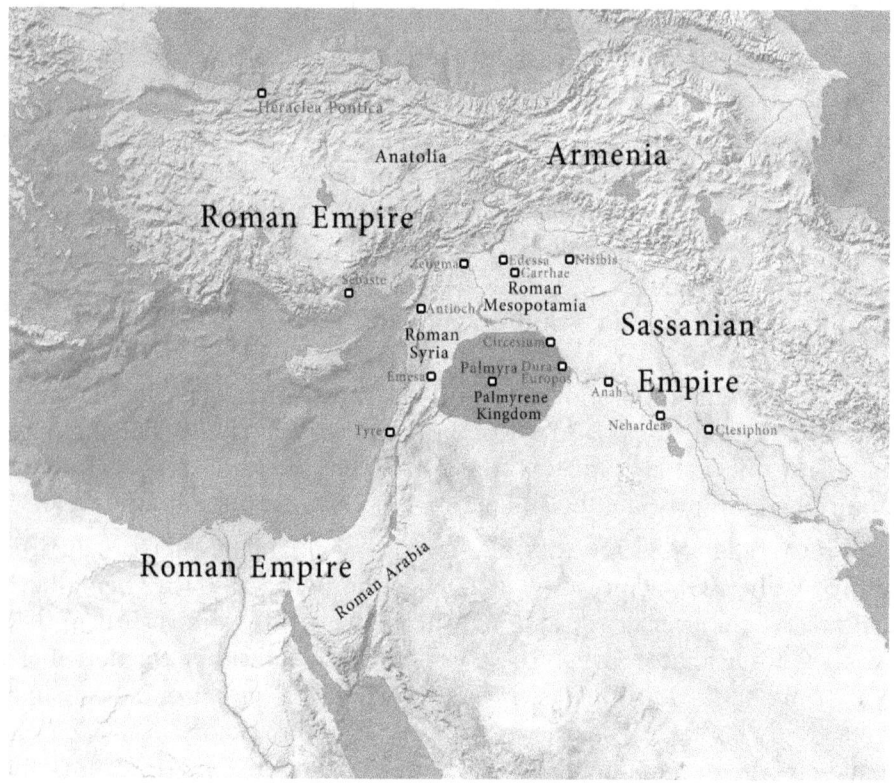

Regions under the authority of Odaenathus of Palmyra.[55]

In 265, Gallienus turned his attention to Postumus and his newly formed Gallic Empire. Although sources claimed that Postumus never intended to invade the Roman Empire, Gallienus was ready to face him and reclaim the provinces. The battle was at its peak when Gallienus laid siege on an unnamed city in the Gallic Empire. However, luck was running out for the emperor, as he was pierced by an arrow, forcing him to leave the ongoing battle. The Gallic Empire remained independent. Gallienus managed to heal from his severe wound, only to be assassinated three years later.

The throne then belonged to Claudius II, who also had his eyes on the Gallic Empire. As he prepared to march on Postumus's empire, the emperor was forced to change his plans after receiving news about an invasion of modern-day Serbia by the Goths. With haste, the Romans engaged in a battle with the invaders near Naissus in 269. Even with the exceptional cavalry units led by the future emperor Aurelian, the fierce battle inflicted extreme casualties on both sides. The Romans eventually won the battle after successfully tricking the Goths into a brutal ambush. In the aftermath of the devastating battle, the Goths were said to have lost at least fifty thousand lives. Claudius II became known as the "Conqueror of the Goths."

The same year, Rome was threatened by yet another invasion attempt, this time by the Alemanni at Lake Benacus. Just as in the previous battle, the Romans managed to overpower them and drive them out of the empire. Sometime later, Claudius II received news that likely eased his mind. The founder of the Gallic Empire, Postumus, had been killed. Sensing an opportunity to seize the Gallic provinces, Claudius quickly moved his troops to Hispania. The emperor showed great promise as a leader, but after his success in recapturing Hispania, he lost his life to the Plague of Cyprian.

While the late Claudius II had his hands full putting his life on the line to reclaim the Gallic provinces and defend the Roman Empire from further invasions, Zenobia, regent and queen of Palmyra in the east, was trying to cement her authority. When the news of Claudius's sudden death reached her, she took the opportunity to proclaim her son, Vaballathus, as emperor. Through Zenobia's efforts, the Palmyrene Empire was born. By 271, Egypt and most regions of central and eastern Anatolia were absorbed into the empire. The reason behind this independence is uncertain; some claim that Zenobia was becoming less confident with Roman protection, while others suggest that she simply intended to strengthen the dominance of Palmyrene.

Back in the west, the imperial throne was passed to Aurelian, a battle-hardened soldier who was soon known as the emperor who reunited the Roman Empire. The new emperor took the reins when Rome was shrouded in multiple threats from foreign tribes and independent empires. He was well aware that he had to secure the loyalty of the military before he could march to the battlefield and exterminate the vicious barbarians. By seizing control of the imperial mint in modern-day Croatia, Aurelian managed to gain enough gold coins to distribute to his army. With their loyalty firmly in his hands, Aurelian could begin his battles.

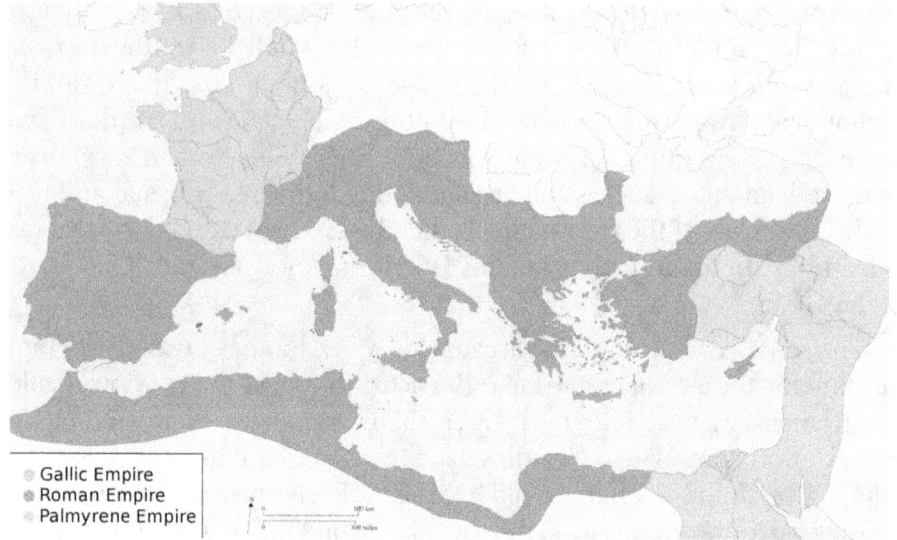

- Gallic Empire
- Roman Empire
- Palmyrene Empire

The Roman Empire before Aurelian's reconquest campaigns of the Palmyrene and Gallic Empires.[56]

Not wasting a single opportunity, the emperor destroyed the Vandals who had been invading northern Italy. He also led his legions to face the Juthungi, who were already planning to leave Italy with their precious plunder. However, Aurelian managed to intercept the tribe, which led to a battle on the Metaurus River. Aurelian and his troops were victorious; however, another concerning matter surfaced that required his immediate attention.

Rome was thrown into a grain crisis when the Palmyrene Empire successfully claimed Egypt. Aiming to put a stop to Zenobia's growing influence, Aurelian journeyed to the east in 272. The emperor faced little resistance, as most cities of the Palmyrene Empire decided to open their gates to him when he offered mercy. This peaceful strategy did not last long, as he was left with no choice but to engage in a military battle with Zenobia's forces. In less than a year, the emperor emerged victorious. Zenobia and her son attempted to escape but were captured and paraded through the streets of Rome in a triumph held by Aurelian. With the fall of Zenobia's Palmyrene Empire, Rome was able to secure the eastern provinces again.

The only part of the Roman Empire left for Aurelian to reconquer was Britannia and Gaul—both of which were still under the Gallic Empire. Wishing to avoid more bloodshed, the emperor resorted to diplomacy, an attempt that failed. He was forced to lay an attack on the empire. The Battle of Châlons took place in 274 and was won by Aurelian's forces. Sources claim that Aurelian lost six thousand men, while Tetricus I, the emperor of the Gallic Empire at the time, lost nearly fifty thousand. After thirteen years of independence, the Gallic Empire finally collapsed, and its provinces were returned to the Romans.

Despite Aurelian's success in restoring the empire, he did not end the Third Century Crisis, although he set in motion the events that led to its end. After Aurelian's death, six more emperors rose to the throne and continued to help the empire solve the ongoing crisis. It was not until the reign of Diocletian that Rome finally began to see the light at the end of the tunnel. Although Diocletian's reign was filled with warfare and violence, the emperor brought glory back to the Roman Empire and ended Rome's fifty-year-long turmoil with his carefully planned strategies and reforms.

Chapter 5 – From the Tetrarchy to the Fall of the West

It was the year 285 CE, and the people of Rome had gathered around to celebrate the return of Diocletian, their emperor who had just emerged victorious from the Battle of the Margus. Some might have assumed that Diocletian was no different from any other emperor before him and that it was nearly impossible for the empire to rise after suffering from the fifty-year-long crisis. After all, Diocletian came from a rather humble background, despite having vast experience in the military. However, his intelligence and reforms finally dragged Rome out of its misery.

From Diocletian's point of view, he saw the empire as too big. One man could not oversee every single matter. Two men should be put in charge to ensure the empire was at its best. So, Diocletian decided to call upon his close friend he had known from his days in the military. His name was Maximian. Diocletian made him his co-emperor, bestowing him the title of Caesar. Not long after that, he gave him the most honorable Roman title: Augustus. With two emperors on the throne, Diocletian split the empire into two: East and West. While Diocletian chose to oversee matters in the East, Maximian was put in charge of ruling over the West. Nicomedia (an ancient city once located in modern-day Turkey) was made the capital of the Eastern Roman Empire. Maximian chose the city of Milan as the capital of the Western Roman Empire.

Diocletian began securing the East from future threats, meeting little to no obstacles. He made peace with the Persians and secured alliances with the Arab tribes that had once acted against the empire. However, Maximian faced a different situation. A self-proclaimed emperor in Britain threatened his position. He worked on eliminating the threat by launching an attack on Britain, which proved challenging, especially when Germanic tribes invaded the western provinces. Diocletian soon journeyed to the West, and the two emperors joined forces to push back the barbarians and put the other threats to rest.

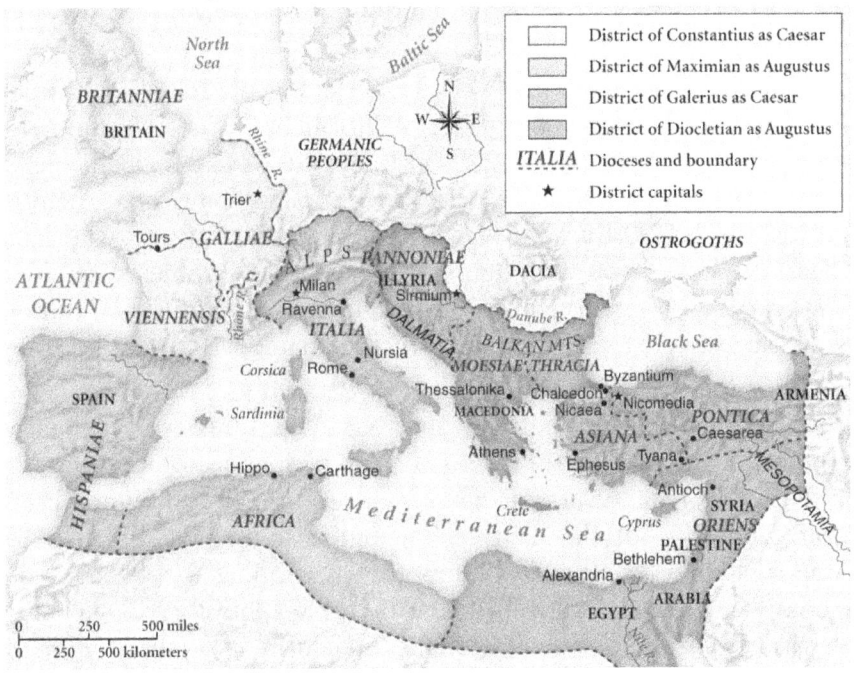

Map of the Roman Empire under the Tetrarchy. [57]

After witnessing multiple invasions and other problems, the emperors came to the conclusion that they needed more assistance. Diocletian suggested they appoint one emperor each who would rule under their supervision. Diocletian's chose a man named Galerius, while Maximian appointed Constantius—both of these men were the prefects of their Praetorian Guard. The two men were given the title Caesar (junior emperor) and would rule alongside their respective Augustus (senior emperor). Four emperors now controlled the vast Roman Empire. This reform is known to historians as the Tetrarchy, and as much as it brought the Roman Empire back to its feet, it would also cause troubles as the years passed.

How the Tetrarchy Began to Crumble

With the abdication of Diocletian and Maximian in 305, the empire's leadership was put on the shoulders of their Caesars, who were promoted to the rank of Augustus. Galerius ruled over the East with his newly appointed Caesar, Maximinus, while the West was put under the control of Constantius and his subordinate, Severus. However, the appointments of the new Caesars were not accepted by all, especially Maxentius (the son of Maximian) and Constantine (the son of Constantius), both of whom were initially seen as the next in line. It did not take long for the empire to witness another succession issue.

In 306, the Augustus of the West, Constantius, marched to Britain to lead a campaign against the Picts. Unfortunately, he succumbed to leukemia the same year, leaving his throne open for a new capable leader to claim. His Caesar, Severus, was quickly named the new Augustus. However, this was not acknowledged by Constantius's army, who hailed the late emperor's son, Constantine, as the ruler of the West (some sources claim Constantius named his son the next Augustus). To calm the strained succession issue, Galerius officially named Constantine Caesar instead.

Another matter arose the following year. Maxentius, who had earned the support of the Praetorian Guard and the people of Rome, proclaimed himself emperor. Since no one acknowledged his self-proclaimed power, all four emperors of the Tetrarchy planned to remove him. In 307, Severus marched to Rome with his troops, hoping to put an end to Maxentius, but the defection of his army forced him to retreat. He was soon captured and murdered. As Maxentius's army grew, he resumed his unofficial rule over Italy alongside his father, Maximian, who had resurfaced from his retirement a few years earlier. Sometime in the same year, Galerius attacked them to no avail; his army also defected to Maxentius's side.

Following the advice of the retired Diocletian, the emperors chose another man to replace the now-dead Severus. The Tetrarchy saw the arrival of Valerius Licinianus Licinius, the new Augustus of the West, while Constantine remained his Caesar. Maximian still craved power and attempted to overthrow Constantine, which failed and led to his demise. Galerius, on the other hand, died after battling a horrible disease, possibly bowel cancer or gangrene. His death was rejoiced by the Christians, as it meant the end of their ruthless persecutions.

Wars among the emperors raged for years to come. Constantine exploited Maxentius's weakness when he lost support from the citizens of Rome by launching an attack and invading Italy. The night before the battle, Constantine was believed to have had a dream of Jesus Christ. He ordered his troops to march into battle with the Christian cross on their shields and banners. His victory against Maxentius at the Battle of the Milvian Bridge allowed him to gain complete control of the West.

Constantine shifted his focus to Licinius, who had successfully seized control of the East following Maximinus's defeat. The two fought multiple times before Licinius finally surrendered in 324. After crushing the Tetrarchy and reuniting the empire, Constantine became the sole emperor.

An illustration of Constantine leading his army against Maxentius at the Milvian Bridge. [58]

Constantine, the First Christian Emperor of Rome

As the sole emperor of Rome, Constantine was free to rule over the vast empire as he pleased without facing any threats or disagreements from other Roman rulers. After seeing the decaying state of Rome, the emperor sought out a new location for his capital. He first thought of the site of the ancient city of Troy but changed his mind. Nicomedia was not on his radar since it once belonged to Diocletian; Constantine wanted a place untouched by previous emperors. So, he chose the ancient city of Byzantium. Its strategic location and great harbor made it the perfect choice.

Constantine began working on his new capital. He invited artisans throughout the empire to rebuild the city and used the rich resources obtained from the provinces. Walls were built, and avenues were constructed, along with several statues of powerful figures of Roman history, including himself. Constantine even commissioned the construction of Christian churches, cisterns, and pagan temples in his new capital. By 330, Byzantium, renamed Constantinople, was exactly how he had envisioned it.

After experiencing a dream of Jesus Christ in 312, right before his big battle, Constantine was said to have converted to Christianity; some sources, however, claim he was baptized on his deathbed. Nonetheless, the great emperor showed signs of his devotion. As soon as Constantine acquired the throne, he immediately sent his mother, a devoted Christian, on a pilgrimage, which resulted in the construction of the Church of the Nativity at Bethlehem. Gladiatorial games ended since killing for entertainment was against the beliefs of Christianity. Pagan sacrificial rituals also ended.

Constantine's best-known contribution to the Christians was the Edict of Milan, which was established in 313, before the war with Licinius. Since Christianity was functionally illegal in the Roman Empire at the beginning of the religion's existence, many Christians had perished due to persecution. Emperor Nero blamed the Christians for the terrible Great Fire, leading to many of their deaths. Even Diocletian passed a decree allowing for the official persecution of Christians in 303. Although Constantine was not the first to legalize Christianity, his edict was effective. The Edict of Milan officially declared the abolishment of the persecution of Christians while protecting the rights of Christian citizens. Those arrested were released from prison, and their confiscated properties were returned. The edict also declared tolerance for all faiths. Even though Christianity did not become the empire's official religion—this happened during the reign of Emperor Theodosius in 380 — Constantine no doubt contributed to the spread of the religion.

During the years of his blossoming reign, the great emperor remained a military commander and had dozens of successes defending his empire against foreign threats. With his son, Constantius II, by his side, he defeated several barbarian tribes on the battlefield and reconquered the territories once lost to the Dacians. He planned to capture Persia, but his illness prevented him from doing so. He died in 337 after ruling over the reunited empire for over thirty years.

From glory and stability, the empire was again thrown into another set of skirmishes after the passing of Constantine. Power struggles between his family members were brewing, and they all fought for the throne. However, in the end, Constantine's three sons rose to power after eliminating their rivals.

With one matter resolved, another arose; the empire was facing constant trouble, with wars and rebellions happening almost weekly. While trying to return stability and peace to the empire, two of Constantine's ruling sons perished, leaving Constantius II as the sole emperor. Seeing all the ongoing issues in the empire, Constantius II decided to appoint a co-emperor to rule the West. His cousin, Julian, was chosen, who would soon prove to be a highly efficient ruler. Threatened by Julian's success, Constantius II aimed to bring down his own appointed co-emperor. However, he died of an illness before their battle, thus leaving Julian as the only ruler.

In addition to his military successes, Julian was also known for his effort to revive paganism. He even reversed some of the Edict of Milan that had restrained pagan practices. The emperor, also known as Julian the Apostate to the Christians, faced his demise during his campaign against the Sassanid forces. He died due to a spear wound. The battle with the Sassanids was only the beginning, as peace and glory were no longer on the horizon for the Roman Empire.

The Fall of the West

The empire soon sensed even bigger troubles when they saw the beginning of the Germanic tribes' migration. The extreme pressure from the powerful Huns had caused these barbarians to seek refuge within the empire; some entered peacefully, while others did not. The Visigoth, for instance, approached the frontiers of the empire by 376, hoping for a safe refuge. They were welcomed by the ruling emperor, Valens, with the condition that they defend the borders from any threats. However, the situation quickly went south, as the Romans failed to accommodate the large tribe—it was estimated that there were nearly eighty thousand of them. Combined with the hostility portrayed by most of the Romans toward them, the Visigoths rebelled, which led to a bloodbath called the Battle of Adrianople.

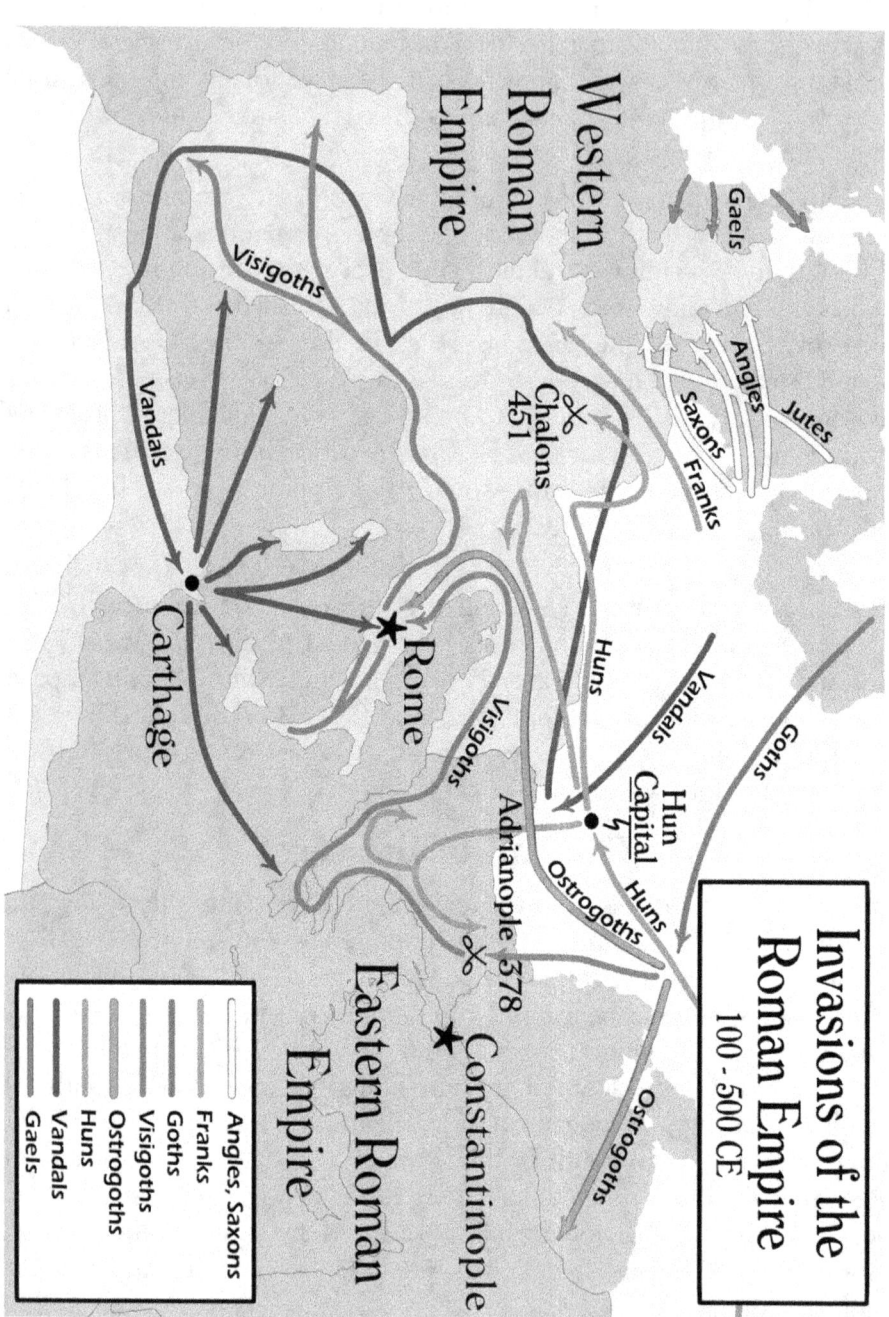

Routes taken by barbarian invaders of the Roman Empire during the Migration Period.

The large Roman infantry was headed by Valens, while the Germanic Visigoths were led by Fritigern. The Visigoths were also aided by the Ostrogoths. On August 9th, 378, the battle began with an attack launched by a few Roman commanders. Since the assault was launched without an order, the rest of the troops were confused, which opened an opportunity for the Ostrogothic cavalry to charge from the mountains and annihilate the Roman infantry. Over forty thousand Romans were killed, including Valens. With the emperor's body lying lifeless on the battlefield, the barbarians emerged victorious, although it was only for a short while. They were soon pushed back to Thrace by the Roman army, which was led by the next emperor, Theodosius.

A 19th-century painting possibly depicting the sacking of Rome.[60]

Theodosius successfully ran campaigns against the Goths and suppressed two civil wars during his sixteen years on the throne. But the Roman Empire was far from achieving peace, as it was split into two again in 395. It was passed to Theodosius's two sons: Arcadius and Honorius. Since the well-fortified Eastern Roman Empire remained impenetrable, many aggressors shifted their focus to the West. In 410, the Visigoths, under the leadership of King Alaric, launched an attack on Rome. The old, decaying city, which was once the most glorious part of the empire, was beyond saving. It received no help from the East. The great city of Rome was sacked, marking the beginning of the end of the Western Roman Empire.

Decades after the fall of Rome, the Western Roman Empire was forced into another ferocious battle. This time, it was against the great army led by Attila the Hun. Attila had been rampaging all over the empire, causing extreme fear. His advance was put to a halt by Flavius Aetius, a brilliant Roman commander.

Acknowledging the Huns as extremely formidable warriors, the Roman commander resorted to unlikely allies—the Visigoths, Franks, Burgundians, and Alans. After forming alliances with these Germanic tribes, Aetius led his entire army to the Catalaunian Plains (located in modern-day Champagne, France), where he would clash swords with Attila and his fierce warriors. Making use of his past experiences on the battlefield, Aetius successfully defeated Attila, who was forced to withdraw from the war.

The Battle of the Catalaunian Plains was indeed a great success for Aetius, but it was not enough to bring the Western Roman Empire back to its glory. The death of Attila the following year was seen as good news for the Romans, for without his leadership, the Hunnic Empire would not thrive, thus saving the empire from further threats. However, the Germanic tribes never stopped their conquests of the Western Roman Empire. In 476, the Germanic soldier Odoacer managed to overthrow the young emperor, Romulus Augustulus, and claimed the title of the first king of Italy. While the East remained strong, later on becoming the Byzantine Empire, the disposal of the last Western emperor marked the end of the Western Roman Empire.

Chapter 6 – Trade and Transportation

The Roman Empire might have gone down in history for its flourishing wealth, economy, architecture, art, warfare, and successful conquests. But many are not aware that the vast empire was also known for its long stretches of road networks, some of which still exist today. Of course, roads were not invented by the Romans; the first road was constructed by the early Mesopotamian civilizations. The Romans borrowed the idea and expanded the concept, mostly for military reasons. The first ever *via* or Roman road is known as the Via Appia, more popularly referred to as the Appian Way.

An illustration of the Appian Way. [61]

Parts of the Appian Way that survived the centuries.⁶⁸

Constructed in 312 BCE, this ancient road was commissioned by Appius Claudius Caecus, a brilliant statesman who served the Roman Republic as a censor or magistrate. The road initially ran for over 200 kilometers (about 125 miles), beginning in Rome and ending in the ancient city of Capua in Campania. Almost seven decades later, the road was extended for another three hundred kilometers (nearly two hundred miles) to Brundisium, which was located along the Adriatic Sea. Back then, it was common for Roman roads to be built as straight as possible. The first ninety kilometers (fifty-five miles) of the Appian Way, for instance, was constructed in a straight line until it reached Terracina, a city situated on the coast of the Tyrrhenian Sea. From there, the road took its first turn and was built inland to reach Capua. Later on, more road networks were established, mainly to ease the movements of the military. The Roman Empire was believed to have had a total of 372 roads that connected over a hundred of its provinces. Out of the 400,000 kilometers (about 250,000 miles) of roadways, more than 80,000 kilometers (50,000 miles) were stone-paved highways.

The process of building these roads was a difficult task, especially since they were expected to last for centuries. Since the Romans preferred their roads to be built in a straight line, surveys had to be conducted to determine the correct engineering methods. They would scout the route where the road was supposed to run and observe any natural obstacles in the way. They would cut down forests, drain lakes and marshes, divert creeks, and cut through mountainsides just so the roads could be constructed without turns. Arched bridges were built to cross heavy streams, while tunnels were used to cut through mountains and avoid lengthy detours.

The Roman roads were one of the empire's greatest architectural achievements. Many agree that these road networks were the arteries of the empire and the main key to its impressive might. Other than being used by legionnaires to march toward a captured city and perhaps outmaneuver their enemies, the road system also allowed Roman civilians to travel across the provinces in just a matter of days to visit family members or conduct trade or business. Supplies, emergency help, and reinforcements could easily reach even the most isolated parts of the empire since the roads were specifically designed with speed in mind.

The first emperor of Rome, Augustus, made the decision to establish the *cursus publicus*, the very first courier service in the empire. Historians believe that the establishment of *cursus publicus* was influenced by the Persians. These messengers were put in charge of delivering different types of messages, be they from high officials or senators or even tax revenues from provinces at the end of the western frontier.

Most of the time, the messengers would ride on a horse; sources state it could be plausible that they rode an average of eighty kilometers (fifty miles) a day. The strategic road network no doubt shortened the amount of time needed for the couriers to reach their destination. From Rome, it took roughly seven and a half days to reach the Gallo-Roman town of Lutetia (modern-day Paris). The task of a messenger might have sounded decent, but it was often a dangerous job. Since couriers carried valuable supplies and important mail, they were often targeted by thieves.

The messengers would also travel across the provinces in a light carriage pulled by a couple of fast horses. A birota, a slow, two-wheeled cart pulled by oxen, was used, though it was strictly reserved for delivering official government letters and documents. Since the wheels of Roman carriages were made out of iron, loud and unpleasant sounds were often produced whenever they passed by. Roman law strictly prohibited any kind of carriage from entering the cities during the day.

At every twenty-five kilometers along the Roman roads, one could find a *mansio*. Directly translated as "staying place," a *mansio* was a way station. They were normally commissioned by the government to act as a resting spot for couriers and travelers. Starting off as a simple structure that served drinks and sometimes food, the area surrounding a *mansio* would often attract many other businesses, resulting in the emergence of small towns. Although military camps were a common sight near *mansiones*, some suggest that these resting areas had a rather bad reputation due to the frequent visits of prostitutes and criminals.

The Different Types of Roman Transportation

While *biga*, the two-horse chariot, was often used in races and various ceremonies, the Romans used another type of swift chariot called *essedum* to traverse cities. A much slower version of this was a *cisium*. Unlike the *essedum*, the *cisium* featured a seat for two passengers.

A bronze figurine of a *biga* from Roman Gaul. [68]

For longer journeys, Roman citizens would opt for a *raeda*, a Roman wagon that could trace its roots to the Celts. Almost equivalent to modern-day buses, some of these ancient carriages had cloth roofs to protect passengers from the weather, although those without coverings were pretty common. Inside, the wagon had several benches that could fit multiple passengers. Even though there was a space to place supplies and luggage, the Roman law set a maximum weight limit; each carriage was only allowed to carry less than a thousand Roman *libra* (about 330 kilograms or 730 pounds) of luggage. When a *raeda* was not drawn by four healthy horses, oxen and mules were used to pull the carriage.

The wealthy would travel short distances on a litter, which was carried by six bearers or slaves. This mode of transportation was especially popular among wealthy women since it was a safer option when traveling the city streets. While middle-class Romans used *raeda* to travel in groups, the wealthy rode in a *carpentum*, which was more comfortable than the simple carriage. Not only was it entirely covered with an arched wooden roof, but it was also adequately adorned and spacious. A smaller version of a *carpentum* was known as *carruca*, which could only fit two passengers.

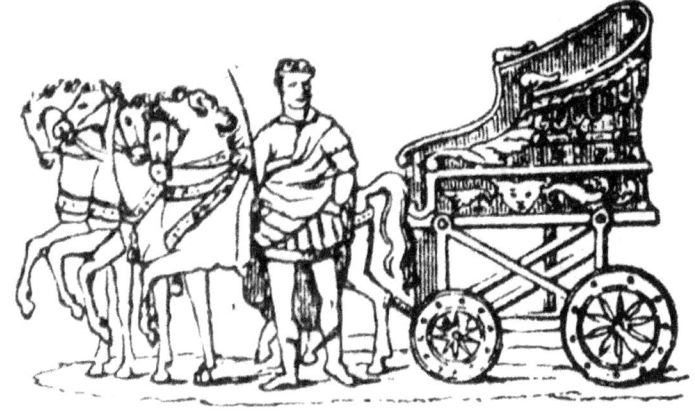

A Roman *carruca*, which was often used by the rich.[64]

An illustration of a *plaustrum* carrying heavy items.[65]

Plaustrum, an open wagon pulled by oxen, was also a common sight. Made entirely out of wood and two to four solid iron-shod wheels, this particular form of transportation was used to transport heavy goods. Construction materials, such as bricks and stones, along with agricultural goods, including olive oil, grapes, wines, cereals, and grains, were some of the items this wagon carried.

How the Roman Empire Gained the Majority of Its Revenue from Egypt

The Eternal City had always been interested in Egypt due to the vast wealth held by the Ptolemaic rulers. When two of Rome's most influential rulers, Augustus and Mark Antony, agreed on an alliance and formed the Second Triumvirate, the two split their powers, with Antony securing the rule over the East, including precious Egypt. There, he formed an alliance with Egypt's queen, Cleopatra VII, who was also a descendant of Ptolemy, one of the four generals who served under Alexander the Great. With Cleopatra by his side and her wealth within reach, the Roman general planned to launch a campaign against the Parthian Empire—an ambition that seriously damaged Egypt's economy. Despite the region's gradual decline, Antony set his eyes on war campaigns instead of restoring Egypt's decaying infrastructure. The canals, for instance, were completely neglected, which disrupted Egypt's irrigation and transportation systems.

Despite the province's gradual decline, Augustus managed to obtain most, if not all, of the treasures that once belonged to the Ptolemaic rulers, including the valuable religious offerings gathered by Cleopatra. However, instead of putting this great fortune in his personal coffers, the young emperor used it on his people; Roman citizens were said to have received nearly four hundred sesterces each, while the military was showered with generous gifts. This move not only guaranteed the emperor's popularity among his subjects but also played a profound role in the empire's economy. The Roman Empire began to witness a consumer boom, which soon led to increased prices on all types of goods, thus attracting more foreign merchants and traders to Rome.

Seeing that the Eternal City was beginning to welcome an increasing number of merchants from outside the empire, Augustus turned his attention to the Egyptian Red Sea ports and its sea lanes. He began restoring Egypt to its former glory, ordering several construction projects across the once-neglected land. Due to these rapid restorations, Egypt was able to resume its flourishing agricultural activities. Roads and trade routes were also greatly improved under the emperor's supervision, with caravan stations built along the way to grant the traveling merchants some respite. Military outposts and watchtowers were installed to ensure smooth communication and safety. At times, merchants who carried extra precious cargo were given the convenience of an escort by the Roman army. The emperor also paid attention to the several harbor cities along the Nile, especially the city of Coptos, which was considered the main hub for receiving exotic goods imported from Arabia, India, and Africa.

These restoration efforts, combined with the Roman administration, no doubt impacted the empire's import and export industries. With the growing number of ships beginning to sail out of Egypt to as far as India, the empire was able to gain attractive revenue from import taxes. One ship known as the *Hermapollon* was said to have returned to Egypt from India with exotic spices and goods worth at least nine million sesterces. From this ship alone, the empire collected 25 percent on tax, which was equivalent to approximately two million sesterces. Records claim the empire collected about 250 million sesterces per year through import taxes and another 25 million sesterces per annum through export taxes.

Under the reign of Augustus, Egypt alone contributed to almost half of the empire's income. The revenue produced by the province continued to grow as the years passed. By the mid-1st century CE, Egypt produced at least six million sesterces per annum, which made up two-thirds of the imperial coffer.

Trade Goods in Imperial Rome

While Egypt was the main entry point for goods originating from the Far East, the Western Roman Empire had Ostia as its main port, as it was located closest to Rome. Its location right at the mouth of the Tiber River made it possible for imported goods to arrive in the Eternal City in just a matter of days. Since transporting goods via the roads was rather expensive, merchants and traders preferred to travel the seas, although it was riskier given the unpredictability of the weather and sea conditions. Because of this, the Romans did their best to ensure the sea routes were safe. Several lighthouses were built, and the Roman navy was deployed to clear out any pirates sailing the waters.

The Romans did not only import goods internationally; they also received goods from their own provinces. Britannia, for instance, supplied Rome with wool, tin, lead, and silver, which they often used to craft jewelry and mint coins. The provinces in the East, on the other hand, provided color dyes for clothing, along with cotton, perfumes, and spices. Grains arrived in the Eternal City from North Africa, which also provided wild animals that were typically used in gladiatorial games. Different types of food and consumables were common trade goods among the Roman provinces, such as the fish sauce garum, olive oil, cereals, and, of course, wine, which was considered an important part of the Roman diet. Internationally, Rome was known to have exported a variety of goods to different parts of the globe, with grapes, pottery, and papyrus being some examples.

The Romans loved wearing silk, especially those in the upper class—though, according to the historian Marcellinus Ammianus, garments made out of silk began to be worn by almost every social class by the late 4th century CE. The Romans were greatly pleased when they finally made direct contact with China in 166 CE. From there on, silk became a common sight in the empire, as the Romans began to welcome imports from China through the Silk Road. In regards to India, Rome was believed to have imported over a hundred items, including exotic spices, sandalwood, glass beads, ivory, and even peacocks. Slaves were also imported into Rome from regions and kingdoms outside of the empire.

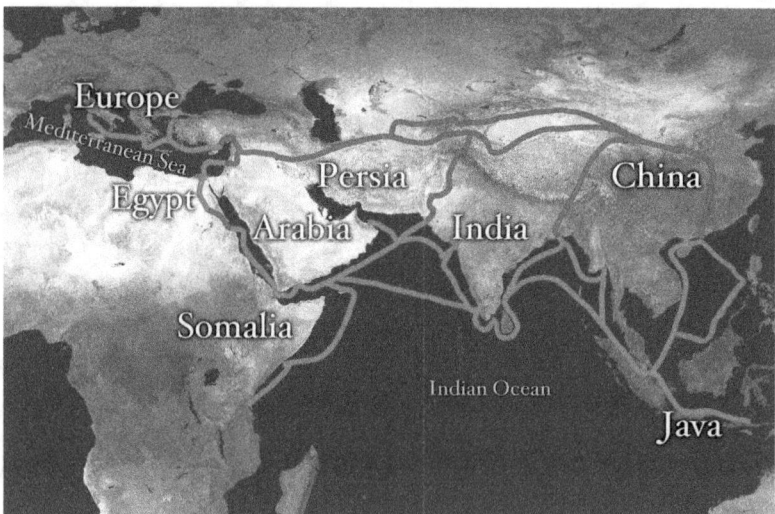

The Silk Road was used for trading goods. The land routes are shown in red, and the maritime routes are in blue. [66]

Trade and commerce in the Roman empire lasted for centuries and kept Rome financially stable. It was only when the Goths captured Ostia that its trade economy started to plummet. Without the control of the harbor, the Romans were unable to import grains and other food supplies, leading to mass starvation—which was the key to the Goths' victory. When the Western Roman Empire collapsed, the Mediterranean was yet again surrounded by dangers, blocking many merchants and traders from conducting business in the Eternal City.

Chapter 7 – Central and Provincial Governing

Somewhere within the safe walls of the Eternal City, a man could be seen rushing his way through the bustling crowds in the ancient Forum. He was probably nearing his fifties and wearing a toga with a broad Tyrian purple stripe: a symbol of high status. On one of his fingers was a special golden ring, a sign that the man indeed belonged to the higher social class of Rome. The man finally arrived at his destination, the Curia Julia, one of the most prominent structures in ancient Rome, commissioned by the great Julius Caesar and completed by Augustus himself. The man continued his pace and entered the Senate house. He then proceeded to take his seat among his fellow senators and got ready for a meeting where they would discuss Rome's next leader.

Roman senators discussing state matters.[67]

Before Augustus gained victory over Mark Antony at Actium, Rome was basically put under the control of the Senate. According to Roman tradition, the birth of the Senate could be traced back to when the Eternal City was first founded. Its first legendary king, Romulus, was the one responsible for the establishment of the Senate. It was believed that Romulus had handpicked a hundred of his best men as the first senators. They were entrusted with a simple task: to provide advice to the sovereign. Although records of how crucial the Senate played a part back then are rather vague, historians agree that the Senate began to grow in power when the Roman monarchy was nearing its end.

Rome became a republic when the seventh king of Rome, Lucius Tarquinius Superbus, was finally overthrown. The absence of a crown on top of the hierarchy paved the way for the Senate to rise and expand its power. Beginning with only a hundred men, the number of senators increased to six hundred. It then grew to nine hundred under the order of Caesar but decreased back to six hundred when Augustus took the reins. Although placed at the top of the social classes, being a senator was not a walk in the park. First and foremost, to become a part of the Senate, one had to be wealthy enough, as senators were not paid any salary and were strictly prohibited from getting involved in commerce and trade. In fact, they were expected to fund the state. Once appointed, senators would serve until their dying breath. If they were caught in a dishonorable act or if their wealth was depleted for some reason, the senator must resign.

During the early period of the republic, the Senate was mainly responsible for advising the magistrates, such as censors and consuls. The senators had no power to pass laws; they could only suggest decrees to the magistrates. After a formal discussion and gaining votes, decrees became laws and were implemented throughout the state. However, by the 4th century BCE, the Senate's authority grew. It was in charge of almost every aspect of the government, including religious matters. Not only was the Senate put in charge of the city's money flow, but it was also powerful enough to appoint favored officials to govern a certain province or promote someone to the rank of *legatus* or general. The senators also had the authority to declare war against their enemies; Julius Caesar and Mark Antony were once branded as public enemies. During desperate times, they could also appoint someone—typically one who had an exceptional background in the military—as dictator.

The Senate was no doubt the most powerful official body in Rome for centuries. After the rise of Rome's first emperor, Augustus, the Senate saw its power gradually wane. During the early imperial period, the Senate still held a considerable amount of influence within the empire; senators were allowed to debate and disagree with the emperor's decisions. They retained some of their authority, both in the military and over religious matters. The Senate was also allowed to appoint governors but only for certain provinces—typically those that were not put under the direct watch of Augustus. The court of law was handled by the senators, and their rulings were final—not even the emperor could overturn them.

However, as time went by, the Senate continued to face various threats to its power and prestige, especially when the military began to gain the upper hand at the start of the Third Century Crisis. The Senate finally lost most of its authority when the emperor's official seat was moved to the East. Although the Roman Senate was split into two bodies—one remained in the crumbling Rome while the other in Constantinople—they were involved only in minor and local matters.

The Roman Emperor, a Man Who Held True Power over the Empire

Even though the early days of the empire retained the Roman Republic's political structure, the Senate's powers were in name only, especially after the reign of Augustus. At this point, the Senate existed only to endorse the emperor's decisions. If the senators refused, they could face serious punishments, including death.

The ruling emperor had complete control over the empire's coffers; they could spend any sum of money on anything they wished, be it the construction of a new temple or even a statue depicting their likeness. Their words were also final. Nero, who was described by many as an emperor who was always in need of money, freely pointed his fingers toward those he disliked, saying they were involved in a certain conspiracy. The person would get arrested and often be murdered. His wealth would be confiscated and given to the emperor. Nero often used this method to fund his expensive construction projects.

The emperor also had control of the majority of the military. Augustus himself was the commander of twenty-six legions, which comprised approximately 125,000 highly trained soldiers. None could run for office without the emperor's approval. The emperor was very involved, even in the city's religious affairs. Augustus and the emperors after him assumed the title of Pontifex Maximus or "Chief Priest," signifying that he had the ultimate authority over every religious ceremony.

The provincial governors were put under close supervision, and the emperor was allowed to call upon his people for assembly should he feel the need to enact new laws. In short, the emperor was the only man who held true power over the vast empire to the point that, even after their deaths, some were deified—a religious tradition the Romans possibly assimilated from the East.

How the Roman Provinces Were Governed

The empire's rapid expansion made it impossible for the emperor to oversee every matter across the hundreds of provinces. During the republic, each of the provinces was put under the watch of a Roman magistrate appointed by the Senate. They would rule over the provinces while being supported by a quaestor, a lower-ranking magistrate whose main responsibility was the treasury, along with three lieutenants. However, extortion and abuses were common in these Roman provinces, as the governors were given complete control.

During the early Roman Empire, reforms for the provincial governments were introduced. Procurators were appointed to curb extortion issues and financial mismanagement. Governors were chosen among either consuls or praetors, who would then draw lots to determine which provinces they would assume control over. The governors then had to issue the *lex provinciae*, sets of laws to help the administration of the provinces.

After Augustus rose to power, the provinces were split into two different classes. While the senatorial provinces were still governed by appointed consuls and praetors, the imperial provinces were put under the control of propraetorian legates, who were the ruling emperor's representatives. Although the provinces were overseen by different types of governors, Augustus set a general governing policy to lessen corruption and unjust administration.

As governors, they had four main responsibilities. Since they were in charge of a province's taxes and financial matters, they were expected to oversee every single local authority and private tax collector. Their second duty was to supervise all construction projects and ensure the flow of money was in line with the projects. Other than paying close attention to the province's financial situation, a governor also carried the responsibility of a supreme judge. They had the power to impose death penalties. While major provinces across the empire had more than one legion ready for battles, smaller provinces typically consisted of auxiliaries. Nevertheless, governors were the ones expected to command the army if there were any threats.

How the Military Asserted Their Power in Imperial Rome

As time passed, the six hundred senators were no longer considered serious contenders to the imperial throne, as their power slowly diminished. However, as the vast empire continued to grow, expanding its borders farther to the east and west, emperors began to rely on the military. Without them, the empire would fall into pieces in no time, especially since the empire had made a lot of enemies as the years progressed. The imperial government was left with little choice but to ensure the military remained loyal to the emperor. They showered the military with gifts, attractive salaries, prestigious awards, and many other promises, hoping they would never turn their backs on the ruling emperor and continue to protect the empire's frontiers from any impending foreign threats.

However, the military quickly noticed how their emperor held a slight fear of them. Many emperors who had just risen to the throne resorted to buying the military's loyalty, but sometimes, the promised payments never arrived, which led the military to take matters into its own hands. Rebellions, threats, and even assassinations were carried out by the military whenever the imperial government showed signs of negligence. These violent episodes of bloodshed, mutinies, and killings were common, especially during the Third Century Crisis.

Out of all the military classes, historians believe the Praetorian Guard was the empire's third power player. Although the Praetorian Guard was said to have been established shortly after Rome transformed into an empire, this elite military unit traces its origins back to the Roman Republic. Back then, the Praetorian Guard was mainly responsible for providing escorts to high-ranking officials of the Senate and the Roman legions. It was only during the beginning of Augustus's reign in 27 BCE that the Praetorian Guard saw some changes. Instead of providing security to elite officials, the Praetorian Guard was tasked with keeping the emperor and his family safe.

A relief of the Praetorian Guard.⁶⁸

The number of men in the Praetorian Guard varied as the years went by. It began with a total of 4,500 handpicked soldiers during the reign of Rome's first emperor and grew to 15,000 by the late empire. This elite unit lived in special barracks referred to as Castra Praetoria, which was said to be right on the outskirts of Rome. The salary of the Praetorians was rather lucrative; they earned about three times more than a regular soldier. They were also entitled to *donativum*, a form of gift money worth several years of pay each time a new emperor took the reins. The highest rank within this special elite force was called a Praetorian prefect, and some of them were known for playing major roles in the harsh political sphere.

As part of protecting the ruling emperor, the Praetorian Guard had to act as anti-riot forces, secret police, and sometimes fire brigades. They often went undercover, dressing as normal citizens and eavesdropping on suspicious conversations, especially at gladiatorial games and theatrical performances. Those who showed even the tiniest signs of treason would be arrested and interrogated. The Praetorians even secretly assassinated those who they deemed an imminent threat to the government and emperor. The Praetorians performed their duty well during the first few decades of the Roman Empire. However, with Augustus's passing and the rise of Tiberius, the Praetorian Guard began to show its true colors.

The first prefect who successfully elevated the involvement of the Praetorian Guard in Rome's political sphere was Sejanus. Many agree that Sejanus was a highly ambitious man whose ultimate goal was to secure the entire empire. In fact, he briefly realized his dreams when the state's matters were left to his judgment after he successfully persuaded Tiberius to leave the imperial seat and reside in his luxurious mansion away from Rome. However, in the end, Sejanus's own greed and thirst for power sealed his fate.

Although Tiberius never left the prefect as the de facto ruler of Rome, Sejanus began to gain political influence, especially from his loyal comrades. The Senate eventually grew fond of him but only for a short while, as he was quick to abuse his power. Treason trials were brought back, and many perished due to his greed. At this point, the government was in shambles, and the people of Rome lived in fear. Sejanus shifted his focus to Drusus, Tiberius's only son and heir apparent to the imperial throne. With the help of Livilla, the wife of Drusus, whom Sejanus had managed to seduce, Sejanus poisoned the only son of Tiberius, thus eliminating the emperor's heir. (It should be noted that scholars aren't entirely certain whether Sejanus did this, but it is likely.)

Sejanus arrested and condemned to death.⁶⁹

To make himself a legitimate heir to the throne, Sejanus attempted to marry Livilla, although this move was denied by Tiberius. The emperor soon learned of Sejanus's true intentions and, with careful planning, managed to execute the ambitious prefect. Due to Sejanus's troublesome rule, the Senate immediately ordered *damnatio memoriae* or condemnation of memory. All of Sejanus's actions and previous achievements might have been excluded from official Roman accounts, but his influence remained within the Praetorian Guard. The Praetorians' power grew tremendously after their success in assassinating Caligula. They not only had the power to eliminate emperors—the Praetorians were famously known for killing thirteen Roman emperors throughout the centuries—but could also select the next ruling emperor.

Although the Praetorians began as an elite military unit with a noble cause, they turned power-hungry and became feared and despised by many, including the emperors. In the 4th century CE, the Praetorian Guard's terror finally ended. After a long series of treasonous actions, Emperor Constantine decided the Praetorian Guard could no longer be trusted, resulting in their permanent disbandment.

Chapter 8 – Imperial Army and Warfare

Farmers, merchants, fishermen, artisans, bakers, and blacksmiths—these were some of the most common occupations that existed in the Roman Empire. Indeed, one could be free from any life-endangering situations should they choose any of these career paths since their jobs were often conducted within the safety of fortified walls, but not all of these professions promised great fortune. Farmers could plant more than a hundred different crops each year, but their chances of owning their own land were slim; bakers could sell dozens of loaves and other goods, but it was nearly impossible for them to move out of their dilapidated high-rise apartments and into a landed house with paved streets and guaranteed security. Back then, fortune and wealth were enough to push Roman citizens into enlisting in the military—one of the few occupations with steady pay.

Being one of the biggest and most powerful empires at the time, it is not surprising that the Roman Empire gathered its fair share of enemies whose sole ambition was to dethrone the reigning emperor and claim every one of his vast regions. Even ancient historians agreed that the empire was synonymous with warfare almost all the time. Because of that, the empire always welcomed recruits who were headstrong in lending the emperor their ultimate loyalty and sword. As much as the Romans would like to defend their empire from foreign forces, they chose to devote themselves to the military because of the lucrative rewards that came with it. Retired soldiers were promised land of their own and a lifetime pension—that is, if they survived the many battles and had served the empire for twenty-five years.

Those interested in joining the military had to fulfill several requirements before raising their swords on the battlefield. The minimum age for a man to enlist as a legionnaire was eighteen, and they must be of Roman birth. Slaves were strictly prohibited from joining the ranks; if one were caught trying to sneak their way in, they would be slain mercilessly. Initially, only those with a height of over five foot ten were allowed to sign up, but as the empire grew more desperate for soldiers—probably due to the constant warfare and terrible plagues that had robbed many lives—the height requirement was lowered to five foot eight. Soldiers were also expected to have great strength and the ability to march at least twenty miles a day while carrying multiple weapons, tent equipment, cooking pots, and other essential items on their backs. The potential recruits were put to the test, as they had to showcase their battle prowess along with their athletic and medical skills. Once all the requirements were checked and the tests passed, they were allowed to swear an oath to the emperor and head to the barracks.

The legionnaires were not only exposed to risks and dangers during a raging war but also during their daily training. They were no strangers to cruel punishments, especially those who portrayed cowardice or were deemed incompetent by their strict commanders. During a march, centurions or commanders would keep a close eye on their soldiers while holding a vine staff in one of their hands. One small mistake, and the soldier would receive a terrible beating. One man known as Lucilius was recorded by the ancient historian Tacitus as one of the most brutal centurions in Roman history; he was believed to have beaten his legionnaires until his staff broke in two. The beating did not stop there, as he then yelled for a new staff so that he could continue the punishment. His excessive brutality proved too much for the soldiers, and he was targeted and murdered by his comrades.

Severe beatings were not the only punishments soldiers had to endure. They could also face execution if they made a serious mistake. Many commanders, even Augustus himself, used decimation, an infamous form of punishment. During decimation, the soldiers would be put into groups of ten and forced to draw lots. The unfortunate man who drew the shortest straw would be the one to get executed, often by the remaining nine soldiers in the group who bludgeoned him to death.

When it was finally time to leave the barracks and prepare for a vicious confrontation, the imperial army would ensure they were armed to the teeth. For protection, a legionnaire would wear iron armor over his simple wool tunic, along with a metal helmet, which was usually made out of either iron or bronze, depending on one's rank and wealth. A *scutum* shield, which often hung on a legionnaire's back, might have been the heaviest item they had to carry. However, the shield's versatility made it extremely useful in battle. Initially, the shield was crafted in a circular shape, but it eventually evolved into a large rectangle that covered the entire torso. While in conflict, the shield would be held in the soldier's left hand and used to parry close combat blows or to protect the body from a rain of arrows. The *scutum* also featured an iron knob at its center, which could be used to bash and stagger an enemy.

The Roman shield, *scutum*. [70]

The Roman *gladius*. [71]

Legionnaires seldom carried ranged weapons, as those weapons were mostly reserved for the auxiliaries or non-citizen troops, whose main role was to assist the imperial army. Along with a *scutum*, legionnaires carried a javelin called a *pilum*. At the start of a battle, the soldiers would hurl the javelin toward their charging opponents. Some would aim at the enemies' shields to limit their defense, while others would aim for the torso. It was extremely difficult for the enemy to remove the javelin from t either their shields or body armor, thus limiting their mobility. The *pilum* was carefully designed to bend once it hit the target to prevent the enemies from reusing them. Once the enemies were overwhelmed by the javelins, the legionnaires would unsheathe their *gladius*, a type of sword, and charge toward them. With their *scutum* held tightly in their left hand, shielding them from any ranged attacks, the Roman soldiers would thrust their *gladius* into the abdomen of their enemies—a fatal spot—followed by a few short slashes. If they were too close to the enemy and had little space to maneuver, the legionnaires would switch to their secondary weapon called *pugio*, an efficient dagger used to perform quick stabs.

The Roman army always preferred facing their enemies on the battlefield head-on, but in certain cases, they were left with no choice but to form a completely different strategy. If their enemies decided to choose defense and remain within their heavily fortified walls, the Romans' clever art of siege warfare was applied. Formidable siege towers were often used to besiege enemy settlements. To topple fortified towers surrounding a city, the army used a catapult called an onager, which could launch circular boulders weighing up to 80 kilograms (176 pounds). Other siege weapons, such as *carroballista* and *scorpions*, were used because of their high accuracy. Instead of rocks and boulders, these two ballistas fired hard iron bolts that could easily pierce armor. To break open the city walls and splinter wooden gates, battering rams were used, which were made out of long, heavy timber and a pointy metal front.

Battle Tactics and Formations

The Romans were believed to have borrowed various influences from the Greeks, including war techniques. Initially, the Roman troops were comprised of hoplites armed with a spear and shield. During a battle, they formed a type of formation known as the phalanx, which was effective, especially against cavalries. Standing less than fifty centimeters (twenty inches) apart, the hoplites interlocked their shields to provide protection and attacked enemies close by with their long spears.

However, despite the phalanx's great effectiveness and mobility, this battle formation had a major flaw; the flanks of the phalanx were often left exposed. By the 3rd century BCE, a new tactical unit was introduced, along with different formations. The military unit was known as maniple. Under a manipular legion, the army was divided into three main units: *hastati*, which comprised of heavy infantry carrying a sword and *scutum*; *principes*, which were more experienced soldiers who were typically in their late twenties; and *triarii*, the most experienced soldiers who often had enough wealth to afford the best armor and weapons. These units were also supported by cavalry units called *equites* and *velites*, the latter of which were young and less skilled soldiers who were normally placed in the front lines. At the start of a battle, the *velites* would throw their javelins toward the oncoming enemies before retreating to the back, giving way for the more experienced soldiers to advance.

By the late 2nd century BCE, the Roman military welcomed a new change in their classes and formations. The Marian reforms replaced the maniple system and entirely removed the military classes, resulting in the soldiers becoming equally trained and equipped. These heavy infantrymen were then divided into cohorts, a unit in a Roman legion. A full-strength Roman legion had about 4,800 to 5,000 well-equipped soldiers. There were ten cohorts within a legion, and each of these cohorts was split into six centuries of eighty men. Centuries were led by centurions, military commanders appointed either by the emperor or the Senate, although their comrades could also elect them. The Marian reforms also changed the way the military obtained its supplies. Soldiers were no longer expected to supply their own weapons and armor, as the reforms placed the responsibility of providing supplies on the shoulders of the military generals.

Some of the most famous battle formations used by the Roman legions were the hollow square and testudo. The hollow square, sometimes called the infantry square, was often used against cavalry. The Romans would arrange themselves closely next to each other, forming a square or, sometimes, a rectangle. This particular formation took time to form; however, once the soldiers were in position, it meant certain death for cavalrymen who dared to charge directly at them. The hollow square was famously used against the Parthian cavalry at the Battle of Carrhae. Unfortunately, the Parthians were a step ahead of the Romans, as their continued use of arrows greatly impacted the formation, breaking the Romans' defense.

The Roman army forming the testudo formation.[73]

Testudo, on the other hand, was often used during a siege. The Romans, along with their heavy *scutum*, would align to form a packed formation resembling the shell of a tortoise. Testudo helped the Roman troops protect themselves from attacks coming from above, behind, and in front of them. Those at the front of the formation would hold their shields up to their eye level, while those in the back held their shields over their heads to defend themselves from any arrows or spears. However, the troops moved slowly while in this formation, as they had to move in unison. Nevertheless, testudo was used by many commanders, one of them being Mark Antony, who, according to Cassius Dio, commanded his troops into a perfect testudo formation. It was reportedly so strong that even a horse could be ridden over it.

Military Awards and Honorary Gifts

Apart from stable and attractive pay, the Roman military enjoyed several awards and gifts from the emperor. While these awards were given to honor their sacrifice and bravery, they were also used to maintain morale and loyalty. The *hasta pura*, for instance, was a type of military decoration awarded to distinguished soldiers who had proven their skill during their first campaign. Shaped to resemble a spear—though it was non-lethal due to the lack of iron in its production—the *hasta pura* was normally awarded to the chosen soldier during a victory triumph and in front of a crowd. According to Suetonius, Emperor Claudius once presented this award to his most loyal supporter and highest-ranking magistrate in Rome, Tiberius Claudius Balbilus, after he emerged victorious from a mission in Britain.

A pair of Roman *armillae* in the shape of snakes.[78]

Another type of military award popular during ancient Rome was an *armilla*. This award was strictly reserved for Roman soldiers below the rank of centurion; non-citizen soldiers were not eligible for this honorary award. Recipients would receive a type of bracelet made from bronze, silver, or gold, depending on their rank and social status. These bracelets were only worn by awarded soldiers during victory triumphs or any official ceremony taking place in the Eternal City. The tradition of gifting the soldiers with bracelets first began in the mid-3rd century BCE when the Romans were at war with the Celts. The elite Celtic warriors often trampled the battlefield while wearing golden necklaces and armbands, symbols of authority and prestige. So, when the Gallic chieftain was finally defeated, Roman General Titus Manlius Torquatus took the chieftain's torque and wore it around his own neck. From there on, torques were often gifted to Roman soldiers as awards, with the addition of bracelets in the empire's later years.

During an official ceremony, some Roman soldiers could be seen with one or more circular insignia fastened on their armor. Known as phalera, which was synonymous with award medals, they often carried the images of the ruling emperor or the Roman deities, especially Jupiter and Mars. Like most Roman military awards, a phalera came in bronze, silver, and gold and could be awarded to individual soldiers or the entire unit. If it were bestowed upon a unit, the medal would be attached to their banners. At times, centurions would wear these medals on their armor to inspire their troops.

A set of phalera. [74]

Crowns and wreaths were also given as awards to the Roman military. The rarest award was the Grass Crown, which was only awarded to generals and commanders who had saved their legions from certain death on the battlefield. Presented by the army that he had saved, a Grass Crown, just as its name suggests, was made out of grass or plants taken from the battlefield. The Camp Crown was given to the first soldier who managed to penetrate the enemy's base or camp during a raging battle. Sometimes known as the Vallary Crown, as part of this award, the soldier would receive a golden crown in the unique shape of a palisade (high fences made out of stakes).

Those who saved the lives of Roman citizens, typically when a city was besieged, were eligible for the Civic Crown. However, the saved citizens had to confirm the soldier's bravery. Almost like the Grass Crown, the Civic Crown was not made of gold but rather oak leaves, which were then woven into a wreath. The Civic Crown was the second-highest honorary award in ancient Rome. The Roman author and naval commander of the early empire Pliny the Elder claimed that when a person with a Civic Crown on his head came to the Roman games, everyone, including the Senate, had to rise from their seats as a sign of respect.

Chapter 9 – Social Structure and Status

Many years had passed since the success of Augustus Caesar transformed the Roman Republic into a powerful empire. Although the empire was plunged into chaos after the passing of its first emperor, Rome was brought to its ultimate glory during the reign of the Five Good Emperors. A great number of military victories were achieved, many structures in Rome were successfully restored, and the empire's defense was greatly upgraded. Around this time, imperial Rome was considered one of the wealthiest and most powerful empires to exist. However, despite the empire's flourishing condition, not everyone had the opportunity to live their life peacefully.

Even before the reign of Augustus, Roman law considered those who were born in Italy as Roman citizens or *cives Romani*. Those who were born outside of Italy were referred to as *peregrini*. Although *peregrini* mostly inhabited the empire in the 1st and 2nd centuries CE, they were not considered citizens and did not have the same rights as Roman citizens. In criminal law, for instance, a *peregrinus* who had become entangled in any kind of serious crime could be tortured during official interrogations, while Roman citizens were exempted from such poor treatment. In fact, the citizens could even insist on a trial and choose to appeal his criminal sentence, be it jail time or a death sentence.

Peregrini were also subjected to an annual poll tax, *tributum capitis*, while Roman citizens were exempted from it. Since joining the military was one of the few ways to obtain wealth—should one survive the twenty-five-year-long service term—many would join the ranks without hesitation. While citizens could sign up and train as a legionnaire, a *peregrinus* was restricted from doing so. They were only allowed to enlist as auxiliaries, which offered little pay compared to the legionnaires. However, they and their children could be granted citizenship should they survive the service term.

In 212, Roman Emperor Caracalla passed the *Constitutio Antoniniana*, an edict that granted citizenship to every free man and woman in the empire. They no longer had to face different treatment than the Roman citizens. However, they were quick to realize that life as a Roman citizen was not always rainbows and sunshine, as the empire's social structure was strictly based on four main aspects: heredity, freedom, property, and wealth.

Just like many other empires and kingdoms of the ancient world, the social structure of imperial Rome was based on a hierarchical system. At the top of the hierarchy was none other than the emperor. As the person at the very top of the social pyramid, he had the ultimate authority over every matter in the empire and led a lavish life. During times of peace, they remained in the finest dwelling on Palatine Hill. Augustus established his own palace on this very hill, followed by Tiberius, who oversaw some huge expansion projects. It was only in 81 CE, during the rule of Emperor Domitian, that Palatine Hill became enclosed, separating the imperial palace from the rest of the citizens.

An emperor's wealth was poured into not only the construction of palaces, temples, and statues but also lavish banquets and parties. While sources claim that certain emperors, such as Augustus, Aurelius, Hadrian, and Trajan, never promoted excessive dinners and preferred to stick to modest banquets, other rulers never hesitated to indulge themselves with only the best foods and wines. Marcus Gavius Apicius, a Roman epicure, was believed to have served honey-glazed nightingales stuffed with prunes to Tiberius's sons.

Roman emperors often donned a solid purple toga to distinguish themselves from their subordinates and subjects—a tradition started by Julius Caesar. He may have gotten the idea from the ancient Etruscan kings. The Roman emperor's abundance of wealth and power came with a price; their position on top of the social structure was almost never perfectly secure, and assassinations and conspiracies were almost always on the table.

Nevertheless, emperors were supported by the ruling classes: the senators and patricians. Placed at the top of the hierarchy—right below the ruling emperor—both were usually wealthy landowners and leaders of Rome's most powerful and oldest family lines. Patricians (simply translated as "fathers") were the ones who held power over Rome's political sphere, religious matters, and military leadership. They were also granted many privileges compared to the rest of the social classes. For instance, patricians were exempted from certain military duties typically done by normal citizens. Only senators and patricians could become emperors.

With such privilege and power, patricians were expected to be highly educated. Young boys would be taught by private tutors in a wide range of subjects and fields, from history to geography, literature, and poetry. Some even had the opportunity to master different languages, including Greek. Wealthy girls likely would have been educated more than their plebeian counterparts. Since most men would embrace a career in the harsh political world of Rome, young patricians were taught the art of public speaking and law. But, like the Roman emperors, the life of a patrician was not simple; they were the ones who often got wrapped up in palace intrigue.

Right below the patricians was another high-ranking social class known as the equestrians, who were responsible for ensuring the empire never stopped growing. Just as the name suggests, equestrians consisted of the Roman cavalry. Early on, one could qualify as an equestrian if they were rich enough to own a horse. However, as time passed, an equestrian had to be worth at least 400,000 sesterces.

Due to the *Lex Claudia*, a Roman law passed in 218 BCE that prohibited the senators from getting involved in commercial roles, the equestrians were often involved in trade and business. Equestrians were also given several privileges, although they were not as extensive as the patricians and senators. Should an equestrian gain enough wealth throughout his career, he could step up to the next rank and become a senator. Those who belonged to the equestrian class were allowed to wear a tunic decorated with a clavus, a set of purple vertical stripes that ran from the top of their shoulders down to their leg. The stripes were, of course, thinner than those worn by the senators to distinguish their rank.

As their numbers increased to the point where they surpassed the senators, Augustus began to take notice of their importance. He reorganized the equestrians into a military class and gave them more positions in the government. Those who portrayed great potential while serving in the army had the chance of getting promoted to prefect, government administrator, or even procurator or imperial governor.

Moving down the hierarchy, we find the plebeians, which comprised the majority of Roman citizens. These working individuals, which included farmers, craftsmen, artisans, bakers, and blacksmiths, were neither rich nor poor. Historians suggest that most plebeians were illiterate compared to the elites, who had easy access to education. Most of the plebeians lived their lives with the simple aim of earning enough money to pay taxes and support their families. Those ambitious enough to rise through the social pyramid worked hard to save money and take their place among the equestrians. Despite having no power in politics and official government matters, plebeians could become a threat to the elites whenever there were cases of injustice. Even Augustus was well aware of the danger the plebeians posed; hence, he always ensured the commoners were well-fed and reasonably entertained.

At the bottom of the Roman social structure were the slaves. The Romans obtained their slaves in various ways. Since Roman slavery was not based on race, prisoners of war, captured enemies, and unfortunate individuals sold by pirates were the most common sources of slaves. There were also plenty of cases where poor parents were forced to sell their children into slavery so that they could live to see another day.

A depiction of a slave market in ancient Rome.[75]

Like all forms of slavery around the globe, slaves had no personal rights, and their days were filled with nothing but hurdles and obstacles. Once they had been bought, they became the property of their owners. One small mistake, and they could face several different harsh punishments. Beatings were not unusual, and all of the slaves were familiar with the cruel insults thrown into their faces every single day. Their owners could also kill them at any moment without worrying about being persecuted by the Roman court of law.

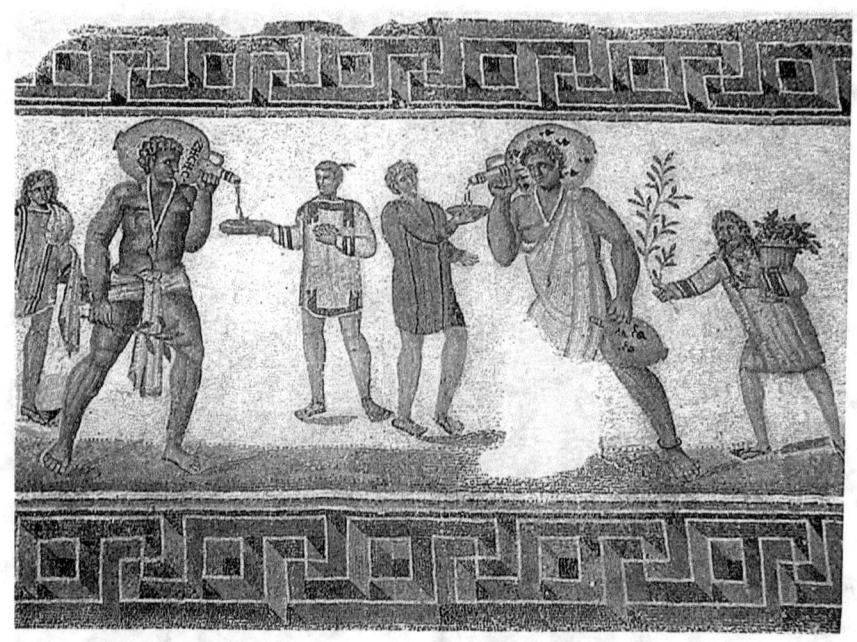
Roman mosaic depicting two slaves in their typical clothing carrying wine.[76]

Work never ended for the slaves, and their owners could send them to various places. Some worked in private households, where their main responsibilities were to take care of their owner's children, while some were sent to mines, factories, or farms. Many also worked to complete all kinds of construction projects across the empire; they built long stretches of roads for the military, as well as pavements, aqueducts, sewer systems, statues, and other structures. A great number of them—usually those who had been prisoners of war—were forced to fight to their death in gladiatorial games.

However, the slaves could obtain freedom. Those lucky enough to have been bought by kind-hearted owners were sometimes freed after several years of loyal service. Those who were less fortunate had to resort to manumission. Once slaves earned enough savings, they could buy their freedom. Freed slaves were granted citizenship and allowed to work the same jobs as plebeians. The father of the famous Roman poet Horace was believed to have been a freedman who had successfully bought his freedom after being enslaved for several long years. Freedmen and Freedwomen gained personal rights and were only prohibited from holding official positions in the government. However, a different law applied to children born to freemen; they were allowed to rise through the ranks and hold office.

The Roles of Women in the Roman Empire

Historians believed that women in ancient Egypt generally had the same rights and standards as men; not only were they allowed to have their own businesses, but female rulers were also common in Egypt. Greeks, on the other hand, had different views. Women in ancient Greece rarely enjoyed privileges and were confined to the home. But what about the roles of women in the Roman Empire? Did they get to live on the same level as the men, or did they have to endure different treatment and perhaps injustice?

It is safe to assume that the two genders were, of course, treated differently. Marriage was one of the most important aspects of a Roman woman's life. It was common for girls to be married off to the man of her father's choosing at a young age—some were expected to tie the knot as soon as they reached puberty, but most were married at the age of twenty. Once a woman had a family of her own, her main responsibility was tending to the household and taking care of the children. But this was not always the case with women of higher classes. The elites would often leave their children under the care of servants or hired caregivers. With their children off of their hands during the day, elite women would spend their time studying either philosophy or literature. Women of all classes were allowed to go to the theater, public baths, races, and gladiatorial games. Some women even chose to become gladiators and competed in the arena.

In the eyes of the Romans, women were seen as fully dependent on their husbands or the male leader of their families. Cicero viewed women as having weak judgment compared to men. He suggested placing restrictions on them when it came to managing their property. But much to his disappointment, the suggestion was not legalized. Although some men agreed with Cicero's point of view, Roman law stated that parents were allowed to distribute properties among their sons and daughters evenly. This explains why one could sometimes find women who actually had their own estates and businesses.

The Roman political world was fully reserved for men. Regardless of social stature, women were not allowed to cast their votes or voice their opinions in political assemblies. However, some women were clever enough to assert their influence indirectly. Mothers would voice their interests regarding a certain political matter through their sons. This can be seen during the reigns of a few emperors. For instance, it is said

Tiberius's mother controlled his decisions until he finally removed her from his life. Some believe that the barrack emperor Severus Alexander was heavily influenced by his mother's ideas, eventually leading to their demise.

Early 18th-century depiction of the dedication of a Vestal Virgin.⁷⁷

Perhaps the most esteemed position a woman in the empire could hold was the priestess of Vesta, known as the Vestal Virgin. However, the role was not voluntary; they had to be chosen from a highborn family. Once a girl was chosen (they were handpicked at the age of six to twelve) by the chief priest, the priestess had to remain chaste for at least thirty years. To ensure they could dedicate themselves entirely to Vesta, the goddess of the hearth, the priestess would be removed from her family and made legally independent. She also had to move out of her family home to the House of the Vestal Virgins, which was next to the sacred temple. After thirty years of serving the goddess with their chastity, these women would end up with enough wealth to last for the rest of their lives. Although they were free to marry once they were freed from the priesthood, many chose to remain independent.

Chapter 10 – Arts and Architecture

Military campaigns, warfare, and assassinations might have been familiar to the ancient Roman world. But aside from the continuous skirmishes and conspiracies, the Romans were well known for their exquisite architecture and complex engineering. Take the Roman aqueducts for example. Historians believe the Romans began building aqueduct systems as early as 312 BCE. Using gravity and natural slopes, the aqueducts typically transported fresh water from natural lakes or springs. The Romans used the clean water for various purposes: drinking, farming, mining, and supplying the many public baths, fountains, and even latrines scattered throughout the highly populated Roman cities.

The Roman emperors often commissioned these stone-arched aqueducts to improve the lives of the citizens. Each structure had its own specific design, source area, and water quality. Archaeologists claim that by the 3rd century CE, the city of Rome alone had eleven aqueducts in total, supplying clean water to over ninety kilometers away. Some of these ancient aqueducts survived for us to marvel at today, such as the Aqua Virgo, which was built during the reign of Augustus and is currently used to supply the world-famous Trevi Fountain.

The Roman Forum

The Eternal City was believed to have embraced seven different hills within its ancient walls. Two of the most popular ones were Capitoline Hill and Palatine Hill. While the latter went down in history as the "Nucleus of the Roman Empire," Capitoline Hill was regarded as Rome's most sacred site. On top of the enchanted hill, which was also known as Mons Saturnius, was the Temple of Jupiter. Although the temple is forever lost to history, it was once considered the most important Roman temple. Constructed in 509 BCE to honor Jupiter—the Roman equivalent of Zeus—the temple faced many destructive episodes. It was continuously restored and rebuilt by the Roman emperors until a terrible attack by the Vandals in the mid-5th century CE permanently destroyed it.

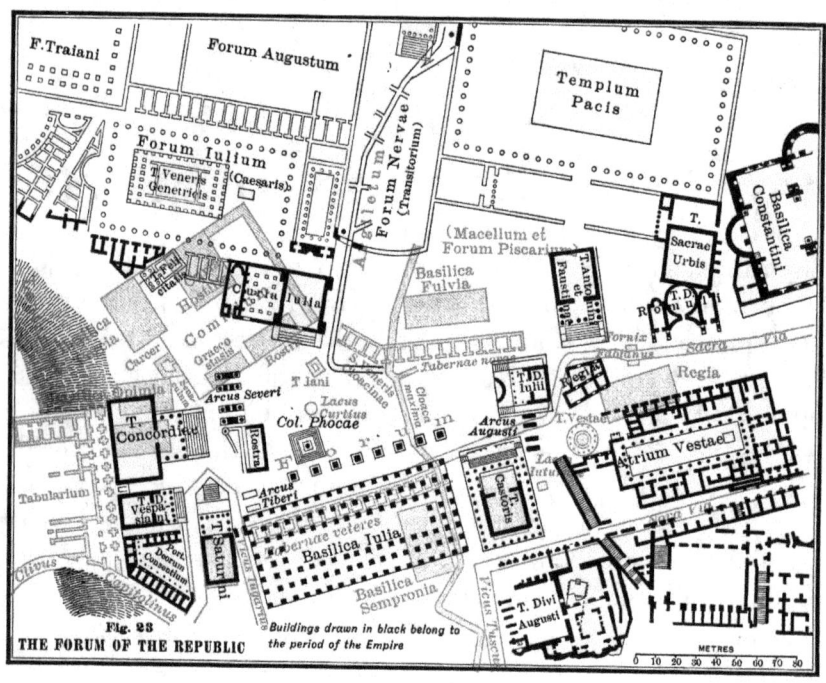

Map of the Roman Forum.[78]

About 40 meters (131 feet) below the two hills was the Roman Forum. Since a huge lake occupied the majority of the site, the Romans had no choice but to drain the water before they could start building anything. Using an underground sewer system called Cloaca Maxima, the water was successfully diverted to a nearby river. Initially, the area was developed as a marketplace, but as time went by, several massive construction projects began to take place, converting the valley into the center of the Eternal City.

Back in those days, the Roman Forum almost never slept; it was constantly filled with Roman citizens conducting both formal business and religious matters. The Basilica Julia, built to commemorate Julius Caesar, was one of the most prominent structures in the Forum. It was mainly used as a court of justice, but when Christianity was made the empire's official religion, the basilica acted as an important church. The Temple of Vesta, which housed the sacred fire of the hearth goddess, Vesta, could also be found at the Forum.

Remains of the ancient Roman Forum. [79]

Aside from temples, columns, and statues of emperors, the Romans were also known for their triumphal arches. While the oldest triumphal arch is the Arch of Augustus, the Triumphal Arch of Septimius Severus is perhaps the most intricate and complex. Still standing today, despite being heavily damaged, the triple triumphal arch was erected to commemorate the Romans' victory over Parthia in the 2nd century CE. Certain scenes of the successful military campaign were depicted on the relief panels, along with ornate columns and sculptures of ancient gods, especially Mars, occupying the rest of the arch.

The Colosseum, the Roman Empire's Largest Amphitheater

The Roman Colosseum is a notable structure, not only during the ancient period but also in modern times. Today, the partly destroyed amphitheater remains a sight to behold, but back then, this spectacular structure was built not only to impress but also to hold bloody and vicious events: the gladiatorial games.

The plan to construct the enormous amphitheater was first laid out sometime around 70 CE. However, Emperor Vespasian did not get to see the completed structure since he died several years later. The project was carried on by Emperor Titus, and in 80 CE, the Colosseum was finally opened to the public. Known as the Flavian Amphitheatre back then, Titus announced a hundred days of games when the amphitheater opened. Gladiatorial and wild animal fights were some of the games held, keeping the Roman citizens greatly entertained.

The construction of such a massive stone structure required a lot of plans, complicated calculations, and, of course, labor. Its location, for instance, was chosen for a reason. The Colosseum was built to the east of the Roman Forum, right on the site of Nero's golden palace: the very same palace that he had built for himself after confiscating many Roman citizens' properties. Vespasian, who sought to reverse the damage that Nero and his successors had done a few decades back, chose the site of Nero's palace on purpose and commissioned the construction of the Colosseum as a gift to his people.

The world-famous Roman Colosseum.[80]

The iconic amphitheater was carefully designed by professional Roman architects, engineers, and artists, but the heavy construction work was mostly done by Jewish slaves—it was believed that at least twenty thousand of them (if not more) were involved in the building of the massive structure. The main construction material, travertine stones, could only be quarried in Albulae, a location believed to be located near modern-day Tivoli. Transporting the stones was no doubt a hassle due to the distance, so new roads were built from the quarry straight to the construction site. It is said that over 200,000 carts filled with travertine stones were transported in the span of the 8-year construction period.

Aside from its size—sources claim that the full size of the Colosseum was about 190 by 155 meters (623 by 508 feet)—the most prominent features were its columns and arched entrances. The structure consisted of three stories and eighty arched entrances, which were fully supported by impressive semi-circular columns. The columns varied depending on the stories. The first story featured simple Doric columns. The second floor had Ionic columns, while the third story featured a set of ornate Corinthian columns. Inside, the Colosseum could fit up to fifty thousand spectators. However, it is plausible that seating was arranged according to social class.

The amphitheater was used for nearly four centuries. Later on, as gladiatorial fights and other forms of ancient entertainment were put to a stop—especially when the Western Roman Empire was about to collapse—the structure was abandoned, and its materials were quarried for new construction projects. Due to a series of natural disasters that struck the empire and the erosion of time, only a third of the Colosseum has survived today.

Roman Baths

As part of providing entertainment for the people, the Roman emperors commissioned the construction of public baths. Historians suggest this idea originated when the Romans visited the towns of the ancient Greeks. The Romans were well known for assimilating the architectural styles of the Greeks, so it is not surprising that they decided to create a public bath in each Roman town across the empire. Typically built near the forum of Roman cities, the Romans expanded the concept of these public baths to include several other facilities. While the Greeks only had hip-baths, the Romans included a set of changing rooms called the *apodyterium*, an exercise room or gymnasium, an open-air swimming pool referred to as *natatio*, massage rooms, and much else. Fountains, gardens, libraries, and lecture halls were also among the features of a Roman public bath.

These baths were often swarmed by the Romans, especially around noon to dusk. Everyone was allowed to spend time at the baths, no matter their social status. Slaves would normally enter if their owners chose to bring them along; they were usually tasked with carrying their owner's belongings, ranging from bathing garments to linen towels, sandals, and other equipment. While entrance to other forms of entertainment in Rome, such as the gladiatorial games, was free, Romans had to pay an entrance fee to use the public baths. However, the fee was so small that even the poorest of citizens could easily afford it. Scholars claim that by the time of Diocletian, the entrance fee for public baths was placed at only two denarii. Free entrance to the baths could be enjoyed during public holidays or any other important festivities.

Augustus's right-hand man and closest friend, Marcus Vipsanius Agrippa, was responsible for constructing Rome's first public baths or *thermae*. It was completed as early as 25 BCE, and the waters of the bath were supplied through the aqueduct Aqua Virgo, which was thought to have been built mainly for the baths. Other outstanding examples of Roman baths were the Lepcis Magna, the Baths of Diocletian in the heart of Rome, the Antonine Baths, and the Baths of Caracalla in southern Rome. The latter is considered by historians and archeological experts alike as the best-preserved Roman baths to ever survive.

Built sometime around the 3rd century CE, the Baths of Caracalla were regarded as the most luxurious Roman baths to ever exist, not only in the ancient period but also by modern standards. The entire complex was said to have been built with nearly 7 million bricks and consisted of over 250 interior columns. The size of the complex was so massive that it could cater to up to eight thousand visitors a day. Two sumptuous libraries, a watermill, a gymnasium, an Olympic-size swimming pool, six-foot long fountains, and a waterfall were some of the Baths of Caracalla's most prominent features.

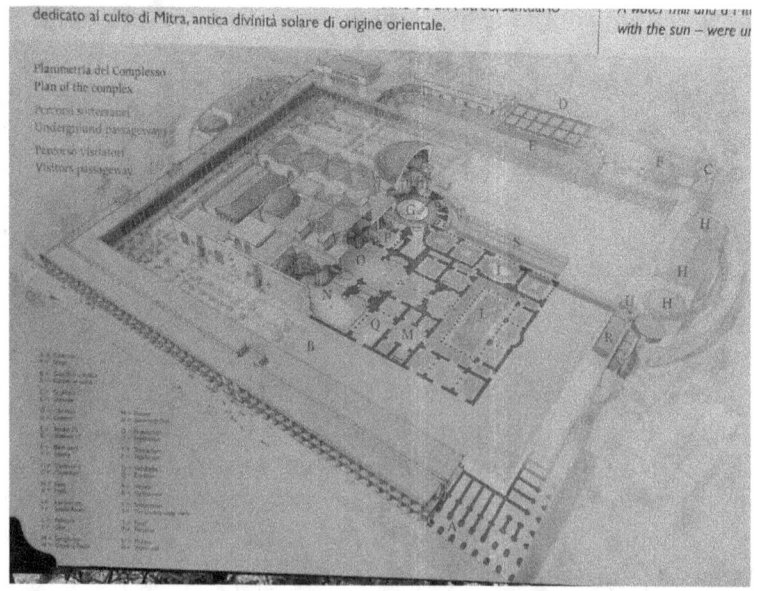

An Overview plan to Baths of Caracalla. [81]

Back in the baths' heyday, one could look around and find exquisite marble and granite adorning every inch of the walls. Parts of the ceiling were made out of finely crafted glass mosaic, which created unique iridescent patterns of the pool when light was reflected at certain angles. Separating two of the three main chambers of the baths—the *frigidarium* and the *tepidarium*—was the great hall, which showcased vaulted nave ceilings, a feature that influenced most churches during the medieval period. By the 5th century CE, the Baths of Caracalla earned its spot as one of the seven wonders of Rome. However, decades later, the baths were abandoned due to the attacks on Rome. It finally fell into disuse by the 7th century, with most parts of the complex destroyed when an earthquake struck the city in 847.

Roman Art and Sculptures

Aside from figure painting, sculptures were regarded as the highest form of art in the eyes of the imperial Romans. Just like many of the empire's architectural styles, it is safe to assume that Greek art had a powerful influence on the Romans, as many of the empire's paintings and sculptures sported obvious features that were only visible in ancient Greece. The Romans were known to have a fondness for Greek-style sculptures and commissioned many marble versions of popular Greek works, such as the *Doryphoros*. The original *Doryphoros* was believed to have been made out of bronze, but it was lost sometime in the 5th century BCE. Thanks to the Romans, a few marble copies of this well-known Greek sculpture were preserved, allowing us to get an idea of what the original looked like.

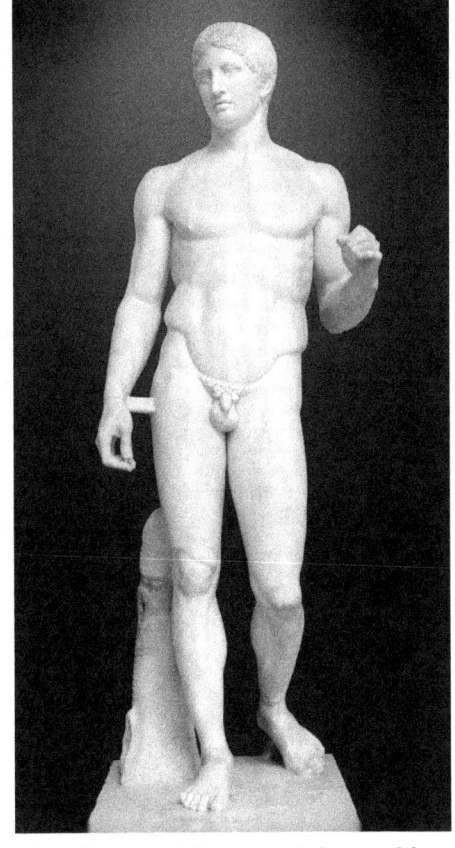

A well-preserved Roman period copy of the *Doryphoros*.[32]

Even historians agree that Augustus and the rest of the emperors from the Julio-Claudian dynasty were fond of classical Greek art. The best example of Roman sculpture could be the *Augustus of Primaporta*, which was commissioned at the end of the emperor's long life. Although Augustus was seventy-five when he died, the fine sculpture depicts a younger version of him, back when he first brought the empire to its utmost glory.

Emperor Hadrian, a lover of all things Greek, collected copies of the most famous Greek mosaic paintings at his villa. The *Battle of the Centaurs and Wild Beasts* by the Greek painter Zeuxis was one of his many prized possessions.

Augustus of Primaporta with a depiction of Cupid by his right leg.[88]

As the years passed, Roman art moved away from the classical Greek-inspired style and welcomed the art of late antiquity. Unlike the realistic sculptures of the classical period, the arts produced during this era were stiff and less realistic. This can be seen in the relief panels on the late Roman Empire's triumphal arches, such as the Arch of Septimius Severus or the Arch of Constantine in Rome. This form of art usually featured deep, full lines with the most important figure a larger size compared to the others. Despite its differences from the previous art style and the lack of naturalism, this form of art continued to be widely used during the reign of Constantine and his successors.

War relief on the Arch of Septimius Severus, a great example of the Roman art of late antiquity. [84]

Chapter 11 – Daily Life and Customs

It was a day almost like any other; a fellow Roman, belonging to neither an aristocratic family nor the rich, had risen from a short sleep and readied himself for yet another tiring day. Dressed in his simple tunic, the man walked through the narrow streets of the ancient Roman city to the shores of the Mediterranean, where he would embark on his boat and spend the rest of the day in the middle of nowhere, surrounded by the deep sea. While fishing was not one of the Roman Empire's main activities, this man was not a typical fisherman who spent his day under the sun waiting for red mullet to take the bait. Instead, he harvested snails collected in traps he installed on floats a few days before. The snails were *Hexaplex trunculus*, commonly known as the banded-dye murex, and used to produce purple dye for the emperor's togas.

Using techniques discovered by the Phoenicians, the man would crush these spiky snails once he had collected enough—at least ten thousand of them were needed to produce a gram of dye—and leave them under the sun to oxidize. The snails were then boiled in tin vats for a few days, filling the air with an unpleasant odor. Producing this dye was time-consuming and required a lot of labor and experience, thus making it extremely valuable.

As the sky darkened, the man returned to the shore and made his journey back home. The narrow street, once quiet during the day, was now filled with all kinds of noises that would keep people from sleeping at night. Unlike those with loads of wealth, the man lived in an *insula*, a high-rise apartment building three to seven stories high—sometimes even higher. Typically built to provide shelter, especially for those not rolling in wealth, the *insulae* were known for their poor construction, despite having running water and sanitation.

Tenants were charged a certain amount of money, which was either paid annually or weekly, depending on the spaces and rooms they occupied. The ground floor, which was paid for annually, was usually more spacious and had several rooms for different activities, such as dining and sleeping. Spaces on the higher floors were much more confined and did not have many windows. It is safe to assume that even during ancient times, no one would say that an *insula* was the best place to stay. One's safety was not guaranteed, and the rooms were usually too hot during the summer and too cold when winter arrived.

Nevertheless, the *insulae* were mostly found in Rome, the heart of the empire itself. By 150 BCE, the city already had over forty-six thousand *insulae* built for its citizens. This was due to the limited space and land in Rome, making it difficult for the city to house the increasing population; the empire had already reached at least forty-five million (some scholars believe sixty million) by the reign of Augustus. However, with brick, timber, and later Roman concrete as the *insulae's* main construction materials, they were susceptible to fire and cave-ins. Given the dark, narrow, and broken roads that led to these apartments, any sort of aid or emergency help wouldn't have been able to reach the people in time if any catastrophic situations happened. These roads were reconstructed and widened under Emperor Nero's reign after the events of the Great Fire of Rome, which burned two-thirds of the city.

Surviving *insulae* in the Roman harbor city of Ostia.[85]

While the commoners spent their lives in the easily destroyed and crowded *insulae*, the rich made themselves comfortable in a type of townhouse called a *domus*. Unlike the *insulae*, which housed several families on multiple stories, the Roman *domus* was inhabited by only a single family. The size of a *domus* varied: some people lived in a very small yet safe and comfortable house, while others lived in huge, luxurious mansions. However, what they had in common was their location: they were built close to buildings of importance and faced away from the busy streets to ensure both safety and privacy.

The atrium of a Roman *domus*.[86]

In contrast to the dilapidated *insulae*, which were rather confined and lacked natural lighting, the *domus* featured at least five different spaces and rooms, each with beautifully painted walls. Indoor courtyards, gardens, bedrooms, a dining room, private bathrooms, and a kitchen were the most common spaces in a *domus*, although some featured an office with its very own library. The most important part of this luxurious house was the atrium, which housed either an altar or a statue of a god worshiped by the household. While the rest of the atrium was usually covered by high-ceilinged porticoes, the center was left open to allow rainwater into the *impluvium*, a pool or basin designed to catch water. It was located beneath the roof opening.

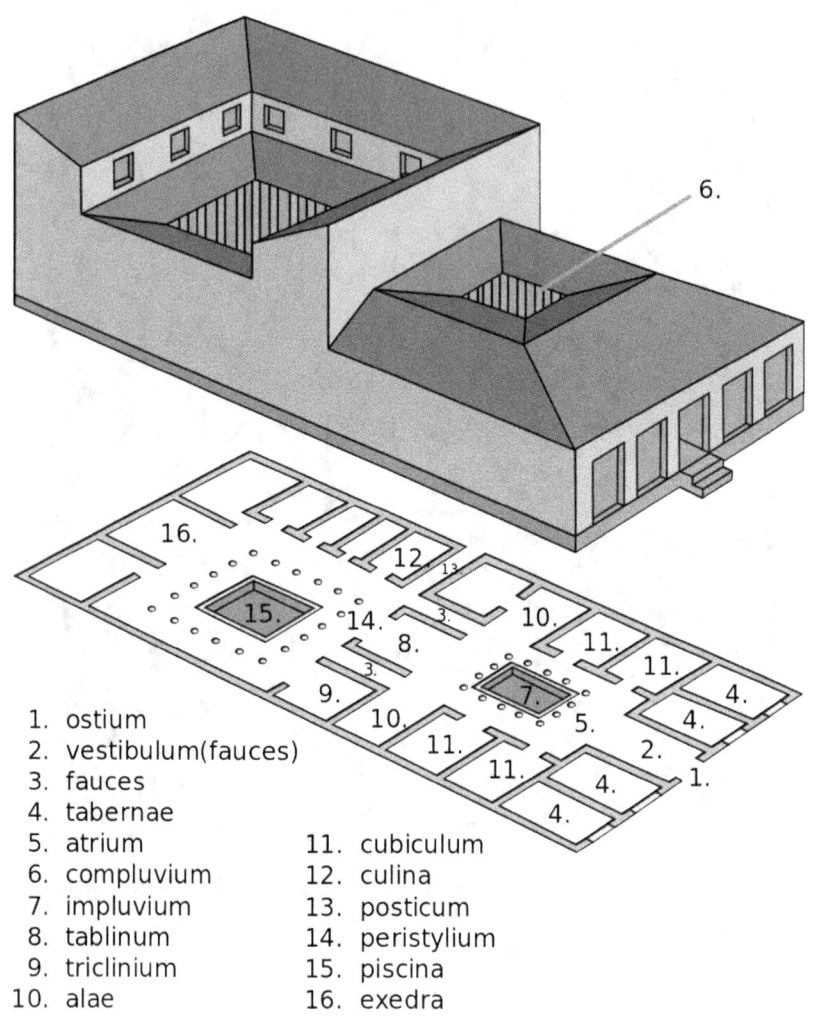

1. ostium
2. vestibulum(fauces)
3. fauces
4. tabernae
5. atrium
6. compluvium
7. impluvium
8. tablinum
9. triclinium
10. alae
11. cubiculum
12. culina
13. posticum
14. peristylium
15. piscina
16. exedra

A schematic of a *domus*.⁸⁷

Weddings, Family Customs, and Tradition

Most marriages in ancient Rome did not start with a romantic relationship. Instead, they were arranged between two families. Parents with a son who had just stepped into his early twenties would seek a woman of their choice, although she would normally be a teenager. Once they found the perfect match, the couple had to meet a few requirements set by the law before proceeding with the wedding ceremony.

In the early years of the Roman Republic, it was strictly prohibited for freed slaves to tie the knot with any Roman citizens, but the first Roman emperor, Augustus, lifted the restriction. One of his reforms, *Lex Julia*, allowed freed slaves to marry anyone except senators. Citizens were also forbidden from marrying their close relatives, prostitutes, and actors (these two professions belonged to the lowest class). As long as these rules were met, a couple would be granted permission called *conubium*, which allowed them to continue with the wedding.

Wedding ceremonies could take place anytime throughout the year, but most Romans chose to get married in June in conjunction with Juno, the goddess of marriage (June is named after her). When the day of the wedding ceremony finally came, the groom would lead a procession to the bride's family house, which was followed by an exchange of gifts and the bride's dowry. The bride and groom signed a written document containing each other's agreement and then sealed it with a kiss. The joyous ceremony would continue with a generous feast and another procession of the newlyweds to their new home.

The process of divorce was rather simple in comparison. A couple who no longer saw eye to eye only had to declare their divorce, although some sources suggest they had to do so in the company of seven witnesses. Once divorced, the dowry had to be returned to the ex-wife so that she could begin a new life or remarry. Children were put under the custody of their father.

Ancient Rome was undoubtedly a man's world; men were on top of every matter across the empire, whether it came to politics or family matters. In a Roman household, the husband or the family's leader was referred to as the *paterfamilias*, meaning "father of the family." To put it in simple words, *paterfamilias* held absolute power in their household and could decide on a matter without question. A father could disown his child no matter the reason. Cold-hearted ones would kill their children if they did not sit right with them, while those who were not so brutal would sell their offspring as slaves. This not only applied to grown children but also newborns. Once a wife gave birth, the midwife would place the newborn on the ground. The father would approach and pick the newborn up if he wanted to accept the baby, while unwanted babies would remain on the floor.

The family's property and wealth were also owned and managed by the *paterfamilias*. They even provided a special allowance called a *peculium* to their sons. It was normal for the Romans to treat their sons differently than their daughters, as sons were considered valuable to the family line; they were expected to carry their family name should their father pass. Those families who did not have a son usually resorted to adoption.

Roman Fashion

Speaking of ancient Roman fashion, many might have imagined the Romans wearing off-white togas and a pair of sandals. However, to the surprise of many, the Romans did not always dress in the iconic toga pictured in many modern movies and TV shows. In fact, a toga was formal attire usually worn to distinguish high social statuses. There was more than one type of toga worn by the rich. *Toga virilis*, an all-white toga, was donned by wealthy young men who had just reached adulthood, while candidates for office typically wore the chalk-white *toga candida*. The *toga praetexta*, which was decorated with a purple stripe, was only allowed for senators and high priests. The rarest of all was the solid purple and golden embroidered *toga picta*, which were strictly reserved for emperors.

As for women, their formal attire was called the stola. The long, sleeveless garment could only be worn by married women. Since a stola was rather simple, women often elevated their looks with elaborate hairstyles and jewelry. Unmarried women wore only a simple tunic—similar to what lower-class men and children would have worn.

Indoors, the Romans often wore sandals—the very ones often depicted in films and paintings. However, whenever they were outdoors or on a long journey, they changed into a pair of boots typically made out of leather. These boots were available to all social classes, though the rich often opted for a more complex design. Soldiers owned a pair of more durable boots known as *caligae*.

What Did the Romans Eat?

At daybreak, it was normal for the Romans to start their day with *ientaculum* or a simple breakfast. Since it was the first meal of the day, a piece of bread from the bakery would suffice, which, most of the time, would be enjoyed with slices of cheese and watered-down wine. Those who could not afford bread would eat staple porridge made from boiled spelt, wheat, or millet. A few aromatic spices and vegetables were added to the porridge to enhance the flavor, and there was usually some fruit on the side.

At high noon, the Romans would rest and sit for a quick lunch called *prandium*, which consisted of salted bread, cheese, fruit, and possibly fish, meat, or eggs. While all Roman citizens ate chicken eggs, large goose eggs were considered luxurious and more often consumed by the rich. Dinner was the main meal of the day. Lower-class citizens typically ate dinner after sunset in taverns, inns, or market stalls. Aristocrats might eat their supper while reclining on intricate couches in a luxurious dining room.

Those of the upper class started their dinner with a *gustatio* or appetizer, indulging themselves with seafood and eggs. Moving on to the main course, they would often get served with heavier options—meats and vegetables for the commoners and more exotic items, such as sea urchins, raw oysters, boars, and sometimes even flamingos and peacocks, for the wealthy. Garum, a type of fish sauce, was commonly used in dishes to elevate the taste. When in season, apples were a favorite dessert. Grapes, dates, pomegranates, and figs paired with honey, cream, or cheese were common desserts.

What Did the Romans Do for Leisure?

The Romans were lovers of entertainment. The Forum, the center of Rome where citizens conducted their business, was often busy at the crack of dawn, but it would be quiet in the evening and sometimes right after lunch. Markets began to close their doors, the elites would disperse from their important meetings, and the farmers would put down their hoes and sickles to get ready for some entertainment. Some would spend the evening watching plays and musicals. Those who preferred a more relaxing activity would travel to the public baths. They enjoyed hot baths, socializing, swimming, reading, and exercising at the gymnasium.

A depiction of a chariot race held in the Circus Maximus. [88]

The most popular types of entertainment in imperial Rome were none other than chariot races and gladiatorial fights, both of which were some of the most violent sports to ever exist in history. Chariot races were held in the Circus Maximus, the largest Roman stadium or hippodrome nestled in between the two hills of Rome. This extreme sport, which could trace its roots back to the early foundation of Rome in the 8th century BCE, was believed to be intertwined with the ancient Roman religion. Because of that, the event always began with a sacred procession of the chariot drivers, who were accompanied by a big group of dancers, musicians, and several statues of Roman gods through the streets of Rome.

The race would take place on the two-thousand-foot-long sand track. The chariot racers would burst through the gates at the starting line once a white handkerchief was dropped on the ground by the game's sponsor. These daring drivers would then steer their chariots to maximum speed—some reached at least forty miles per hour—before testing their skills at the turns. Chariot crashes and injuries were a common sight, which explains why there were always attendants near the tracks ready to rush in and clear the way before another lap took place. After a total of seven laps, the chariot racer who finished first would be celebrated with the sounds of trumpets before being led to the judges' box, where they would be given their victory wreath and prize money.

Gladiatorial fights were held in the famous Colosseum. The bloody fights were held around eight to twelve times per year. They were normally sponsored by the ruling emperor to not only provide entertainment to his subjects but also avoid revolts. Other than weapon combat and wild animal fights, there were reenactments of naval battles, though this particular event was extremely rare.

During a gladiatorial fight, the entire stadium would be filled with loud chants from the fifty thousand spectators. The gladiators, most of whom were either prisoners of war, criminals condemned to death, or slaves, would enter the arena bearing weapons they had mastered—the *gladius* and mace were among the most used weapons. They would then fight, swinging and thrusting their blades into one another while the crowds cheered.

A scene depicting a gladiatorial game. [89]

Although death and bloodbaths were fairly common in a gladiatorial game, losing a fight did not always mean certain death. Their fates also depended on the sponsors of the games, as they were the ones who set the rules. If the sponsors were not planning to watch a fight to the death, the winning gladiator could accept their opponents' surrender. The spectators could also influence the winning gladiator's decision on whether to spare or kill their losing opponent.

While the gladiatorial games were considered one of Rome's main entertainment forms, their prominence began to deteriorate as the empire began to embrace Christianity. In 325 CE, the emperor Constantine banned the games due to humanitarian reasons; the fights were seen as the opposite of civil and domestic peace.

Chapter 12 – Religion and Education

Rome was one of the most powerful empires in the Western world. However, the empire was not the Western world's earliest civilization. In fact, Rome only sprang to life in the 8th century BCE, millennia after the birth of Greece. However, the Italian Peninsula was known to have been in contact with Greece for a very long time, which led to the assimilation of Greek culture and religion. Like the Greeks, the Romans were a polytheistic civilization, which meant they worshiped multiple gods at once.

Since they were influenced by the Greeks, the Roman pantheon mostly corresponded with the Greek Olympians. Three of Rome's most important gods were Jupiter, Juno, and Minerva, who were respectively referred to as Zeus, Hera, and Athena in the Greek pantheon. Other important deities of the ancient Roman religion included Neptune, Venus, and Mars, who corresponded to Poseidon, Aphrodite, and Ares in Greek mythology. The ancient Romans also believed these gods played a role in the founding of their city.

Mars, the god of war, was believed to have born two sons with a woman named Rhea Silvia—there are some sources that claim Hercules bore these children instead of Mars. But since Rhea Silvia had sworn a vow of celibacy, her pregnancy meant certain death. At that time, it was common for those who had broken their vows to be buried alive. However, Amulius, the king of a pre-Roman city called Alba Longa, chose to spare Rhea Silvia to avoid the wrath of Mars. Instead, the king sent her to prison while he condemned her two infant children to death by one of three methods: live burial, exposure to the elements, or death by drowning in the Tiber River. The king did not want to stain his hands, so he directed his servant to carry out the murder.

The shepherd bringing Romulus and Remus home to his wife.⁹⁰

Looking at the infants, whose names were Romulus and Remus, the servant couldn't help but feel pity. He decided to place them inside a basket and allowed them to float down the River Tiber. Under the care of the river god Tiberinus, the two infants survived and were found by a she-wolf who suckled them. Later on, both Romulus and Remus were discovered and adopted by a shepherd and his wife. They grew up to become shepherds, but the two got in trouble, which led to Remus being captured and presented before King Amulius himself. With haste,

Romulus went to save his brother, killing the king in the process. They were then offered the throne by the citizens; however, the brothers insisted on starting their own city.

So, they set out on a journey to find the best location for their new city. Romulus suggested building the foundation on Palatine Hill, while Remus chose Aventine Hill. This disagreement turned into a quarrel, which led to Romulus building trenches and walls surrounding Palatine Hill. To mock his brother, Remus made fun of the walls and attempted to jump over them. Most stories say that Romulus then killed his brother, which some believed to be a sign from the gods that they favored Romulus's location.

Mourning the death of his brother, Romulus buried him with full respect. On the same day of the funeral, which was, according to tradition, April 21st, 753 BCE, Romulus founded Rome, a city named after himself. As the first king of Rome, Romulus ruled the city until his death. Due to his accomplishments, Romulus was believed to have become a god—a practice that was normalized by emperors due to their claim of being descended from the gods themselves. Later on, under the Roman imperial cult, the Senate would cast votes on whether or not their deceased emperor would rise to a state of divinity.

As Rome grew into a bigger city, expanding its power over different kingdoms and eventually becoming a huge empire, the Roman religion saw an explosion of various festivities and celebrations. Sometime in mid-December, the Romans gathered around to celebrate Saturnalia, a celebration in honor of Saturn, the Roman god of agriculture. During this time of the year, all businesses, schools, and even the court of law would close their doors to prepare for a grand celebration. Out of all the religious celebrations in Rome, Saturnalia was considered the most exciting and lively. Catullus, the Roman poet, described it as the best of times. Even the Roman author Pliny had to lock himself inside a soundproof room to work due to the joyous noise of the people celebrating.

The Romans celebrating Saturnalia.[91]

Houses in Rome would be decorated with wreaths and much greenery. The week was filled with nothing but feasts, gambling, singing, and music. A gift exchange was a common practice, with taper candles called *cerei* being the most popular gift. When the Temple of Saturn was built in the 4th century CE, another ritual was brought to life, as young pigs were sacrificed in front of the public.

Another major festival was called Cerealia. It was celebrated in honor of the grain goddess Ceres, who was especially honored by the commoners. Held around mid- to late April—possibly from the 12th to the 18th—the week-long Cerealia festival was celebrated in hopes that the goddess would bestow good harvests.

The common activities that took place during Cerealia were circus games called Ludi Ceriales, which were normally held in the Circus Maximus. According to the records made by Ovid, the famous Roman poet, during the games, women could be seen dressed in all white, running around the arena while holding lit torches. This was done to symbolize an event in Roman mythology where Ceres searched for her daughter, Proserpina, who had been taken to the underworld by Pluto. The celebration also included horse races and theatrical performances.

Other religious festivities celebrated by the Romans included Liberalia in March to commemorate Liber, the god of wine, freedom, and fertility, and Lupercalia. The latter was celebrated every February 15th, and in contrast to the lively Saturnalia, this festival was rather bloody and violent, as it aimed to ward off evil spirits and avoid infertility. Its ritual included a sacrifice of male goats and a dog, with Roman priests smearing the sacrificed animals' blood on their faces. However, after Christianity became the official religion of the Roman Empire, these ancient celebrations began to disappear, although some fused with the new religion.

The Harsh Beginning of Christianity and How the Religion Prevailed

Rome witnessed the emergence of many religions and cults and tolerated some of their beliefs and practices, but not everyone enjoyed the same treatment. Certain religions and cults were banned or even persecuted if the Romans found them unnatural or unfit. For instance, the Celtic Druids who practiced the sacrifice of humans were wiped out by the Roman military. The Romans were also against Judaism, probably due to Rome's prolonged conflict and conquest of Judea. Tiberius was said to have forbidden the religion, and Emperor Claudius even went to the extent of banishing the Jews from the Eternal City.

Another religion the Romans were strictly against was none other than Christianity. The reasons behind this vary, but the most plausible one was due to the Christians' belief in a single god. Ancient Rome had been worshiping multiple gods ever since the earliest days of its existence. It is safe to say that Roman paganism focused more on the present; there were no exact details about the afterlife and salvation. That being said, the Romans believed the main reason to worship the gods was to gain their blessings and avoid their wrath. Refusing to do so would only result in a terrible sickness or perhaps famine or a plague. If the gods were properly worshiped and honored, the Romans would be showered with wealth, health, and military success.

The Christians believed in only their god, which led the Romans to conclude that this was a way of stating that their gods were false. Christians also refused to offer sacrifices to either the Roman gods or the emperors, a decision that was seen as disloyal to the empire. The Romans feared that the Christians' refusal to participate in any sort of pagan practice would only anger their gods, thus inviting great chaos and trouble. Every time the empire was overwhelmed with a certain crisis, even as small as a raging mob in the city, the Romans tended to point their fingers at the Christians. The persecution of Christians gradually became the norm, especially in Rome.

The greatest and most infamous persecution to ever take place within the Roman Empire was done by Emperor Nero. The emperor was already unpopular among some, if not all, of his subjects. So, when a sudden fire broke out that engulfed almost two-thirds of the Eternal City, the emperor was left with no choice but to look for a scapegoat in order to shift the citizens' anger and blame. The easiest targets were the Christians, who had already been demonized by many. Nero put the blame for the fire on the Christians, which resulted in a mass execution. Emperor Decius also mercilessly persecuted many Christians in 250 CE when he discovered their refusal to make a sacrifice to the Roman gods in front of officials.

When Constantine took the mantle, Christians began to see the light at the end of the tunnel. Although the persecution of Christians had ended before Constantine's reign, they were still living in fear. That was until Constantine claimed to have seen a miraculous vision of the Christian cross in his dream the night before the Battle of the Milvian Bridge in the 4th century CE. Since he emerged victorious, Constantine called himself a devout Christian, although sources suggest that he was baptized only on his deathbed. Nevertheless, Constantine was named the first Roman emperor to accept the religion with open arms.

The baptism of Constantine: [92]

The emperor went on to fund and commission the construction of churches in his new capital, Constantinople. Although paganism was still practiced by some of the Romans, coexisting with Christianity and other religions, Christians could now leave the safety of their houses and participate in Roman civic life. Through the Edict of Milan, Christianity was granted legal status for the first time in history. However, after Constantine's death, Christianity's fate was yet again hung in the balance, as some reigning emperors were still skeptical of the religion. But by this period of time, the religion was growing in popularity. Finally, under the rule of Theodosius I, Christianity was made the Roman Empire's official religion, while the old pagan religion was suppressed.

Education in Imperial Rome

Education was very important in ancient Rome. However, not everyone in the empire had the luxury of being taught at school. Although the poor and commoners received some basic education, formal education, which was mostly based on the Greek system, was typically reserved for children born to wealthy families.

Girls, on the other hand, were restricted from receiving advanced education. They were only taught how to write and read, and these lessons could only be taught at their home. Some would be taught by their own mothers, while those in the higher social classes were put under the care of hired instructors. From the Romans' point of view, girls were expected to focus more on achieving their ultimate goal in life: marriage and having children. So, a Roman girl's childhood would often be filled with lessons on how to be a good wife and mother.

However, on the bright side, girls could avoid obtaining injuries caused by teachers. Education in ancient Rome was said to have been based on fear—there was even an old Roman saying that those who were never flogged were not trained. Staying true to these sayings, instructors or teachers would often beat their students with a cane or a leather whip should they make even the tiniest mistake in class. In some cases, those who made too many mistakes in a short amount of time would be held still by two slaves while their teacher beat them multiple times with a leather whip.

There were different stages of education in imperial Rome. The first one was rather informal, as it focused more on moral education, which the children received from their parents. At this stage, children would be taught various skills needed to live a life in the city, from agriculture to military skills to civil responsibilities. They were also educated about Roman tradition and ways to respect it. Basic reading, writing, and arithmetic were normally taught by the *paterfamilias* or the male leader of the family.

While the rich continued their education with private tutors, middle-class boys were sent to *ludus litterarius*, a primary school taught by a teacher referred to as a *litterator*. Back then, there was no exact location for a primary school, as it could change from one place to another. Some studied in gymnasiums or private residences, while there were others who studied in the streets. At this stage, students would mostly focus on improving their reading, writing, and mathematics. Literature was the most common teaching material, with works from Homer and Hesiod being used. Since parchment and papyrus were rather expensive at that time, students were only allowed to write on a wax tablet. Once they showed great improvement in their writing, their instructors would provide them with papyrus to write on.

At the age of nine, the rich would go on to learn more important skills from a *grammaticus*, who would sharpen his students' speaking skills. Those who had not yet mastered Greek would take this opportunity to hone their skills in the language since elite Romans were expected to be bilingual. Most of the time, these students would spend their day listening to their *grammaticus's* lectures, or *narratio*, and practicing expressive reading of poetry.

Elite students who had proved themselves through the years would be given a chance to further their studies as an orator. This level of education was crucial for those who aspired to be lawyers and politicians. Possibly originating from Greece, this level of education was not strictly taught by a teacher; instead, it was mostly done through careful observations of their elders and mentors. At this point, orators mainly focused on learning the art of public speaking while still receiving new knowledge in geography, literature, music, philosophy, mythology, and geometry—some of which were absolutely important in order to get a chance to run for office one day.

Conclusion

The Roman Empire launched numerous campaigns and introduced various laws to its many provinces. But in the end, the once-flourishing empire crumbled when Rome was taken away from its people—an event that definitely shook the world back then. The fortified walls of Rome were finally penetrated by the headstrong barbarians. Under a new ruler, the empire was split into a series of feudal kingdoms with their own code of laws, customs, and traditions. But despite the fall of Rome, the empire still managed to leave its mark and influence. In fact, certain aspects of Roman life survived and were practiced in some of these new kingdoms.

The Eastern half of the Roman Empire survived and maintained its presence in the world for about a thousand more years after its Western counterpart's defeat. With Constantinople now acting as the "New Rome," the Romans resumed their lives. Although they considered themselves part of the Roman Empire still, most scholars refer to the Eastern Roman Empire as the Byzantine Empire.

Although the mighty Roman Empire is a thing of the past, its influence can still be felt today. It had a tremendous impact on architecture, technology, law, arts, literature, and even religion. Especially in Western cultures, one could find an array of traces left by the Romans. For instance, many Roman structures survived, and some of their construction techniques were borrowed and are still used in the modern world. The Arc de Triomphe du Carrousel in Paris is often associated with Roman architecture; its design bears a striking resemblance to the Arch of Septimius Severus in Rome.

William Shakespeare has forever been immortalized as the greatest English writer of all time, thanks to Ovid and a few other poets born during the golden period of Roman literature. The Romans' mother tongue Latin was used as the basis for the English language. Certain months in the calendar that we've come to know today owe their name to the Romans; January, March, May, and June were all named after the ancient Roman gods, while July and August were named in honor of Julius Caesar and Augustus.

The Roman concepts of laws and justice systems were widely used as a rough outline for modern-day legal systems, especially in Europe and the United States. The Roman Empire also played a key role in spreading Christianity. Although the monotheistic religion was initially rejected by the Romans, when it was finally made the official religion, its influence began to impact almost every aspect of the Romans' lives. Christmas, the most popular holiday celebrated by Christians today, traces its origins back to the Roman Empire. Some of the festivity's traditions, including gift exchanges, feasting, singing, and lighting candles, are still widely practiced today; however, they were borrowed from Saturnalia, an ancient Roman winter celebration.

With all of the triumphs and achievements obtained by the once-booming empire, it is not a surprise that the world can still feel its presence today. The Roman Empire might have faced its end over a thousand years ago, but many agree that the Romans undoubtedly helped us lay the foundations for almost every aspect of the modern world. It might be hard for us to imagine the similarities that we bear with the Romans since their lives constantly revolved around bloody wars and conquests, but it is also impossible to deny that Rome is ingrained in our lives. Despite the many violent episodes that took place throughout the years of the Roman Empire, its legacy will continue to live on and set examples for future generations to come.

Part 3: The Byzantine Empire

An Enthralling Overview of the Byzantium

Introduction

The ultimate dissolution of the Roman Empire in 476 CE was a major event that shaped the future development of rudimentary European states. These events, occurring more than 1,500 years ago, established the fundamentals of modern-day Europe. Prior to the fall of Rome, the heritage, tradition, and power of ancient Rome moved eastward to the city of Byzantium or Constantinople, the capital of a new empire that is today known as the Byzantine Empire.

While the West was rediscovering the inventions and culture that lay in the remnants of Rome, the Byzantine Empire continued the Roman tradition. The Byzantine Empire inherited the political structure, military organization, and intellectual tradition of the old Roman Empire and started building upon these rich foundations.

The most important innovation brought on by the Byzantine Empire was, of course, the acceptance of Christianity. Constantine the Great, with his Edict of Milan, facilitated the development of a religion that took the world by storm with incredibly far-reaching consequences. It is impossible to overestimate the importance of this event. Christianity became the foundation of not only the Byzantine Empire but also of all European medieval states. It brought a major route of intellectual development in the period known, somewhat unjustified, as the "Dark Ages." The truth is that Christianity brought at least some sense of structure and hierarchy, especially in western Europe, which had been ravaged by wars and incessant barbarian invasions. It also represented a major pillar for the development of the Byzantine Empire. In turn, the Byzantine Empire allowed for the development of Christianity, with a series of councils aimed at codifying Christianity into a well-defined religious movement that could be further propagated across Europe and the world.

The Byzantine Empire managed to spread its influence across the Balkans into Russia. Serbia, Bulgaria, Romania, Montenegro, North Macedonia, Bosnia and Herzegovina (to a certain extent), Armenia, Georgia, and, last but not least, Turkey. These nations all bear marks of the Byzantine Empire, whether in terms of Orthodox Christianity, scripture, or culture. Modern-day Greece is equally proud of its ancient origins as it is proud of the days of the Byzantine Empire.

So, let's delve into the history of the Byzantine Empire, where we will discover numerous illustrious emperors, less illustrious court intrigues, and its final and inevitable decline.

Section One:
The Early Years
(330–565 CE)

Chapter 1: From Rome to Constantinople

Prelude to Byzantium

The sheer extent of the Roman Empire in the late 3rd and early 4th centuries CE made effective governing of Roman lands no small feat. We must not forget that in those days, information moved at a slower pace, as did people and goods. Moreover, the Roman government was heavily centralized, which is a challenge for today's modern governments, let alone an ancient empire where it took weeks to go from one corner of the empire to the other. Even though "all roads lead to Rome," and in spite of Rome's success in Latinizing the lands it conquered, the Roman Empire was fairly diverse, with many different languages, cultures, religions, and histories.

Thus, it is not hard to understand why Emperor Diocletian, who reigned between 284 and 305 CE, decided to divide the empire. First, he divided it into two parts, himself being the head of the Eastern Empire and his chief officer, Maximian, being the head of the Western Empire. Not only that, but Diocletian (who was always the real emperor, it has to be said) formed what is now called the Tetrarchy, "the rule of the four," in 293 by appointing junior officers as co-rulers, Galerius to himself and Constantius to Maximian.

Many emperors had co-rulers. Between 161 and 169 CE, Marcus Aurelius ruled jointly with Lucius Verus as co-emperors—the first formal diarchy in Roman imperial history. In 166, Marcus appointed his son Commodus as Caesar (junior emperor), marking him as his heir.[i] Septimius Severus ruled alongside his sons, Caracalla and Geta, between 209 and 211. In a lot of cases, co-rulers, *Caesars* or *Augusti*, were mostly ceremonial, formal titles. Diocletian's Tetrarchy was more pragmatic and real. All four rulers had significant responsibilities and powers.

It seems that the most pressing demand to create the Tetrarchy was war. The Roman emperor at the time was very much the chief military commander. As war was raging in multiple corners of the empire, the most logical thing seemed to be to add more emperors who would direct the military efforts in his part of the empire. Namely, the Roman Empire faced the prospect of an "anti-emperor" elected in Britain, as well as Persian advances in the east.

It has to be stated that the Roman Empire in the late 3rd and early 4th centuries CE still had a very vivid memory of half a century of tumult, later called the Crisis of the Third Century (lasting from 235 to 284). As the Severus dynasty was sinking into its inevitable demise, the empire was plunging into anarchy. There was a long line of bad emperors, starting with the relatively stable Septimius Severus, who was followed by his unfortunate older son Geta, who was murdered by his brother Caracalla, a capricious emperor known for his ruthlessness and coarseness. Caracalla, in turn, was murdered by Macrinus, the head of his guard, who was himself murdered by the supporters of Elagabalus. His reign is remembered for unprecedented debauchery. The Roman Empire finally entered a period of serious decline during the reign of Severus Alexander in 235, a weak emperor who did not manage to gain obedience and respect from the military.

As can be seen, even the decades leading up to the Crisis of the Third Century were marked by instability, but the crisis itself plunged the Roman Empire into near collapse. Between 235 and 284 CE, the empire fractured into three rival entities: the Gallic Empire in the west, the central Roman Empire, and the Palmyrene Empire in the east. Over the course of this fifty-year span, approximately twenty-three emperors ruled in rapid succession, many of whom met violent ends.

Emperor Aurelian (r. 270-275) succeeded in reuniting the empire by

---

[i] Waldron, Byron Lloyd. *Diocletian, Hereditary Succession and the Tetrarchic Dynasty*. PhD diss., 2018.

defeating both the Gallic and Palmyrene breakaway states. However, despite his achievements, he was assassinated in 275 by members of his own entourage. After another decade of turmoil and six more emperors, Diocletian rose to power in 284. His ascension marked the beginning of comprehensive reforms aimed at ending the chaos and restoring stability to the Roman world.

The solution, as we have already emphasized, was obvious. The Roman Empire had to be formally divided. Besides fighting the uprising in Britain and the Persian threat, the emperors also had to deal with constant barbarian invasions in central Europe, as well as significant threats in Spain and North Africa.

Formalizing the Tetrarchy might have also been a way to ensure a smooth succession, a problem that was at the very heart of the Crisis of the Third Century.[i]

One of the tetrarchs was Constantius, surnamed Chlorus ("The White"). An able general and an experienced soldier, a necessary prerequisite for a good emperor, Constantius rose through the ranks and was declared co-ruler to Maximian around 293. A person of "great mildness, self-possession, and philosophic virtue, just, and a Neo-Platonist of the best type, a monotheist and philanthropist," Constantius was a man of great ability and power.[ii]

It is possible that he bequeathed at least some sort of enlightened spirituality to his son, Constantine. Interestingly, the times of Diocletian and his co-rulers were the last periods of Christian persecution before Constantine the Great finally granted religious freedom to Christians in 313.[iii] Although we don't really know that much about the religion of Constantine's father, we do know that Sol Invictus (Apollo) might have been Constantius's patron deity.

Diocletian established a sort of heavenly patronage system. Jupiter was the protector of Diocletian himself. Hercules was Maximian's patron, quite likely owing to the latter's physical prowess. Interestingly, a medallion that honored Constantius and his conquests in Britain bore the inscription REDDITOR LUCIS AETERNAE ("restorer of eternal

---

[i] Ibid.
[ii] Richardson EC, Schaff P, Wace H. The life of Constantine. A Select Library of the Nicene and Post-Nicene Fathers of the Christian Church, ser. 1890;2:481-540.
[iii] Smith MD. The religion of Constantius I. Greek, Roman, and Byzantine Studies. 1997 Jun 6;38(2):187-208.

light"), which was possibly a direct reference to Apollo, the deity of light. Truth be told, the parallels between the deities and tetrarchs are not clear, and scholars sometimes find variations in the deity patronage system.

Constantius, the father of Constantine the Great.[98]

There are some indications that Constantius wasn't that diligent about Diocletian's persecution of Christians. In 303, Diocletian issued an edict that ordered the closing of the churches, the forced worship of pagan gods, and the destruction of the holy Christian scriptures.[i] All Christian believers, followers, and priests were subjected to persecution. Even before this, Christian priests were ordered to make sacrifices for pagan gods, but now the whole Christian community was supposed to do it. The persecution, however, was somewhat random. In some parts of the empire, it was quite rough, but in regions governed by Maximian and Constantius Chlorus, Christians enjoyed relative peace. The two co-rulers

---

[i] Carlan, C.U. "Life and Death in the Ancient World: The Tetrarchy and the Last Persecution of Christians (303-311)."

made some symbolic gestures in favor of the edict.

It's likely that Constantius remained steeped in the pre-Christian religious landscape of the Roman Empire. An early chronicler recalls the speech of an orator at Constantius's funeral: "The temples of the gods were opened for him, and he was received by the divine conclave, and Jupiter himself extended his right hand to him."[i]

When Constantius died in 306, his son Constantine came to the forefront, the man who would revolutionize the Roman Empire and start a new empire that would last for over one thousand years. It bore the same name, but this time in Greek (Βασιλεία Ῥωμαίων), and it was, in a lot of respects, radically different than the old Roman Empire.

However, before we delve deeper into the social, economic, and political aspects of the Byzantine Empire, we will first focus on the man who made it happen: Constantine the Great.

Constantine the Great

Born in the town of Naissus (modern-day Niš in southern Serbia), in a province where his father likely grew up, Constantine was pretty far away from the illustrious Rome. However, long gone were the days in which Roman emperors were chosen from the crème de la crème of Roman society. With the Crisis of the Third Century, it became obvious that the crown was up for grabs and that quite literally anyone could get it, provided he had enough power and ambition. Over the years, it had become a more common phenomenon for legions stationed in important provinces to declare their military leaders as emperors. This contributed to the instability of Rome; there were many provinces, many legions, and many powerful military leaders.

In the times of Diocletian, it was very much the same. Powerful legions, which drew its military strength from the local people, were stationed in the Balkan region. Diocletian was from roughly the same region as Constantine and his father (Diocletian was born in Dalmatia, modern-day Croatia). Maximian was from Sirmium (modern-day Sremska Mitrovica in Serbia), and Galerius was from Serdica (modern-day Sofia, capital of Bulgaria). These individuals came from provinces at the borders of the empire and had much humbler backgrounds in comparison to the typical emperors of the 1st and 2nd centuries CE.

---

[i] Ibid. 194

Constantinus Chlorus was hailed by both the armies he led and the people in the western region of the empire. Consistent with the Roman tradition fostered in the preceding tumultuous decades, the armies greatly favored their generals and would often willingly act in the interest of their generals and against the interest of the state. In York, where Constantinus had died, Constantine was proclaimed Augustus by the armies that had been under the command of his father.

Early Reign

Constantine first assumed control of his father's vast territories, which included Gaul and Britain (the modern-day United Kingdom, France, and western parts of Germany). By this time, the Tetrarchy had started to devolve into the sort of chaos so characteristic of the Roman Empire. Without going into too much detail about every person involved in the civil wars of Constantine's early reign, we're going to paint the basic backdrop of the landscape of the early 4th-century city of Rome.

Although Diocletian's Tetrarchy aimed to divide imperial power and provide solid checks on the power of each emperor, internal strife was inevitable. In theory, Diocletian and Maximian held the senior imperial title of Augustus, each overseeing half of the empire. Under them were their junior colleagues, Galerius and Constantius Chlorus, who held the subordinate title of Caesar. When the time came, Diocletian and Maximian would be replaced by the two Cesares, which would ensure a smooth and peaceful succession. Both Diocletian and Maximian, miraculously for Roman emperors, abdicated in 305. The Tetrarchy wouldn't last for much longer.

A few unfortunate events made a smooth succession much more complex. First of all, Galerius didn't really want to let Constantius and Maxentius (son of Maximian and contestant for the throne) dominate the Roman Empire after the two Augusti had abdicated. Shortly after the departure of Diocletian and Maximian, Galerius promoted two people of his own choosing to the rank of Ceasar: Severus II and Maximinus Daza. The matter was made even more confusing when Constantius died and left control of Rome's northeastern regions under his son's command. The armies under Constantine's command were too powerful and loyal for Galerius to immediately face Constantine.

Galerius's disregard for Maximian's son, Maxentius, cost him dearly. Maxentius launched an attack on Galerius in Italy in 307, defeating

Severus II, who had been sent by Galerius. He assumed control of Italy and North Africa and held his positions until 312.

Constantine the Great.[94]

Meanwhile, Constantine decided to lay low, avoid the conflict in Italy, and get things sorted out in his provinces. He was popular very early on due to the people's vivid and positive memories of his father. Constantine earned a reputation for his able leadership of his provinces, focusing on infrastructure (such as building roads), stability, and peace.

The event that laid the foundation for the next millennia of the emerging Byzantine Empire came in 312. Constantine decided to conquer Rome to reunify the Roman Empire under his authority. To this end, he formed an alliance with Licinius, a former friend of Galerius, who was in Gaul at the time. Thanks to this alliance, Licinius would become Augustus and ruler of the East.

Constantine's army of twenty-five thousand men crossed the Alps. Once they were in Italy, they took the city of Susa, defeated Maxentius's troops in Turin, and captured Milan in a series of blistering victories.

Maxentius was preparing for a final battle to preserve his reign in Rome and decided not to let Constantine lay siege to another city. Instead, he decided to face Constantine's army in an open battle, which would turn out to be a fatal error.

On October 28th, 312, a few kilometers north of Rome on the Milvian Bridge, the two armies clashed, reshaping the history of the Roman Empire.

According to Eusebius, Constantine said that about noon, when the day was already beginning to decline, he saw a cross of light in the heavens, above the sun, bearing the inscription IN HOC SIGNO VINCES ("conquer with this sign"). It was said he was struck with amazement and that his whole army also witnessed the miracle.

"He said, moreover, that he doubted within himself what the import of this apparition could be. And while he continued to ponder and reason on its meaning, night suddenly came on; then in his sleep the Christ of God appeared to him with the same sign which he had seen in the heavens, and commanded him to make a likeness of that sign which he had seen in the heavens, and to use it as a safeguard in all engagements with his enemies."[i]

Maxentius's army has been said to be so numerous that its formation was as deep as it was wide, counting as many as thirty thousand men. Yet, the risky tactic left Maxentius's army without room for maneuver or retreat and encouraged Constantine to attack. His veteran army managed to push the cavalry toward the Milvian Bridge, at which point Maxentius and his reserve infantry tried to run across the Tiber. Some of the fleeing infantry managed to get away, but most of Maxentius's men were cut down. Maxentius himself fell onto the wooden boat bridge built prior to the battle, which got destroyed, and he was swallowed by the Tiber, ending his life.

---

[i] Hunt, E.D. *Eusebius of Caesarea, Life of Constantine.* Translated by Averil Cameron and Stuart G. Hall. *The Journal of Ecclesiastical History* 52, no. 2 (2001): 338-396.

Meanwhile, to the north, the Praetorian forces surrounded by Constantine's army made their final stand. Amazed by their courage, newly Christian-converted Constantine decided to spare their lives.

Amassing Power

Following this victory, Constantine claimed the entire Western Roman Empire for himself, while his ally, Licinius, claimed the Eastern Roman Empire. Constantine became the first Christian emperor of Rome.

Constantine sought to elevate his brother-in-law, Bassianus, possibly to the rank of Caesar, and entrusted him with authority in Italy. However, before the appointment could be finalized, Bassianus was implicated in a conspiracy against Constantine, allegedly at the instigation of his brother Senecio, a close ally of Licinius. When Constantine demanded that Licinius hand over Senecio for punishment, Licinius refused. This breakdown in diplomacy contributed directly to the renewal of civil war between the two emperors.

In 316, Constantine won the Battle of Cibalae despite being outnumbered. He conquered the entire Balkan Peninsula, apart from Thrace and Lower Moesia, and made Licinius agree to a peace deal. Nevertheless, in 324, the conflict resumed when Constantine's army went into Licinius's territory in pursuit of a raiding force of Visigoths, which Licinius interpreted as a direct attack on his own forces. Licinius placed his army in a two-hundred-stadia-long defensive formation in the Battle of Adrianople, but Constantine used a clever trick.[i] He sneakily crossed the river to make the enemy withdraw. Once

Licinius.[95]

Licinius's army took a defensive position on a higher ground, an

---

[i] A stadion (plural stadia) was an ancient unit for measuring length. One stadion equaled about 150 meters. The unit got its name from ancient stadiums used to host games, such as the Olympics.

onslaught ensued, from which Constantine emerged as the victor.[i]

Following the defeat, Licinius retreated to Byzantium, which Constantine besieged. Constantine's son Crispus commanded the fleet in the Battle of the Hellespont, where he inflicted another defeat on Licinius's forces. Following this naval victory, Constantine the Great faced Licinius's army in the final battle of the war, Chrysopolis. After the ultimate defeat of Licinius, Constantine became the first man to rule the entirety of the Roman world since Maximian became Diocletian's co-emperor in 286.[ii]

From Byzantium to Constantinople

The city of Constantinople was built on the foundations of a much older town, Byzantium. Byzantium was founded by the polis of Megara, a mid-sized city-state between Corinth and Athens, in 657 BCE. To this day, scholars don't know for sure why it was placed on the eastern side of the Bosphorus, given that the tides are more favorable on the western side. A common explanation is that unfavorable tides made it harder for enemies to approach by sea, and if Byzantium was attacked by land, the enemy army would be forced into a narrow strip, giving Byzantium a unique military advantage.

The city saw a period of expansion during the reign of Emperor Septimius Severus, who ruled between 193 and 211. New sets of defensive walls were built, as well as other great structures, such as the Baths of Zeuxippus and the Hippodrome. These structures were Severus's most important and enduring legacy.

Following the victory over his rivals in 324, Constantine renamed Byzantium, firstly to New Rome and later to Constantinople, making it his new capital.

---

[i] Zosimus, Historia nova, English translation: R.T. Ridley, Zosimus: New History, Byzantina Australiensia 2, Canberra (1982).
[ii] Dunstan, W.E. (2010) Rome, Rowman & Littlefield Publishers, Lanham MD. ISBN 9780742568341

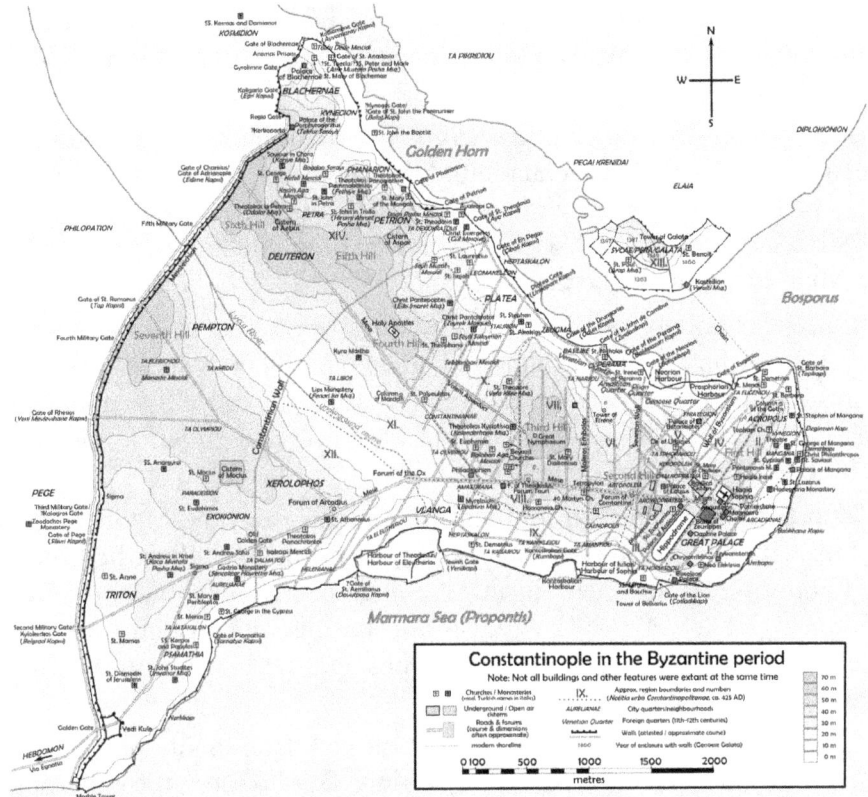

Map of Constantinople.[96]

By Constantine's time, the center of power had shifted to the east, where three-quarters of the Roman population and wealth were located, making relocation of the capital a politically viable move. A factor that also played a great role was that Constantine, even though he was the son of an emperor, did not come from an aristocratic Roman family. He was looked down upon by Roman aristocrats. By being the sole ruler in Byzantium, his own city, he would ensure the stability of power far away from the intrigues of Rome.

Constantine's first step in making Constantinople was the construction of the Walls of Constantinople, outgrowing the city's former boundary. Even though they were outdated by 420, and the city continued to add new fortifications, some parts of the Walls of Constantinople can still be seen in modern-day Istanbul.

Constantine also enhanced and decorated the Baths of Zeuxippus with around eighty statues of numerous historical figures, such as Homer and Demosthenes, along with various heroes and gods. The fact that pagan deities stood in the middle of the newly founded city of Constantinople debunks the myth that Constantine's intention was to create an entirely Christian city.

The Hippodrome, another construction rebuilt by Constantine, remained one of the key centers until the fall of the Byzantine Empire. It was a place where the emperor could observe the people and allow them to let off steam. It was also a place where great tumult and revolts, such as the Nika riots, would take place.

Once the Hippodrome was renovated, it was about 450 meters long and 130 meters wide, capable of holding 100,000 spectators. The Kathisma (the emperor's lodge) was accessible directly from the Great Palace of Constantinople through a passage only the emperor and other members of the imperial family could use.

Constantine relocated important monuments from the Mediterranean and placed them at the center of the Hippodrome, including the Obelisk of Thutmose III (erected during the Eighteenth Dynasty by Pharaoh Thutmose III (r. 1479-1425 BCE)) and the Serpent Column (made to celebrate Greece's victory over Mardonius and the Persians in the Battle of Plataea in 479 BCE).

Emperor Constantine the Great dedicated Constantinople on May 11th, 330, by performing a bloodless sacrifice. He honored the city's deity, Tyche, and some traditions suggest he named her Anthousa. However, he also placed the city under the protection of the Virgin Mary, marking its Christian foundation.

Constantine the Great built a statue of himself, holding the protector of the city, Anthousa (Tyche), in his right hand. Constantine ordered that on the day of the races held in honor of the city's founding, his statue should be brought into the Hippodrome accompanied by soldiers dressed in cloaks and campagi (ceremonial lace-up boots traditionally worn by emperors, consuls, and high-ranking officials) while carrying candles. The statue was placed on a cart and taken around the track in a ceremonial circuit before being brought to a stand opposite the imperial box. At this point, the reigning emperor would rise, face the statue of Constantine—alongside the city's divine protector—and bow in a gesture of reverence.[i]

---

[i] Jeffreys, Elizabeth. "The Beginning of Byzantine Chronography: John Malalas." In *Greek and Roman Historiography in Late Antiquity*. Brill, 2003. pp. 497-527.

By far the most important and most fascinating building in Constantinople was Hagia Sophia, the temple of the empire's new religion, Christianity. Initially, the city must have looked fairly similar to ancient Roman or Greek cities, with the Hippodrome dominating the landscape. However, Constantinople and numerous other cities in the Byzantine Empire would oversee the construction of an entirely new category of buildings: early Christian temples.

In the next chapter, we'll address the roots of Christianity and how it managed to take over the Byzantine Empire.

Chapter 2: The Empire of Christ

Early Christianity: Not the Christianity We Know Today

The Byzantine Empire's development was influenced by the organization of the Roman state, Greek culture, and the Christian faith. That merging happened as a consequence of the decentralization and decline of the Roman Empire due to the Crisis of the Third Century. As mentioned before, the Crisis of the Third Century left the empire in a state of chaos. But from this chaos emerged a sort of structure, a blend of Greco-Roman culture and Christianity, which provided fertile ground for the development of a new European powerhouse fueled by the growth of the Orthodox Church.

To truly understand the origins of Christianity, we must first briefly delve into some predecessor currents of religious thought.

Origins of Christianity

During the Bronze Age, in the regions of ancient Israel and Judah, the religion of the Israelites (Yahwism, as scholars today call it) arose.[i] It was initially polytheistic. Yahweh and his consort, Asherah, were seen as superior to the second-tier divinities, such as Baal, Shamash, Astarte, Yarikh, and Mot. All these gods and goddesses had their own priests,

---

[i] Miller, Patrick D. (2000). The Religion of Ancient Israel. Westminster John Knox Press. ISBN 978-0-664-22145-4.

prophets, and royalty among their devotees.[i] Priests of the time largely advocated for henotheism, calling for adherence to one particular god, Yahweh, while still recognizing other gods. The Temple in Jerusalem was the most significant place of worship to the Israelite king, who was seen as God's worldly governor.

The Kingdom of Israel fell to the Assyrians, and the nearby Kingdom of Judah and its capital, Jerusalem, managed to keep the Israelite religion alive, with the Temple of HaShem (meaning "the name," Yahweh) as its center. Once the Kingdom of Judah was conquered by the Babylonians, the Temple was destroyed, and Judah's elites were carried off to Babylon, an occurrence we now remember as the Babylonian Exile, which lasted from 586 to 516 BCE. From that point in time, the Israelites became known as Jews, named after the fallen kingdom.

The Persians who had conquered the Babylonians allowed the Jews to return to Jerusalem and rebuild the Temple, thus marking the era of the Second Temple, which lasted from 516 BCE to 70 CE. The importance of this cannot be understated, as the original Israelite religion became highly influenced by Persian philosophy. The religion of the Persian Empire at the time was Zoroastrianism, one of the oldest monotheistic religions, which largely influenced the belief systems of Judaism, Christianity, and Islam. It is most likely that the concept of Satan and the divine battle between good and evil, in which good will emerge victorious, came from this ancient Persian religion. Zoroastrianism is still practiced to this day, with about 120,000 followers worldwide.

Four sects of Judaism existed at the time, one of which became the foundation of Judaism as it exists today. The Sadducees were active in Judea during the Second Temple period up until its destruction in 70 CE. They were associated with the elites of Judean society, and their priests ran the Temple since they were the most open to Hellenistic influences.[ii]

The Pharisees, on the other hand, were associated with the common man. Its scholars studied Hebrew scriptures. They emerged around 150 BCE and resisted Hellenistic influence. While the Sadducees emphasized the importance of the Temple and its rituals, the Pharisees focused on Mosaic law and oral tradition. After the Romans destroyed the Second

---

[i] Handy, Lowell K. (1995). "The Appearance of Pantheon in Judah". In Edelman, Diana Vikander (ed.). The Triumph of Elohim: From Yahwism to Judaism. Peeters Publishers. ISBN 90-5356-503-5.
[ii] "The Antiquities of the Jews (13.298)".

Temple in 70 CE, the Sadducees lost their influence, while the Pharisees' adaptable model of worship and law interpretation survived. Many Jews were killed or enslaved during the siege, but Pharisaic teachers regrouped in other regions, eventually evolving into the rabbinic leadership that shaped what is now known as Rabbinic Judaism—the foundation of modern Jewish practice.

The Essenes were the sect known to be the most mystical. They usually lived apart from mainstream society and had a keen interest in angels and the spiritual Messiah, seeing themselves as the genuine remnants of Israel who upheld the true covenant with God. Scholars believe that the Dead Sea Scrolls are the library of the Essenes. In contrast to the Essenes, the Zealots worked toward real-world change, namely the political freedom of Jews and the overthrow of the Roman government.

Early Christianity

The fifth Jewish sect is Christians. A large number of Christian denominations have come about and perished over the centuries. The term "early Christianity" refers to the period between Jesus' death and the Council of Nicaea in 325 CE.

Early on, in the 1ˢᵗ century CE, almost all Christians were Jews. Apostle Paul, a former Pharisee, was the one responsible for attracting the Gentiles (God-fearing non-Jews) who were somewhat sympathetic toward Judaism but were not Hebrews. (Gentiles could not convert to Judaism, mostly due to the fact that Judaism, especially at the time, was closely related to the Hebrew ethnicity, so one could rarely convert to Judaism if they had not been born as a Hebrew Jew.)

Many early Christians were merchants who created churches (in that time, the term was taken in its literal sense, ἐκκλησία, meaning "gathering" or "congregation"). More accurately, they held services in small private homes.[i] More than forty Christian communities existed in cities around the Mediterranean by the end of the 1ˢᵗ century, laying the foundation for its expansion.[ii]

Early Christianity was very much influenced by Judaism, but it also influenced the Jewish community in a major way. Numerous Jews

---

[i] Liddell, Henry George, and Robert Scott. *A Greek-English Lexicon*. The Perseus Project.
[ii] Hitchcock, Susan Tyler, and John L. Esposito. *Geography of Religion: Where God Lives, Where Pilgrims Walk*. National Geographic Society, 2004. p. 281.

converted to Christianity. While the Zealots were primarily a political-religious movement that opposed Roman occupation, it is possible that some individuals with Zealot sympathies later embraced Christianity. One of the apostles, Simon the Zealot—also referred to as Simon the Canaanite—is traditionally believed to have had such associations, although the exact meaning of his title remains debated. Some scholars have also noted the influence of the Essenes on early Christianity. Their emphasis on divine revelation, dualism, and the coming of a messianic age bears resemblance to certain early Christian themes.[i]

Before we delve into the Council of Nicaea, it is important to know that it was not the first Christian council. A common misconception people often hold is that Christianity was a free-for-all in terms of interpretation of the scripture. For example, a number of post-apostolic councils were held in Rome and elsewhere sometime in the 2nd and 3rd centuries. The problem that emerged during the mid-2nd century was the rise of Montanism, a belief system that stated the Trinity consisted of only a single person, meaning that Christ's humanity was absorbed by his divinity. This sect was also more radical, discipline-wise. For instance, according to Montanism, once a Christian fell out of grace, they could not be redeemed. Their restoration to the church would be impossible.

During that time, many other belief systems that were associated with Christianity were influential. Gnosticism was one of them. Gnosticism was not a single, unified belief system but rather a collection of diverse teachings and sects that are grouped under the umbrella term "Gnostic." They believed that the physical world was imperfect and evil and that through knowledge (*gnosis* means "wisdom"), they could access the perfect spiritual world. They downplayed Jesus' humanity, placing emphasis on his divinity. Yet, some sources describe Yahweh as being a malevolent lesser deity who created this vile world.[ii] Even though early church fathers condemned Gnosticism as heresy, its schools of thought were very influential. More orthodox Christians did their best to destroy the Gnostic scriptures, a task in which they were almost fully successful.[iii]

---

[i] Hamidovic, David. "About the Links Between the Dead Sea Scrolls and Mandaean Liturgy." *Aram Periodical* 22 (2010): 441–451.

[ii] Pagels, Elaine. The Gnostic Gospels. Knopf Doubleday. (1989) ISBN 978-0-679-72453-7.

[iii] Layton, Bentley. "Prolegomena to the study of ancient Gnosticism". In White, L. Michael; Yarbrough, O. Larry (eds.). (1995) The Social World of the First Christians: Essays in Honor of Wayne A. Meeks. Minneapolis: Fortress Press. ISBN 978-0-8006-2585-6.

Valentinianism and Sethianism, two distinct Gnostic teachings, spread across the Persian Empire, and a related movement called Manichaeism spread all the way to China. To this day, there is a Gnostic religion in modern-day Iraq called Mandaeism (sometimes referred to as Sabianism or Nasoraeanism) that considers Adam (the first human, according to the Bible) to be the founder of the religion and John the Baptist its greatest prophet. Jesus is considered to be a false prophet.[i] Its adherents today range somewhere between sixty thousand and one hundred thousand.[ii] They manage to keep their belief system alive even though they suffer oppression.

To illustrate early divisions in Christian theology, let's look at Marcionism, a movement founded by Marcion of Sinope around 144 CE in Rome. Marcion, the son of a bishop from Pontus (modern-day Turkey), was influenced by dualistic and Gnostic ideas. He rejected the Hebrew Scriptures (the Old Testament), viewing the God described there—the creator of the material world—as a lower, imperfect deity known as the Demiurge. He believed the God revealed in the New Testament was the true, supreme, and benevolent deity.[iii]

Marcion dismissed many Christian writings that did not align with this view and compiled his own version of the Christian canon, including a heavily edited Gospel of Luke and ten of Paul's epistles. He considered the Apostle Paul the only true apostle who correctly understood Jesus' message.[iv] Although Marcion's teachings were declared heretical by the early church, they sparked significant debates and influenced the early development of Christian doctrine and the biblical canon

Just how powerful these non-orthodox teachings were can be seen in the fact that Augustine of Hippo, who lived in the 4th and 5th centuries CE and was born decades after the Nicene Creed was created, was, for a long time, a Manichean. He became a Manichean after arriving in Rome.

The landscape of Christianity was incredibly diverse, and while there were more or less orthodox currents, centuries would have to pass before the establishment of an institution that could be referred to as an official

---

[i] Edmondo, Lupieri. "Friar of Ignatius of Jesus (Carlo Leonelli) and the First 'Scholarly' Book on Mandaeaism (1652)." *ARAM Periodical* 16 (2004): 25-46.
[ii] Thaler, Kai. "Iraqi Minority Group Needs U.S. Attention." *Yale Daily News*, 9 March 2007. Retrieved 4 November 2021.
[iii] Ehrman, Bart D. *Lost Christianities: The Battles for Scripture and the Faiths We Never Knew.* Oxford: Oxford University Press, 2005. pp. 95-112. ISBN 978-0-19-518249-1.
[iv] Ibid.

church in the modern sense.

Establishment of the Official Faith

While there are many events that shaped Christianity as we know it today, two major decisions made by Constantine are arguably the most important.

In February 313, via the Edict of Milan, Emperor Constantine, together with Licinius, granted Christianity legal status in the Roman Empire, ending centuries of persecution of Christians and paving the way for the Christian faith to become the foundation of the Western world we know today.[i] This did not mean that Christianity became the official faith of the Roman Empire; it only meant that Christians were now allowed to worship freely and without fear of persecution.

Some historians argue that this edict shouldn't be seen as an act of genuine faith on Constantine's part; instead, it should be seen as a pragmatic political decision. Constantine considered the Christian god to be such a strong and influential deity that an alliance had to be made to ensure the stability of the empire and avoid his wrath.[ii] Nevertheless, it is more probable that it was an act of true faith since Constantine's favors to Christianity in his lifetime were many.[iii]

This leads us to the Council of Nicaea. There is a common misconception regarding the first ecumenical council that needs to be addressed. It is often mentioned that in Nicaea, bishops agreed upon which scriptures would become part of the canon and which ones would be discarded. The most important bishops gathered in Nicaea because there was a big crisis within the Christian faith, and this crisis threatened to divide Christianity.

---

[i] The Cambridge History of Christianity - Cambridge University Press.
[ii] Sordi, Marta. *The Christians and the Roman Empire.* Norman: University of Oklahoma Press, 1994. p. 134.
[iii] Maier, Paul L. *Eusebius: The Church History.* Grand Rapids: Kegel Publications, 1999. p. 374.

A later icon depicting the Nicene Creed.[7]

The problematic teaching was a heresy called Arianism, named after Bishop Arius of Alexandria. In his attempt to defend the oneness of God, he separated the Father (a transcendental being not confined by the universe) from the Holy Spirit and the Son, Jesus Christ. He referred to Christ as *homoiousios* (a term coined in Greek, with *homoios* meaning "similar" and *ousia* meaning "essence"). This means he thought that Christ the Son was subordinate to God, which diminished his divinity.

To resolve this division, Constantine called for an ecumenical council (a council of all the church's bishops) to ensure religious stability. Constantine's personal involvement in Christian affairs set a precedent that many kings and emperors would follow. He convened an ecumenical council in Nicaea and summoned all 1,800 bishops of the known Christian world.

The debate raged for sixty-six days, from May 20th to July 25th, 325.[i] Out of 381 bishops that were present near Constantine's summer palace, the loudest proponents of opposing views were Arius of Alexandria, after whom Arianism was named, and Athanasius of Alexandria, whom Christians came to worship as a saint both by the Eastern Orthodox Church and the Catholic Church.[ii, iii] The debate was fierce, and upon being cleverly questioned, Arius admitted that Christ is a created creature, which implies he is a limited being and that his death for humanity's sins couldn't have redeemed us. That meant both Christ and the Holy Spirit were separate from the Father, bringing polytheism back into the game. According to Damaskinos, an Athenian monk, Saint Nicholas of Myra, at one point stood in front of Arius and slapped him in front of all of the church fathers and Constantine, who was present for the entirety of the council.[iv]

By the end of the sixty-six-day council, the Nicene Creed was agreed upon. Christ was to be referred to as *homoousion,* the same in being and the same in essence as the Father. Those who "assert that the Son of God is of different hypostasis or substance, or created, or is subject to alteration or change" would be looked down on.[v] Furthermore, Constantine issued an edict that Arius's writings were to be burned to erase his teachings, going as far as to command "that if someone should be discovered to have hidden a writing composed by Arius, and not have immediately brought it forward and destroyed it by fire, his penalty shall be death."[vi]

Yet, the story of Arianism lived on until the 7th century. Following the establishment of Nicene Christianity, there were issues with Athanasius.

---

[i] Wheeler, Joe L. *Saint Nicholas.* Thomas Nelson, 2010.
[ii] Theodoret of Cyrus, The Ecclesiastical History of Theodoret, Book 3, Chapter 31
[iii] "Online Chapel - Greek Orthodox Archdiocese of America". *www.goarch.org*
[iv] Wheeler, Joe L. *Saint Nicholas.* Thomas Nelson, 2010.
[v] The Nicene Creed, which was agreed to at the council in 325.
[vi] "Emperor Constantine's Edict against the Arians." *fourthcentury.com.* 23 January 2010. Archived from the original on 19 August 2011. Retrieved 20 August 2011.

He was accused of murder, sorcery, and treason. The First Synod in Tyre was convened in 335 to address these allegations, and Athanasius was excommunicated. This synod, interestingly, also saw Arius be absolved of his wrongdoings.[i] Constantine himself was baptized by Eusebius of Nicomedia, a priest sympathetic to Arius, on his deathbed.[ii] His son, Constantinus II, who inherited the throne, was also somewhat sympathetic to Arianism. Constantine's grandson Julian was the only emperor of the Byzantine Empire who rejected Christianity, seeing himself as a pure "Hellene."

Even though Julian's successor, Jovian, was a Christian, he only reigned for eight months, never even entering Constantinople. That's when Valens, an Arian, became the ruler of the empire for fourteen years, from 364 to 378. Having an Arian emperor for nearly fifteen years led to the restoration of lost rights for Arians. This continued the debate and the somewhat precarious status of Christianity within the Byzantine Empire throughout the rest of the 4th century.

It was not until Theodosius I, a devout Nicene Christian, that Christianity finally became the official religion of the empire. The Edict of Thessalonica was issued on February 27th, 380 CE, by Emperor Theodosius I of the Eastern Roman Empire and the Western co-emperors Gratian and the young Valentinian II.[iii]

Theodosius I was able to restore political stability in the East, which allowed the Goths to settle in Roman territory. With his increasing power, he defeated the usurpers Magnus Maximus and Eugenius. In 381, he convened the second ecumenical council, known as the First Council of Constantinople, which condemned paganism and established

Theodosius I.[98]

---

[i] Socrates of Constantinople. *Church History*, Book 1, Chapter 33. In Anthony F. Beavers, *Chronology of the Arian Controversy*.
[ii] Gonzalez, Justo. *The Story of Christianity*, Vol. 1. Harper Collins, 1984. p. 176. ISBN 0-06-063315-8.
[iii] Ehler, Sidney Zdeneck; Morrall, John B (1967). *Church and State Through the Centuries: A Collection of Historic Documents with Commentaries*

Nicene Christianity over Arianism. He was the last emperor to hold power over both the Eastern and Western parts of the empire.

Arcadius took the throne in the East, while the Western soldier-emperors were under the rule of his son Honorius. After the death of Arcadius, his heir, Theodosius II, entrusted a loyal ally, Anthemius, and other officials with the task of building the Theodosian Walls to defend Constantinople. Since he had others deal with the matters of the capital, his focus shifted toward theological disputes and the formulation of the *Codex Theodosianus*. The codex aimed to clear up confusion and establish a single code of law, reinforcing Christianity as the empire's official religion. It contained some of the first laws granting tax exemptions to the church, which were originally passed by Constantine and Constantius II. In 431, Emperor Theodosius II convened the third ecumenical council, the Council of Ephesus, to address the teachings of Nestorius, who believed that Jesus had two separate persons, human and divine. The council condemned Nestorianism and affirmed Mary's title as Theotokos, or "mother of God."[i]

Eutyches, in contrast to Nestorius, denied the humanity of Christ and held a Monophysite view of Christ's nature. The Second Council of Ephesus in 449, called by Theodosius II toward the end of his rule, addressed this new view. It was one of the most controversial councils of the time. However, the decisions made at this council were ultimately rejected by the wider Christian community, leading to further divisions in the church.

Theodosius's successor, Marcian, almost immediately convened another council in 451, the Council of Chalcedon. This council affirmed the Chalcedonian definition that declared Christ to be perfect in godhood and manhood. Eutyches's Monophysitism was rejected, marking a significant turning point in theological debates.

Although there were sporadic and short-lived returns to paganism, such as with Emperor Julian, the Eastern Roman Empire was strongly defined by Christianity.

---

[i] Ostrogorsky, George, *History of the Byzantine state*, Rutgers University Press, 1969, p.78

Chapter 3: Separation from the West

Wars with Germanic Tribes, the Invasion of the Huns, and the Battle of Adrianople

The Western Roman Empire was heading toward its complete demise due to ongoing internal instability, economic challenges, and barbarian invasion. In 375, the nomadic confederation known as the Huns breached Europe through the passage between the Caspian Sea and the Ural Mountains, sometimes colloquially referred to as "the gate (or passage) of the peoples."[i] The Roman Empire faced numerous battles along its northern and western borders, but most of the power was situated in the Eastern Roman Empire. It was up to the Eastern emperor to fight on two fronts.

---

[i] It seems there is no definitive translation of this term, but it is frequently used in many Slavic languages.

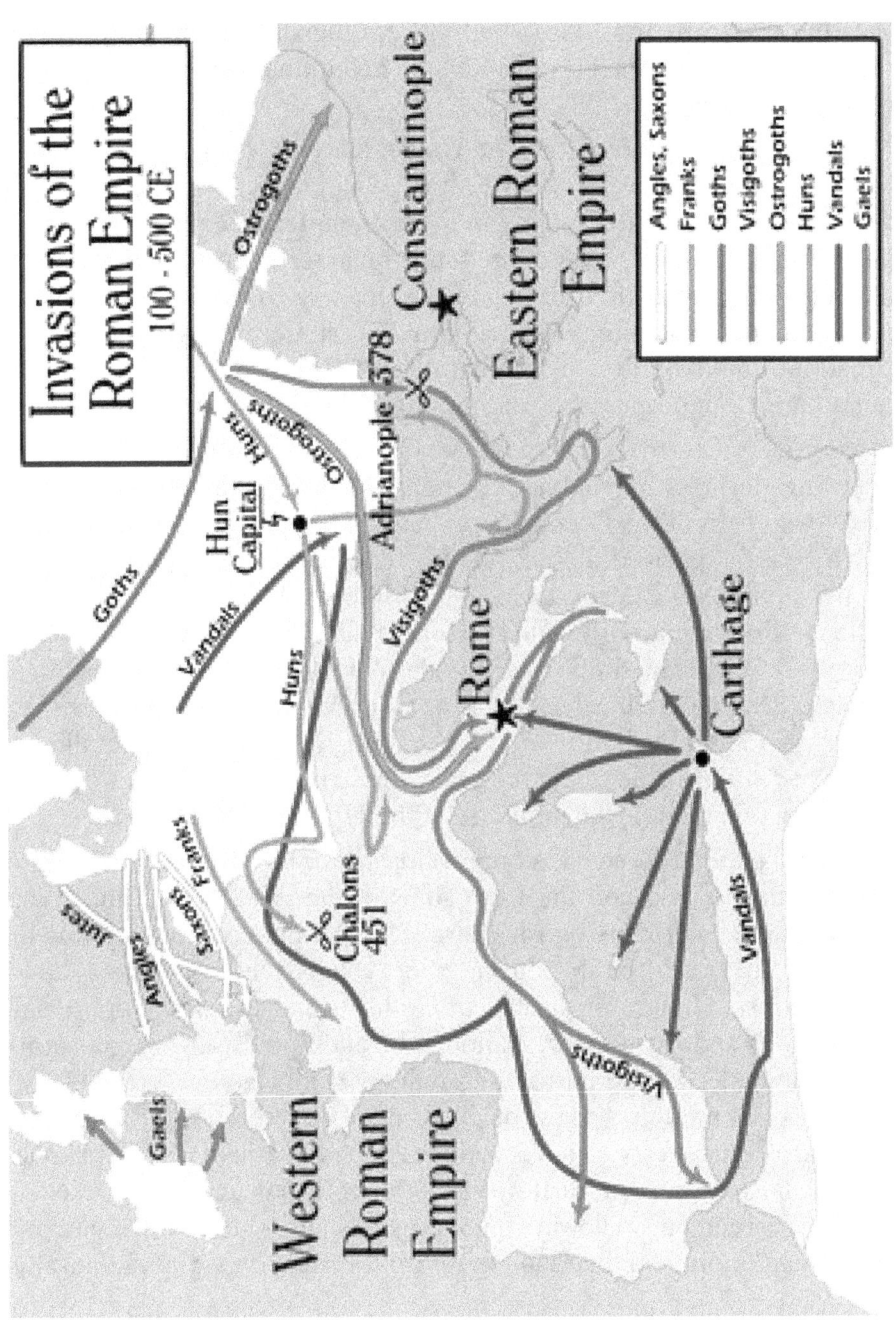

Map depicting the invasions of the Roman Empire.[99]

Valens (r. 364-378), who ruled in the East, was the first emperor to face this two-front war. He aided his brother, Valentinian II, in the western provinces while simultaneously defending the Eastern Empire from Persian attacks.

An Eastern Germanic tribe, the Goths, played a significant role in the decline of the Western Roman Empire. They fled from the advancing Hun army, which left devastation in its wake, and the Goths sought refuge in the Roman Empire. They arrived in Roman territory in 376.[i] However, they were mistreated by Roman officials, leading to a revolt. One of the most significant outcomes of the Hun threat was the Goths' sack of Adrianople in 378. Emperor Valens, who had been dealing with the Persian army on the eastern front, moved to the Balkan Peninsula.

Ignoring pleas from his nephew Gracian, Valentinian's successor, Valens insisted on confronting the enemy alone. He underestimated the size and strength of the Gothic forces, and he and his army were defeated after the Goths pillaged Thrace.[ii] This event marked a significant shift in the perception of Roman invincibility. It emboldened other tribes to challenge Roman authority and led to increased instability in the region. The attack highlighted the vulnerability of Roman military tactics to nomadic cavalry-based armies. This demonstration of cavalry supremacy served as a model for future wars.[iii] Even though the Huns did not directly participate in the battle, their presence compelled other tribes to engage in action, strengthening the influence of the Huns in Europe.

Following the Hunnic invasion, two major Gothic groups emerged: the Visigoths in the west and the Ostrogoths in the east. The Gothic Wars predated the reign of Theodosius I (r. 379-395) but continued during his rule after he took over the throne after Valens died. Seeking to quell further unrest, Theodosius dealt with Gothic tribes, primarily suppressing the Visigoths and Ostrogoths. Although he attempted peace negotiations, he ultimately decided to engage in a military campaign in Thrace in 380, which was not entirely successful. Nevertheless, Theodosius managed to conclude a peace treaty with Visigothic King Athanaric in 382. This treaty was a significant moment in Roman-Gothic relations and set a precedent for future agreements, allowing the Goths to settle within the empire and maintain autonomy on their land in return for military service and loyalty.

---

[i] Painter, Sidney, *A History of the Middle Ages 284-1500*, The MacMillan Press LTD, 1973, p.33
[ii] Ostrogorsky, George, *History of the Byzantine State*, Rutgers University Press, 1969, p.72
[iii] Bury, J.B. *The Invasion of Europe by the Barbarians*, W.W. Norton & Company, 2000, p.42

Wars with Sasanian Persians

On the eastern border, the Eastern Roman Empire and the Sasanian Persian Empire were involved in several wars and other minor conflicts during the 4th century. Although the conflict predated and lasted after the 4th century, some of the longest and most significant wars between the two empires took place during this century. It started during the reign of Constantine the Great (r. 306-337) and continued into the reign of Emperor Julian the Apostate (r. 361-363), and it involved multiple campaigns and battles. After King Shapur II (309-379) regained control of the territory that is now Afghanistan and Pakistan, he launched a campaign against the Romans in 359.[i] In response, Emperor Julian launched a major campaign spanning the next four years, culminating in the Battle of Ctesiphon in 363, where Emperor Julian was killed.

The conflict ended with his successor, Jovian, signing a treaty that returned the territories the Romans had taken from the Sasanian Empire. During the reign of Theodosius I, relatively peaceful relations were maintained with the Sasanian Empire, partly due to internal challenges and threats from other powers. However, conflicts arose as Theodosius I solidified the power of the Eastern Empire. Disputes over the division of Armenia between the Romans and Sasanians sparked this conflict. Both empires wanted to exert their influence, and in 387, a major revolt erupted in Armenia against Sasanian rule. The rebels sought assistance from the Eastern Roman Empire, leading to increased tensions. Under King Shapur III, the son of Shapur II, the Sasanians invaded Roman territories in Armenia and Mesopotamia. The war ended with the signing of the Treaty of Acilisene, which did no more than reaffirm the existing status quo in Armenia.

Separation of 395

The Roman Empire underwent Christianization and was unified under the rule of Theodosius I. He was the last emperor to rule a unified empire. On his deathbed, he divided the empire. It's important to note that the empire remained divided until the fall of the Western Roman Empire. The division was a significant moment in the history of the Roman Empire since it marked the beginning of separate political and administrative entities.

---

[i] Shapur II acquired the title at birth and held it until his death at age seventy, making him the longest-reigning monarch in Iranian history.

The already fractured empire was split between Theodosius's sons. Honorius was appointed as the leader in the west, with the capital first in Milan and later in Ravenna. His territories included Italy, Gaul, North Africa, and a part of the Balkans. Arcadius encompassed eastern Europe, Macedonia, Egypt, Asia Minor, and Thrace, holding his power from the capital in Constantinople.

This formalization of separating the administration had been developing since the time of Diocletian in the late 3rd and early 4th century. This separation led to distinct political, cultural, and religious identities, eventually contributing to the fall of the Western Roman Empire and the flourishing of the Eastern Roman Empire.

Considering Arcadius was eighteen and Honorius only eleven years old, they were under the influence of their officials. In the Western Roman Empire, the real power was in the hands of Vandal Stilicho, a military commander close to Theodosius I.[i] Even though he was a Germanic barbarian, Stilicho was allowed to marry Serena, Theodosius's niece, setting a precedent that allowed barbarian personnel to rise through the ranks.

The main threat came from the Visigoths, who were led by Alaric. Stilicho made a deal with Alaric but was killed soon after in 408. Alaric, who was of Germanic ancestry, once again proved that the Germanic tribes could acquire important positions. After Stilicho's death, Alaric attacked Rome and successfully sacked and pillaged the city in 410. It took him many attempts over the course of two years, but it is considered the final blow might have been possible with inside help from a slave or a Roman traitor.[ii] For three days, the city was burned, destroyed, and raided. Even though he was Arian himself, Alaric spared the churches, allowing the Roman people a few safe spots during the havoc.[iii] Other buildings didn't share the same fate; an archaeological site in Aventine contains remains of buildings burned during this invasion.[iv]

---

[i] Mashkin, Nikolai, *A History of the Ancient Rome*, Gospolitizdat, 1956, p.406
[ii] Bury, J.B. *The Invasion of Europe by the Barbarians*, W.W. Norton & Company, 2000, p.66
[iii] Mashkin, Nikolai, *A History of the Ancient Rome*, Gospolitizdat, 1956, p.406
[iv] Bury, J.B. *The Invasion of Europe by the Barbarians*, W.W. Norton & Company, 2000, p.67

Sack of Rome by Joseph-Noel Sylvestre (1890).[100]

The damaged empire was unable to resist fierce attacks from the Goths. Other parts of the empire began succumbing to their inevitable fate. Around 409, the Vandals and Alani took some parts of Spain. In 420, the Vandals solidified their position, and by 429, they had taken control of North Africa. The Huns, who were united by Attila in the 430s, posed a specially serious threat. The death of Emperor Honorius in 423 started a period of turmoil until the Eastern Roman government installed Valentinian II as the Western emperor in Ravenna.

Theodosius II, the new Eastern emperor and son of Arcadius, saw Aetius rise to the rank of magister militum.[i] Aetius was able to somewhat stabilize the military situation of the Western Empire. The Germanic general Ricimer succeeded Stilicho as a defender of the empire. Despite being German, these men proved to be capable of attaining the highest ranks and even married into the royal family. However, they were aware that as foreigners, they could never legally become rulers. During this time, the power lay in the Eastern Roman Empire.

The Fall of Attila and the Huns

The Huns, led by Attila (434-453), pillaged and scourged the Balkans, causing the fall of many cities, such as Sirmium, Singidunum, Naissus, and Emona.[ii] Peace treaties were signed with Attila, but they were short-lived. After the death of Theodosius, his successor, Marcian, refused to pay the established fee to the Huns. Attila responded to this by sacking Gaul in 451. The Battle of Chalons, also known as the Battle of Maurica, occurred near the Catalaunian Plains.

The Roman forces were led by Flavius Aetius and faced a coalition of Hunnic and Germanic forces led by Attila. The battle involved tens of thousands of soldiers on both sides and resulted in heavy casualties. Although neither side achieved a decisive victory, the Romans managed to halt the Huns' advance. Attila later invaded Italy but was forced to retreat due to attacks by Marcian on the Danube.

Attila's sudden death in 453 did not prevent the deterioration of the Western Roman Empire. Chaos ensued even after the deaths of Aetius and Valentinian III. Petronius Maximus emerged as emperor, eventually leading to the formation of new Germanic kingdoms in North Africa, Gaul, and Spain. The collapse of the Roman Empire was marked by the dominance of Germanic military leaders over ineffectual puppet emperors.

New Battle Tactics of Eastern Armies

The Roman military strategy emphasized defensive warfare and the use of fortified positions. The army continued to utilize combined arms tactics, integrating infantry, cavalry, archers, and siege machines in coordinated

---

[i] Magister militum was a term that referred to a senior army commander with significant influence.
[ii] Romans perceived Attila as a divine punishment sent from Gods, giving him the nickname whip or scourge of God, referring to his brutal and fearsome reputation.

maneuvers. Skilled commanders and disciplined troops proved to be good assets but had flaws. Byzantine commanders sometimes employed tactical deceptions, known as feigned flight. This required effective coordination and discipline but could be highly effective in surprising and defeating the enemy. Investing in the development of new systems and exploiting enemy weaknesses was useful in countering new threats that came in the coming centuries.

The Collapse of the Western Roman Empire

The gradual collapse of the Western Roman Empire unfolded over several decades. While historians debate the exact causes and timeline, several key factors undoubtedly contributed to its downfall.

- Political instability and internal division: Frequent changes in leadership, often through assassination or usurpation, weakened central authority and hindered effective governance.
- Military decline: The once formidable military force gradually weakened due to budget cuts, corruption, and recruitment difficulties. Strained capabilities left the empire vulnerable to incursions by Germanic tribes, pressure from the Sasanian Persians, and the rise of the Huns.
- Economic crisis: High taxation, inflation, and corruption led to a downfall in trade and productivity, resulting in economic stagnation.
- Social unrest: Slave revolts, peasant uprisings, and urban unrest destabilized the empire, leading to the depopulation and decline of many cities while trade routes shifted.
- Loss of territory: Further invasions by Germanic tribes weakened the empire's strategic position, resulting in the loss of North Africa to the Vandals and Italy to the Ostrogoths.

Petronius Maximus was succeeded by other prominent generals, firstly Avitus and then by Ricimer. After the death of Ricimer in 472, it seemed his cousin Gundobad would inherit the leadership role. Gundobad couldn't come to an agreement with Eastern Emperor Leo (r. 457-474.). Leo's candidate was Julius Nepos. This conflict was resolved when Gundobad departed to Burgundy following his father's death. Julius Nepos was free to overtake the Western throne. He appointed Orestes, a former secretary of Attila, as magister militum while he himself retreated to Dalmatia.

Orestes crowned his young son as the new emperor with the name Romulus Augustus. Considering that Julius Nepos wasn't dead or overthrown, Romulus was not recognized by the Eastern court. Julius Nepos was still the legal emperor. In September 476, Odoacer, the leader of the Germanic *foederati* in Italy, seized Ravenna, killed Orestes, and deposed Romulus.[i] Julius Nepos did not return to Italy and continued to rule from Dalmatia, where he was in exile.

By law, there were still only two legitimate emperors, Zeno in the East and Julius Nepos in the West. Romulus Augustus was an illegitimate sovereign who was overthrown in a coup, but he never objected to Zeno's power. Odoacer accepted Zeno and eventually invaded Dalmatia after the murder of Julius Nepos in 480. Zeno abolished the title and position of the Western Roman emperor and assumed the role of Odoacer's sovereign. Odoacer was simultaneously the king of the Goths as well as the magister militum.

The position of the Roman emperor would never again be divided, though some candidates for the Western emperor position were proposed in the 6th century. After the Western Roman Empire crumbled, various Germanic tribes led Italy and its provinces. The new Germanic rulers maintained most of the Roman laws and traditions, and many tribes were Christianized, although they mostly followed Arianism.

---

[i] The foederati were tribes bound by a treaty.

Chapter 4: Justinian's Dream of Restoration

Renovatio imperii: Reconquering the West

Emperor Zeno's reign (r. 474-475 and 476-491) was defined by internal revolts and religious conflicts. His successor, Anastasius I (r. 491-518), tried to stabilize the economy and implement financial reforms. Although known for his construction projects, his rule was not very successful. Justin I, an elderly officer, was chosen as emperor after Anastasius I passed away and remained on the throne until his death in 527. These emperors set the stage for Justinian I, who would go on to have a profound impact on the Byzantine Empire and the lands beyond. Justin's reign focused on internal stability and preparing his nephew Justinian for succession.

Justinian was born to a peasant family of either Illyro-Roman or Thraco-Roman origin. The name *Iustinianus* was indicative of his adoption by his uncle Justin, who brought him to Constantinople and looked after his education. Others who contributed to Justinian's success included his finance ministers, John the Cappadocian and Peter Barsymes, who collected taxes more efficiently than anyone before, funding the wars that his talented generals Belisarius and Narses led. Justinian's reign is known for his ambitious but only partly realized idea of *renovatio imperii* ("restoration of the empire"). Justinian rose through the ranks of the Byzantine bureaucracy and became a close advisor to Emperor Justin I. In 527, he was named co-emperor, and shortly after, his uncle died, leaving him to become the sole emperor at the age of forty-five.

During Justinian's rule, the Eastern Roman Empire managed to overcome the crisis that had led to the fall of the Western Roman Empire. Justinian was instrumental in shaping the empire's policies during this time. A noteworthy aspect of his reign was the reconquest of the western Mediterranean. As a Christian and a great connoisseur of Roman history, he felt it was his divine duty to restore the Roman Empire to its ancient boundaries.

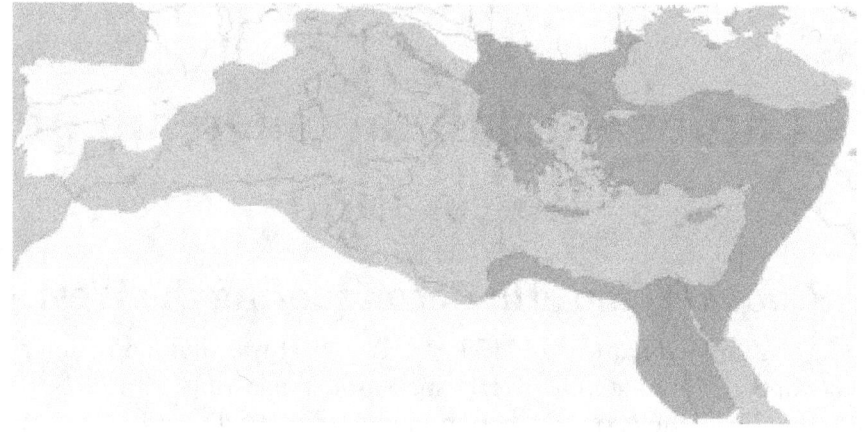

A map depicting Justinian's expansion to the west.[101]

The first of the western kingdoms Justinian targeted was the Vandal Kingdom in North Africa. King Hilderic, who had maintained good relations with Justinian, was overthrown by his cousin Gelimer in 530. This event prompted Justinian to demand the return of the kingdom to Hilderic.

Justinian inherited ongoing hostilities with the Sasanian Empire from his predecessors. In 530, the Persian forces suffered defeats at Dara and Satala, while the Romans faced a loss near Callincium. Justinian attempted to form alliances with the Axumites of Ethiopia and the Himyarites of Yemen and lay a final blow to the Persians, but these efforts were unsuccessful.

After Gelimer refused his demands to return the Vandal Kingdom to Hilderic, Justinian knew he had to secure one of the frontiers. Following the death of King Kavadh I of Persia in 531, Justinian established an "eternal peace" with Kavadh's successor, Khosrow, in 532. With the eastern frontier secured, he turned his attention to the west, where Germanic tribes had been established for decades.

Justinian prepared an expedition against the Vandals in 533. The emperor's trusted general Belisarius sailed to Africa with a fleet of ninety-two dromons (a type of galley) and five hundred transports carrying a large number of men, counting up to eighteen thousand.[i] The forces landed in modern-day Tunisia and caught the Vandals off guard, defeating them at Ad Decimum in September and Tricamarum in December of the same year. Belisarius captured Carthage, and King Gelimer, who initially fled, surrendered the following year. Gelimer was taken to Constantinople, where he was paraded during a triumph. Word of Belisarius's plan to proclaim himself as king of Africa could be heard throughout the empire but was overshadowed by the glorious parade.

In the same campaign, Belisarius also recovered Sardinia and Corsica, as well as the Balearic Islands and the stronghold of Septem Fratres (later named Gibraltar). Although the area was not completely pacified until 548, it remained peaceful and experienced a measure of prosperity.

As in Africa, dynastic struggles in Ostrogothic Italy provided an opportunity for intervention. The young king Athalaric had died in 534, and the usurper Theodahad had imprisoned and assassinated the widowed queen Amalasuintha, the mother of Athalaric. So, Belisarius invaded Sicily and advanced to Italy, sacking Naples and capturing Rome in December 536. By that time, Theodahad had been deposed by the army, which elected its commander, Vitigis (also spelled Vitiges), as the new king. Vitigis gathered a large army and besieged Rome for over a year between 537 and 538.

His efforts weren't enough to retake the city. Justinian sent Narses to aid Belisarius, but tensions between them hampered the campaign's progress. Milan was taken but soon recaptured by the Ostrogoths. Not very long after that setback, Justinian recalled Narses to settle the tensions between the two generals. By 540, Belisarius had reached the Ostrogothic capital Ravenna. The Ostrogoths tried to lure Belisarius to their side by giving him the title of Western Roman emperor. He feigned acceptance and entered the city to reclaim it for Justinian.

In the face of renewed hostilities by the Persians, Belisarius was recalled to the eastern front. King Khosrow I broke the eternal peace and invaded Roman territory in the spring of 540. The following years were characterized by upsets on Roman territory. Justinian suffered some defeats and lost a few smaller quarrels.

---

[i] Ostrogorsky, George, *History of the Byzantine State,* Rutgers University Press, 1969, p..89.

While military efforts were directed to the east, the situation in Italy took a turn for the worse once again. Under their respective kings, Ildibad, Eraric, and Totila, the Ostrogoths made quick gains in the lands not secured by Justinian I. They reconquered some major cities and almost managed to take the entire Italian Peninsula. Belisarius was sent back to Italy in 544, but he lacked troops and supplies after the clash with the Persians. After making no progress, he was relieved of his command in 548. During these four years, Rome changed hands many times between the Ostrogoths and Byzantines. Finally, Justinian dispatched a large force of approximately thirty-five thousand men under the command of Narses. In 552, they reached Ravenna and defeated the Ostrogoths decisively at the Battle of Busta Gallorum (Battle of Taginae), where Totila was slain. There was another smaller battle to finish the Ostrogoth resistance. In 554, a large-scale Frankish invasion was defeated at Casilinum, and Italy was secured for the empire. It would take Narses several more years of continuous efforts to reduce the remaining Gothic strongholds in occasional smaller clashes.

A mosaic of Emperor Justinian in the Basilica of San Vitale, Ravenna.[102]

In addition, the Byzantine Empire established a presence in Visigothic Hispania, where the usurper Athanagild requested assistance in his rebellion against King Agila I. The Byzantines took Cartagena and other cities on the southeastern coast and founded the new province of Spania. The newly crowned king of the Visigoths acknowledged the suzerainty of the empire, which marked the highest point in Byzantine expansion.

In the end, Justinian's ambitions were only partly realized, with noteworthy sustainable conquests in Africa. In the West, the successes of the 530s were followed by years of stagnation. The dragging feuds with the Goths were a disaster for Italy. The enlarged area of Byzantine influence eliminated naval threats, and the empire reached its territorial zenith in 555.[i] Truth be told, not every ex-Roman territory was under Justinian's rule, but having conquered North Africa, Spain, and Italy, he once again made the Mediterranean Sea a "Roman lake."

Nika Riots

Justinian's rule was not universally popular. He almost lost the throne during the Nika riots, and a conspiracy against his life was discovered as late as 562. Amidst turbulent external affairs, internal unrest flared up rapidly. Heated altercations between the autocratic centralized government and various political organizations divided the empire.

The riots were sparked by social, political, and sporting rivalries that had been building up for some time. The two main factions involved were the Blues and the Greens, names that originated from chariot racing teams but also represented broader factions within the city.[ii] Although Justinian was fond of the Blues in the beginning, his support abated once he took a more neutral stance and sought to limit the power of all the factions. Contrary to Anastasius I, Justinian wanted to free himself of the deme's influence and imposed punitive measures on fighting organizations.[iii]

As early as January 532, unrest arose in Constantinople at the Hippodrome during a chariot race. Unsatisfied attendees yelled, "Nika" ("win," "triumph," or "conquer"), a chant that would become the symbol and the name of these riots.[iv]

---

[i] Ostrogorsky, George, *History of the Byzantine State*, Rutgers University Press, 1969, p.89.

[ii] There were initially four factions: Blue (*Veneti*), Green (*Prasini*), Red (*Russati*), and White (*Albati*), but by the 6th century, most of the influence was distributed between the Blues and Greens.

[iii] In ancient Athens, *deme* was a municipality. In the Byzantine Empire, however, *deme* signified the chariot racing factions (perhaps based on municipal borders), as well as political factions that formed around these groups, such as the Blues and Greens.

[iv] Mitchell, Stephen, *A History of the Later Roman Empire AD 284-641*, Oxford: Blackwell, 2007, p.198.

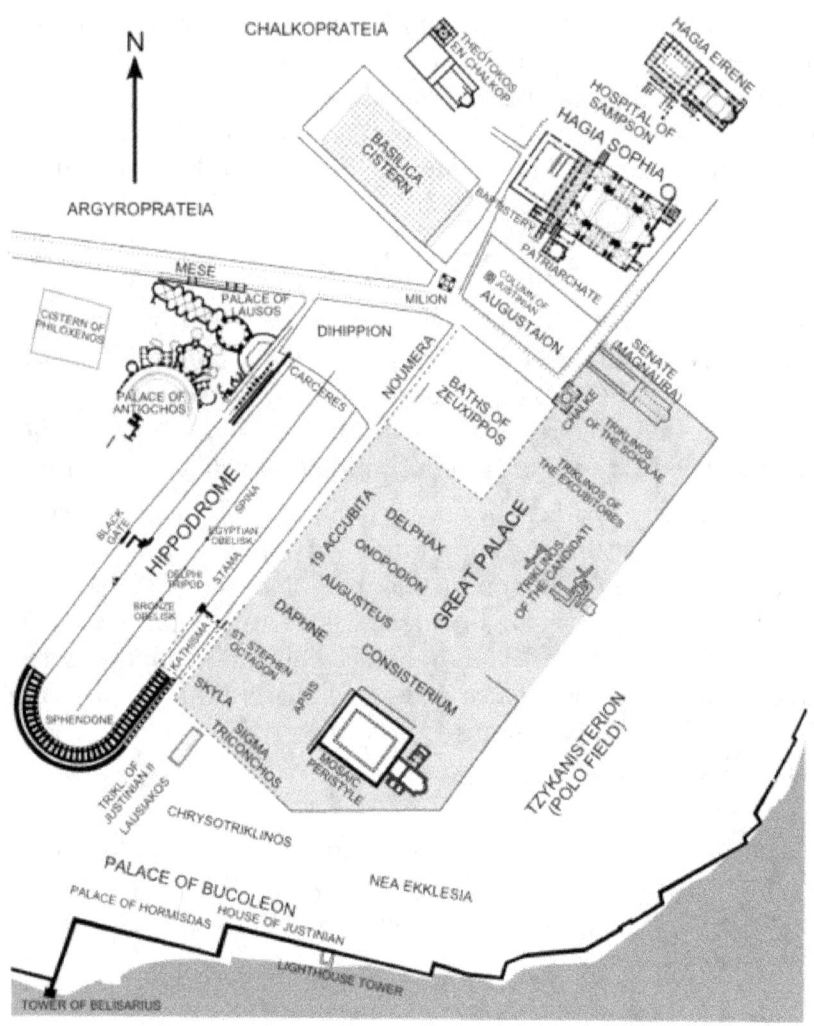

A map of the palace and Hippodrome during the riots.[108]

The riots began as a verbal protest but quickly escalated into widespread violence and chaos. Soon, the capital of the empire was engulfed in flames. Most notably, Hagia Sophia, the Praetorium, and the city's main granaries were set ablaze. The united rioters proclaimed Hypatius, Anastasius's nephew, as the new emperor, which incited Justinian to contemplate fleeing the city. Empress Theodora was the one who convinced him to stay, while Belisarius and Nerses managed to break the unity of the protesters.[i]

---

[i] Ostrogorsky, George, *History of the Byzantine State*, Rutgers University Press, 1969, p. 91.

The commanders moved into the Hippodrome and trapped the rioters. Narses tried to bribe the Blue faction, reminding them that Justinian was fond of them and also mentioning that Hypatius was a sympathizer of the Greens in order to divide them. Blinded by the gold, the voracious rioters were caught off guard when Belisarius began killing anyone left in the Hippodrome, whether they were Blue or Green supporters. Hypatius and his associates were also killed during the carnage. This "maneuver" in the Hippodrome marked the end of the uprising. Justinian used the opportunity to consolidate his power and undertook significant reforms and construction projects, including rebuilding the burned Hagia Sophia.

This riot was a pivotal event in Byzantine history, as it shaped the reign of Justinian and the subsequent development of the entire empire. This bloodbath took thirty thousand lives and remains the most controversial aspect of Justinian's rule.[1] One of the more interesting things is the importance Justinian attached to this episode. He announced victory by proclaiming he had removed tyrants from all the cities, obviously exaggerating the magnitude of the outcome. Justinian emerged as a more confident and sterner ruler after this success.

The Great Hagia Sophia

Whether it was fate or projected unrest, the events that transpired in the city gave the emperor a chance to stamp his mark deeper on the capital. The main project he focused on was the church known as Hagia Sophia, which was not only the most spectacular church of late antiquity but also inspired Christian and Muslim architectural traditions in the centuries to come. Justinian enlisted architects Isidore of Miletus and Anthemius of Tralles for the restoration. The shape of the church shifted the focus from the cross toward the dome as a representation of the sky and a symbol of the divine. Materials were brought from every part of the empire.

Considering the scale of the project and the technology of the time, it is surprising that the construction took only five years to complete. The dedication ceremony was grand and attended by Justinian, a multitude of clergy, and the citizens of Constantinople and other parts of the empire.

---

[1] Mitchell, Stephen, *A History of the Later Roman Empire AD 284-641*, Oxford: Blackwell, 2007, p. 194.

The knowledge about domes at the time was not advanced enough, resulting in its collapse in 558. During Justinian's final years of rule, the newly upgraded dome was finished and is standing to this day as part of the mosque in what is now Istanbul. This achievement exemplifies Justinian's ambition and dedication to restore Constantinople as the center of the Roman Empire and to leave his mark on the history of the empire.

Empress Theodora

Mosaic of Empress Theodora in the Basilica of San Vitale, Ravenna.[104]

Empress Theodora's early life is characterized by humble beginnings. Her father was a bear trainer at the Hippodrome and an ally to the Green faction, but after his death, Theodora's favor shifted toward the Blues. Her acting career gave her access to influential circles and brought her to the attention of Justinian, who was the heir to the throne.

Procopius colorfully wrote that Theodora made a name for herself with her pornographic portrayal of Leda and the Swan.[i] The accuracy of Procopius's portrayal is unclear because sexual promiscuity was ascribed to many females of low origin or who had acting careers. It was rumored she was a dancer in brothels instead of being an actress, but despite conventions and prejudices, Justinian wanted to marry her. A law that had been in power since Constantine I barred anyone of senatorial rank from marrying an actress. But in 524, Justinian passed a law allowing reformed actresses to marry outside their rank if approved by the emperor. In 525, he married Theodora. This marriage caused a scandal and inspired animosity toward her, though she became very influential in the politics of the empire later on.

After Justinian succeeded the throne in 527, she was crowned Augusta and became empress against all odds. She shared Justinian's vision that there could be no Roman empire that did not include Rome itself. Being relatively young as an emperor and empress compared to their predecessors, they weren't content to maintain the status quo. During the Nika riots, her role was of vital importance to the outcome and Justinian's decision-making. She persuaded him not to flee and to take a stand. According to Procopius (a source not to be believed blindly), she interrupted the emperor and his counselors to motivate them with a speech.[ii]

Theodora was known for her intelligence and political savvy. She often advocated for policies that benefited the lower classes and worked to curb the power of the aristocracy. She was very involved in helping underprivileged women. Theodora championed the rights of women and enacted laws to protect them, such as protection for women against abusive husbands. She bought girls sold into prostitution and freed them, providing for their future. In 528, she ordered the closure of brothels and arrested keepers and procurers. This probably reflected the remorse she had regarding her (alleged) past choices.

Her death is recorded by Victor of Tunnuna, and the cause is uncertain, but many believe it to have been a serious illness.[iii] Theodora

---

[i] A story from Greek mythology in which the god Zeus seduces a Spartan queen in the form of a swan.
[ii] Procopius, *The Secret History*, Penguin Books, 1982, p. 38.
[iii] A bishop from North Africa and a chronicler of the time known for his outward resistance toward Justinian I.

was known for her strong sympathy toward the Miaphysite Christians, who rejected the Chalcedonian definition of Christ having two distinct natures. Although Justinian remained officially committed to Chalcedonian orthodoxy, he made significant efforts later in his reign to reconcile the two factions, efforts that many historians believe were influenced by Theodora, even after her death in 548.

The imperial couple is famously depicted in the mosaics of the Basilica of San Vitale in Ravenna, completed around 547, shortly before Theodora's death.

Law and Administration

Justinian was known as "the emperor who never sleeps" for his devotion to the empire. He achieved lasting fame through his judicial reforms, particularly the complete revision of all Roman law, something not previously attempted. Justinian's law and administration are among his most enduring legacies, influencing legal systems to this day. His legislation is now known as the *Corpus Juris Civilis* (Body of Civil Law). The *Corpus Juris Civilis* consists of several components, the most important of which are the following:

1. **Codex Justinianus** – The Codex Justinianus (Code of Justinian) was a collection of imperial enactments and laws issued by previous emperors known as Theodosian, Gregorian, and Hermogenian codices organized thematically and intended to simplify and update existing laws. Early in his reign, Justinian appointed the quaestor Tribonian to oversee this task. The first draft of the Codex Justinianus was issued in 529 and then again five years later as a supplemented edition.[i]

2. **Digesta** (or **Pandects**) – The Digesta was a compilation of legal opinions and writings published in 533. Classical Roman jurists were often contradictory to one another, and for the first time, their works were systematically reviewed and organized in a more functional way.

3. **Institutes** – The *Institutes* was a textbook that served as an introduction to Roman law for law students, ensuring future law representatives would have a better understanding of implemented changes.

---

[i] Ostrogorsky, George, *History of the Byzantine State*, Rutgers University Press, 1969, p. 94.

4. **Novellae Constitutiones** (or **Justinian's Novels**) – These were new laws or amendments issued by Justinian himself after the completion of the codex. While the Codex Justinianus, Digesta, and *Institutes* were published in Latin, *Justinian's Novels* were written in Greek. Justinian decided the other three parts should also be translated into Greek and spread across the empire in both languages.[i]

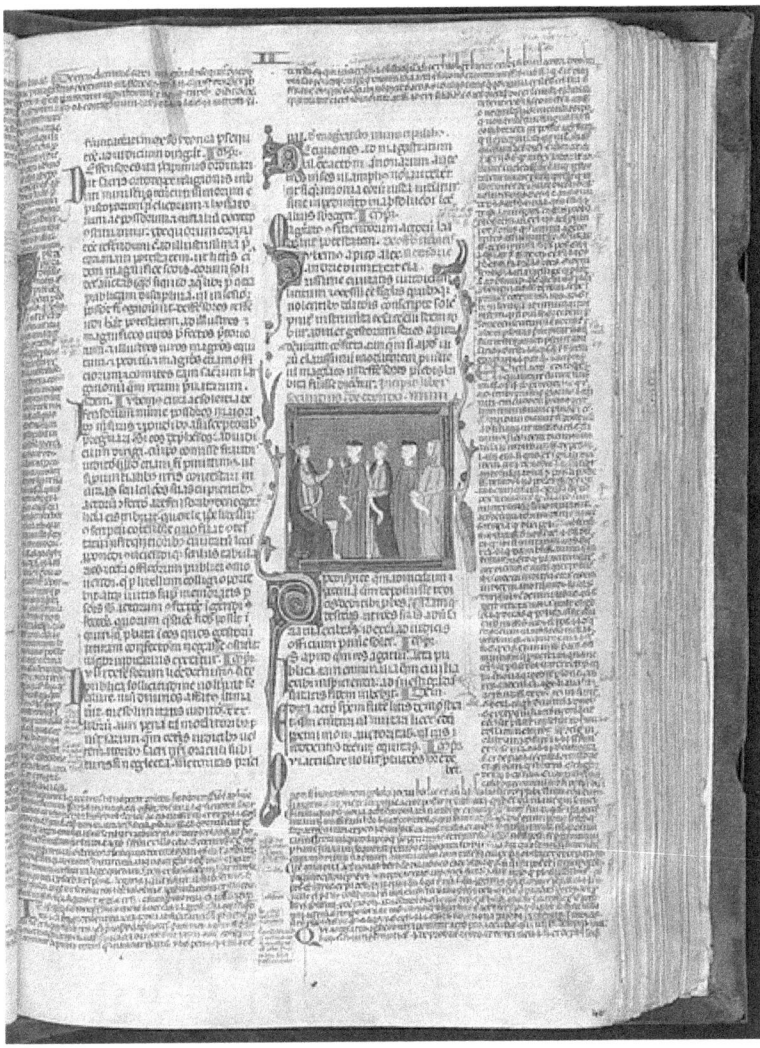

Medieval copy of the famous Code of Justinian, copied by Franciscus Accursius in the 13th century. Preserved in the Ghent University Library.[105]

---

[i] Ibid.

By participating in different parts of the empire's legal system, Justinian succeeded in his attempt to untangle obsolete law codices. The codification of Roman law provided a strong legal foundation for the centralized state. It outlined regulations for public and private life and societal and family matters while also aligning them with Christian ideals and morals with notable Hellenistic influences.

In 541, there was a discontinuation of the regular appointment of consuls. The empire's social welfare program aimed to prevent hunger, with free bread provided at twenty state bakeries and free access to public baths for all residents. Additionally, the Byzantine administration was reorganized to enhance efficiency and centralization. Skilled administrators and legal experts were appointed to key positions to streamline governance and improve tax collection. Provinces were grouped into larger administrative units called dioceses, each under the control of a governor.

Section Two:
From Latin to Greek Empires
(565–867 CE)

Chapter 5: New Enemies at the Gates

The great conquests of Emperor Justinian restored the glory and power of the former Roman Empire and once again turned the Mediterranean Sea into a "Roman lake." The Byzantine Empire utilized all its available resources to allow the old empire to experience its final political and cultural resurgence.[i] The territorial expansion to the west was successful, and there was a flourishing in literature and art. Justinian's efforts failed to restore the empire, but it briefly and superficially revived the splendor of the aging Roman state apparatus.

With his grand endeavors, Justinian aimed to start a new era in the empire's history, but he did the opposite, causing its final collapse and transformation. The territorial restoration of the Roman Empire lacked a solid foundation and internal reforms, leading to its disintegration by the end of Justinian's reign. The empire he left to his successors was internally exhausted and economically and financially shaken due to extensive military undertakings. Justinian left a vast empire that could not be defended, so subsequent rulers had to correct all of the great emperor's mistakes and salvage what could be saved.[ii]

Justinian sacrificed certain border territories in the east and along the Danube limes through his military and financial efforts in the policy of

---

[i] Ibid
[ii] Runciman, *Byzantine Civilization.*

western expansion.[i] The Sasanian dynasty in Persia, led by Khosrow I (r. 531–579), managed to capture a large amount of Byzantine territory in northern Mesopotamia and Armenia at the beginning of Justinian's reign.[ii] However, Justinian's famed general Belisarius managed to gain the upper hand in the war, resulting in the so-called "eternal peace." The Persians broke the peace in 540, taking advantage of the Byzantine army's engagement in Italy. They crossed the border and captured Antioch in Syria. Persia's breakthrough to the Mediterranean was crowned with a ritual bath of Khosrow I in the Mediterranean Sea and the offering of sacrifices. The imperial army, with great effort, managed to defend the crucial fortress of Dara and forced the Persians to withdraw from Edessa and retreat from Syria. Another peace treaty was signed in Dara in 562 called the Fifty-Year Peace, and Justinian spent the final years of his reign with peaceful borders in the East.[iii]

After Justinian

Justinian's successors inevitably shifted the focus of their policy toward the East, with the primary task of consolidating the empire's weakened position in central Asia. A firm stance toward Persia became a characteristic feature of Byzantine policy over the next few decades. The peace that had financially and militarily cost Byzantium so much was disrupted by Justinian's nephew, Justin II (r. 565–578), who, in 572, stopped paying the agreed tribute to Persia.

The entourage around the emperor advised exploiting the troubles in Persia and extending Byzantine influence over all of Armenia. Turkish tribes invaded northern Persia, devastating the region, which encouraged the Caucasian Iberians and Armenians to revolt against Khosrow in alliance with Justin II. Emperor Justin II sent his commander Marcian to gather an army in the east and station them at the fortress of Dara. Supported by the Iberians and Armenians, he attacked the Persian city of Nisibis in Mesopotamia.

Before the decisive clash with Khosrow's approaching army, Emperor Justin II ordered a change in command and transferred all of Marcian's authority to Acacius, who failed to organize the army. Due to a communication and command error, the military collapsed, and the

---

[i] A lime is a border separating the empire from barbarian lands.
[ii] Ostrogorsky, *History of the Byzantine State*.
[iii] Ibid.

Persians ravaged the Byzantine province of Syria and reached the Mediterranean again. This time, the Byzantines lost their famous fortress, Dara.

News of the catastrophic defeat reached Constantinople in 574 and further deteriorated the already shaken mental health of Emperor Justin II. Meanwhile, Khosrow continued to devastate Byzantine territories in the northeast. The war with Persia was continued by Justin II's successor, the energetic Emperor Maurice (r. 582-602), but this time, he managed to take advantage of the unrest that broke out in Persia. With his support, the young Khosrow II Parviz (r. 590-628), grandson of Khosrow I, ascended to the Persian throne. Maurice succeeded in securing peace by signing a treaty with the young Khosrow in 591, regaining the lost territories.[i]

The Italian Situation

The heaviest blow to Byzantium occurred in Italy, the most important region of the restored empire whose reoccupation had required great efforts and sacrifices. Pressured by the Avars, the Lombards invaded Italy in 568 and quickly conquered a large part of it. Alboin (r. c. 560-572), the Lombard king, united the major Germanic tribes in an alliance with the Lombards and defeated the Gepid Kingdom of King Cunimund in the Pannonian Plain. Due to the significant pressure from the advancing Avars, he had to retreat from Pannonia to the old Roman province of Raetia, where he waited for a better opportunity to invade war-ravaged Italy.

In the first months of 568, a large group, mainly consisting of the Lombards, penetrated into Italy, swiftly capturing cities like Padua, Mantua, and Cremona. The famous Byzantine general Narses was tasked with defending Italy in the Po Valley, but he was around ninety years old, and his army and subordinates were unable to stop the conquests.[ii] The only city that offered more resilient resistance was Pavia, which held out against the Lombards for three years but eventually surrendered in 571. With the fall of Pavia, King Alboin controlled half of Italy, which he divided into thirteen Lombard duchies.

---

[i] Ibid.
[ii] Bury, *A History of the Later Roman Empire*.

Africa

In North Africa, the Byzantine Empire maintained its position despite constant exhausting battles with the Moorish tribes until the Arab invasion. Even in Italy, provinces remained under Byzantine rule for several centuries.[i] Thus, the remnants of Justinian's conquests long formed the foundation on which Byzantine power in the West rested. However, the aspiration for world domination vanished forever.

Emperor Maurice (r. 582–602), unlike Justin II, was a statesman of high caliber. Through shrewd policies in the East, he secured the long-needed peace but had to relinquish territories in the West that the Germanic peoples were beginning to conquer. During Maurice's reign, significant measures were taken to preserve Byzantine authority in the newly conquered regions. By reforming the state apparatus in the remnants of these areas, military governorships were established: the Exarchate of Ravenna, which included the remaining Byzantine holdings in Italy, and the Exarchate of Carthage, which encompassed the North African coast. Because of their strong military organization, the exarchates were capable of defense and became the vanguard of Byzantine power in the West. Exarchs, the governors, were in charge of both military and civil administration in their territories. The establishment of the exarchates in Ravenna and Carthage marked the beginning of the Byzantine administration's militarization. The organization of the exarchates would later serve as a model for the arrangement of themes, which were administrative districts of the Byzantine Empire (the region of modern-day Turkey was at one point divided into more than a dozen themes).[ii]

Iberia

Right from the start, Byzantine holdings in the Iberian Peninsula were attacked by their former Visigothic rulers. Visigothic Kings Athanagild and Leovigild conquered the interior territories of the province of Spain, reducing Byzantine control to the coastal areas along the Mediterranean. Many territories were lost during King Leovigild's offensives in 571 and 577, but the Byzantines continued to control key cities in the region of Baetica, such as Carthago Nova, and occasionally reclaimed lost areas. Emperor Maurice managed to consolidate the remaining territories of the

---

[i] Ostrogorsky, *History of the Byzantine State*.
[ii] Ibid

province of Spain and signed a peace treaty with King Reccared I of the Visigoths (r. 586-601) through the mediation of Pope Gregory I the Great. However, the province of Spain did not undergo the exarchate reforms like other territories due to the difficulties in maintaining it and its distance from Constantinople.

After the violent death of Emperor Maurice and the turmoil in the Byzantine Empire, the Visigoths took a firmer stance toward the Byzantine holdings. Over the next twenty years, they managed to conquer all the cities and reclaim their former territories in the Iberian Peninsula except for the Balearic Islands, which were later conquered by the Arabs.[i]

The Balkans

The preoccupation of Justinian's troops with conquests in the West and the defensive policy toward Persia in the East left the Danubian frontier undefended. Even during the reign of Justinian's predecessor, Emperor Justin I, the Antes launched an attack on Byzantine territories. In the early years of Justinian's reign, the Slavic tribes, in alliance with the Bulgars, began continuous incursions into the Balkan provinces. In response, Emperor Justinian erected an entire system of fortifications along the Danube and in the interior of the threatened provinces.[ii] However, the defense of the frontier lacked manpower rather than fortifications. While the Byzantine army celebrated its great victories in the West, the Slavs flooded the Balkan Peninsula from the Adriatic to the Aegean and from the Danube to the Gulf of Corinth.

The Slavs were initially content with plundering the central Byzantine provinces, transporting the loot across the Danube into their territories. Over time, Slavic migrations began to spread into the interior of Byzantium, marking an era of constant Slavic settlement in the Balkan Peninsula.

The tumultuous state of the Byzantine Empire due to frequent Slavic incursions across the Sava and the Danube was further exacerbated by the appearance of the Avars in the Pannonian Plain. According to the Byzantine historian Menander, the Avars established their state (khaganate) under the rule of Khagan Bayan, who governed large groups of Slavs. Byzantium now faced a new formidable enemy on its Danubian borders who coordinated attacks on its territories. Bitter battles began

---

[i] Bury, *The Invasion of Europe by the Barbarians*.
[ii] Ostrogorsky, *History of the Byzantine State*.

over crossings of the Sava and the Danube with the aim of capturing the first major stronghold and former imperial city of Sirmium. Sirmium was besieged in 579 and managed to hold out for the next three years, but unfortunately for Byzantium, Emperor Tiberius II Constantine (r. 574–582) failed to secure peace through diplomatic means.[i] The city fell into Avar hands in 582 after the emperor's death, becoming a base for further incursions into the empire's interior.

While the Avars besieged border fortresses, Slavs from the central Danubian region, following Bayan's orders, plundered Hellas in 580. Slavic tribes settled in the former Roman province of Dacia ravaged the territory of Thrace. According to the Byzantine historian Theophylact Simocatta, these Slavic tribes were not subordinate to Bayan and independently carried out raids. Simocatta refers to their territory as Sclavinia.[ii] Two years after the conquest of Sirmium, the Avars captured Singidunum, which would change hands multiple times. In the same year, 584, Viminacium and Augusta also fell, dismantling the Byzantine defensive system and allowing the Avars and Slavs to spread across the Balkan Peninsula. In the following years, 584 and 586, the first Avar-Slavic attack on Thessalonica occurred, and more importantly, the permanent settlement of certain Slavic tribes in Byzantine territories began. The Slavs were no longer content with just plundering. They transitioned into a sedentary way of life, occupying territories on Byzantine soil.

---

[i] Diehl, *History of the Byzantine Empire*.
[ii] Bury, *The Invasion of Europe by the Barbarians*.

Migration of Slavs in the early medieval age.[106]

Foreign Policy and the Internal Situation

Among the significant foreign policy changes of the early Byzantine period, none had nearly as much impact on the Byzantine Empire as the penetration of the Slavs into the Balkans. All other barbarian incursions that the empire experienced at that time were transient. Even the great migration of the Germans, which shook the empire profoundly, ultimately bypassed Byzantium. In contrast, the Slavs remained in the Balkans permanently, greatly influencing Byzantine history.[i]

By saving territories in the West and engaging in constant wars with Persia in the East, Justinian's successors failed to take any action to save Byzantine possessions in the Balkans. Only after the victorious conclusion of the war with Persia in 591 did Emperor Maurice (r. 582-602) manage to transfer a significant portion of the army from the East and initiate an offensive against the Slavs in the Danube region. Maurice appointed his generals who had distinguished themselves in the Persian War, such as Comentiolus, who was tasked with defending the interior

---

[i] Ostrogorsky, *History of the Byzantine State*.

territories, and the strategos (general) Priscus, who was to defeat the Slavs from the other side of the Danube.

In 594, Priscus launched a major raid into Slavic territories (Sclavinia), where, according to sources, he managed to kill one of the Slavic leaders and return with significant spoils of war. The following year, Maurice's brother, the curopalates Peter, led the Byzantine army in an incursion into Slavic territories, successfully disrupting their organization, recovering plundered Byzantine treasures, and capturing a leader.[i]

In addition to the campaigns against the Slavs, Maurice ordered his generals Priscus and Comentiolus to penetrate the Avar Khaganate in 597 and 599, thereby inflicting the first defeat on the Avars deep within their territory.[ii] The struggle dragged on, leading to a war in the remote Danube region, which was difficult and exhausting. There was no significant impact on the large masses of Slavs, causing the combativeness of the Byzantine army to decline.

After the collapse of Justinian's restoration, Byzantium lost much of its authority. In reaction to Justinian's absolutism, the political importance of the Senate increased, and the urban population's desire for freedom grew. Discipline in the army greatly declined, often leading to open manifestations of dissatisfaction, especially as the government frequently delayed soldiers' pay.

Rebellion

In 602, the curopalates Peter was tasked by Emperor Maurice to lead the army across the Danube, but a rebellion broke out. The rebellious soldiers acclaimed Phocas, a man with barbarian origins, as emperor. The army then abandoned its positions and marched on Constantinople after an uprising supported by the Senate erupted in the city. Emperor Maurice was deposed and executed in the square with his supporters, and the Senate crowned Phocas as the new emperor in Constantinople. The collapse of the Byzantine army on the Danube, after a futile ten-year struggle, sealed the fate of the Balkan Peninsula, which was left to the Slavs.

---

[i] Curopalates was a court title. It formally designated a person who was in charge of handling imperial palace matters. Females could rise to the rank of courapalates.

[ii] Bury, *The Invasion of Europe by the Barbarians*.

Byzantium faced a catastrophe that had long been postponed by the struggles of the previous decades. The complete collapse of Byzantine defensive strength occurred both in the Balkans and in the east toward Persia. The Persians crossed the border and penetrated deep into Asia Minor up to Caesarea (modern-day Israel) after capturing the fortress of Dara in 605. During this time, the Balkans again fell into turmoil due to Slavic-Avar incursions. Not even Phocas increasing the tribute to the Avars helped. Soon, the entire Balkan Peninsula was flooded with enormous Slavic masses, and the entire Byzantine Empire found itself on the brink of collapse.[i]

The years of anarchy under Phocas marked both the final years of the old empire and the end of the post-Roman early Byzantine era. After the severe crisis experienced by Byzantium, it would emerge as a new state under the new emperor, Heraclius (r. 610–641). It was liberated from the decaying post-Roman state and strengthened by new forces.[ii] Now, the true history of Byzantium begins, or rather, the history of the medieval Greek empire.

Depiction of Heraclius on a coin.[107]

---

[i] Ostrogorsky, *History of the Byzantine State*.
[ii] Ibid.

Chapter 6: The Arab Invasion

After the conclusion of the first major religious war of the Christian era, the Byzantine-Sasanian War (602–628), Emperor Heraclius managed to completely destroy the power of the Persian state and reclaim all territories that belonged to Byzantium.[i] As the enemy evacuated from Byzantine provinces, Heraclius symbolically returned the Holy Cross to Jerusalem and celebrated a victory in the spring of 630.[ii]

Amidst this great war, which had repercussions for all states and peoples located east of Byzantium, Muhammad laid the foundations for a new religious and political unity in the Arab world. Muhammad's persona and deeds injected a new driving force among the numerous tribes of the Arabian Peninsula. In the same years when Heraclius celebrated his triumph in Jerusalem, Muhammad triumphantly entered Mecca. Just a few years after the Prophet's death, a great Arab migration began.[iii] They abandoned their barren territory and advanced unstoppably, subjugating neighboring peoples. Their initial goal was not the spread of Islam but rather the conquest of new lands.

---

[i] Howard-Johnston, *East Rome, Sasanian Persia and the End of Antiquity*.
[ii] Diehl, *History of the Byzantine Empire*.
[iii] Kennedy, *The Great Arab Conquests*.

The Rise of the Arabs

The centuries-long struggle between Byzantium and Persia weakened both empires, thus facilitating the rise of a new religious and state entity: the Rashidun Caliphate.[i] The Rashidun ("rightly guided") Caliphate was the first Islamic state established after the death of the Prophet Muhammad. His four immediate successors and close companions—Abu Bakr, Umar, Uthman, and Ali—held the title of caliph and significantly expanded the Islamic state through military conquests and administrative reforms. It lasted from Muhammad's death in 632 to 661, when it was succeeded by the Umayyad Caliphate.

The first major victim of their onslaught was the defeated Sasanian Empire, which was engulfed in chaos. A civil war broke out among the sons of Khosrow II after the defeat in the Battle of Nineveh and the Byzantine conquest of the capital. The eldest son, Sheroe (Kavad II), led a conspiracy that resulted in the death of his father and half-brother, and then he crowned himself as Kavad II. The situation in the Persian realm allowed the renowned Arab commander Khalid ibn al-Walid to, upon the order of Caliph Abu Bakr (r. 632-634), launch the first incursion into Sasanian territories in 633. He captured a large part of Mesopotamia and subjugated the Lakhmid Kingdom.[ii]

In the years following the initial Arab incursions, the Muslim armies were engaged on multiple fronts, including their ongoing conflict with the Byzantine Empire. In a decisive campaign, General Sa'd ibn Abī Waqqāṣ led a victorious army at the Battle of al-Qādisiyyah in 636, which resulted in the permanent Arab conquest of Mesopotamia and the collapse of Sasanian control over the region. The new frontier was eventually established along the Zagros Mountains, marking the loss of the western territories of the Sasanian Empire.[iii]

The conquest of Persia continued under Caliph Umar (r. 634-644) when a great victory was won at the Battle of Nahavand in 642, resulting in the subjugation of the entire territory of the great Sasanian Empire in the following years.[iv] The last king from the Sasanian dynasty, Yazdegerd III, was killed in 651, and his relatives found refuge in China. Under

---

[i] Howard-Johnston, *East Rome, Sasanian Persia and the End of Antiquity*.
[ii] Nicolle, *The Great Islamic Conquests, AD 632-750*.
[iii] Kennedy, *The Great Arab Conquests*.
[iv] Nicolle, *The Great Islamic Conquests, AD 632-750*.

Caliph Uthman (r. 644-656), the caliphate had expanded in the east to the border with India in less than twenty years.[i]

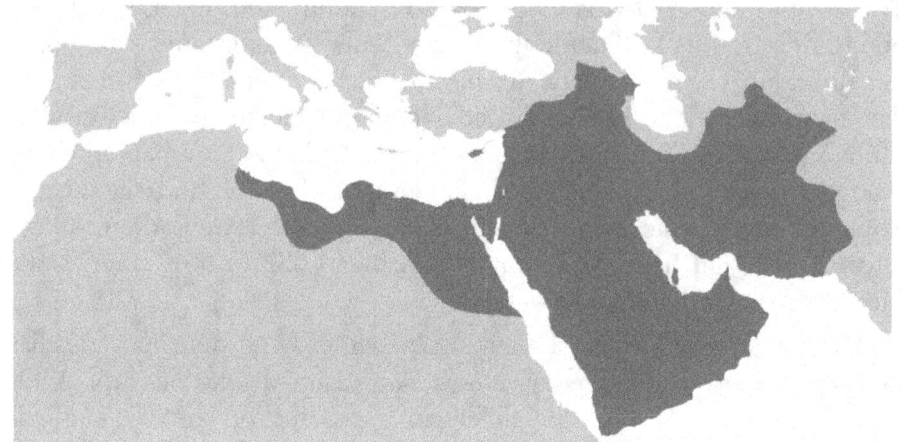

The Rashidun Caliphate in the mid-7th century CE.[108]

Unlike Persia, the victorious Byzantine army was exhausted by the long and arduous war that was being fought on multiple fronts. Within the empire, religious tensions were prevalent along the stretch from Constantinople to the eastern provinces. These tensions fueled aspirations among the Coptic and Syrian populations, which undermined the defensive ability of these regions.

Two years after Muhammad's death in 634, the Arabs invaded the Byzantine Empire under the leadership of Caliph Umar (r. 634-644) and rapidly advanced through the territories of the Ghassanids (modern-day Syria, roughly speaking) and the recently reclaimed provinces from the Persians. The battle that would herald the further expansion of the Arab army and the complete collapse of Byzantine defenses took place at the Yarmouk River on August 20th, 636.[ii, iii] The Byzantines lost this fateful battle, enabling the Arabs to conquer all of Antioch without resistance, as well as all the cities in Syria. The only significant resistance encountered by the victorious conquerors was in Palestine. While Jerusalem managed to withstand the siege, the persistent Caliph Umar compelled its inhabitants to surrender the city in 638.

---

[i] Howard-Johnston, *East Rome, Sasanian Persia and the End of Antiquity*.
[ii] Ostrogorsky, *History of the Byzantine State*;
[iii] Howard-Johnston, *East Rome, Sasanian Persia and the End of Antiquity*; Hoyland, *In God's Path*.

After the conquest of Syria, the Arab army continued its advance into Persia and occupied the Byzantine part of Mesopotamia in 639.[i] By the following year, 640, the strongest fortress in Armenia, Dvin, surrendered. Thus, all Byzantine territories east of the Mediterranean fell under Muslim control in less than ten years. The fate of Egypt remained uncertain.

While Emperor Heraclius (r. 610–641) personally led the empire's successful campaign against the Sasanian Persians, his involvement in the struggle against the emerging Arab Muslim forces was far less direct. Initially, he attempted to oversee military operations from Antioch, but after the catastrophic defeat at Yarmouk, he lost all hope. Before his eyes, his life's accomplishments had fallen away, and as it turned out, his heroic victory against Persia was futile. All the Byzantine Christian lands he had liberated from the Persians were lost with the advent of the new religion, against which no one had the strength to resist.[ii] This physically and mentally broke the old emperor to the extent that he could no longer endure sea voyages.

In addition to the defeat at Yarmouk, matters became even more tragic in Constantinople. Political struggles over the issue of succession began with the ailing Emperor Heraclius, who died on February 11th, 641, from illness. After Heraclius died, unrest engulfed the empire, which divided itself in support of his sons. In his will, Emperor Heraclius designated his sons Constantine III and Heraclonas to rule jointly as co-emperors, with Martina—Heraclonas's mother—acting in a supervisory role. His eldest son from his first marriage, Constantine III, briefly ruled but died of tuberculosis.[iii] His death was exploited by Heraclius's younger son from his second marriage, Heraclonas, who, along with his mother Martina, seized the crown. Martina supported Monothelite teachings and restored the exiled Pyrrhus to the position of patriarch (the religious leader of the Byzantine Church), who, in turn, appointed the zealous Monothelite Cyrus as bishop of Alexandria. This caused significant religious unrest in Constantinople and great opposition against the emperor and his mother.[iv]

---

[i] Kennedy, *The Great Arab Conquests*.
[ii] Hoyland, *In God's Path*.
[iii] Ostrogorsky, *History of the Byzantine State*.
[iv] Ibid.

The Threat Rises

The new government in Constantinople considered further resistance against the Arab invasion futile and ordered Bishop Cyrus to negotiate with the Muslims in Alexandria. Cyrus concluded a peace treaty in which virtually all of Egypt was surrendered to the conquerors. Dissatisfaction with these decisions spilled over to the troops in Asia Minor, which supported the population of Constantinople and deposed the hated Heraclonas, Martina, and Pyrrhus from power.

After the old ruler's exile to Rhodes, the Senate chose the ten-year-old son of Constantine III, Constans II (r. 641–668), as the new emperor.[i] The new emperor, under the tutelage of the strengthened Senate, had to fulfill the signed agreement to surrender Alexandria to Patriarch Cyrus and the Arabs. Byzantine troops left Alexandria on September 12th, 642, embarking for Rhodes. The Arab commander Amr ibn Kulthum entered the city and extended his authority along the North African coast to Tripoli.[ii] The new caliph, Uthman (r. 644–656), recalled Amr ibn Kulthum with his army from Alexandria due to obligations in the east, which emboldened the Byzantines to launch an offensive. A strong fleet from Constantinople, under the command of Manuel, disembarked in Alexandria and captured the city by surprise. However, this victory was short-lived, as Amr ibn Kulthum besieged and recaptured Alexandria in 646. Manuel left Egypt with his garrison, while the Coptic population, along with their Monothelite patriarch, submitted to the Arabs. This act marked Byzantium's permanent loss of its richest and economically strongest province.

From Egypt, the Arab forces continued their advance westward toward the Exarchate of Carthage, where Exarch Gregory the Patrician had proclaimed himself emperor in defiance of Constantinople.[iii] The usurper Gregory was supported by the local Monophysite population and Moorish tribes. Exploiting the revolt, the Arabs sacked the usurper's residence in Sufetula in 647 and killed Gregory, after which they received a large tribute from the legitimate authorities to withdraw to Egypt.

The territories of the Byzantine Empire in the remaining part of Armenia, as well as Anatolia itself, were threatened by the governor of

---

[i] Bury, *A History of the Later Roman Empire*.
[ii] Kennedy, *The Great Arab Conquests*.
[iii] Hoyland, *In God's Path*.

Syria, the capable military leader Muawiyah. In 642 and 643, Muawiyah launched a major incursion into Armenia, besieging fortresses with the aim of cutting off Constantinople. Amassing large contingents of troops, in 647, he penetrated into Cappadocia, capturing Caesarea before advancing into Phrygia. While plundering the wealthy province, he failed to take the heavily fortified city of Amorium. However, his return to Damascus was crowned with rich spoils and numerous captives.

Muawiyah's military genius is evidenced by the fact that he was the first statesman to recognize that the struggle against Byzantium was impossible without a strong fleet.[i] The governorship of Syria and access to the Mediterranean enabled Muawiyah to redirect resources that had been acquired through conquests into building the first Arab fleet. However, he did not have the support of Caliph Umar in this endeavor. Circumstances changed after Umar's death when Caliph Uthman assumed power and lent support to Muawiyah's plan.[ii]

Muawiyah.[109]

Personally leading the first Islamic fleet he created, Muawiyah attacked Cyprus in 649 and captured the capital, Salamis (Constantia). After signing a three-year truce with Byzantium, Muawiyah used the respite to build an even larger and better fleet. In 654, the Arabs devastated Rhodes, carrying off the famous Colossus of Rhodes to their territory. Crete and several Cycladic and Sporadic islands were also ravaged. Following these attacks, Kos, Rhodes, and Cyprus remained in Arab possession. There is no doubt that Muawiyah's primary goal was

---

[i] Nicolle, *The Great Islamic Conquests, AD 632-750*.
[ii] Hoyland, *In God's Path*.

Constantinople even then. This was clear to the emperor and those around him, prompting them to assemble a strong fleet near the Anatolian coast to confront Muawiyah. Emperor Constans II (r. 641-668) personally led the fleet in the naval battle of 655, which also happened to be the first Arab-Byzantine battle. It ended in catastrophe for the Byzantines, with the emperor narrowly escaping death.

Further major offensives against Byzantium were averted by the civil war in the Rashidun Caliphate, which followed the assassination of Caliph Uthman in 656. The First Fitna, a prolonged civil war between the two proclaimed caliphs, Ali and Muawiyah, lasted until 661 and provided temporary relief for Byzantium.[i]

In the last five years of his life, Emperor Constans II spent his time in Italy and Sicily, relinquishing his involvement in Eastern politics due to the seemingly hopeless situation. He was assassinated in 668 in Syracuse in a palace conspiracy led by close associates of the court. The usurpers proclaimed one of their own, Mezezius, as the new emperor, but he was killed by the army of the Ravenna Exarchate, which quelled the uprising in 669.[ii] Upon the emperor's assassination, his young son, Constantine IV (r. 668-685), ascended to the throne, injecting new energy into the Byzantine-Arab conflicts.

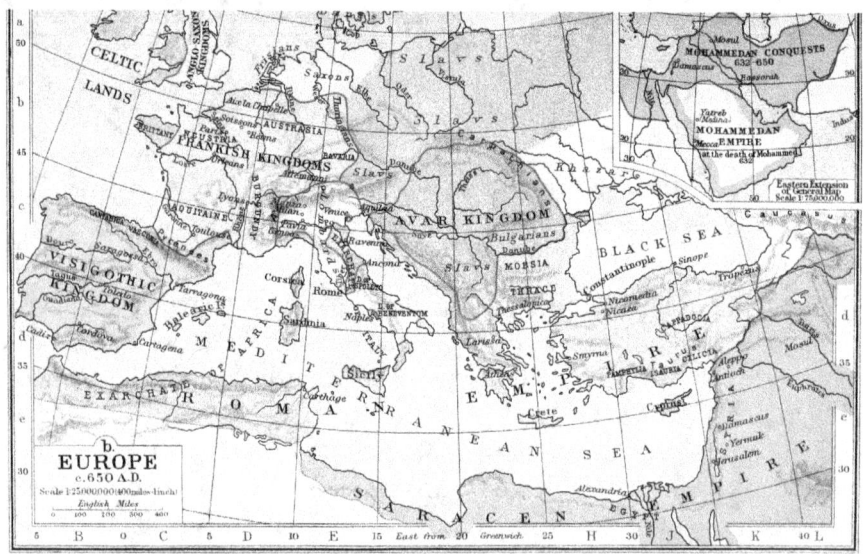

Europe in the mid-7th century.[110]

---

[i] Nicolle, *The Great Islamic Conquests, AD 632-750*.
[ii] Ostrogorsky, *History of the Byzantine State*.

The Umayyad Caliphate

Muawiyah I (r. 661-680) achieved victory in the First Fitna after a five-year struggle. He founded the Umayyad Caliphate and transferred the state's center to Damascus. By winning the civil war, Muawiyah introduced the rule that succession to the throne was heredity rather than by election, as was the case in the Rashidun Caliphate.

After pacifying the situation in the caliphate in 663, the Arabs renewed their struggle against Byzantium. Their raids became more frequent, and each year was marked by Arab devastation for the next fifteen years.[i] Their incursions reached as far as Chalcedon on the Bosphorus, where some units spent the winter and continued to ravage the once-rich Byzantine Anatolian provinces. The Arabs briefly occupied the island of Chios in 670, and one of Muawiyah's commanders managed to conquer the Peninsula of Cyzicus, located in the immediate vicinity of Constantinople.[ii] This created a solid base for an attack on Constantinople, which Muawiyah had long coveted.

Before the attack, his fleet secured complete control of the Lycian and Cilician coasts, as well as the conquest of Smyrna in 672, giving him complete control of the rear. In the spring of 674, the main action of the attack on Constantinople began. The city was initially besieged by sea with a large Arab fleet, which was supported by infantry advancing from Cyzicus. The battles lasted throughout the summer, with the Muslim fleet withdrawing to Cyzicus in the autumn. The next spring, the fleet reappeared and once again besieged Constantinople throughout the summer, a pattern that repeated in the following years. Constantinople, as the largest fortress of the time, could not be conquered, and due to their great losses, the Arabs were forced to abandon the naval siege in 678.[iii] The Arabs suffered heavy losses in battles under the walls of Constantinople because of the Byzantine use of Greek fire, which was first mentioned in contemporary sources during this siege.

Greek fire was an invention of the architect Callinicus from Syria. It was an explosive material composed of saltpeter, the ingredients of which were known exclusively to the Byzantines. Using siphons mounted on ships, Greek fire was thrown onto enemy vessels, causing intense fires. It

---

[i] Nicolle, *The Great Islamic Conquests, AD 632-750.*
[ii] Ibid
[iii] Kennedy, *The Great Arab Conquests.*

was first used in the Arab siege of Constantinople (674-678) and, from then on, frequently served in offensive and defensive actions, ensuring the Byzantines' technological superiority over surrounding enemies.

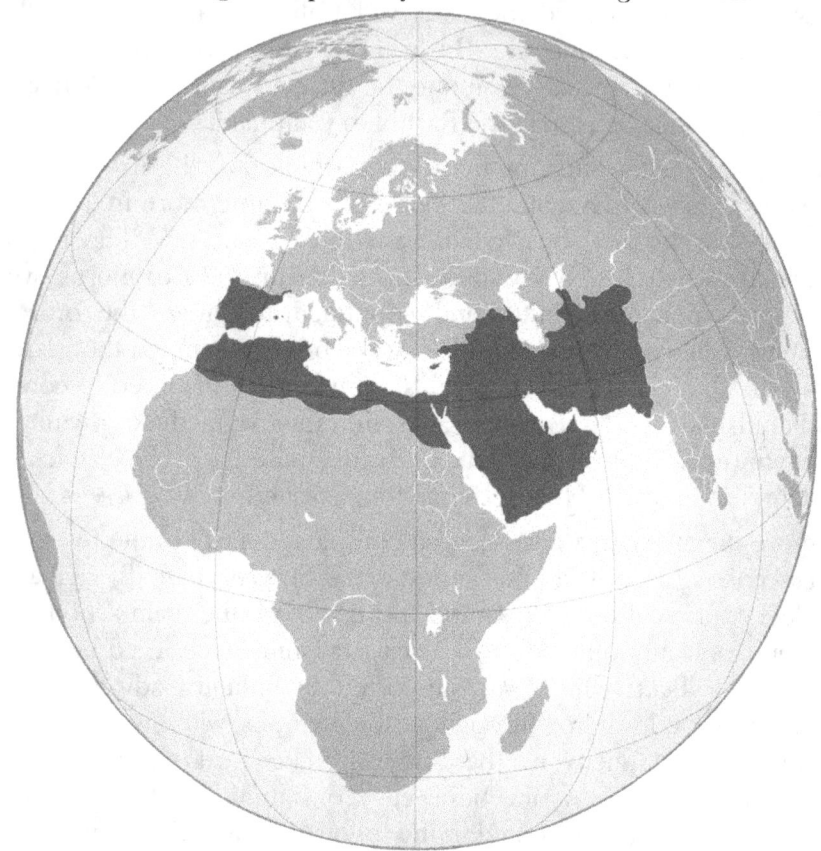

The Umayyad Caliphate at the height of its power in the early 8th century CE.[iii]

Muawiyah's fleet suffered losses in a storm that struck near the Pamphylian coast (a region in the south of Asia Minor), and simultaneously, the Arab army was defeated in Asia Minor.[i] All of this forced Caliph Muawiyah I to negotiate a peace treaty with Byzantium for thirty years with an annual payment of tribute. As the historian Theophanes notes in his work, "And great peace reigned in the East and in the West." The unsuccessful long siege of Constantinople resonated far beyond the Byzantine Empire's borders and restored the shaken position of the empire.[ii]

---

[i] Nicolle, *The Great Islamic Conquests, AD 632-750.*
[ii] Ostrogorsky, *History of the Byzantine State.*

The Succession of Constans II

Emperor Constans II was assassinated in 668 while bathing, likely as part of a conspiracy aimed at installing Mezezius, a Byzantine-Armenian general, as emperor. His son, Constantine IV, suppressed the usurpation and assumed the throne. Constantine IV successfully resisted the Arab siege of Constantinople (674-678) and became one of the first emperors to confront the rising Bulgarian threat in the Balkans. Despite setbacks in the Danube region, his reign had a lasting impact on Byzantine internal stability and foreign policy. He died around the age of thirty-three in 685 and was succeeded by his sixteen-year-old son, Justinian II (r. 685-695, 705-711), a capable but autocratic ruler. Thanks to his father's victory over the Arabs, Justinian enjoyed peace in the East during the early part of his reign.

After the death of Muawiyah I, the caliphate fell into an internal crisis until the next caliph, Abd al-Malik (r. 685-711), consolidated power and signed a new treaty with Byzantium. This treaty was more favorable than the previous one, as it brought the emperor a larger annual tribute along with the division of revenues from Armenia, Iberia, and Cyprus.[i]

Encouraged by his successes against the Slavs in the Balkans, Justinian II continued the policy of resettlement throughout the empire. He resettled a large part of the population of Cyprus to the devastated Cyzicus, refusing to inform the caliphate about it. Disregarding the caliph's protests, Justinian II reignited hostilities with Muslim forces around 691. In 692, at the Battle of Sebastopolis, he suffered a major defeat, partly due to the defection of Slavic troops that switched sides at a critical moment. As a result of this loss, Justinian was forced to sign a treaty that ceded tax revenues and influence in Armenia and Iberia to the Umayyads.

New problems for Byzantium were caused by a revolt against Justinian II in 695, which the Arabs knew how to exploit. The turmoil that followed paralyzed defensive operations in distant parts of the empire for the next twenty years. The Arabs broke through in 697 and captured Carthage, prompting Emperor Leontius (r. 695-698) to send a fleet to restore the Exarchate of Carthage. The fleet managed to regain the city briefly, but by the following spring, the Arab fleet had forced the Byzantines to permanently abandon their North African territories.

---

[i] Hoyland, *In God's Path*.

The new emperor, Tiberius III (r. 698-705), did not even attempt to restore the Exarchate of Carthage, so no one slowed down Arab advances until Ceuta, where the last Byzantine garrison was located.[i] With the fall of Ceuta in 711, the caliphate seized control of the entire coast of North Africa and reached the Atlantic Ocean. This would be the starting point for the fateful crossing of Arab commander Tariq ibn Ziyad into Europe in 711.[ii] He took a detour through Africa since the strong walls of Constantinople prevented a direct route from the east.

From the eastern front, the Arabs continued to exploit the unrest in the Byzantine Empire, and in 709, they besieged the fortress of Tyana, where they dealt a heavy blow to the Byzantines. This defeat again broke the Byzantine defense system and led to Arab raids in Cilicia in 710 and 711. Emperor Anastasius II (r. 713-715) attempted to counterattack to suppress the attacks, but it failed due to internal crises. Once again, the fate of Byzantium was decided under the walls of Constantinople. In August 717, Constantinople was besieged for the second time by both land and sea, just like forty years prior. This time, the Byzantines managed to destroy the enemy fleet with Greek fire while the walls withstood the Arab assaults. Furthermore, the winter of 717-18 was unusually cold, causing famine, epidemics, and deaths among the Muslim forces. The decisive contribution to a victory was made by twenty thousand Bulgarian cavalry troops led by Khan Tervel, an old ally of Emperor Justinian II, who inflicted heavy losses on the Arabs. Due to significant losses, on August 15th, 718, the Arab ships left the waters of Constantinople, thus ending another siege of Constantinople.[iii]

After another unsuccessful attempt to conquer Constantinople, the Arabs consolidated their troops and again threatened Asia Minor in 726 by capturing Caesarea and besieging Nicaea. The end of Byzantine troubles in regards to their territory would be resolved by Emperor Leo III the Isaurian (r. 717-741) with a great victory at Akroinon in 740 and his alliance with the Khazars to reduce the major incursions of the Arabs.[iv]

With the liberation of Constantinople and Asia Minor from the Arabs, an important stage in the Byzantine-Arab struggle came to an end. Constantinople would no longer experience any siege by the Arabs in the

---

[i] Ostrogorsky, *History of the Byzantine State*.
[ii] Nicolle, *The Great Islamic Conquests, AD 632-750*.
[iii] Ibid.
[iv] Diehl, *History of the Byzantine Empire*.

future, ensuring the survival of the Byzantine Empire. Just as in 678, when Constantine IV halted the Arab invasion for the first time with the defense of Constantinople, Leo III's victory in 718, like the success of Charles Martel at Poitiers in 732, determined the fate of Europe. Constantinople was the last barrier standing in the way of a Muslim invasion, and the city's survival was not only a salvation for the Byzantine Empire but also for European culture and civilization.

Chapter 7: Iconoclasm

Introduction

The Byzantine Empire at the end of the 7th century was shaken by military, internal, religious, and even natural crises. The combination of these dangers and geopolitical realities required a different climate in the Eastern Roman Empire. It was trying to find an outlook that would make peace in the state, security in the region, and renew the relationship with the divine. Iconoclasm was the manifestation of the latter, but it was caused by all of the mentioned factors.[i]

The 7th century was particularly hard, and Byzantium saw a decrease in its geopolitical significance. In 602, the Eastern Roman Empire fought for the domination of the Middle East with the Persian Sasanian Empire. The Sasanian army won Armenia, Syria, Palestine, and Egypt. A few years later, the Sasanian army was camping outside of Constantinople.[ii]

In the end, this political crisis was successfully managed by the Byzantine Empire, but the most significant effect of these wars was the neglect of the events unfolding in the Arabian Peninsula by both empires. At this time, Muhammad was going from Mecca to Medina, spreading the seed of a new religion. Just a decade later, the followers of the new religion would control the whole Arabian Peninsula, forming the Rashidun Caliphate, which started after the death of Prophet Muhammad in 632 and ended with the internal conflict of 661.

---

[i] Brubaker and Haldon, *Byzantium in the Iconoclast Era (ca. 680-850)*.
[ii] Howard-Johnston, *East Rome, Sasanian Persia and the End of Antiquity*.

During this period, the Arabs saw the conquest of both Byzantine and Persian territory. The Byzantines lost all the territory they regained from the Sasanians, including Egypt, Palestine, and the Caucasus, thus losing undisputed control of the Mediterranean. The Persian Empire had suffered dire consequences and was consumed by the Arab conquest.[i]

The 7th century saw the demise of the Heraclian dynasty, which ended with internal instability. The Twenty Years' Anarchy is a term used for the period of internal instability in the Byzantine Empire. This period saw the rapid succession of several emperors to the throne between the first deposition of Justinian II in 695 and the ascent of Leo III the Isaurian to the throne in 717, marking the beginning of the Isaurian dynasty.[ii]

The Byzantine Empire in the early 8th century.[iii]

Leo III (r. 717-741) successfully ended the period of military coups and instability, but the state he inherited was much weaker than it had been a century earlier. The hegemony of the Mediterranean ended, with the Levant and North Africa being under Arab control, the Balkans being attacked by the Bulgars, and lost influence over Italy and the papacy to the growing power of the Franks. His rule also marked the beginning of the First Iconoclasm, which occurred between 726 and 787.

Iconoclasm is the deliberate destruction of a culture's religious images and other symbols or monuments, usually for religious or political motives (from Greek εἰκών or *eikón*, "figure" or "icon" and κλάω or *kláō*, "to break"). Conversely, people who revere or venerate religious

---

[i] Nicolle, *The Great Islamic Conquests, AD 632-750*.
[ii] Bury, *A History of the Later Roman Empire*.

images are derisively called "iconolaters" (εἰκονολάτρες).[i] They are normally known as "iconodules" (εἰκονόδουλοι) or "iconophiles" (εἰκονόφιλοι). These terms were, however, not a part of the Byzantine debate over images; rather, they have been brought into common usage by modern historians. The Byzantine term for the debate over religious imagery was iconomachy, meaning "struggle over images." The breaking of the icons was an attempt to stop the already established practice of depicting Jesus, Mary, and the saints through canonized imagery. So, if that tradition already existed, what caused the controversy and change of heart?

First of all, the Arab conquests didn't only change the eastern borders of the Byzantine Empire; they also brought some old ideas about the depiction of God. Judaism, as the first Abrahamic religion, had a strict understanding of God as the impersonal and omnipotent. God was a universal force beyond human comprehension. As such, depictions of God were strictly forbidden, and any attempt at a physical representation of God was seen as blasphemous and idol worship. We can find that directly in the Old Testament in Exodus 20:4: "You shall not make for yourself a carved image, or any likeness of anything that is in heaven above, or that is in the earth beneath, or that is in the water under the earth," thus forbidding any depiction of God.

However, with Christ understood as God in the flesh, with his human and divine nature coexisting, the Christians argued that God intentionally came closer to humanity by becoming flesh. This is confirmed in the New Testament in Colossians 1:15: "The Son is the image of the invisible God, the firstborn over all creation." Thus, the veneration of icons was not understood as idol worship since they were a means of worship, not the object of worship.

Islam brought the idea of iconoclasm back into the spotlight. Muslims have a very strict policy on not depicting God in any shape or form. This is extended to prophets, such as Muhammad and Jesus, who are understood to be prophets in Islam. With the expansion of Islam, this view was reintroduced to the Byzantines.[ii]

What is important to understand is that theological dilemmas were taken very seriously in this period. Religion had roles that are today being

---

[i] Kolrud and Prusac, *Iconoclasm from Antiquity to Modernity*.
[ii] Ibid.

done by science, art, and politics. In other words, Christianity explained that "God's will" manifested in military and political successes. In other words, military losses and political crises were observed as a way of God correcting the path of an empire.

With the loss of territory and power in the region, the Byzantines observed the rise of Islam. The Eastern Roman Empire was also stricken by the volcanic eruption of Santorini, which was paired with external and internal political crises. These were all seen as a sign from God that something was wrong with Christian devotion.

The First Iconoclast Era

Another reason that might explain the introduction of iconoclasm by Leo III is his Syrian roots. The Byzantine Empire had two roots: Western, which was more Roman or Greek, and Eastern, which was associated more with the Levant and closer to ideas of Islam. Leo was the first ruler of the first non-Greek or Roman dynasty, which might have affected him to search for spiritual rebranding in Eastern traditions.

An icon of Mary, the mother of Jesus, 6ᵗʰ century.[118]

Leo's stance against religious images became evident when he ordered the removal of a particularly revered icon of Christ from the imperial palace in 725.[i] This symbolic act marked the beginning of a movement that would soon engulf the empire. The situation further culminated in the official ban on icons, which happened in 730.

Leo's iconoclastic policies drew condemnation from Pope Gregory II in Rome, sparking a rift between the Eastern and Western branches of Christianity. The pope vehemently opposed Leo's ban on icons, which culminated in the pope's declaration of iconoclasm as heretical that same year, further exacerbating tensions between the Byzantine Empire and the papacy.

The iconoclastic fervor continued after Leo's death under Constantine V (r. 741-775, who enforced his father's policies with even greater zeal).[ii] The biggest difference is that Constantine persecuted the people who didn't follow the iconoclastic policies with an extensive purge of the military and bureaucracy of icon worshipers. His father, on the contrary, only destroyed the icons.

The reign of Constantine V also witnessed the rise of the iconophile movement, which was led by those who vehemently opposed the destruction of religious images. This culminated in the revolt of iconophiles in 750, which challenged the authority of the emperor and iconoclastic ideology.

The last years of Constantine's reign were also unsuccessful politically. In 751, the Byzantines lost the northern Italian territories for good. The Exarchate of Ravenna was lost to the Lombards, which caused the pope to turn away from the Byzantine Empire even more. Not only were Eastern Roman heretics ignoring the supposedly higher status of the pope, but they were also proving less and less useful as potential allies. They couldn't guarantee the safety of the pope, but the Franks could. The Franks also recognized the pope's superior authority in church matters. This territorial decline further weakened the empire's position on the international stage and strained its relations with neighboring powers.

Constantine V was succeeded by his young son Leo IV, who took full rule in 775.[iii] He died only five years later, in 780. His

---

[i] Besançon, *The Forbidden Image*.
[ii] Ostrogorsky, *History of the Byzantine State*.
[iii] Ibid.

politics were not too influential on the matter of iconoclasm. He agreed with his father, but he did stop the oppression of iconophiles. What is important is that he left the throne to his wife since his son, Constantine VI, was only nine years old at the time. Leo's wife and *de facto* ruler and regent for her son Constantine VI was called Irene, also known as Irene of Athens, and she was the first iconophile ruler after the establishment of the Isaurian dynasty.[i] She wasn't just sympathetic to the icons; she made it her mission to abolish iconoclasm with vigor, intelligence, and ruthlessness.

That was an extremely difficult task, as previous emperors had eradicated support for icons not only from the church hierarchy but also from public life and the army. Irene's first step was to install someone she trusted as the patriarch of Constantinople. However, the church had been purged of iconophile sympathizers. She appointed her trusted secretary, Tarasios, to the position. Although a layman at the time, Irene used her influence at court to fast-track his ordination, allowing him to assume the patriarchate and assist in restoring the veneration of icons.

This raised tensions in the empire, but Irene didn't stop there. In 786, she attempted to condemn iconoclasm as an official heresy at a church council held at the Church of the Holy Apostles in Constantinople. However, iconoclast troops in the imperial army revolted, preventing the council from proceeding. To deal with this opposition, Irene acted strategically: she dispatched the iconoclast elements of the army on a military campaign to Asia Minor, only to inform them upon arrival that they were dismissed from service. With the opposition removed, she convened a new council the following year.

In 787, Irene organized the Seventh Ecumenical Council, also known as the Second Council of Nicaea, which officially condemned iconoclasm and reaffirmed the veneration of religious images within the Byzantine Empire. This council marked the end of the first iconoclast crisis.[ii]

There was also a chance for possibly mending the rift between East and West, not only by condemning iconoclasm and affirming the legitimacy of icon veneration but also with the proposal of marriage between King Charlemagne of the Franks and Irene of Athens. However, this didn't happen. Irene turned out to be the last ruler of the Isaurian

---

[i] Bury, *A History of the Later Roman Empire*.
[ii] Bury.

dynasty. In 797, she—or her supporters—had her son Constantine VI blinded and deposed seven years after he had assumed full imperial authority. Although Constantine became the sole emperor in 790, Irene never ceased to exert considerable influence over imperial policy. Eventually, her supporters conspired to remove him and consolidate her rule. The ruthless court politics and intrigues of Irene's regime made her deeply unpopular, leading to her overthrow in 802 by Nikephoros, her finance minister.[i]

The rule of Nikephoros tried to move from the iconophile versus iconoclast rift, leaving the official dogma as Irene had put it. At that moment, there were still iconoclast supporters but also iconophiles who wanted the persecution of the iconoclasts. However, this situation didn't last. Nikephoros was focused on tax revisions and the new military campaign in the Balkans against the Bulgars. He died in conquest against Krum the Bulgar in 811; his army was decimated after a previously successful campaign. The crown was inherited by his son-in-law, Michael I Rangabe (r. 811–813), who managed to flee from the battlefield back to Constantinople.[ii] His reign was short since he was quickly overthrown by the strategos Leo, who crowned himself as Leo V the Armenian (r. 813–820). The rule of Leo V also marked the second and last iconoclast era, which lasted from 814 to 842.[iii]

The Second Iconoclast Era

Under Leo V, iconoclasm was reinstated, reflecting the enduring popularity of the movement among certain segments of Byzantine society. The sentiment was similar to before the First Iconoclast crisis. The country was going through a difficult time, with the military failures of the Bulgars in the north and the Abbasid Caliphate in the south, which was going through its golden age.[iv] Yet again, this was interpreted as the consequence of icon worship by Emperor Leo V and his advisors, and they started policies to purify the church of icons and persecute iconophiles.

---

[i] Ostrogorsky, *History of the Byzantine State*.
[ii] Ibid.
[iii] Ibid.
[iv] Hoyland, *In God's Path*.

Depiction of Leo V.[114]

The policies of iconophile tolerance were briefly reinstated with Michael II the Amorion (also called the Stammerer), who overturned Leo V in 820. As a ruler, Michael II had a lot of crises to attend to. His conquest of the throne was organized by his followers since he was imprisoned and sentenced to execution by Leo V. In a last-ditch attempt, his followers killed Leo V in church on Christmas Eve in 820, thus starting Michael's reign, which lasted until 829. He had a turbulent and challenging rule with potential usurpers of the throne, such as Thomas the Slav, who represented himself as Constantine VI, the blinded son of Irene. This attempt led to a siege of Constantinople in 823, which was unsuccessful due to the arrival of the Bulgars from the west.

The last thing that Michael II wanted was more problems, so he tried to make peace between iconophiles and iconoclasts by forbidding the discussion of the issue. However, both iconophile zealots and iconoclasts tried to push their cause during this period. For example, iconophile zealots cooperated with the pope in pushing for the full return of icons and a complete ban on iconoclast heresy. As a consequence, the pope sent a convoy to appeal to Michael, but he didn't appreciate this attempt to meddle in his rule, so he imprisoned them for a while, thus dividing Byzantine and Rome even more.

The successor of Michael II was his son Theophilus (r. 829-842), the last iconoclast emperor.[i] The young emperor was a well-educated iconoclast, similar to Constantine V, who was a great admirer of Arab culture. Furthermore, he was a close friend of John the Grammarian, who was one of the most accomplished iconoclast scholars. Apart from being a friend and a mentor to Theophilus, he was also appointed patriarch in 837 by the blessing of the emperor.

This period witnessed the peak of the second iconoclast persecution, which saw emperors and royalists clashing with iconophile zealots. The death of Theophilus in 842 marked the end of the iconoclast persecution. Theophilus left a young son and a very capable iconophile wife in charge of the throne.

The mother of the young emperor Michael III and his regent was Theodora, who brought the end of iconoclasm to Byzantium.[ii] Her reign was a mixture of favorable geopolitical occurrences and well-executed political moves, especially when it came to defeating the iconoclasts. First, the military conquest of Sicily and southern Italy by the Aghlabid Emirate served as evidence that the military downfall of the Eastern Roman Empire was not because of the icons. Additionally, Theodora spread the rumor that Theophilus had repented for persecuting the iconophiles on his deathbed, which served as additional proof. All of these circumstances allowed her to align herself with the zealot party and replace John the Grammarian with an iconophile patriarch, which ended the iconoclast episode. Her politics were further enforced by her son Michael III, which cemented the future of iconoclasm as a fringe movement out of the spotlight of Byzantine politics.[iii]

---

[i] Ostrogorsky, *History of the Byzantine State*.
[ii] Besançon, *The Forbidden Image*.
[iii] Ibid.

The Consequences of Iconoclasm

The iconoclastic controversy was interpreted by scholars as the Byzantine Empire choosing between Western and Eastern traditions. Though this is a very sound explanation, the iconoclastic movement also represents the adjustment to the new geopolitical reality that saw the fall of some important empires, such as Persia, and the rise of new ones, such as the Muslim caliphates. Even though it was a sort of adjustment phase, it also provoked a serious chain of events. For example, it strained the relationship between the Eastern and Western branches of the Christian Church, particularly between the pope and the Byzantine Empire. The divergent views on the use of religious images deepened the schism between the two churches, leaving a lasting impact on the religious landscape of Europe.[i]

In conclusion, the Byzantine iconoclasm era was a complex and tumultuous period in the history of the Byzantine Empire and was characterized by religious fervor, political intrigue, and cultural upheaval. Spanning over a century, this conflict left a profound impact on Byzantine society and its relationship with the wider Christian world. Despite its eventual resolution, the legacy of the iconoclastic controversy continued to resonate throughout the Byzantine Empire and beyond, shaping the course of religious and political developments for centuries to come.

---

[i] Ibid.

Section Three: Byzantium's Heyday (867–1025 CE)

Chapter 8: Christianization of the Slavs

By the 9th century, South Slavs fostered their strongholds in the Balkans and started forming their first states. For centuries, Slavs contributed to the general chaotic state of affairs in the Balkans. We have mentioned previously that Slavs, together with the Avars and Sasanians, attempted to invade Constantinople in the 7th century without success.

The Slavs were a nuisance to the Byzantine Empire, settling in areas that the Byzantines considered their own, engaging in skirmishes, heists, looting, and pillaging. However, South Slavs were there to stay, and they became stronger and stronger. With South Slavic states forming in the Balkans and the Russian state forming in the north, it became clear to the Byzantine emperors that Slavs needed to be placated and pacified somehow. Moreover, if the Byzantines were too slow to exert their cultural influence upon the Slavic peoples, western Europe would most certainly do so, undermining Byzantine influence right at the empire's doorstep. As we will soon see, there was a lot of friction and tension between Western and Eastern Christian missionaries in the Balkans and eastern Europe.

Instead of conquering the Slavs with a sword, the Byzantines conquered Slavs by exerting their culture, most importantly Christianity. For centuries, missionaries from the Byzantine Empire strolled through the Balkans (and farther), bringing enlightenment, literacy, and the monotheistic religion to the Slavs.

The Bulgars, who were among the first to form stable states in the Balkan Peninsula, were also one of the ethnic groups that were influenced the most by the Byzantine Empire. The Bulgars were finally Christianized in the 9th century under their ruler Khan Boris I. After exploring potential ties with western Europe, particularly with King Louis the German, Boris ultimately turned toward Eastern Christianity. Following a military defeat by the Byzantine Empire and ongoing diplomatic pressure, Boris accepted baptism in 864, marking the formal conversion to Christianity.[i] Mass conversion of the Bulgar population began in 865.

The subsequent events are indicative of what typically happens when a country decides to suddenly enforce a completely new religion. Boris faced dissent and bitterness on all fronts. His feudal nobles (boyars) revolted, with the rebellion only subsiding after a number of boyars were executed. Pagan temples were destroyed all around Bulgaria, and the country was flooded by Byzantine preachers. Interestingly, missionaries from other places started to arrive, such as Arab Muslims, contributing to the religious chaos that reigned in the country.[ii]

To make matters even more complicated, Boris started questioning his decision to accept Eastern Christianity. Byzantine Emperor Michael III bluntly refused Boris's demands for the Bulgarian Church's independence, which prompted Boris to turn once again toward the West. Although the talks with Rome turned out to be unsuccessful, the Byzantine Empire, alarmed at the prospect of losing cultural influence over Bulgaria, decided to grant relative religious autonomy to Bulgaria. In 870, the Bulgarian Church obtained the status of archbishopric under the jurisdiction of the Patriarchate of Constantinople.[iii] This was followed by a period of relative religious stability, which saw Bulgaria become a center of Eastern Christianity, helping spread Byzantine cultural influence throughout the Balkans. Bulgaria became a foothold of missionaries, which included Clement, Nahum, and Angelarius, who were disciples of Cyril and Methodius, two important Byzantine missionaries of the period.

There is evidence pointing to a possible early Christianization of Serbs in the Balkan Peninsula, way back in the 7th century.[iv] These efforts were

---

[i] DIMITROV, Ivan Zhelev. Bulgarian Christianity. The Blackwell Companion to Eastern Christianity, 2007, 47.
[ii] Ibid.
[iii] Ibid.
[iv] Ilić, Nikola. *Da li je srpski knez Višeslav bio Hrišćanin?* Teološki Pogledi, 55(1), 95-112

made during Emperor Heraclius's reign, with Roman missionaries arriving in the Balkan Peninsula to Christianize Serbs. However, it seems that these initial efforts, in the case of the Serbs, were not successful or at least not as successful as the later efforts of Emperor Basil I in the 9th century, which saw a large part of the Serbian population adopt Eastern Christianity.

We know quite a bit about both of these Christianization attempts thanks to a later emperor, Constantine VII Porphyrogenitus (r. 913-959), and his manuscript Πρὸς τὸν ἴδιον υἱὸν αὐτοῦ Ῥωμανὸν ("To my son Romanos"), widely known as *On the Governance of the Empire*. The manuscript was essentially a how-to-guide made by Constantine VII for his son Romanos and included a lot of information on ethnic groups deemed important for the politics of the Byzantine Empire.

Constantine VII writes that during the reign of Emperor Basil I (r. 867-886), Croatian and Serbian emissaries came to Constantinople to ask the emperor to dispatch missionaries, who would complete the previous Christianization attempts of the 7th century.[i]

Preaching in the Language of the Slavs

A major game changer in the Christianization of the Slavs was the strategy taken by Byzantine missionaries. Cyril and Methodius, venerated as saints by all major Christian churches, are today known as the "apostles" of the Slavs.[ii] Cyril (826-869) and Methodius (815-885) were brothers from Greece, spending their early years in Thessalonica, a major city in modern-day northern Greece, northwest of the Chalcidice Peninsula. By that time, the Slavs had already reached deep into the Byzantine Empire, so Cyril and Methodius were able to get acquainted with the language and culture of Slav immigrants fairly early on.

---

[i] Ibid.
[ii] Radic, Radmila. Serbian Christianity. The Blackwell Companion to Eastern Christianity, 2007, 231-248.

Saint Cyril and Methodius.[116]

The father of Cyril and Methodius was a high-ranking military official, and thanks to his influence, the brothers received the best education possible. They weren't simply theologians; they were also intellectuals and able to converse in a number of different languages. This would prove crucial in their efforts to spread the Christian faith among Slavs.

Cyril and Methodius were appointed by Patriarch Photius around 860 as Byzantine missionaries to the Khazars and Slavs. The most significant turning point came with an appeal from Great Moravia (modern-day Czechia and Slovakia) and Prince Rastislav, who, similar to the Bulgarian ruler Boris, vacillated between the East and West and was looking to get the best deal possible. Rastislav was territorially and militarily more under the influence of the West, but he sought to get better terms of cooperation by bringing Eastern preachers into his territory. Perhaps Rastislav wanted to tell the Western rulers that they should offer him better terms or else he would side with the Byzantine Empire.

Whatever the scenario, Cyril and Methodius started developing a new script, the Glagolitic script, in order to transcribe Old Church Slavonic, which is the first standardized literary language of the Slavs. The language was probably in development for some time before Cyril and Methodius standardized it and developed the Glagolitic script to accompany it.

Cyril and Methodius then translated the Bible using Old Church Slavonic and their Glagolitic script. They also developed the Slavic liturgy. Cyril and Methodius were fairly successful in spreading their newly developed script in Great Moravia, but this wasn't always received positively. Cyril and Methodius would encounter missionaries coming from the West, much to the latter's dissatisfaction. Moreover, as they were preaching in Great Moravia, the so-called Photian Schism was reaching its peak.

Patriarch Photius baptizing Bulgarians.[116]

Patriarch Photius, the one who sent Cyril and Methodius on their mission in the first place, ascended to his post in a somewhat dubious fashion. He replaced Patriarch Ignatius, who was probably deposed due to his hostility toward Bardas, a high-ranking noble who managed to become the de facto regent of the young Emperor Michael III after deposing his mother, Theodora. This sort of scenario wasn't really that unusual in Byzantium or Rome. Photius came from an influential family, his uncle being a high-ranking theologian and patriarch in the early 9th century. Photius did not meet numerous prerequisites for becoming a patriarch, so he was quickly made into a monk, a deacon, and then a priest. Rome did not accept Photius and regarded him as an illegitimate patriarch. In 863, Pope Nicholas officially condemned Photius and sought to reinstate the old patriarch, Ignatius.

The situation was made even worse by the Bulgarian question that was unraveling at the time. As already mentioned, in the 860s, Bulgarian Khan Boris was deciding whether to accept Eastern or Western influence, finally settling for the East.

In the meantime, debates started to arise over the differences between Latin and Greek Christianity. This threatened to turn into a major schism, especially when Photius condemned Pope Nicholas for heresy, thereby excommunicating the whole Western Church in 867. However, that same year, Basil, the closest advisor to Emperor Michael III, assassinated the emperor. Although he had initially supported Photius, Basil later deposed him and reinstated Ignatius as patriarch, partly to improve relations with the papacy. The assassination marked the end of the Phrygian (Amorian) dynasty and the beginning of the Macedonian dynasty.

This put an end to the Photian Schism, and the two churches gradually rekindled their relationship, although the underlying factors of the schism were never completely removed.

Going back to our main topic, the Christianization of the Slavs, we can now better understand the general context in which Cyril and Methodius operated. They must have had a fairly stressful and challenging job, as they constantly came across other missionaries who ostensibly preached the same faith but served a different master. Cyril and Methodius, however, were fairly well respected in theologian circles and were positively received in Rome in 868. Pope Adrian, who became the next pope after Nicholas, a major antagonist in the Photian Schism, finally granted Cyril and Methodius freedom to continue to spread Christianity with the help of their new script and also accepted the Slavic liturgy. It's possible that Cyril and Methodius, in a way, functioned as a sort of positive mediator between the East and West, helping establish a positive image of the Byzantines among the Roman clergy.

Cyril died in 869, but Methodius continued to preach alone in the regions of Great Moravia and Pannonia. A testament to the still-existing fluidity between the East and West is the fact that Methodius was appointed as archbishop of Pannonia/Moravia by the pope and not by the Constantinople patriarch. He probably resided in Sirmium (modern-day Sremska Mitrovica in Serbia). However, he was quickly captured by Adalwin of Salzburg, Ermanrich of Passau, and Anno of Freising, who considered Methodius a threat to German interests in the region. Methodius was kept in Bavaria.[i]

Thanks to his reputation in Rome, Methodius was quickly released in 873 and got back to spreading the faith. Apparently, he was advised not to use the Slavic liturgy, but he largely ignored this advice. Due to this, animosities with the Western-influenced preachers in Pannonia and Moravia continued, with Methodius having to justify his decisions several more times to authorities in Rome. Methodius finally died in 885. Gorazd, Methodius's student, inherited his position, but he was deposed by the Western clergy. Followers of Cyril and Methodius in Pannonia and Moravia were forced to flee, and they found a new home in Bulgaria, which was much closer to the Byzantine sphere of influence.

After Cyril and Methodius

This event perhaps shaped the future development of Glagolitsa (the Glagolitic alphabet). In Bulgaria, the disciples of Cyril and Methodius—Clement of Ohrid, Naum of Preslav, and Constantine of Preslav—continued the work of their predecessors, spreading the Eastern version of Christianity, as well as their newly developed alphabet. They formed two schools: the Ohrid Literary School (Ohrid is in modern-day North Macedonia) and the Preslav Literary School. While the Ohrid School was more focused on Glagolitsa, the Preslav School was focused more on the standard Greek alphabet, which culminated in the development of the Cyrillic script. The Cyrillic script of the Preslav School still bore some marks of Glagolitsa but had obvious inclusions from the Greek alphabet.

---

[i] Imre, Boba. The Episcopacy of St. Methodius. Slavic Review, 1967, 26.1: 85-93.

This Cyrillic script completely replaced Glagolitsa and entered into use in numerous countries influenced by the Byzantine Empire. To this day, Serbs, Bulgarians, Macedonians, Montenegrins, and Russians use different variations of the Cyrillic script.

Chapter 9: The Bulgar Wars

Even though the Bulgarians accepted Eastern Christianity, heralded by the shrewd rule of Boris I, who was able to maintain control over a fairly large area in the Balkan Peninsula, encompassing modern-day Bulgaria, southern Romania, most of Serbia, North Macedonia, and Greece, the situation couldn't remain calm forever.

A Monk Versus a Wise Man

Boris I abdicated in 889, with his son, Vladimir, inheriting the throne. Vladimir wasn't really like his father; he had other plans for Bulgaria. First of all, it seems that Vladimir didn't care that much about the nascent Bulgarian Christianity and would rather go by the ancient Bulgarian pagan tradition. In fact, Vladimir possibly ordered the destruction of Christian temples and persecuted the clergy. Moreover, he wanted to turn away from the Byzantine Empire altogether and focus more on fostering an alliance with the Germans.[1]

In the meantime, Boris became a monk, hoping to live peacefully in a monastery. However, he had to reclaim the throne and topple his rebellious son Vladimir, who was blinded and removed from political life altogether in 893. Instead of Vladimir, Simeon, Boris's younger son and a monk, was brought to the throne.

---

[1] Leszka, Mirosław J. "The Monk versus the Philosopher: From the History of the Bulgarian-Byzantine War 894–896." *Studia Ceranea* 1 (2011): 55–70.

Therefore, it was up to Simeon, who had received extensive theological education and spent a lot of time in Constantinople, to lead Bulgaria. Simeon was more of an intellectual type and was surrounded by the disciples of Cyril and Methodius. Importantly, he wasn't initially destined for a political or military career; his father wanted Simeon to become the head of the Bulgarian Church. After ascending to the throne, Simeon is said to have remained very humble, steering away from the lush imperial life and choosing to live more like a monk, as he did before.

Emperor Leo VI the Philosopher, son of Emperor Basil, the founder of the Macedonian dynasty, ruled the Byzantine Empire. Much like Simeon, Leo VI was a true intellectual, a wise individual, and active in numerous areas, including theology, legislation, and the military. Also, like Simeon, Leo VI wasn't originally meant to become the emperor; it was only after his older brother Constantine died that Leo had to accept his unexpected promotion to the rank of emperor.

Bulgaria and the Byzantine Empire were led by two very wise gentlemen who weren't really that pretentious or hungry for fame and power. After all, neither of them had much hope of ascending to the throne as they were more steeped in the areas of education and theology.

So, what could go wrong in the relations of these two wise rulers? It is possible that the reasons for the war are purely economic. There's a story about Leo's closest advisor, Basileopator Stylianos Zaoutzes. Zaoutzes had an enslaved eunuch, Musikos, who was connected to Staurakios and Kosmas, two wealthy traders and speculators. They managed to gain approval for several questionable decisions, thanks to their connection with Musikos. First, they raised taxes on Bulgarian goods. Second, they relocated the Bulgarian market within the Byzantine Empire from Constantinople—closer to the source of those goods—to Thessalonica, a city that was both less profitable for Bulgarian merchants and situated along a more dangerous trade route.[i]

---

[i] Ibid.

Emperor Leo VI.[117]

When Simeon complained to Emperor Leo VI, he was rebuffed, the latter receiving reassurance from Stylianos Zaoutzes that everything was going great and that there were no reasons to succumb to the Bulgarian pressure.

Escalation

That's how the war started between Bulgaria and the Byzantine Empire. The war started in 894 and is known mainly as the Trade War in order to distinguish it from earlier and later conflicts between Bulgarians and Byzantines. Initial military actions were mainly confined to East Thrace, where the Bulgarians were able to defeat the Byzantine expeditionary forces led by Procopius Crenites, who was killed in the battle. Bulgarians allegedly managed to get a hold of a Khazarian regiment, which battled on the side of the Byzantine Empire, proceeding to cut their noses off and sending them back to Constantinople.

Fearing the power of the Bulgarians and angered by what the Bulgarians did to the Khazars, Leo VI managed to convince the Hungarians (or "Turks" as they were referred to back then) to join the war on the Byzantine side. However, the Hungarians had to be ferried across the Danube, which was heavily fenced and blocked by the forces of Simeon, who had received news of the Hungarians' involvement. The Byzantine navy managed to pass the blockade and ferried Hungarians into Bulgaria.

Facing a war on two fronts, south and north, Bulgaria suffered heavy losses, especially from the Hungarians, who managed to penetrate deep into Bulgaria, reaching its biggest cities and plundering and pillaging everything on their way. The Bulgarian army had to seek refuge in fortresses (Hungarians lacked machinery and siege equipment), such as the fortress of Mundraga.

For a little while, it seemed that the war was over and that the Byzantines had won. The year 895 brought more of the same for the Bulgarians, and Simeon once again could do little but sit in a fortress and look as the Hungarians pillaged his lands.

A Turn of Fate

However, in 895, Simeon managed to regain his composure and inflicted a devastating counterattack on the Hungarians, together with the Pechenegs (the Hungarians' neighbors who were ethnically closely related to them). By the spring of 896, the Bulgarians and Pechenegs had managed to drive the Hungarians out of Bulgaria and forced them to settle farther away in the confines of modern-day Hungary.

Around this time, the Byzantines decided to send another emissary to attempt to negotiate some kind of peace with the Bulgarians. Simeon imprisoned an emissary who had been sent earlier when the situation on the battlefield had been much less favorable to the Bulgarians. Now, Simeon was ready to engage in some kind of dialogue with the current emissary, Leo Choirosphaktes. It is thanks to their correspondence that we know quite a lot about Simeon as a ruler, negotiator, and person. Simeon comes across as fairly straightforward and honest but also a hard negotiator. He would not succumb to Leo's pleas for the release of thousands of Byzantine prisoners in Bulgaria and constantly implicitly mocked the alleged clairvoyant ability of Emperor Leo VI. Simeon, simply put, was trying to get the best deal possible, knowing that the Byzantine Empire didn't have anything else to throw at him. The Hungarians had been defeated, and the Bulgarians repelled the attacks from the Byzantine mainland.

In the summer of 896, Simeon decided to march once again into East Thrace. Emperor Leo VI sent a general to lead the battle instead of him. While previously relying on a very able general, Nikephoros Phokas, Leo VI now turned to Leo Katakalon, the protégé of Stylianos Zaoutzes. It is fairly evident that Zaoutzes had a prominent influence during Leo VI's reign, so much so that he was apparently able to shift public policy and replace high-ranking officials for his own profit.[i] Zaoutzes replaced Nikephoros and bought in Leo Katakalon, a general with lesser merit and experience.

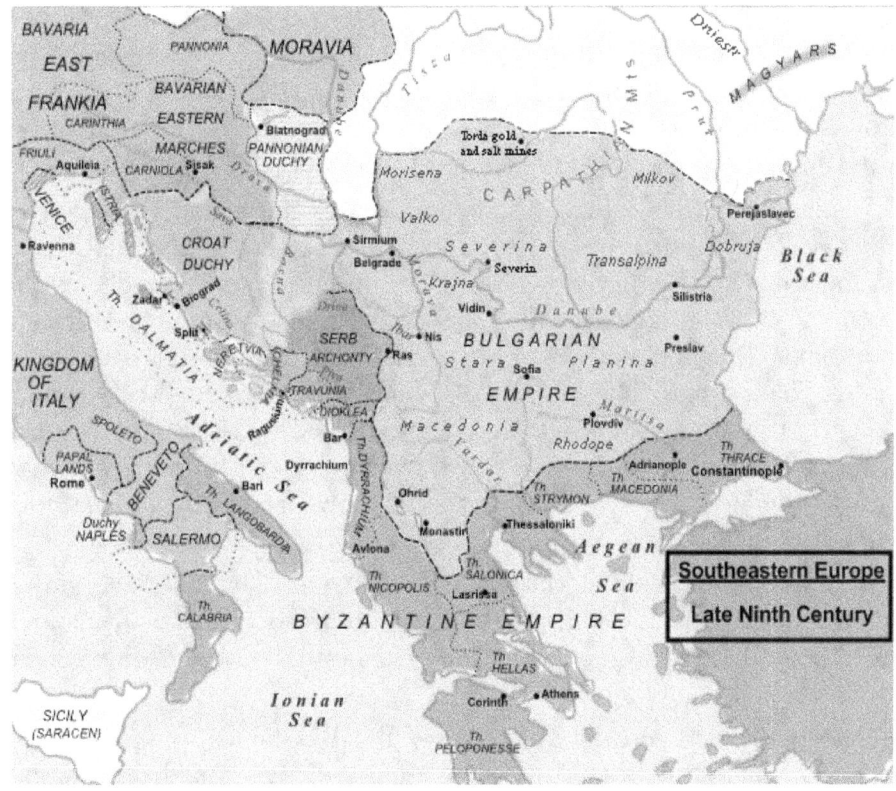

The Bulgarian Empire in the 9ᵗʰ century.[118]

---

[i] Hupchick, P. Dennis, *Simeon's Campaigns for Imperial Recognition*, 894–927. The Bulgarian-Byzantine Wars for Early Medieval Balkan Hegemony: Silver-Lined Skulls and Blinded Armies, 2017, 149-219.

Bulgarian Victory

The final battle occurred in the vicinity of the village Boulgarophygon ("Bulgar's Bridge"). The battle ended with a decisive Bulgarian victory, and there was more hardship for the Byzantine Empire to come. Katakalon's first officer, Theodosius, was killed in battle, and Katakalon just barely managed to save his own life. The road to Constantinople was open, and Simeon decided to plunder the areas surrounding the Byzantine capital, as he lacked resources for a full-blown siege of Constantinople.

For the time being, in 896, the Bulgarians obtained more favorable trade agreements and forced the Byzantine Empire to pay a hefty tribute. Twenty-five thousand prisoners held by the Bulgarians were handed over to the emperor as part of the agreement.

Taking all of this into consideration, it can be argued that Simeon didn't really obtain that much from the Byzantine Empire; his victory, for the most part, was symbolic. He was recognized as a great leader by the Byzantine Empire, and his supremacy in the Balkans was acknowledged and tolerated, if not accepted. He was also venerated among Bulgarians for his political and military prowess.[i] Simeon developed Preslav into a capital worthy of a great commander. Preslav became the cultural capital of Bulgaria and a major center of the development of Orthodox Christian thought. Simeon, once a humble monk, now proudly wore luxurious symbols of his power:

"...dressed in his gold-woven mantle, wearing a golden necklace, girded with a velvet belt, his shoulders sprinkled with pearls, girded with a golden sword ... with bracelets on his arms, his boyars adorned with golden necklaces, belts, and bracelets."[ii]

The peace between the Bulgars and the Byzantines was marked by countless small Bulgarian expansions at the expense of the Byzantine Empire. The matter was made worse by the Arab expansion. Arabs took over Sicily completely in 902, launching numerous small attacks on the Byzantine coastline. Leo of Tripoli, a Greek captured in Attaleia (modern-day Antalya in Turkey), led numerous devastating attacks on Byzantine coastal towns, the most devastating being the sack of Thessalonica in 904. Leo was once a slave, and he rose to the rank of

---

[i] Ibid.
[ii] Ibid. 165

naval commander and governed Tripoli (modern-day Lebanon), from where numerous Arab raids were launched. Leo Tripolites took advantage of the weak defensive systems of Thessalonica, capturing it and wreaking havoc among the local population.

Simeon, in turn, took advantage of the Thessalonica raid and launched operations in Macedonia. Gathering Slavs along the way, who inhabited the province of Macedonia in great numbers, the Bulgarians threatened Thessalonica, which had already been weakened by the Arab raid. Once again, Leo Choirosphaktes, who had spent years negotiating with the Bulgarians on behalf of Emperor Leo VI, brokered a deal that at least temporarily halted the Bulgarian invasion. However, Bulgaria was not the only threat Byzantium faced.

The Varangians Versus Byzantines

The Varangians were Viking conquerors who founded Kievan Rus'. They started the Rurik dynasty and eventually assimilated with the surrounding and much more numerous Slavic population, whom they dominated in a sort of feudal system. The Ruriks were the aristocrats (and possibly the most able and best-equipped soldiers), and the Slavs were peasants and servants.

The Ruriks attacked the Byzantine Empire in 830 and 860. It is likely that the reasons for these conflicts were mostly economic, with the Ruriks aiming to inflict swift defeats and get as much goods and money as possible before leaving. In 907, the Ruriks, led by Oleg of Novgorod, sought better trade terms and effectively coerced the Byzantines into paying them to leave the empire in peace, though this peace would, of course, prove temporary.

There are scant reports about the Ruriks invading the Byzantines or returning home from their bountiful Byzantine exploits. What we have is preserved in the *Primary Chronicle* (*Tale of Bygone Years*), one of the oldest Russian written pieces (it was written in the 12th century by Nestor).[i] "Oleg went to the Greeks ... and came Oleg to Kiev taking gold and silks, and vegetables, and wines."[ii]

---

[i] Rukavishnikov, Alexandr. "Tale of Bygone Years: the Russian Primary Chronicle as a family chronicle." Early Medieval Europe 12, no. 1 (2003): 53-74.
[ii] Ibid. p. 66

A modern painting of Oleg, the leader of the Varangians.[119]

The conquest was incredibly bloody:

"They waged war around the city, and accomplished much slaughter of the Greeks. They also destroyed many palaces and burned the churches. Of the prisoners they captured, some they beheaded, some they tortured, some they shot, and still others they cast into the sea. The Russes inflicted many other woes upon the Greeks after the usual manner of soldiers. Oleg commanded his warriors to make wheels which they attached to the ships, and when the wind was favorable, they spread the sails and bore down upon the city from the open country. When the Greeks beheld this, they were afraid, and sending messengers to Oleg, they implored him not to destroy the city and offered to submit to such tribute as he should desire. Thus Oleg halted his troops."[i]

Therefore, it isn't surprising that the Byzantines ultimately decided to pay off the Ruriks and give them what they wanted. The 12th-century Russian chronicler Nestor recorded some of the peace terms between the Ruriks and Byzantines:

---

[i] Nestor. Primary Chronicle. P. 64. https://www.mgh-bibliothek.de/dokumente/a/a011458.pdf

1. The Greeks would pay a hefty tribute directly to the Ruriks who conquered them.
2. The Ruriks would receive as much grain as they wished.
3. They would receive six months' worth of bread, wine, fish, meat, and fruit.
4. Baths (yes, baths) would be prepared by the Greeks for the Ruriks.
5. The Ruriks could engage in tax-free business with the Greeks.
6. The Ruriks should not inflict violence on the Greeks.
7. The Rus' who came to Constantinople would be required to apply to a sort of Rus' consulate in Saint Mamas district in Constantinople so that they could get their monthly allowance.

Chapter 10: Basil II: The Bulgars' Demise

Continuation of Conflicts between Bulgaria and Byzantium

In the early 10th century, Byzantium had a lot of internal problems. Emperor Leo VI was desperate for a male heir, and finally, one of his mistresses, Zoë Karbonopsina (Karbonopsina means "coal black eyes"), gave birth to his first male child, Constantine VII. After marrying Zoë, Emperor Leo VI had four marriages under his belt, which didn't really sit well with the religious authorities. This contributed to a rift between religious and political authority in Byzantium.

Leo the Wise died in 912, leaving the empire to Constantine VII, who was only seven years old at the time. Alexander, Leo's brother, was supposed to act as Constantine's co-ruler, but he quickly gathered all the power in his hands, allying with people previously hostile to his brother Leo. Alexander seemed to have been less wise than Leo, as he failed to acknowledge the importance of the Bulgarian threat. Alexander refused to honor the peace agreements made between Leo and Simeon. Even worse, he insulted the Bulgarian delegation, which came to express their condolences over the death of Leo VI, treating them in a despicable and condescending way.

Simeon harbored hopes of becoming the head of a joint Bulgarian-Byzantine Empire, so he launched a new war against Byzantium.

Campaign after Campaign

Emboldened by his successful wars against the Byzantine Empire, Simeon started to nurture hopes of much larger exploits. In 913, Simeon marched into the Byzantine Empire once again, this time in an even more powerful and dominant fashion. During the conflict that lasted from 894 to 896, the Byzantine Empire was led by a wise and able emperor, Leo VI. In 913, it was nominally led by Constantine VII, Leo's son, who was only around eight years old at the time: his co-ruler, Alexander, died that same year. There was a battle of intrigue, gossip, and political wit in Byzantium. Alexander appointed Patriarch Nicholas Mystikos as Constantine's regent. Mystikos, in turn, feared Zoë, who had been exiled by Alexander, as Mystikos was a bitter opponent of the marriage between Zoë and Leo VI. Mystikos, as if wanting to completely shatter the empire's military organization, ordered the execution of Constantine Doukas, the supreme commander of Byzantium's military.

Simeon found little resistance on his way to Constantinople. The Byzantines, led by Patriarch Mystikos, hurriedly accepted the Bulgarians' terms. Mystikos even ceremonially crowned Simeon, acknowledging him as the emperor of the Bulgarians in 913. Simeon managed to get another concession. One of his daughters would be married to Constantine VII. While this temporarily averted the Bulgarian threat, it came at the expense of undermining the exclusivity of Byzantine imperial authority. There was now another emperor, or tsar to be specific, who was dangerously close in power to the Byzantine emperor.

Zoë gathered people hostile to this surrendering of imperial authority to the Bulgarians, rising to become her son's regent. Mystikos kept his position as patriarch, but Zoë was now at the head of state. One of her first moves was to reject all terms negotiated by Mystikos, as well as the coronation of Simeon. The year 914 was thus a repetition of 913, but this time, instead of marching on Constantinople, the Bulgarians marched on Adrianople, managing to take it over by bribing the heads of the city. Zoë, alarmed, begrudgingly accepted the annual tribute previously negotiated by Leo VI.

Simeon returned once again, uncertain as to whether the Byzantines would live up to Mystikos's concessions. Simeon was well aware that Zoë was hostile toward Mystikos and his concessions to Simeon regarding imperial authority and that she wouldn't let her son, Constantine VII, marry a Bulgarian princess. In fact, Zoë quickly started to forge a plan to completely destroy the Bulgarian Empire by drawing the Serbians, Magyars, and Pechenegs into the conflict.

By 917, the Serbs and Pechenegs had seemingly been drawn into an alliance with Byzantium, and the Byzantines marched into Bulgaria. The soldiers were paid, and commanders were chosen carefully and based on merit. Moreover, Byzantium got some much-needed truce deals with the Armenians and Arabs, who were now free to face the Bulgarian threat.

Things didn't start well for Zoë. The Pechenegs and Serbs failed to honor their part in the war, and the Byzantines had to face the Bulgarians alone. When the day of the decisive Battle of Achelous came, it was just the Byzantines against the Bulgarians. The Byzantines, led by Leo Phokas, pushed the Bulgarians into a retreat.

After stopping to rest his soldiers, who had been battling for a long time on a very hot summer's day, Leo Phokas dismounted his horse. For some reason, his horse quickly ran away. Some soldiers recognized the horse as belonging to their supreme commander and immediately started spreading the word that their great commander had been killed in battle. The battle that had seemed to be going in the Byzantines' favor became a catastrophic defeat, with numerous soldiers trampled and killed in a chaotic withdrawal from the battlefield. Leo Phokas himself perished.

The Byzantine army reassembled in Katasyrtai, a suburb of Constantinople. Simeon was determined not to give the enemy enough time to rest and recuperate, and he organized a night attack on the enemy camp in Katasyrtai, inflicting yet another devastating defeat on the Byzantines. That same year (917), Simeon dispatched a regiment to depose the leader of Serbian Rashka, Petar Gojniković, making Rashka into a sort of client state led by Pavle Branovic, a Serb leader friendly to the Bulgarians.[i]

The campaign of 917 ended inconclusively. Zoë didn't even want to hear about the tribute or the previously arranged marriage between Constantine VII and one of Simeon's daughters. So, the conflict spilled into 918, and this time, Simeon decided not to focus on Constantinople, instead turning to provinces like Thessaly. Macedonia, and Thrace. He just barely managed to recover from years of plundering, which was the main reason why Simeon decided to attack provinces (or themes) that lay far away from Constantinople. In 918, the Bulgarians destroyed Thebes

---

[i] Rashka was an early medieval Serbian state in the southern Balkans.

and reached Corinth, only to return soon to Bulgaria with bountiful loot and numerous prisoners.

The Macedonian Dynasty under Pressure

By this time, matters in Constantinople had become very murky and confused. In 919, Zoë was removed from the regency, probably owing to the terrible casualties suffered in the war against the Bulgarians. Romanos Lekapenos, the head of the Byzantine navy, which was instrumental in keeping Constantinople safe from sieges, was put in her place with the help of the previous regent, Patriarch Mystikos. Lekapenos married his own daughter to Constantine VII, drastically reducing Simeon's own chances of mingling with the Byzantine imperial family. This prompted Simeon to launch yet another campaign. He was determined to conquer the city of Constantinople, hoping to obtain much-needed naval help from the Arabs. The Arabs, however, didn't make it, as they were stopped by the more powerful Byzantine navy. So, Simeon camped for a while near the Dardanelles and returned to Bulgaria.

Romanos Lekapenos on a coin.[190]

Lekapenos managed to fend off the Bulgarian and Arab threats, convincing the young Constantine VII (who was sixteen years old at the time) to promote him to the rank of co-ruler in 921. Romanos Lekapenos, as we can see, wasn't really content with being the regent of the young emperor; he wanted to become the main man himself. He also convinced Constantine VII to accept Christopher, Lekapenos's own son, as a legitimate heir.

Lekapenos was a shrewd political player, as he was able to draw Serbian Rashka into conflict with Bulgaria. During his annual campaigns in the Byzantine Empire, Simeon regularly left his western borders with Serbian Rashka unguarded. Having been installing client rulers there for quite some time, Simeon was certain that his rear was safe while he was campaigning in Greece.

However, the current ruler of Rashka, Zaharija Pribisavljević, spent a lot of time in Constantinople (he might have been a protégé of the current emperor, Lekapenos) and was previously captured and held in captivity by Simeon when Zaharija tried to take power from another Serbian ruler, Pavle Branovic. Simeon believed that Zaharija had, for all intents and purposes, turned into a good Bulgarian client ruler, and when Branovic started to show signs of weakness and a growing alliance with the Byzantine Empire, Simeon removed Branovic and brought Zaharija to the head of Rashka. Simeon believed that during Zaharija's years of captivity in Bulgaria, he had gained a Bulgarian-friendly attitude. Zaharija wasn't put in a dungeon. He had been under a sort of house arrest, and his rank and dignity had been completely respected by Simeon.

However, Zaharija remained friendly to the Byzantines, and this proved instrumental in 923. While Simeon was in the Byzantine Empire, plundering as usual, Zaharija gathered Serbian forces to strike into Bulgaria. Simeon learned about the plot and sent two of his ablest generals to quench the rebellion. Both, however, were killed in the rugged mountains of Rashka, their heads and armor sent to Lekapenos.

Determined to crush the Serbs, Simeon settled the matters in Greece and turned to Rashka, which was quickly ravaged and turned into a wasteland. Then, Simeon turned to Croatia, which was more unified than Rashka, with significant naval forces. The Bulgarians managed to penetrate deep into Croatia, but due to the challenging and unknown terrain, they fell into a trap and were decimated by the Croatian king, Tomislav, in 926.

Simeon never abandoned his grandiose plans and high hopes, planning yet another excursion into the Byzantine Empire and a potential alliance with the Arabs. However, it was not to be, as he died, probably due to a heart attack, in 927.[1]

---

[1] Hupchick, Dennis P. Simeon's Campaigns for Imperial Recognition, 894-927. The Bulgarian-Byzantine Wars for Early Medieval Balkan Hegemony: Silver-Lined Skulls and Blinded Armies, 2017, 149-219.

The Inevitable Decline of Bulgaria

The great expansionist period of Bulgarian history essentially ended with Simeon's death. The Bulgarian Empire, although fairly powerful immediately following the death of Simeon, would gradually succumb to the same problems faced by the Byzantine Empire: internal strife and external threats. These issues gradually weakened the Bulgarian Empire.

When military and political command is surrendered to strong personalities, the road is open for the perversion of dictatorial, autocratic power. What then ensues is periods of relative stability, thanks to the prominence of leaders who merit adoration, but also periods of chaos when less honorable people take power. This happened in ancient Rome. The republic laid foundations that were finally shattered by powerful people like Julius Caesar, Octavian Augustus, and Tiberius. And the same thing happened to Bulgaria. The Bulgarians had their share of fame, wealth, and strength, and after Simeon died, the historical pendulum shifted and marked a drastically different period of Bulgarian and Byzantine history.

Constantine VII and the Succession Crisis

Although already mature, even by modern standards, Constantine VII was only formally the emperor of the Byzantine Empire. Romanos Lekapenos and his family firmly held the imperial reins. Lekapenos knew how to keep the Bulgarian threat at bay.

Although Constantine VII wasn't ultimately married to a Bulgarian princess, Simeon managed to marry his son Peter to Irene Lekapene, granddaughter of Romanos Lekapenos, in 927. This event mitigated the Bulgarian threat and put an end to conflicts that had been raging since the late 9th century.

While Lekapenos was dealing with the military and politics, Constantine VII mainly spent his time on scholarly pursuits; you may recall that we mentioned him as the author of an important text that gives us a glimpse into a number of important historical topics, such as the Christianization of the Slavs. However, starting in 944, Constantine VII started to profit from the animosities between Lekapenos and his own sons, who hoped to grab some of the imperial power for themselves. Constantine removed the intruders and assured that future emperors would come from the Macedonian dynasty, to which Constantine VII belonged.

Constantine VII on an ivory plaque.[121]

Constantine VII quickly appointed Romanos II, his son, as co-emperor. Constantine VII died in 959, but the death of Romanos II came quickly in 963, putting the Byzantine Empire once again at the will of court intrigue and a battle of interests among the nobility.

The wife of Romanos II, Theophano, made sure to safeguard their two sons, Basil II and Constantine VIII. She was on friendly terms with the two most powerful men in the Byzantine Empire after the death of her husband: Nikephoros II Phokas and John Tzimiskes. The two men successively became emperors and were closely related to Theophano, who seemed to have had all the reins in her hands.

Nikephoros II Phokas, who came to power after the premature death of Romanos II, was instrumental in the reconquest of Crete, which had been in the hands of the Arabs for a long time. Nikephoros was also instrumental in the empire's eastern conflicts with the Arabs. He participated in the capture of Tarsus (modern-day southern Turkey), which was a starting point for many Arab naval raids. The Byzantines, spearheaded by Nikephoros II Phokas, marched farther south, reaching Syria and overtaking cities such as Antioch, Laodicea, Larissa, and many others. Antioch was a particularly tough nut to crack. The Byzantines planned to besiege the city and use hunger as a weapon against the Antioch defenders.

Nikephoros II Phokas.[122]

Nikephoros II Phokas was assassinated in 969, possibly at the request of Theophano and her lover John Tzimiskes, another important general. It is also possible that the events surrounding the siege of Antioch were to blame. When besieging Antioch, Nikephoros's aim was to make the city surrender. He left Michael Bourtzes and Petros (previously a eunuch servant in the Phokas family) in Bagras Fortress to oversee the siege of

Antioch during the winter. Bourtzes and Petros received explicit orders not to attack Antioch, as Nikephoros wanted the city walls to remain intact.

Bourtzes, however, was able to reach the officers in Antioch who were responsible for the city's towers and defense walls. Through bribery, he managed to get himself and a few hundred men into the city, after which the bulk of the Byzantine forces were let in, led by a somewhat reluctant Petros. After learning of Bourtzes's disobedience, Nikephoros had him removed from his post and disgraced. Bourtzes then decided to join or form a plot to kill Nikephoros II Phokas. He might have found enthusiastic supporters in John Tzimiskes and Theophano.[i]

It's possible that Nikephoros II Phokas, due to his illustrious heritage, experience, and merit, was feared by Theophano and that she recognized him as a threat to her young sons. She turned to John Tzimiskes (Nikephoros II was his maternal uncle), another influential and able general who might have been easier to control.

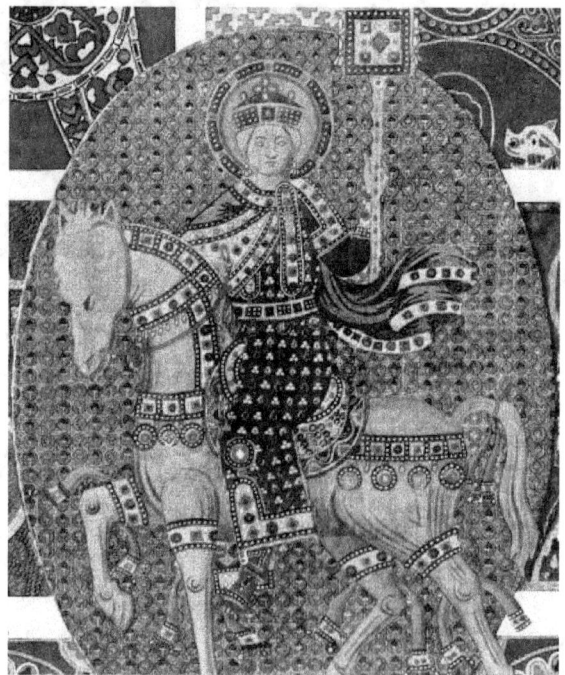

John Tzimiskes, a reproduction of a lost portrait.[128]

---

[i] Krsmanovic, Bojana; Dzelebdzic, Dejan. John Tzimiskes and Nikephoros II Phokas: The background and motives of a premeditated murder. Zbornik radova Vizantoloskog instituta, 2010, 47: 83-120.

It is likely that a plot was devised by John Tzimiskes, Empress Theophano, General Bourtzes, and other conspirators to assassinate Emperor Nikephoros II Phokas. He was murdered in his bedchamber in December 969; his head was severed from his body. Shortly afterward, Tzimiskes was crowned emperor. To deflect blame, he reportedly found scapegoats (their names are not known). The coronation was arranged to take place on Christmas of that same year.

Tzimiskes and Nikephoros II had a troubled relationship. Tzimiskes, a proven and able military strategist in his own right, was removed from his military post as soon as Nikephoros II Phokas became the emperor in 963. Since the earliest days of Rome, the return of a triumphant military general had been one of the most cherished and attended events. A triumph could turn a military general into a figure of veneration, respect, and fear. Tzimiskes wanted to prove himself, this time in the attire of a Byzantine emperor.

Tzimiskes as Emperor

For all intents and purposes, Tzimiskes continued the same expansionist policy as his predecessor. He managed to fend off the Kievan Rus' (Varangian) attacks in a conflict for supremacy over Bulgaria. Tzimiskes fought the Kievan Rus' leader, Sviatoslav, in a series of battles in Bulgaria. Sviatoslav's forces were finally besieged in the fortress of Dorostolon (modern-day northern Bulgaria), and Sviatoslav was forced to concede. Tzimiskes also captured Boris II, the Bulgarian leader who was forced to side with Kievan Rus' to try and fend off the Byzantines. Bulgaria was officially annexed by the Byzantine Empire.

In the following years, Tzimiskes focused on the situation in the southern parts of his empire, particularly on warfare against the Abbasid Caliphate. He managed to conquer numerous cities, reaching as far as Nazareth and Caesarea (modern-day Israel).

When Tzimiskes died in 976, the Byzantine Empire seemed to have been in a much better position than in the early 10th century when Bulgarians, Varangians, and Arabs posed major threats. By the end of the reign of John Tzimiskes, the Byzantine Empire had a firm grip over the Balkans and Mesopotamia.

Macedonians Back in Power

The sons of Romanos II, Basil II and Constantine VIII, were mature enough to lead the empire by this time. The Macedonian dynasty was ready to return to the scene and lead the Byzantine Empire to the peak of its power. The transition, however, wasn't entirely peaceful or elegant.

By gathering extensive warfare experience and quickly learning the cunning ways of Constantinople's politics and intrigues, Basil II managed to remove opposition after ascending to the throne. It's important to emphasize here that although Basil II and Constantine VIII were formally co-rulers, Constantine VIII, who was younger than Basil II and less interested in politics, was a more peripheral figure, while Basil II took the main stage. He ended the rebellions of two of the most powerful Byzantine families, Phokas and Skleros, in the years following his ascension to power.

Bardas Skleros was the governor of Byzantine Mesopotamia. He learned about John Tzimiskes's death and the subsequent proclamation of Basil II and Constantine VIII as emperors in 976. Skleros immediately gathered an army with the intent of taking the imperial throne by force. He was defeated by Basil II, who had to muster the forces of another eventual contender, Bardas Phokas, who, for the time being, was allied with Basil II. In fact, Phokas dealt the final blow to Skleros in 979. Bardas Skleros went into exile in Iraq, where he was well received by the Muslim authorities.[i]

Basil II feared that Skleros would return at some point to the Byzantine Empire, perhaps aided by the Muslims, who were already a major threat. He considered handing Aleppo to the Muslims if they handed Bardas Skleros over to him. Although this would have been a shrewd move, this offer wasn't received positively by the elite in the Byzantine Empire, especially by Bardas Phokas.

---

[i] Holmes, Catherine. Basil II and the Government of Empire (976-1025). 1999. PhD Thesis. University of Oxford.

Basil II.[194]

After Bardas Skleros was released from Baghdad in 987, he quickly formed an alliance with his previous rival, Bardas Phokas, and another rebellion against Basil II started. Basil II personally commanded his forces in the war against the rebels, and he was helped out by the Russian forces. Basil II was instrumental in the conversion of Russians to Christianity. The first Christian Russian ruler, Vladimir I, was married to Basil's sister, Anna. By 991, Basil II had been able to grind down the rebels completely.

These turbulent events of Basil II's early reign meant that he couldn't stop the Bulgarian expansion. While John Tzimiskes inflicted a devastating blow to the Bulgarians and captured their ruler, the Bulgarian state recovered and managed to reclaim a portion of its previous territory, once again threatening the Byzantine Empire's center of power.

Basil II, the Uncontested Emperor

Once the internal conflicts were settled, Basil II could turn to the Bulgarian threat. He was determined to end it once and for all. The Bulgarians, led by Emperor Samuel, reclaimed some territories conquered by possibly the greatest Bulgarian ruler, Simeon. During his turbulent early reign, Basil II tried to eliminate the Bulgarian threat, but he was forced to retreat in a humiliating fashion. In 1001, he initiated another offensive, which was much more successful and bloodier.[i] Slowly but surely, Basil II weakened the Bulgarian center of power, cutting the Bulgarians' supply sources and undermining their recovery.

Forced to face Basil II in an open battle, the Bulgarians offered a last resistance effort in 1014 at Kleidion, where they were decisively defeated by Basil II. The Byzantines managed to capture around fifteen thousand Bulgarian soldiers. Almost all were blinded, and a small number of soldiers had one eye spared so that they could guide the mutilated army home.

Over the next few years, Basil II annexed the whole Bulgarian territory to the Byzantine Empire.

The Reign of Basil II

After defeating the rebels, Basil II sought to further weaken the aristocracy by reducing their influence in regions where they held significant amounts of land. Namely, Basil II forbade aristocrats to hold land and public offices in the same region, thereby mitigating their influence in the areas where they had the most interests.[ii]

Basil II was able to placate, or at least stabilize, support among the poorer segments of society by restoring village lands that had been acquired—often unjustly—by wealthy elites. These estates were returned to

---

[i] Goodyear, Michael. "Compromised Defense-The Conquests of Basil II." *The Michigan Journal of History*, 5.
[ii] Holmes, Catherine. Political elites in the reign of Basil II. In: Byzantium in the Year 1000. Brill, 2003. p. 35-69.

their original holders without compensation, and new laws discouraged the further accumulation of land by the aristocracy.[i]

Basil II was able to assert his dynasty as the sole ruler of the Byzantine Empire, but members of the Skleros family continued to hold high offices. While this wasn't the case for the Phokas family, they still retained some land and status.

Basil II also fought another kind of war. Although he succeeded in removing his great-uncle and closest advisor, Basil Lekapenos, in 985, the latter was able to form an intricate web of alliances and quid pro quo networks within the government, which continued to function and undermine his influence. By 996, Basil II had not only removed the rebels who dared face him in an open battle but also inflicted a final blow to the more tacit resistance that was going on. It was possibly due to this long struggle for power that Basil II was determined to present himself in a truly imperial, imposing, and grandiose style.

Basil II is remembered for his purported war exploit: the blinding of an entire Bulgarian army. While his strategy in Bulgaria was devastating and inhumane, Basil II also knew the importance of solid civil governance and conquest by culture. He was able to fortify the frontiers of his country, not only through conquest and military command but also through religious, cultural, and political influence.

At the end of his reign, Basil II faced another rebellion, this time fomented by Nikephoros Xiphias, Basil's most important general, and Nikephoros Phocas, in 1021. Xiphias was a major factor in numerous military victories of Basil's reign, including the crushing victory against the Bulgarians at Kleidion in 1014.

The ironlike Basil II was able to crush this last rebellion. Having significantly expanded and stabilized the Byzantine Empire, Basil II died in 1025. Constantine VIII, Basil's younger brother, himself already an old man, came to power after Basil's death.

---

[i] Holmes, Catherine. Basil II (AD 976-1025). De Imperatoribus Romanis, 2003.

Chapter 11: Signs of Destabilization

Prelude to a Decline

After the death of Emperor Basil II in 1025, the question of succession was simple. Basil II had no offspring and had not prepared anyone to be his successor. So, his younger brother Constantine was proclaimed the new emperor. The accession of Emperor Constantine VIII (r. 1025-1028) to the throne led to the strengthening of the influence of court eunuchs, who were appointed to high positions in the state, which resulted in the return of court intrigue. Whenever the administrative matters were left to the court personnel, whether it be in the times of ancient Rome, the Byzantine Empire, or the Russian Empire, there was a high risk of intrigue, corruption, and mishandling of governmental affairs. This is exactly what happened during the reign of Constantine VIII. Constantine VIII, a son of Romanos II and a child during the reigns of powerful men like Nikephoros II Phokas and John Tzimiskes, lurked in the shadows of his much more powerful brother Basil II for some time. He patiently waited his turn. However, by this point, Constantine VIII had become fairly indifferent to the allure of the imperial throne. Nominally, Constantine VIII reigned for sixty-six years alongside Nikephoros, then Tzimiskes, then Basil, and then for three years on his own. He ultimately left a faint mark on Byzantine history.

Emperor Constantine VIII's reign was short-lived, and before his death, the question of succession arose again, even more seriously this time because he had no sons, only three daughters—Eudokia, Zoë, and Theodora.[i] Since Eudokia had taken monastic vows, Zoë (978-1050) inherited the legitimacy of the Macedonian dynasty, and her husband, Romanos Argyros, Prefect of Constantinople, who was related to Emperor Romanos I Lekapenos (who served as a co-emperor to the young Constantine VII in early 10th century), was chosen as the new emperor, in 1028. This decision did not provide a lasting solution to the imperial throne but merely postponed it, as the fifty-year-old Zoë was too advanced in years to bear children.

Romanos Argyros, now Emperor Romanos III Argyros (r. 1028-1034), continued the court policy of the previous emperor, generously granting and bribing the support of the ruling segments of society. In 1034, Emperor Romanos III died under suspicious circumstances, after which Zoë's lover, Michael, was chosen as the new emperor and became her husband.

Michael IV (r. 1034-1041) belonged to the Paphlagonian family, which included several influential figures at court, most notably his brother, John the Orphanotrophos, a powerful eunuch who served as chief minister. Although the family was not of noble origin, they rose to prominence due to the decline in traditional aristocratic influence and the increasing dominance of court intrigue, petty officials, and eunuchs in Byzantine politics. Michael was able to rise quietly through the ranks, eventually beginning an affair with Empress Zoë, which led to his elevation to the throne. Full of ambition to establish their lineage as the new imperial dynasty, they persuaded Empress Zoë to adopt Michael IV's nephew, also named Michael, as her son, ensuring the continuation of the Paphlagonian dynasty.

Wishing to further secure support for their regime, the Paphlagonians promoted their own supporters to high positions in the spiritual centers of the empire and in the military.[ii] One of the family's leaders, the influential eunuch John the Orphanotrophos, attempted to secure the position of patriarch of Constantinople in 1037, but his efforts were blocked by the reigning patriarch and church opposition, preventing the family from extending its control into the highest ecclesiastical office. The following year, the Paphlagonians launched an unsuccessful military campaign in Sicily, compromising their position with the army.

---

[i] Ostrogorsky, *History of the Byzantine State*.
[ii] Kaldellis, *Streams of Gold, Rivers of Blood*.

After the death of Emperor Michael IV in 1041, his nephew and the empress's adopted son, Michael V, succeeded him. Believing he had enough support in Constantinople, Emperor Michael V banished Empress Zoë under charges of a coup and exiled her to Principo in April 1042. This was followed by the forced exile of the popular Patriarch Alexios. Upon hearing this news, the people of the capital rebelled. A mob led by General Constantine Cabasilas forcibly took Zoë's sister, Theodora, to Hagia Sophia, where they crowned her empress, stripping Emperor Michael V of any remaining legitimacy. The short-lived Paphlagonian dynasty, which had started with court intrigues, ended with public unrest.

Sixty-five days later, Zoë married again, this time to Constantine IX Monomachos, who assumed the imperial responsibilities. He had been previously exiled from the empire by Michael IV but was brought back by Empress Zoë. His rule was shaken by various political, military, and church intrigues, which he tried to overcome.[i] Constantine continued the purge instituted by Zoë and Theodora, removing the relatives of Michael V from the court.

The instability of the throne and the empire made him prone to violent outbursts over suspicions of conspiracy. This caution wasn't unfounded. In 1042, Constantine relieved General George Maniakes from his command in Italy, and Maniakes rebelled, declaring himself emperor in September. He transferred his troops to the Balkans and was about to defeat Constantine's army in battle when he was wounded and died on the battlefield, ending the crisis in 1043.

Constantine also waged wars against groups that included the Kievan Rus', the Pechenegs, and the rising Seljuk Turks. Despite the varying success of these campaigns, the Byzantine Empire

Constantine IX.[185]

---

[i] Ibid

largely retained the borders established after the conquests of Basil II, even expanding eastward when Constantine annexed the wealthy Armenian Kingdom of Ani.

In 1054, a year before Constantine's death, the Great Schism between the Eastern Orthodox and Roman Catholic Churches took place, culminating in Pope Leo IX excommunicating Patriarch Michael Cerularius. Constantine was aware of the political and religious consequences of such an event and made unsuccessful efforts to prevent it from happening.

The End of the Macedonian Dynasty

With the death of the ruling couple, Empress Zoë in 1050 and Emperor Constantine IX in 1055, Empress Theodora, as the last legitimate representative of the Macedonian dynasty, assumed power. Despite Constantine IX having already designated a successor, Nikephoros Proteuon, the governor of Bulgaria, Empress Theodora, together with her supporters, seized the imperial palace in a coup, which led to the exile of Nikephoros. The empress then appointed her own representatives to the main positions of the state, headed by the chief minister, eunuch Leo Paraspondylos, while simultaneously dismissing Isaac Komnenos, a powerful and popular military commander, from his position as stratopedarches (a high-ranking military officer).[i]

At the end of August 1056, Empress Theodora died at the age of seventy-six, marking the end of the Macedonian dynasty. On her deathbed and with the influence of her advisor, Leo Paraspondylos, the bureaucrat Michael Bringas was selected as her successor and crowned Emperor Michael VI. Although he had administrative experience, Michael VI lacked military credibility, which soon led to tensions with the army and set the stage for his brief and troubled reign. Leo Paraspondylos continued to exert considerable influence during Michael VI's rule.

Upon ascending the throne, Emperor Michael VI generously distributed promotions to officials in the capital while ignoring promotion requests from the officer corps led by Isaac Komnenos. The military commanders once again tried to secure promotions, this time through eunuch Leo Paraspondylos, but they were again rejected, prompting them to retreat to Asia Minor. On June 8th, 1057, in Paphlagonia, they proclaimed Isaac Komnenos as emperor.

---

[i] Ostrogorsky, *History of the Byzantine State*.

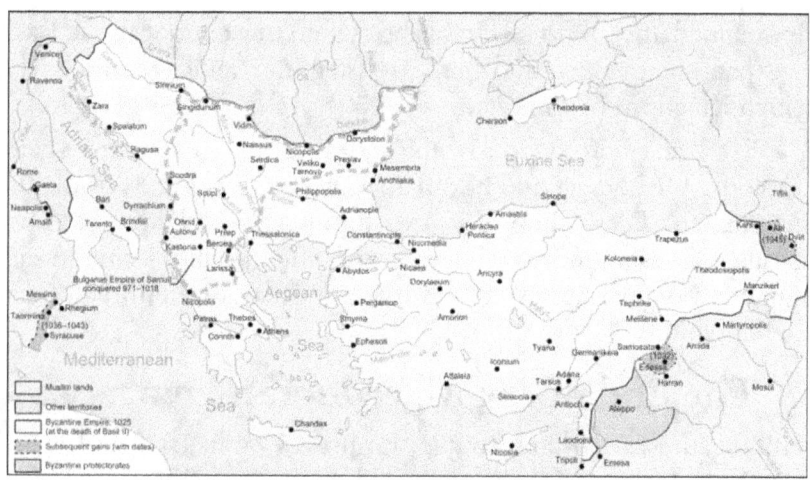

The Byzantine Empire in the 11ᵗʰ century.[196]

Insurgency

Thanks to the falsification of imperial orders and the provision of their own resources, the insurgents were able to gather a large army. They captured Nicaea and then won a victory over the legitimate forces at Hades. Faced with the possibility of being overthrown, Emperor Michael VI entered into negotiations with the insurgents, offering Isaac Komnenos the title of Caesar and recognition as his successor in exchange for ending the rebellion. However, at the urging of his fellow commanders, Isaac rejected the offer. Although Michael VI had been lawfully appointed by Empress Theodora, his rule lacked broad support, particularly from the military. In contrast, Isaac, a respected general with strong backing from the army, was a compelling alternative to the unpopular emperor.

Meanwhile, during the negotiations between the emperor and the insurgents, the people of the capital were won over to the side of the insurgents, thanks to Patriarch Michael Cerularius, which led to Michael VI's abdication and departure for a monastery where he spent the rest of his life. Constantinople was then peacefully occupied by the insurgents on August 31ˢᵗ, which was followed by Isaac Komnenos's coronation as emperor on September 1ˢᵗ, 1057.[i]

Once in power, Emperor Isaac I promoted the accomplices who had helped him gain power, after which he implemented reforms aimed at reducing state expenditures, such as bureaucratic salaries and pensions,

---

[i] Ibid.

which had been increasing since the reign of Emperor Constantine VIII, who frequently awarded court titles and was lenient toward church estates, often at the expense of the military.[i] Due to reforms that encroached on the wealth of individuals and the church, Emperor Isaac I quickly lost popularity among the ruling strata of society, which, combined with his poor health, led to his abdication in November 1059. His accomplice in the rebellion and the president of the Senate, Constantine Doukas, was crowned the new emperor. Upon taking power, he annulled all of Isaac I's decisions regarding the abolition of dignities and fiscal measures.

The year after Constantine died, the capable and brave General Romanos IV Diogenes took power. The new emperor fought against the Seljuks until his defeat and capture at the Battle of Manzikert in 1071. Romanos IV managed to negotiate with the Seljuks and returned to Constantinople. However, during his absence, Constantine's son, Michael VII Doukas, became the sole ruler. A civil war ensued, in which Michael was officially confirmed as the ruler while Romanos retreated, believing in assurances of his safety. However, Romanos's eyes were gouged out, and he died from the injuries he sustained in 1072.[ii]

Michael VII Doukas's reign was characterized by numerous rebellions. Two claimants to the throne from military aristocracy circles emerged, one from Europe and the other from Asia Minor. Nikephoros Bryennios entered his native Adrianople as a counter-emperor in 1077 and marched on Constantinople. His namesake, Nikephoros Botaneiates, also advanced on Constantinople with the support of the Seljuks. Botaneiates entered Constantinople first, seized the throne in 1078, and married Empress Maria, the wife of his predecessor.

The Byzantine Empire was in chaos, and a struggle among generals for supreme power began. The most capable proved to be Alexios Komnenos, a nephew of Emperor Isaac I. He was not only an excellent military commander but also a talented politician, which distinguished him from his uncle Isaac and the unfortunate Romanos Diogenes. With him, a more than century-long period of rule by the Komnenos dynasty (1081–1204), one of the most glorious in Byzantine history, would begin.[iii]

---

[i] Ibid.
[ii] Ibid.
[iii] Kaldellis, *Streams of Gold, Rivers of Blood*.

Internal Problems

The period of dynastic change signified the worsening of problems that were typical of Byzantium due to its geographical and political circumstances. Since the emperor was the head of the state and directed the executive power, he always faced two problems. The first was the need for capable people to fill important positions, especially those in the military. However, the most capable individuals were also ambitious, and as such, they represented a potential threat to legitimate power in the event of an open rebellion. The second problem was the need for authority through official institutions, but there was the caveat that emperors had to find ways to maintain personal control over them; otherwise, the rulers would be sidelined themselves.

To manage potential threats to their rule, Byzantine emperors often marginalized or sidelined relatives—especially siblings—who might challenge dynastic stability. While earlier Roman emperors often involved their families in succession, systematic dynastic rule became more formalized under Alexios I Komnenos, whose reign marked the rise of family-based governance as a political norm. Additionally, emperors sought to limit the power of ambitious generals by frequently transferring them to commands far from their native regions, thus preventing them from building regional power bases.

A similar dynamic existed in the Roman Republic, where the Senate attempted to manage military power through a system of checks and balances. Over time, however, powerful generals such as Gaius Marius, Pompey the Great, and Julius Caesar eroded these controls. Julius Caesar famously crossed the Rubicon from Cisalpine Gaul, initiating a civil war that ultimately led to the end of the Roman Republic and paved the way for the imperial system under Augustus.

The plotting of conspiracies was most pronounced among members of prominent families who had extensive networks and connections with members of other significant families and military officers. They had the necessary unity to seize supreme power, and on those occasions, they presented a representative around whom they rallied all available resources. The household guard, or family retainers, initially formed the nucleus of the forces, after which the common people joined the rebellion. To expand the rebellion, the pretenders sought to broaden their circle of supporters, which invariably included military leaders living in Constantinople and the provinces, demobilized soldiers, and prisoners in the capital.[i]

Following a well-conceived plan of conspiracy, the right moment for defection from imperial authority would be seized, as any attempt at usurpation was doomed to fail as long as the reigning emperor resided in the capital, except in the case of Emperor Michael V. Usurpations in the capital typically occurred when the emperor left Constantinople accompanied by the imperial guard, leaving the court unprotected in the event of a coup.[ii] In the provinces, the rebels had more opportunities to act, especially when the main army, led by the emperor, suffered a defeat against the enemy it was fighting (such as Bardas Phokas in 976 and Caesar John Doukas in 1071) or when the army was deep in enemy territory on campaign (such as Leo Tornikios in 1047). The most reliable method was securing the main command over the army (such as Alexios Komnenos in 1081).

It is also important to keep in mind that internal fluctuations either encouraged or indirectly enabled external crises. The loss of territory necessitated the mobilization of the army to the hotspot, leaving the rest of the empire's territories vulnerable, especially at the other end of the empire. Similarly, internal disputes provided additional reasons for foreign powers to dismember or plunder the empire's borders. Also, considering that the emperor had to worry about usurpers, it was extremely difficult to organize his departure from Constantinople to adequately address a military crisis. To make matters worse, even if a commander managed to successfully handle a military incursion, his success would position him as a pretender to the throne, reducing the chances of his re-engagement.

External Problems

The turbulent period in Byzantium following the death of Emperor Basil II marked a turning point, particularly in terms of foreign policy. At the time, the Eastern Roman Empire extended across Asia and Europe, with outposts in southern Italy, placing it at the intersection of three rising spheres of influence: the Latin West, the Islamic world, and the Slavic and steppe regions. These neighboring powers began to grow in strength

---

[i] Ibid.
[ii] Ibid.

during this period, reshaping the geopolitical balance in and around the empire.

In the Balkans, the Hungarians occupied border towns such as Belgrade, and the Slavic population, primarily the Bulgarians and Serbians, rose up in rebellion against Constantinople. Similarly, border tribes like the Pechenegs and Cumans raided border territories and plundered towns. Although the situation in the Balkans was serious, it was the least critical compared to other border areas. By far, the most severe situation was in the East with the fall of Anatolia, which was never fully brought back under Byzantine control. In the West, the Normans strengthened their position, causing Byzantium to lose all its possessions in Italy.

At the beginning of the 11th century, southern Italy was divided between the Byzantine Empire and coastal duchies on the Tyrrhenian Sea, which were partially dependent on Byzantium to some extent due to help with defense against the Lombards from the interior. Beginning in the 9th century, Sicily had belonged to the Arabs. In 1018, Basil II sent Basil Boioannes as the catepan (regional leader of the Byzantines in Italy) to consolidate imperial authority in Italy. Boioannes's administration from 1018 to 1028 marked the peak of Byzantine power and influence in Italy.[i] The emperor planned to proceed from there to liberate Sicily from Arab rule, but his death in 1025 thwarted his plan. The catepan George Maniakes would have more success (though briefly) in that endeavor.

Maniakes was sent by Emperor Michael V in 1038 to conquer weakened Sicily due to internal conflicts among the Kalbid emirs. Maniakes had success at the start, liberating the eastern part of the island with Messina and Syracuse. However, Constantine IX Monomachos, who took the throne in 1042, relieved him of his duties. Maniakes died fighting Constantine IX's forces in 1043 after declaring himself emperor and marching on the capital.[ii] With Maniakes's departure, the Zirids, a dynasty from northern Africa, returned to Sicily, and all the wars that were fought further weakened this area, making it easier prey for the future Norman conquerors, who finally expelled Byzantium from Italy in 1071 by capturing Bari.

---

[i] Ostrogorsky, *History of the Byzantine State*.
[ii] Kaldellis, *Streams of Gold, Rivers of Blood*.

The arrival of the Normans began in the 1040s when they came as a mercenary army fighting for all warring sides in Italy. From 1042 to 1059, they became independent conquerors, establishing themselves in Apulia and Capua. However, the turning point came in 1059 when the pope recognized two Norman leaders, Richard of Aversa and Robert Guiscard, as the rulers of the conquered territories, marking the final confirmation of the Norman presence.

The Great Schism of 1054 between the Eastern Church and Western Church led to a change in the attitude of the new pope, Nicholas II, toward the Normans. The pope wanted to use them to expel the Byzantines from southern Italy. Because of this, the pope went to Melfi, where a synod was held, and Robert was proclaimed duke of Apulia, Calabria, and Sicily. In return, he swore loyalty to the pope and promised an annual tribute. After that, Robert conquered all of Calabria and Apulia and expelled the Byzantines from Italy.

However, the Normans were primarily ambitious opportunists and adventurers, so they seriously considered Byzantium's offer to join the empire just a few decades later. An offer was given by Michael VII Doukas, who had just risen to the throne after Romanos had suffered the loss at the Manzikert. The emperor sought help from Robert in the fight against the Turks. To this end, he sent letters with proposals, offering a marriage between his newborn son and Robert's daughter. Robert Guiscard aligned himself with the Byzantine Empire through a marriage agreement. His daughter was betrothed to Constantine Doukas, the son of Emperor Michael VII, and sent to Constantinople to be raised in the imperial court. However, this arrangement collapsed in 1078 when Nikephoros III Botaneiates seized the throne in a coup. As a result, Michael VII was forced to become a monk, and Robert's daughter was confined to a convent, ending the proposed alliance.[i]

The instability in Byzantium led the Byzantine emperors to use extreme measures to form alliances. The imbalance in the empire caused these alliances to fail. Provoked by this outcome, the Normans entered a phase of expansion, conquering Calabria and Apulia by 1071 and Sicily from 1061 to 1091. However, their influence in Byzantine politics would continue. The Normans, hungry for territory, embarked on plundering and conquest campaigns in Byzantine territory, first in the Balkans and

---

[i] Houben, *Roger II of Sicily*.

then within the Levant. Numerous conflicts culminated in a direct clash with Byzantium (1081-1085).

This westward expansion did not limit itself only to the Normans; it also manifested in the Crusades, during which western European states created kingdoms in the Middle East. The weakening of Byzantium allowed the West to pursue opportunistic policies, and it also showed that Byzantium lacked the capacity to liberate its former territories (many of them holy places for Christians) from the influence of Muslim states. On the other hand, the Great Schism prevented the coordination of the Roman Church with the rest of the Christian world, hindering unity in religion and identity between the East and West.[i]

A similar situation occurred in the East. The eastern part of the empire, centered in Antioch, was one of the most significant cities of the empire. Antioch was important as a strategic border point for the eastern part of the Byzantine state, and it housed the center of the Byzantine army, which was in close proximity to Arab Aleppo, the Arab center of Syria. The governor of this city and region held the title of dux, and in the transitional period between the Macedonian dynasty and the Komnenos dynasty, this title served as one of the stepping stones to usurp the throne. For this reason, due to instability, it was practically a title for pretenders to the throne.

The dux and domestikos (a regional leader) of the East, Philaretos Brachamios, a member of the old Armenian family Brachamios, rebelled against Michael VII Doukas and held Antioch, Edessa, Germanikeia (Marash), and Melitene himself. This area, after the Battle of Manzikert and before the Turkish conquest, was only nominally part of Byzantium.[ii] The Seljuks took advantage of the division within the state and finally conquered the city in 1085.

After Tughril Beg's victory over the Buyids in Baghdad in 1055, the Seljuks emerged as restorers of Muslim unity under the Sunni caliphate. In Byzantium, the Seljuks were hired as mercenaries by various rival Byzantine generals in their behind-the-scenes struggles for the imperial throne in Constantinople, so the Seljuks gradually gained increasing influence over Byzantine political affairs. At the same time, they

---

[i] Fouracre, *The New Cambridge Medieval History Set.*
[ii] Ostrogorsky, *History of the Byzantine State.*

controlled an ever-growing number of territories in Anatolia as allies of the Byzantine emperor.¹ The Eastern province followed the same route.

The court intrigue and uncertain successor to the throne caused ruling families and capable military leaders to shift their focus to Constantinople. In effect, this weakened the state, making it a far easier target for emerging regional powers. Their emergence was nothing new, but in the past, Byzantium had the strength not only to endure these attacks but also to spread its territory. This fall from grace would continue in the future, with capable leaders managing to salvage some things. In the end, though, the Eastern Roman Empire paid the final price of having conspiracies and court intrigue.

---

¹ Ibid.

Chapter 12: The Great Schism

The Great Schism, which occurred on July 16th, 1054, between the Roman Church and the Patriarchate of Constantinople, was a canonical separation and the end of a single liturgical community. This event was the result of numerous factors and cannot be viewed from a single perspective or considered as having a single cause. The fact that the two sides, which were once united through one church, would completely distance themselves and thereby divide the church was evident long before 1054. In the 11th century, problems and tensions between the East and West reached their peak, but they had been developing throughout the Early Middle Ages and increased over time.

The schism of 1054 is one of several schisms that occurred in the history of the Christian Church, but this one was final. The causes are numerous and complex, and they should be studied in historical, political, theological, and cultural contexts. The Eastern and Western parts of the Roman Empire primarily differed in language, tradition, and theological crises, and all of these differences arose due to the different circumstances in which they developed. Because of the division of the Roman Empire, iconoclasm, and various theological and dogmatic issues, the final schism of the Christian Church into the Orthodox Church and the present-day Catholic Church occurred.

The division between the Eastern and Western Churches.[197]

Both churches wanted their independence, perhaps not initially. Over time, they became aware of their political situations, which pushed them in different directions. Over time, the Eastern and Western Churches developed in such different ways that they were unable to share common social conditions or exert meaningful influence over each other's political realities.[i] While Byzantium was surviving incursions from the Muslim states, Rome was becoming a player in the medieval European states that were forming around it.

Factors that would have allowed for the unity of the Christian world had been lacking for centuries. As previously mentioned, the Western and Eastern Churches developed in parallel but were shaped by differing ideological frameworks. In Byzantium, the concept of caesaropapism—where the emperor held significant authority over ecclesiastical matters—was a major factor necessitating coordination between the disputing sides. The Eastern Roman emperor often acted as the de facto authority in

---

[i] Jedin, Dolan, and Holland, *History of the Church*.

appointing patriarchs, a practice that became increasingly problematic as Byzantium lost control over its territories in and around Italy. With the loss of these possessions, Byzantium could no longer guarantee peace and security to Rome, which had to seek another protector and thus become a political player that would build its own sphere of influence. As the West solidified behind the Frankish Kingdom, it forced Byzantium to bring the Slavs under its influence. After bringing the Southern Slavs to heel, the next step was, of course, to Christianize Russia within the patriarchal authority of Constantinople.

Precursors to the Schism

After difficult battles against the Muslims, the Byzantine Empire preserved its central territories and simultaneously blocked the path to Christian Europe while securing its status as a great power. However, the price was high. The extent of the empire significantly diminished in these battles, but Byzantium strengthened within its new borders. The influx of new external forces into the empire, as well as many reforms, revitalized the aging late Roman state. Following the Heraclian restoration, Byzantium was forced into many defensive wars against migrating peoples who settled on its borders, such as the Avars and Bulgars. After these victories, they began their offensives in Asia and the Balkans to regain some of the lost territories.

The Roman Empire, which had been united in the past, could not be revived. Although under the influence of Roman traditions and ideas, Byzantium transformed into a medieval Greek empire, while the West witnessed the formation of Germanic kingdoms in the former territories of the old empire. The future development of Byzantium was guided by the Greek culture and language, creating a new identity for the Byzantine Empire.[i]

In 751, Byzantine rule in northern and central Italy was destroyed. Ravenna was conquered by the Lombards, and the Exarchate of Ravenna ceased to exist.[ii] The newly established Frankish Kingdom, which grew into a new power, assumed the role of protector of the pope. In January 754, Pope Stephen II personally traveled to the Frankish Kingdom across the Alps to forge an alliance with the Frankish king. This act symbolically turned the pope away from the Byzantine emperor. In response, the

---

[i] Cleenewerck, *His Broken Body*.
[ii] Ostrogorsky, *History of the Byzantine State*.

Byzantine emperor separated the Hellenized southern Italian provinces of Calabria and Sicily and the province of Illyricum, which belonged to the Roman Church, from Rome.

Another factor in the distancing of the East from the West was iconoclasm. This deepened the rift between the two ecclesiastical centers and eventually pushed Rome out of the Greek East and Byzantium out of the Latin West. This meant that both the universalism of Byzantine imperial power and that of the Roman Church began to lose ground.

This rift was further deepened by the coronation of Charlemagne as emperor and the establishment of the Papal States.[i] A process was initiated to resist the influence of the East on the West and vice versa. The first step in resisting was taken by the iconoclast Constantine V, who subordinated southern Italy and a large part of the Balkan Peninsula to the Patriarchate of Constantinople. All these were immediate causes and indirect triggers, but direct confrontation between the Patriarchate of Constantinople and Rome could only begin after overcoming the iconoclastic crisis.

The Photian Schism

In 857, Photius became the patriarch of Constantinople. He ascended to this position after Emperor Michael III removed the previous patriarch, Ignatius. Photius was one of the most skilled diplomats and politicians to occupy the seat of the patriarch. The two candidates for the seat sought approval from Pope Nicholas I, an ambitious and energetic politician. A significant obstacle for Photius was that he was a layman who had been consecrated (ordained) within five days without adhering to church tradition. The pope sent his envoys to investigate the matter. To secure his position, Photius bribed the papal envoys, but the pope discovered this and dismissed them. Subsequently, in 863, the pope ordered Photius to abdicate from the seat of patriarch.[ii]

Constantinople was attempting to establish an autonomous position. In light of these events, Photius decided to excommunicate the pope and accused the Roman Church of heresy. The patriarch went further and criticized the Western Church for errors in matters of liturgy and church discipline. He attacked the Western doctrine of the Holy Spirit proceeding from the Father and the Son (*ex Patre Filioque*). Thus,

---

[i] Orlandis, *A Short History of the Catholic Church*.
[ii] Cleenewerck, *His Broken Body*.

Photius, whom the pope thought he could summon as a defendant, accused Rome of heresy in the name of orthodoxy.

In 867, a synod held in Constantinople under the emperor's presidency excommunicated Pope Nicholas I, rejected the Roman doctrine of the Holy Spirit's procession as heresy, and declared Rome's interference in Eastern Church affairs unlawful. A letter from the patriarch that extensively addressed and harshly condemned the different teachings and customs of the Roman Church, especially *Filioque*, was sent to the Eastern patriarchs.

Photius was supported by Emperor Michael until the emperor was killed in 867. The new emperor, Basil I deposed Photius and exiled him to a monastery. Ignatius was reinstated as the patriarch of Constantinople. Pope Nicholas I, having proven his ability to influence the affairs of the Eastern Church, distanced the Byzantines from Rome. This event is considered one of the factors leading to the Great Schism and is known as the Photian Schism.[i]

Political Reasons for the Schism

When discussing the political causes of the Great Schism, one must return to the factor that perhaps led to the greatest tensions in the disagreements between the East and the West: the elevation of the Patriarchate of Constantinople. This elevation occurred in 451 as a result of the Council of Chalcedon and its famous Canon 28, which placed all the territory of the Byzantine Empire under the jurisdiction of Constantinople. Such a provision was unacceptable to Pope Leo I, who refused to accept it since Constantinople was attempting to present itself as the "New Rome." For these reasons, Constantinople was transformed into the main patriarchate of the Christian East, becoming a rival to the Roman papacy. During a period when the Roman Church was distancing itself from the Byzantine Empire, the Eastern Church increasingly identified with Byzantium, leading Rome to turn toward the Frankish and German emperors. This cooling of relations caused a weakening of the church and its unity.

Another significant problem with church universalism between the East and West was the issue of church primacy.[ii] The primacy of the Roman Church played a crucial role in uniting the universal church,

---

[i] Jedin, Dolan, and Holland, *History of the Church*.
[ii] Cleenewerck, *His Broken Body*.

which had previously been divided. The Western Church believed that Jesus Christ chose his apostle Peter as his successor and the builder of the church's foundation as an institution on Earth. By this logic, the task entrusted to Peter was not temporary or limited by his lifetime; rather, it represented the establishment of a church heritage. Peter became the first bishop of Rome, and his successors inherited not only his title but also the right of primacy, establishing themselves as the pinnacle of the church, justified by the will of Christ. In this way, the Roman Church assumed the role of the center of unity for the universal secular church based on heritage.

Rome invoked its historical rights and ecclesiastical primacy based on legacy, which increasingly irritated Byzantium as the years passed. Byzantium wanted to be independent and structure the church according to its own terms rather than being dependent on every decision made by the Roman Church. The moment that highlighted the obvious problem of primacy was the attempted alliance between Rome and Byzantium against the Normans, as it revealed the struggle for primacy between the two sides.

Furthermore, in addition to the question of primacy, the Gregorian reform aimed at freeing the church from secular power and achieving autonomy. This movement was named and endorsed by Pope Gregory VII.[i] He attempted to resist the previous practices of kings, princes, and other nobles who distributed bishoprics and abbeys and exploited the church for financial gain (simony). One of the goals of the movement was to secure the right of church elections to ensure the independence of areas under religious authority. Additionally, the Cluniac reform awakened a sense of dignity and independence in the church and spiritual life. These reforms helped the Christian Church achieve a sense of value and awareness in the West.

One of the major supporters of the Cluniac reforms was Pope Leo IX, who, with the help of Cardinal Humbert, held a series of church synods across Europe from 1049 to 1053.[ii] At these synods, issues such as lay investiture, simony, and clerical marriages were condemned. These decisions soon clashed with the religious views of Constantinople and its patriarch, Michael Cerularius. Pope Leo IX politically attempted to claim

---

[i] Orlandis, *A Short History of the Catholic Church*.
[ii] Jedin, Dolan, and Holland, *History of the Church*.

southern Italy, which was gradually being taken from Byzantium by the Normans, provoking a conflict between the East and the West.

One of the political causes of the schism included iconoclasm.[i] Iconoclasm was initiated by the emperors of the Syrian (Isaurian) dynasty: Leo III the Isaurian, Constantine V, and Leo IV.[ii] They promoted an aristocratic view of the Christian faith, emphasizing the search for the absolute and direct worship of God without the mediation of images and other religious symbols. The movement was partly started because the veneration of icons, supported by the successful sale of saintly images by some monasteries and their art workshops, had reached a level of superstition. Icons were purchased for vows and prayers and celebrated as family saints (sometimes even taken as wedding godparents instead of living people). There were also frequent cases of consuming paint scraped from icons as medicine for various illnesses. Although iconoclasm might be theological and cultural in nature, the iconoclastic conflicts were political since they are remembered as a kind of religious war between the two sides of the church.

In 726, Emperor Leo III decreed a ban on icons in the Byzantine Empire, leading to catastrophic conflicts, the destruction of mosaics and frescoes, the devastation of monasteries, and the persecution and murder of iconophile priests. The conflicts intensified, necessitating military interventions. In 730, an imperial edict by Leo III, influenced by Jewish and Islamic models and church circles that were negatively disposed toward icons, banned the cult of religious images or icons.[iii]

The Seventh Ecumenical Council was convened in 787 under the auspices of Patriarch Tarasius and consisted of eight sessions held from September 27th to November 23rd of the same year. Empress Irene and her son participated in the final session of the council.[iv] The council was attended by over three hundred bishops, including two papal legates, who also signed the council's resolutions. Tarasius rejected the conclusions made in 754 against icons and refuted the iconoclast arguments against the veneration of images inspired by scripture and church tradition. He also defined icons as religious doctrine, viewing them as pictorial representations of Christ, the Mother of God, angels, and saints. He

---

[i] Besançon, *The Forbidden Image*.
[ii] Ostrogorsky, *History of the Byzantine State*.
[iii] Ibid.
[iv] Ibid.

believed they should be allowed because such expressions of faith led to the emulation of the religious ideals depicted in them. It was concluded that worship or *latreia* belonged only to God and was different from the veneration of images or proskynesis, which relates to the prototype and is not equated with God. Those who opposed the conclusions were treated leniently if they showed repentance for their earlier iconoclastic ideals.

During the 9th century, iconoclasm resurged, but after the decisions of the aforementioned council, it eventually succumbed to pressure. The West did not succumb to the temptations of iconoclasm; there, images were initially valued for their moral value. Thus, iconoclasm became one of the disagreements between the West and the East.

The lack of sustained communication and linguistic misunderstandings led to the separation of these two sides. Greek was the official language of the Christian Church for the first three centuries, but at the turn of the 3rd century, Latin was introduced into literature and liturgy. By the end of the 4th century, under the influence of Carthage, Western liturgy fully adopted Latin. This language barrier not only created a rift between the East and the West but also led to mutual suspicion and distrust at a time when the church was shaken by heresies and theological disputes.[i] The division deepened with the introduction of differences in discipline and rites.

Theological Causes

From the formation of the Christian Church up until the Great Schism of 1054, numerous differences emerged between the eastern and western parts of the empire. The theological, doctrinal, and cultural differences that separate the Western and Eastern Churches are not simple issues. Differences exist even among Eastern churches, with some Eastern theologians highlighting distinctions between Russian doctrine and their own. It is generally accepted that the two churches, Eastern and Western, diverge in the doctrines of the procession of the Holy Spirit from the Father and the Son, the primacy and infallibility of the Roman bishop, purgatory, and the two most recent Marian dogmas, especially the Immaculate Conception.

Debates on the doctrine of the procession of the Holy Spirit arose as early as 381 at the Second Ecumenical Council in Constantinople, where the teaching of the third divine person was condemned as heresy. Further

---

[i] Cleenewerck, *His Broken Body*.

disagreements over the Holy Spirit led to the insertion of the Filioque clause into the Nicene-Constantinopolitan Creed.

The Nicene Creed of 381 in its original form states: "I believe in the Holy Spirit, the Lord and Giver of Life, who proceeds from the Father, who with the Father and the Son is worshiped and glorified." In the West, this part reads: "I believe in the Holy Spirit, the Lord and Giver of Life, who proceeds from the Father and the Son, who with the Father and the Son is worshiped and glorified."[i]

The addition "and the Son" (Latin *Filioque*) was added in the West by the 5th century at the latest. This doctrine was based on the theological works of some Eastern Church fathers, such as Saint Cyril of Alexandria, who believed that everything the Father has, he has given to his only begotten Son, thus making the Son consubstantial with the Father. However, many Eastern theologians and churchmen did not find these explanations sufficient. This doctrine clashed with their beliefs, making the Filioque a significant point of contention between the two sides. Patriarch Michael Cerularius was also among those who considered the addition of the Filioque to the Nicene-Constantinopolitan Creed a violation and heresy by the Roman Church, claiming that this act caused it to lose its jurisdiction in the Church of Christ.

Regarding the sacraments, the greatest difference was celibacy. The West reformed the church to enforce celibacy, prohibiting priestly marriages, while the East disagreed, allowing such marriages. Further differences are found in the sacrament of chrismation (confirmation) and baptism. In the East, it was typically performed by an ordinary priest, whereas in the West, this duty was usually carried out by a bishop. Contrary to Catholic belief, Eastern Orthodox theologians hold that chrismation must be repeated for an apostate returning to their faith. Orthodox theologians also criticized the West for deviating from Orthodox teachings on several other points.

A problem also arose in the sacrament of the Eucharist. The West used unleavened bread for the sacrament, which Eastern churchmen criticized, along with the fact that Holy Communion was not given to small children. Another important point of controversy regarding the sacraments was the prayer to the Holy Spirit, which is believed to transform the bread and wine into the body and blood of the Savior. This

---

[i] Cleenewerck.

act, known as the epiclesis, is absent in the Western Church, which believes that the transformation occurs during the recitation of Christ's words and does not require the mention of the epiclesis. Eastern priests, however, believe that the words of the epiclesis must be spoken and that this alone is necessary for the transformation.[i]

Another difference between the two theologies and churches regarding the sacrament is related to confession, specifically the penance imposed by the priest on the penitent during confession. In the Eastern Church, penance or epitimia served instructive purposes, while in Catholic doctrine, it served exclusively for forgiveness.

Finally, Eastern and Western churchmen disagreed on the issue of church councils. Some Eastern Orthodox theologians viewed the Trullan Council as ecumenical, calling it the Fifth-Sixth Council, as it completed the decisions of the Fifth and Sixth Ecumenical Councils.

In conclusion, the theological issues that were prevalent just before the Great Schism of 1054 were old issues that had divided churchmen since the time of Photius and earlier.

The theologian differences were not, as sometimes portrayed, the cause of the Great Schism. They were given as the official reasons, but the actual cause was the separation of political and cultural development. The political separation was finalized with the loss of Byzantine territory in Italy and with Rome's decision to seek protection from the Frankish Kingdom. The cultural separation happened parallel with politics, with exposure to different influences and differences in language.

The Great Schism was one of many crises between two churches, which permitted their relationship before and after 1054. Their distancing continued well into the 13th and 14th centuries. The Great Schism ended without a solution and served as a final, symbolic step in the separation between the East and the West that still exists.

---

[i] Cleenewerck.

Section Four: Decline and Fall (1081–1453 CE)

Chapter 13: The Komnenian Dynasty and the Crusades

Introduction

During the reign of Empress Theodora, who was the last representative of the Macedonian dynasty, there were discussions about the future successor. Given that Theodora was elderly and her death was expected any day, and since she had no offspring, the logical step was to choose a new emperor. Many tried to influence Theodora regarding the appointment of her successor. Finally, Leo Paraspondylos convinced Theodora to name Michael Stratiotikos as the new emperor. Theodora's decision was accepted without any opposition by the patriarch of Constantinople.

Michael was shortly dethroned, and his successor, Isaac Komnenos, reigned from 1057 to 1059.[1] After just two years of rule, Isaac abdicated, and Constantine X Doukas was chosen as the new emperor. The exact reason for his abdication is unknown, but it is presumed that he was a victim of a conspiracy by those dissatisfied with his rule. His short rule would probably have stayed as a footnote in history books if he had not been the first ruler of the Komnenian dynasty, one of the most influential royal families in Byzantine history.

---

[1] Ostrogorsky, *History of the Byzantine State*.

Constantine X Doukas died in 1067, leaving his underage son, Michael VII Doukas, as his heir. His mother, Eudokia Makrembolitissa, assumed the regency. With the empire facing serious military threats, Patriarch John VIII Xiphilinos granted her permission to remarry, overriding a clause in Constantine's will. Soon afterward, she married the general Romanos Diogenes, who was crowned Emperor Romanos IV.

During his reign, Byzantium faced numerous problems. The problems faced by the empire were partially caused by the growing influence and power of the aristocracy, which weakened the empire's military structure. A series of weak rulers after the strong soldier-emperor Basil II disbanded the large armies and stockpiled gold in Constantinople in order to hire mercenaries. Despite the severity of losing Italy, the Byzantine Empire suffered its greatest catastrophe in Asia Minor. The Seljuk Turks, who were primarily focused on fighting the Fatimids of Egypt, launched a series of raids in Armenia and eastern Anatolia, which was the main source of Byzantine recruits. By reclaiming much of this region, the Komnenian emperors halted the Turkish advance in Anatolia for over two centuries. In the process, they laid the groundwork for the Byzantine successor states of Nicaea, Epirus, and Trebizond.

Diminishing Influence in Italy

The Byzantine Empire's last stronghold in Italy fell under Norman control in 1071. The Seljuk Turks attacked Byzantine cities, forcing Romanos to engage around 200,000 soldiers to expel the Turks from Asia Minor. A conflict arose between the Byzantines and Turks near Manzikert in Armenia.[i] During the battle, the Normans deserted, leaving the Byzantines on their own. Initially, they had the advantage, and victory was within reach. However, a false rumor spread by Romanos's rival, Andronikos Doukas, that said the emperor had been killed in the battle led to the army scattering in fear. Many historians believe this defeat was pivotal, as it allowed the Turks to expand farther into Asia Minor and deal a heavy blow to Byzantium from which it never fully recovered.[ii] At the Battle of Manzikert in 1071, the Turks captured Emperor Romanos IV Diogenes and overtook Anatolia, which severely weakened Byzantine influence in the east. There were some exceptions where Byzantine control was still strong, most notably in Lesser Armenia.[iii]

---

[i] Haldon, *Byzantium at War*.
[ii] Ostrogorsky, *History of the Byzantine State*.
[iii] The western part of the former Armenian Kingdom, known as Armenia Minor.

Romanos IV's successor, Michael VII Doukas, appealed to Pope Gregory VII for assistance against the advancing Seljuk Turks. However, Gregory was deeply engaged in the Investiture Controversy with Holy Roman Emperor Henry IV and did not respond to the request. This appeal, though unsuccessful, foreshadowed future attempts by Byzantine emperors to seek Western support, particularly during the era of the Crusades.

The Komnenian dynasty played a pivotal role during this period. From the accession of Alexios I Komnenos in 1081 to the death of Andronikos I in 1185, the Byzantine Empire experienced a period of political, military, and economic revival, often referred to by historians as the Komnenian restoration.

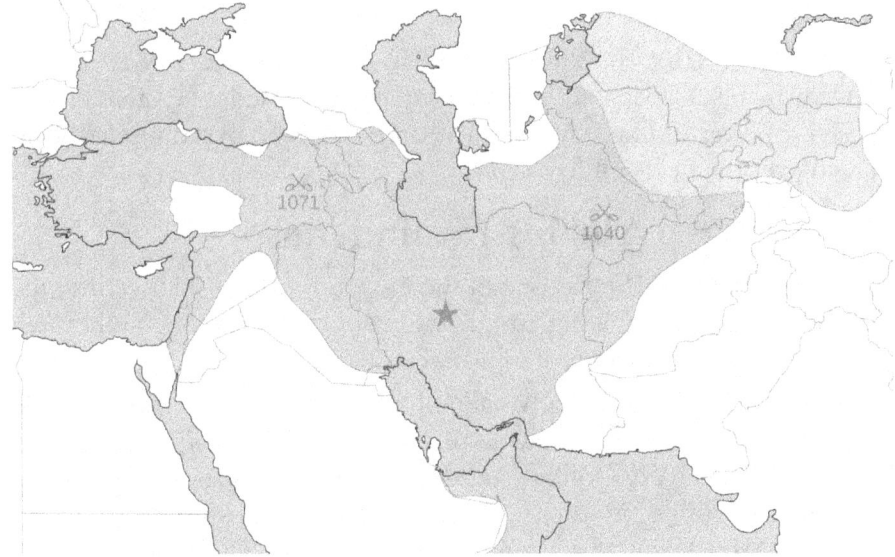

Expansion of the Seljuks in the 11ᵗʰ century.[198]

Michael Doukas

Michael VII Doukas, son of Constantine X, became emperor during a period of profound crisis. Byzantium faced external threats and internal instability, particularly after the disastrous Battle of Manzikert in 1071, which led to the loss of Asia Minor to the Seljuk Turks.

Michael was seen as a weak ruler, ceding much of the empire's administration to the powerful eunuch Nikephoritzes. The latter imposed harsh taxation policies while mismanaging military funding and court spending. These failures caused widespread public discontent, particularly among the military, which led to desertions and mutinies. The devaluation of Byzantine currency under Michael's reign earned him the mocking nickname "Parapinakes," meaning "a quarter less," symbolizing the economic decline.

Meanwhile, the empire's control over the Balkans weakened. The Bulgarians remained restive, and Slavic groups such as the Serbs began asserting greater autonomy, signaling future challenges to imperial authority.

Facing mounting pressure, Michael VII abdicated in 1078 and entered monastic life. While he was spared, Nikephoritzes became a scapegoat for the regime's failures. He attempted to flee to Heraclea Pontica, but he was captured and handed over to the new emperor, Nikephoros III Botaneiates.

Nikephoros III's rule lasted only a few years. In 1081, he was overthrown by Alexios I Komnenos, who started the Komnenian dynasty—a powerful line that would restore some of Byzantium's former strength over the next century.[i]

Alexios I Komnenos

Alexios I (r. 1081-1118) was one of the most powerful nobles of his time. He focused on stabilizing the empire and restoring Byzantine authority in Anatolia through alliances and military campaigns.

Alexios I Komnenos already had a distinguished military career by the time he rose to the throne, having served under Emperors Romanos IV Diogenes, Michael VII Doukas, and Nikephoros III Botaneiates. He and his politically astute mother, Anna Dalassene, conspired to depose Nikephoros III. Anna, who came from the influential Dalassenos family, was a formidable figure in her own right and maintained close ties with Maria of Alania, the former empress to both Michael VII and Nikephoros III.

To strengthen the plot, Anna persuaded Maria to adopt Alexios as her son, a move that enhanced his legitimacy and tied him to the Doukas dynasty. Maria's chief concern was securing the succession for her own son, Constantine Doukas, whose position was increasingly threatened under Nikephoros III. As part of the scheme, Anna might have staged a diversion by seeking sanctuary in the Hagia Sophia, as she allegedly

---

[i] Angold, *The Byzantine Empire, 1025-1204*.

feared a plot to blind her sons. While she occupied the emperor's attention, Alexios and his brother Isaac rallied support and marched on Constantinople, successfully ousting Nikephoros III.

Following Alexios's coronation in 1081, Constantine Doukas was named co-emperor, and Anna Dalassene was granted the prestigious title of Augusta. The Komnenoi and the Doukai forged a temporary alliance, which was further solidified by Alexios's marriage to Irene Doukaina. Although Irene was young and less politically seasoned than Maria of Alania, she became an important figure in the new dynasty. Maria remained at court and likely retained some influence early in Alexios's reign.

With the birth of John II Komnenos in 1087, Alexios secured a direct heir, marking a turning point in his personal authority. Over time, both Anna Dalassene and Maria of Alania receded from political life, and Alexios began to rule more independently. His reign was marked by persistent military challenges, but unlike several of his predecessors, Alexios successfully reasserted control over both the court and the provinces, founding the Komnenian dynasty and ushering in a period of relative stability and military revival for the Byzantine Empire.

The Byzantine Empire was threatened by the Normans under Robert Guiscard, who invaded the Balkans from the west. After inflicting a defeat on Emperor Alexios I Komnenos, Robert was forced to return to Italy to support Pope Gregory VII, who was facing a crisis in Rome. In his absence, Robert left his son, Bohemond, to lead the Norman campaign. Given their mutual opposition to Robert and Pope Gregory, Emperor Alexios found a strategic ally in Henry IV of the Holy Roman Empire, who was then locked in conflict with the papacy during the Investiture Controversy.[i]

The Byzantine emperor also made an alliance with the Venetians. What Byzantine troops lacked on the ground was even worse at sea, so the aid from the Venetian fleet was of great importance. With their help, Alexios managed to defeat the Norman armies led by young Bohemond, marking the beginning of the Komnenian restoration.

---

[i] Ostrogorsky, George, *History of the Byzantine State*, Rutgers University Press, 1969, p. 337.

Shortly after, the Pechenegs, a nomadic group, invaded the empire from the north. Alexios allied with the Cumans, another nomadic group, and with their help, they annihilated the Pecheneg horde in 1091. By making clever alliances and using his advantages at the right moment, Alexios proved himself to be a great leader with good political connections.

During Alexios I's reign, the Byzantine Empire established standing armies known as *tagmata* to respond rapidly to threats. These units consisted of both cavalry and infantry. The Komnenian era focused on recruiting professional, disciplined, and well-equipped soldiers. Reforms also enhanced logistical support for the army, ensuring a steady supply of provisions, arms, and equipment, which enabled Byzantine forces to operate more effectively and for longer periods of time. Additionally, fortifications, roads, and communication networks were developed to facilitate rapid movement. Armies also saw improvements in siege warfare techniques, including the use of more advanced siege engines and tactics. Military manuals and strategic treatises were also revised during the Komnenian period, providing guidelines for future commanders.

Alexios Komnenos.[129]

In 1095, Alexios sent an appeal for military aid to Pope Urban II. Unlike their predecessors, Michael Doukas and Pope Gregory, they struck an alliance. Pope Urban II answered the emperor's call the same year and convened the Council of Clermont in France, calling for participants to fight in a holy war to recapture Jerusalem from Muslim control. He preached that Christians should unite in a fight against Muslims, the common enemies of the Christian faith, and promised to provide indulgences to those who enlisted.

The earliest wave of Crusaders, led by Peter the Hermit, a priest from France, was composed largely of peasants, the poor, and indebted individuals seeking spiritual rewards and escape from hardship. Undisciplined and poorly equipped, they suffered heavy losses shortly after entering Asia Minor. The main force of the First Crusade followed later and was made up of prominent feudal nobles, such as Duke Godfrey of Bouillon, Count Raymond of Toulouse, Count Hugh I of Vermandois (brother of French King Philip I), Duke Robert of Normandy, and Bohemond of Taranto. These leaders agreed to support Emperor Alexios I Komnenos in reclaiming Byzantine territories in Anatolia in exchange for safe passage and logistical support. The Byzantine general Tatikios was assigned to accompany the Crusaders, helping coordinate their efforts in the early stages of the campaign.[1]

Alexios demanded every Crusade leader to take an oath of homage when they arrived in Constantinople, and his former enemy Bohemond was no exception. French knight Hugh de Payen, with eight more followers, swore an oath to be a sort of police escort for the Crusaders. They got a house near the Temple of Solomon, defining them as Knights Templar.

Despite facing financial challenges and resorting to drastic measures, such as melting down church artifacts and selling church lands, Alexios achieved important military victories. He recovered Nicaea, Rhodes, and Ephesus. Alexios's popularity was affected by his financial measures, but he managed to be consistently successful in mitigating dissent by the time of his death in 1118.

In terms of foreign policy, the period between the death of Basil II and the rise of Alexios I Komnenos marked the collapse of Byzantine authority in Asia Minor, the loss of imperial possessions in Italy, and a noticeable weakening of control in the Balkans. These setbacks coincided with the disintegration of the socioeconomic and military systems that had sustained the empire under Basil II. Alexios I's efforts to restore imperial stability were based on new foundations, with his administrative, military, religious, and cultural reforms forming the pillars of the revitalized Byzantine state.

After Byzantium freed itself from danger, it was time to confront new threats. This time, Alexios successfully dealt with Prince Vukan of Serbia

---

[1] Ostrogorsky, George, *History of the Byzantine State*, Rutgers University Press, 1969, p. 342.

(Rashka), who was disrupting the internal security of Byzantium with his raids. Alexios had to be content with the apparent submission of Prince Vukan in 1094, as old Byzantine allies, the Cumans, invaded the empire, causing disorder all the way to Adrianople. This time, they were led by Constantine Diogenes, who claimed the imperial crown. Alexios scattered them and captured the pretender. He finally managed to establish peace in the European part of the empire and intended to focus on Asia Minor. However, during this period, a Crusader army approached Byzantium on its way to Jerusalem, looting Hungary and the Balkan lands along the way.[i]

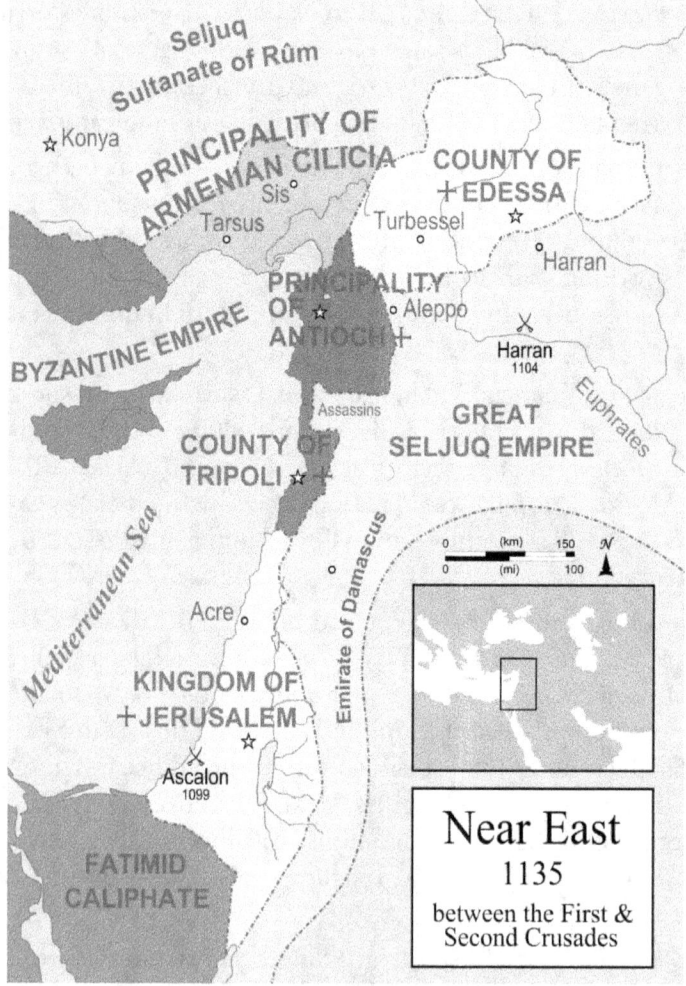

The Crusader States in the Holy Land.[180]

---

[i] Haldon, *Byzantium at War.*

John II Komnenos

John II Komnenos succeeded his father, Alexios I, in 1118 and is often regarded as one of the most successful rulers of the Komnenian dynasty. The third child and first son of Alexios and Irene Doukaina, John was recognized early on as heir, and by 1108, during negotiations with Bohemond of Taranto, he was already acting in an authoritative role.[1]

Known by the epithet Kaloïōannēs, often translated as "John the Good" or "John the Beautiful," John was praised more for his spiritual and moral character than for his physical appearance. William of Tyre, a contemporary, described him as physically unattractive, further reinforcing the view that the nickname referred to his virtuous nature.

John's reputation for justice, discipline, and piety echoed that of his father, Alexios I, and his mother, Irene Doukaina, whose marriage was noted for its stability and mutual devotion. John himself was deeply spiritual, frugal, and famously moderate in his exercise of power. He notably refrained from excessive cruelty or the theatrical punishments common in medieval courts, earning him comparisons to Roman Emperor Marcus Aurelius.

To secure alliances in the volatile Balkans, Alexios arranged for John to marry Piroska of Hungary (later known as Irene) in 1104. This union strengthened Byzantine ties with Hungary at a time when Slavic groups, particularly the Bulgarians and Serbs, were asserting greater autonomy. John's reign brought relative stability and prosperity to the empire, continuing the Komnenian revival.

After taking power, John II did not have time to rest. The Seljuks attacked the southern part of Thrace in 1119. John decided on an offensive, which he launched with

John II Komnenos, a mosaic from Hagia Sophia.[181]

---

[1] Mullett and Smythe, *Alexios I Komnenos*.

his friend John Axouch. He achieved success in the war, crowned by the capture of Sozopolis in 1120. However, John did not have time to celebrate because he had to confront the Pechenegs, who had crossed the Danube and started looting the surrounding areas in 1121. After defeating them and pacifying Rashka, new problems continued with the Serbs, who still frequently rebelled against the Byzantine Empire by allying with Hungary, which was becoming an increasingly strong power in the Balkans and the Adriatic.[i]

The Hungarians eventually decided to attack to establish their influence and power in the Balkans, and in 1128, their army destroyed the fortress of Belgrade. After that, the Byzantine heavy cavalry won a victory over Hungary, following their advance farther south. John's army successfully continued to advance to Zemun. Hungary was forced to agree to peace. John could finally focus on Asia Minor after stabilizing the Balkans.[ii]

John decided to reclaim territories in Anatolia and launched several campaigns toward this goal. The first few were not very successful due to the military situation and conspiracies in Constantinople, which forced the emperor to abandon the campaigns. However, after the death of his wife Irene, John returned to Anatolia. There, he conquered Gangra and Kastamonu in 1135 and achieved victory against the Danishmends, one of the Turkic tribes from Anatolia. After that, he decided to continue his path of conquest and set out for Antioch. On the way, he had to confront the Armenian Principality of Cilicia in 1137. After this victory, the cities of Tarsus, Adana, and Mamistra fell. Finally, John reached Antioch, which he captured after a short siege.[iii]

John did not solve some problems solely with force but also with skillful diplomacy. This is best seen when, after the establishment of Norman rule in Sicily, he established a blockade of the Norman fleet in cooperation with Germany and Pisa.

The emperor planned another campaign and the reconquest of territories in Palestine, but he was prevented by an accident that occurred during a hunting expedition. During the hunt, he was attacked by a wild boar, and in the struggle, he was pierced through the arm by a poisoned

---

[i] Ostrogorsky, *History of the Byzantine State*.
[ii] Haldon, *Byzantium at War*.
[iii] Ostrogorsky, *History of the Byzantine State*.

arrow. The only option was amputation, which he refused. John died on April 8ᵗʰ, 1143.[i]

Manuel I Komnenos

Emperor John II Komnenos decided to bypass his older son Isaac and leave the crown to his youngest son, Manuel.[ii] The new emperor, Manuel I, was born in 1118 and ascended the throne as a young man. It's not entirely clear why John II decided to bypass Isaac and the other older brothers of Manuel, who was fourth in line to inherit the throne. It is possible that Manuel was perceived as the most suitable for the throne out of all his brothers.

Manuel I Komnenos was described as a ruler with a fierier temperament than his father and a much greater inclination toward Western customs than his predecessors. He introduced new forms of behavior, such as participating in knightly tournaments. Additionally, at the beginning of his reign, more and more foreigners arrived in the empire, causing internal unrest. He adopted his father's political goals, although he pursued them much more recklessly. He also continued to develop good relations with Germany and married King Conrad III of Germany's sister-in-law, Bertha of Sulzbach.

Manuel Komnenos with Maria of Antioch, his second wife.[183]

---

[i] Ibid.
[ii] Ibid.

At the very beginning of Manuel's reign, he faced the same problem as his grandfather Alexios: the arrival of the Crusaders, which included his brother-in-law Conrad.[i] It is worth noting that relations between the French king and the Byzantine emperor were quite strained to the point that there was even speculation about a Crusader takeover of Constantinople. Following his grandfather's example, Manuel negotiated the handover of territories that were previously under Byzantine control and then transferred the Crusader army across the Bosphorus to avoid disturbances.

While the Byzantine Empire was preoccupied with the Crusaders in 1147, Norman King Roger II launched a devastating naval raid, capturing the island of Corfu and sacking the wealthy cities of Corinth and Thebes, which were Byzantine territory. On his way back to Germany, Conrad stopped in Constantinople and promised to help Manuel in the fight against the Normans. Venice also joined the anti-Norman coalition, but Byzantium managed to recapture Corfu in 1149.[ii]

Manuel I Komnenos planned a military campaign against Norman territories in Italy, with Emperor Conrad III of Germany initially promising support. However, Roger II of Sicily skillfully used diplomacy and exploited unrest in Germany, forcing Conrad to withdraw. Roger secured alliances with the Kingdom of Hungary and the Serbian principality of Rashka. By 1149, the Grand Župan of Rashka had incited revolts and openly defied Byzantine authority. Roger also sought to ally with King Louis VII of France, who had previously entertained plans for a crusade against Byzantium, though the French knights ultimately refused to take part in such a campaign.

The European states were divided into two camps; on one side were Byzantium, Germany, and Venice, and on the other were the Normans, France, Hungary, and Rashka, with the support of the papacy. After Conrad III resolved the internal problems, everything was ready for the campaign in Italy. However, before the campaign could begin, Conrad died and was succeeded by Frederick I Barbarossa, who was not interested in a joint attack. From that point on, Germany and Byzantium began to diverge in their policies.

---

[i] Riley-Smith, *The Crusades*.
[ii] Angold, *The Byzantine Empire, 1025-1204*.

After the death of King Roger II of Sicily in 1154, Emperor Manuel I Komnenos launched a campaign to reassert Byzantine influence in southern Italy. His fleet arrived at Ancona in 1155. With the assistance of defecting Norman vassals, Manuel's forces managed to seize control of several key cities in Apulia despite operating with a relatively small army.

However, the initial success of the Byzantines did not please their old allies, Frederick Barbarossa and Venice. The following year, Roger's successor, William I, launched a counterattack. The ensuing Battle of Brindisi saw Byzantium inflict a heavy blow to the Normans, forcing them to make peace in 1158. After this successful campaign, Manuel increasingly promoted the idea of restoring the Roman Empire to the time of Justinian, although he lacked the means to undertake such a venture.

Manuel achieved great success in the Latin states. First, he subdued Armenian Prince Thoros, who had entrenched himself in Cilicia, incorporating him among the "Roman servants" in 1158. He then moved against Antioch and its ruler, Reynald. Reynald had to acknowledge the supreme authority of Byzantium and pledge his assistance. After this, the king of Jerusalem, Baldwin III, visited Manuel and placed himself under his protection.[i] This was a significant achievement, as Manuel had secured the loyalty of the Latin states, which viewed Byzantium as their protector.

In his dealings with Hungary, Emperor Manuel I Komnenos continued his father's policy of intervening in succession disputes. Initially, he supported Stephen IV and Ladislaus II—uncles of Hungarian King Stephen III—during a period of civil strife. Although Manuel attempted to install a pro-Byzantine ruler, Stephen III ultimately retained the throne.

To solidify Byzantine influence, Stephen III's younger brother, Béla, was sent to Constantinople, where he was raised in the imperial court and was betrothed to Manuel's daughter. Manuel granted Béla the prestigious title of despotes and named him heir to the Byzantine Empire. In addition, Béla was promised governance over Dalmatia and Croatia, further tying the two realms together politically.

Béla was invited to Constantinople to negotiate terms of an alliance, but the talks ultimately failed since Stephen III resisted Byzantine influence. In response, Manuel I prepared for a military confrontation,

---

[i] Angold.

dispatching troops to intimidate Hungarian factions. In 1164, he personally led a campaign across the Danube and successfully established Byzantine control over the region of Sirmium, securing key territories between the Sava and the Danube. Concurrently, a Byzantine army was sent to Dalmatia, where it managed to seize several coastal cities, further extending imperial influence in the western Balkans.

However, due to health problems, Manuel left the campaign, and command was taken over by his nephew, Andronikos Kontostephanos. Andronikos Kontostephanos, through his strategic maneuvers, managed to force the Hungarian army into battle near the fortress of Zemun in the Sirmium region. After the successful battle, the territories of Dalmatia, Croatia, Bosnia, and the Sirmium region fell to Byzantium in 1167.[i]

During this period of conflict with Hungary, the Byzantine Empire was shaken by frequent uprisings in Rashka. Manuel suppressed these rebellions and replaced the local lords, but his actions did not completely resolve the issues. In 1166, Stefan Nemanja became the lord of Rashka. Stefan also turned against the emperor and dealt him a severe defeat. However, after Hungary's defeat, Rashka was left without a powerful ally in its fight against Byzantium. In 1172, Manuel marched on Rashka with a large army. Nemanja abandoned resistance and became a Byzantine vassal.[ii]

New problems emerged when Sultan Kilij Arslan II of the Seljuk Sultanate of Rum consolidated his power in Asia Minor and failed to honor previous agreements with Byzantium, including the return of several cities and potential military cooperation. In response, Emperor Manuel I Komnenos launched a major campaign in 1176, intending to capture the Seljuk capital, Iconium. Kilij Arslan, recognizing the threat, attempted to negotiate, but Manuel refused.

Anticipating Manuel would take the same route he had used in 1146, the sultan prepared an ambush near the ruined fortress of Myriokephalon, where the terrain was narrow and ideal for a trap. The Seljuks also scorched the land, destroying food and water sources along the way. Despite warnings from his commanders, Manuel ordered a frontal assault into the pass, where the Seljuk forces had already positioned themselves.[iii]

---

[i] Ostrogorsky, *History of the Byzantine State*.
[ii] Ibid.
[iii] Haldon, *Byzantium at War*.

Though the Byzantines managed to break through the pass and avoid total annihilation, they suffered heavy losses in manpower and lost much of their siege equipment. As a result, Emperor Manuel I was forced to abandon his campaign against Iconium. The defeat was significant enough that some contemporaries compared it to the catastrophe at Manzikert in 1071. This turning point ended Byzantine hopes of reclaiming central Anatolia.[i]

Despite all his previous military successes, Manuel's grand plans remained unattainable. His constant warfare exceeded the available strength and resources, creating many enemies. Moreover, during Manuel's reign, the military grew in importance. The population became increasingly impoverished, and more people chose to join the army. To meet the need for recruiting soldiers, Manuel increasingly used the pronoia system, granting land to nobles in exchange for military service, which accelerated the process of feudalization, weakened the state, and undermined the country's defensive strength. These processes would further weaken the Byzantine Empire after Manuel's death.

Alexios II Komnenos and Andronikos Komnenos

After Manuel's death, his twelve-year-old son Alexios II ascended the throne, with Empress Maria of Antioch acting as regent.[ii] However, this arrangement faced opposition from other members of the dynasty and the populace due to Maria's Latinophile policies. Andronikos Komnenos also opposed these policies, thus emerging as an ideal candidate for the new emperor.

Andronikos reached Constantinople without significant resistance; the only opposition came from Protosebastos Alexios, who attempted to block the Bosphorus.[iii] However, a revolt erupted in Constantinople, leading to Alexios being blinded and imprisoned. In May 1182, a massacre occurred in the city, resulting in the killing and plundering of a significant portion of the Latin population.

---

[i] Ostrogorsky, *History of the Byzantine State*.
[ii] Ibid.
[iii] A protosebastos was another title denoting a high court position.

Alexios II fell under Andronikos's influence and was forced to sign a death warrant for his mother. Subsequently, Alexios II became a co-ruler, although this was merely a façade. Two months later, Alexios II was strangled by Andronikos's supporters, and Andronikos officially became the Byzantine emperor. He immediately began addressing the issues of bribery and corruption with strict and merciless measures. He also targeted the nobility, using violent means against them, which created even more enemies. Furthermore, external political problems arose due to the absence of the authority that had characterized Manuel's reign.[i]

By 1181, taking advantage of the political instability following Emperor Manuel I's death, Béla III of Hungary regained control over Dalmatia, Croatia, and the region of Syrmia. With imperial authority weakened, uprisings broke out in Rashka, where the Grand Župan Stefan Nemanja quickly reasserted independence from Byzantine rule. This shift culminated in a joint Hungarian-Serbian invasion of Byzantine territory in 1183. The campaign devastated key cities such as Belgrade, Braničevo, Niš, and Sofia. Nemanja not only secured Rashka's autonomy but also expanded his domain by annexing the strategically vital region of Zeta in what is now Montenegro.[ii]

Asia also faced troubles, with frequent uprisings against Andronikos's rule led by magnate families, particularly the local Komnenians. Their representative, Isaac Komnenos, established independent rule in Cyprus, separating it from the Byzantine Empire. Isaac assumed the imperial title and minted his own coins; he faced no punishment for his actions. Andronikos only executed a few of his friends in Constantinople.[iii]

However, the greatest threat to the Byzantine Empire came from the Normans, who launched a military campaign. They first attacked Durrës in 1185 and then moved toward Thessalonica, occupying Corfu, Cephalonia, and Zakynthos along the way. They reached Thessalonica without significant resistance, where they began a siege by land and sea. The city's defenses were weak, and it was soon captured. After Thessalonica, the Norman army advanced toward Serres. Fears of a Norman conquest of Constantinople grew, and there was mounting dissatisfaction with Andronikos's tyrannical rule.

---

[i] Ibid.
[ii] Ibid.
[iii] Angold, *The Byzantine Empire, 1025-1204*.

The crisis reached its peak when Emperor Andronikos I Komnenos ordered the arrest of Isaac Angelos. Isaac evaded capture by taking sanctuary in Hagia Sophia, where he rallied public support and was quickly proclaimed emperor by a mob. Andronikos attempted to flee, likely toward Kievan Rus', but was intercepted by Isaac's supporters and returned to Constantinople. There, he was subjected to brutal torture. His hair and beard were torn out, and his right hand was mutilated. Eventually, he was dragged through the city and killed in the Hippodrome before a vengeful crowd. With his death in 1185, the Komnenian dynasty came to an end, marking the close of a pivotal chapter in Byzantine history.[i]

---

[i] Ostrogorsky, *History of the Byzantine State*.

Chapter 14: The Fourth Crusade and Recovery

The Fourth Crusade

In letters dated August 15th, 1198, Pope Innocent III called for the organization of a new crusade to the Holy Land. Motivated by the inconclusive outcome of the Third Crusade, disappointment with the failed German expedition under Henry VI, and the continued Muslim control of Jerusalem, Pope Innocent aimed to reclaim the Holy Land in full. He also used the opportunity to assert papal supremacy by taking a central role in organizing the Crusader army and positioning the papacy as a dominant force in secular political affairs.[i]

The recruitment for the Fourth Crusade did not proceed favorably. Due to poor papal diplomacy and continuous international instability, the burden of military leadership fell on counts rather than kings. It is doubtful that the Crusade would have been feasible without investments from the church leaders. A recurring challenge of earlier Crusades was the need to raise vast sums of money, which often influenced the direction and effectiveness of the campaigns. In early 1202, a group of French envoys arrived in Venice to negotiate support for the Fourth Crusade. Six knightly envoys, all of whom had taken the cross, signed a contract with the Venetian doge, Enrico Dandolo. According to the

---

[i] Bartlett, *The Making of Europe*.

agreement, Venice would provide ships and logistical support to transport the Crusader army to Egypt, which was viewed as the strategic gateway to reclaiming the Holy Land.[1]

This risky venture left the Venetians without a significant portion of their financial income for a year, as they invested in a project that did not promise secure profit. Moreover, no one could guarantee that enough Crusaders would enroll and adhere to the terms set by the group of leaders. Although the French counts were extremely wealthy and politically powerful, they had no authority to bind anyone except themselves and their vassals. Due to the gamble by both sides, the agreement became a deadly trap.

Upon arriving in Venice, the Crusaders were housed on the island of Lido at the eastern edge of the lagoon, where conditions ranged from comfortable to desperate depending on one's status, wealth, and connections with the nobles' entourages. The estimated number of thirty-five thousand warriors was not reached. According to some estimates, only a third of the total number arrived: just a quarter of the knights and half of the infantry. However, the empty spaces in the ranks of the ships' galleys and boats led to confusion about covering the costs, which had to be met under the contract terms. Thus, the Venetians pressured the Crusaders to honor the agreement.

The first option to attempt to resolve the crisis was for each Crusader to pay for his own transport. Even though this was insufficient, everyone contributed what they could. Most began selling their equipment and property to avoid the shame of being unable to pay the agreed price and keep their word. Despite efforts, the Crusaders still owed about thirty-four thousand marks, around 40 percent. Many Crusaders were left with barely enough to survive the upcoming winter on the island of Lido. Venetian Doge Enrico Dandolo understood how important it was for the main command to maintain its reputation and promote the Crusade's goals.

At one point, in September 1202, the blind Dandolo granted the Crusaders a temporary moratorium on their debt repayment. In return, the Crusaders were to embark on the ready fleet and help the Venetians capture the Dalmatian port of Zadar. The Crusaders would receive a

---

[1] Nicolle and Hook, *The Fourth Crusade 1202-04*.

share of the spoils to revive their hopes of settling the remaining debt.[i] This move was justified as the first step toward Egypt, which was impossible to reach until spring due to the season.

Pope Innocent III had explicitly ordered the Crusaders, under the conditions of the campaign he had drafted and signed, not to attack, conquer, or destroy Christian lands.[ii] However, the circumstances were such that the Crusaders could not adhere to these conditions because the debt had not been fully paid. It was necessary to keep the army from disbanding and the endeavor from collapsing. Within a month of setting out, they had conquered Trieste and Muggia, followed by Pula. The fleet arrived at Zadar on St. Martin's Day, November 11th, 1202, and captured the port.[iii]

Alexios Angelos and the Agreement with the Crusaders

In the summer of 1202, Alexios Angelos, the son of the deposed Byzantine emperor Isaac II, fled Constantinople and eventually made his way to the court of his brother-in-law, Philip of Swabia, in Germany. There, he learned of the Crusader army gathering in Venice and was advised to offer them an alliance. In exchange for their help in reclaiming the Byzantine throne, Alexios promised substantial military and financial aid, including funding the Crusade and pledging to reunite the Eastern and Western Churches. Burdened by debt and attracted by the offer, the Crusader leaders agreed to support him.

Alexios joined the Crusaders in Zadar in May 1203. At that time, the Crusade nearly came to an end. Almost half of the army balked at the final obligation to restore young Alexios to power. However, persistent arguments convinced the Crusaders to head toward Constantinople, where they arrived on June 24th, 1203. Despite the overwhelming opposing army, Emperor Alexios III refused to surrender, as his subjects did not share the Crusaders' enthusiasm for his nephew. The inhabitants observing the scene did not know who he was and did not express any support, especially when they saw his army was composed of Venetians and Crusaders.

---

[i] Nicolle and Hook.
[ii] Villehardouin, *Memoirs or Chronicle of the Fourth Crusade and the Conquest of Constantinople*.
[iii] Nicolle and Hook, *The Fourth Crusade 1202-04*.

This situation was dire for the Crusader leaders. They were deeply committed and lacked the means to retreat. Open war was their only option.[i]

After successfully achieving naval supremacy in a short but intense battle in Galata and arriving at the gates of Constantinople, the Crusader army surrounded Constantinople's large and strong walls. These walls intimidated the Crusaders but motivated and encouraged the Byzantine army not to surrender a city that had never been conquered since its founding. On July 17th, the Venetians and the Franks launched a joint attack on the front of the Palace of Blachernae, located in the far northwestern corner where it would be easiest to penetrate the city. Due to intense breakthroughs and fires, which got out of control and destroyed vast areas of the central part of the city, Emperor Alexios III withdrew.

Although the city had not yet been conquered, the emperor's retreat showed the final state of the situation. Emperor Alexios III, distressed, unprepared, and outmaneuvered, decided to flee the city. His officials who remained immediately freed his blind predecessor and brother, Emperor Isaac II Angelos, from prison, reinstating him to the throne. They thought this would halt the attack on the city since Emperor Alexios III was no longer on the throne.[ii]

However, this presented a problem for the Crusaders because Isaac was not mentioned in the agreement with his son Alexios. Nevertheless, the Crusaders fulfilled their part of the agreement, and on August 1st, 1203, young Alexios was crowned co-emperor in Hagia Sophia.[iii] As soon as he was crowned co-emperor, becoming Alexios IV, he had partially fulfilled the agreed terms with the Venetians by paying off the debts incurred by the Crusaders at a cost of fifty thousand marks and compensation for his own ascension, which amounted to the Crusaders' debt. Thus, Venice and its citizens received almost 100,000 marks.

Unlike his father, who had sufficient support, Alexios IV lacked a political base among the Byzantine ruling circles. Recognizing that the presence of the Crusaders provided him with security, he decided to hire them in Constantinople as his protectors until March 1204, when it was believed that the campaign could resume its path to Egypt. In return, after the expiration of the agreement with Venice, he would support them

---

[i] Nicolle and Hook, *The Fourth Crusade 1202-04*.
[ii] Ostrogorsky, *History of the Byzantine State*.
[iii] Ostrogorsky.

financially for a year and guarantee them a campaign to the East. Once the Crusaders accepted the emperor's proposal, Alexios IV, together with Boniface of Montferrat, Hugh of Saint-Pol, and Henry of Flanders, toured the Byzantine province of Thrace to establish his authority and prevent a counterattack by Alexios III.[i]

Relations in the Byzantine Empire between the Westerners and the Byzantines deteriorated due to increasing disappointment and distrust in the new regime on both sides. With the accession of Alexios IV to power, the political situation worsened. Payments to the Crusaders were delayed, and the sources dried up, as the Byzantines could no longer endure Alexios's impositions that covered the Westerners' protection. Churches were also plundered by the authorities, seizing gold ingots for the same purpose. Among other things, Isaac began to engage in astrology, and Alexios led a debauched life with his Western allies, showing no concern for preserving their dignity in public, which also strengthened the sense of an impending crisis.

Alexios IV Angelos.[188]

---

[i] Nicolle and Hook, *The Fourth Crusade 1202-04*.

The lack of money to pay the Crusaders and the Byzantines being overwhelmed by defeat, heavy taxation, and the prolongation of the existing order indicated the loss of Isaac's and Alexios's power. Open violence became more common. As the emperors quickly lost track of the events around them, an attack was launched by the anti-Western faction, led by Alexios V Doukas, nicknamed Mourtzouphlos ("melancholic" or "sullen"), who, with the support of the army, civil service, and clergy, successfully overthrew the existing government. On the night of January 27th, he arrested and imprisoned Alexios IV, and soon after, the other emperor, Isaac, died in prison.[i]

In February, Mourtzouphlos's forces continued the war against the Westerners, attempting to crush them. However, when success was lacking in the initial strikes, Mourtzouphlos managed to negotiate with the Crusaders to continue the agreements that had been made with his deposed predecessor, Alexios IV.[ii]

Despite the conciliatory situation, the Crusaders' options were limited since their ships required repairs, equipment, and supplies for people who were seriously endangered because Mourtzouphlos had closed the capital's markets. One must also consider the new Byzantine anti-Western government. The new emperor no longer wanted to negotiate with the Crusaders, and he began preparing an attack and strengthening the city's walls. The severe circumstances pressing on the Crusaders forced them to act quickly; otherwise, their campaign was in danger of collapsing. The option that quickly ripened as the best choice was to conquer Byzantium for themselves, which would open the way to the necessary supplies and resources.

Doges Dandolo, Boniface of Montferrat (a nobleman from northern Italy), Baldwin of Flanders, Louis of Blois, and Hugh of Saint-Pol concluded that conquest was the only choice to preserve the campaign, so preparations for seizing the city, power, and empire began. According to the so-called March Agreement from 1201, all spoils would be collected centrally and distributed so that the final compensation for all the various obligations made by the Venetians, valued at 200,000 marks, would be paid first.[iii] Once this debt was settled, the Crusaders and Venetians would equally share the profit according to the agreement. Women and the

---

[i] Ostrogorsky, *History of the Byzantine State*.
[ii] Nicolle and Hook, *The Fourth Crusade 1202-04*.
[iii] Pears, *The Fall of Constantinople, Being the Story of the Fourth Crusade*.

clergy were to be spared during the looting, and rape and church plundering were strictly prohibited under the threat of death. The future emperor of Constantinople and Byzantium would be chosen by a twelve-member commission—six Venetians and six Crusaders—and he would receive a quarter of the capital and two imperial palaces. Any dealings with Venetian enemies were prohibited, an obvious example of Dandolo's profiteering. If the emperor was chosen from among the Crusaders, the new Latin patriarch had to be a Venetian, indicating secular interference in the election of a church authority.

The remainder of the empire was to be divided by a commission made up of twelve Venetians and twelve Crusaders, with lands distributed as fiefs among the Crusader leadership, including the newly elected emperor. This new political agreement was secured by deciding that the army would remain in Byzantium for another year until March 1205, delaying the campaign to Egypt for the fourth time since 1202.[i] Anyone who broke the terms of the agreement would be punished with excommunication.

The Crusader Attack Begins

The Crusader attack began on April 9th with amphibious warfare techniques, used with the help of Venetian ships, which acted as troop transports and assault siege engines. The attack reached its peak on April 12th when, during desperate hand-to-hand combat, the walls were breached, and a bridgehead was established on a critical part of the battlefield inside the fortifications. The Crusaders cleared a path into the city by killing and looting, making no distinction between soldiers and civilians.[ii] Fearing a counterattack, the Crusaders set a fire that quickly spread from the north to the south of the city.

As the anti-Western faction lost ground, Emperor Mourtzouphlos realized that the opponents had won, and he fled the city during the night. By April 13th, there was no serious resistance to the Crusaders, signaling that the city had been conquered. The victory might not have been achieved without the incredible naval skills of the Venetians and the engineering ingenuity that allowed the ships to be turned into battle towers.

---

[i] Nicolle and Hook, *The Fourth Crusade 1202-04*.
[ii] Nicolle and Hook.

The fall of Constantinople to the Crusaders.[184]

For three days, Crusader leaders allowed their troops to vent their anger, greed, and relief in an orgy of looting. The pillage and killings turned beautiful Constantinople into a heap of ruins. A contemporary source noted that even the Saracens would have shown more mercy than the Crusaders.[i] The original pious goal of the Crusaders had been lost. The fall of Constantinople might never have gained such a notorious reputation for dreadful barbarism if the victors had continued their campaign to the Holy Land the following spring.

The new state system in Byzantium was to be implemented according to the agreement that the Venetians and Crusaders had made in March 1204. It was assumed that Marquis Boniface of Montferrat would be elected emperor. His personal and military capabilities and Byzantine connections made him worthy of this honor, but the doge did not favor this, as he desired a less prominent person. Since the Frankish camp was not united within itself like the Venetians were, he managed to secure the election of Count Baldwin of Flanders as the new emperor.[ii] He was crowned emperor of the Latin Empire on May 16th in Hagia Sophia, and the Venetian Thomas Morosini became the first Latin patriarch of Constantinople.

---

[i] Nicolle and Hook.
[ii] Villehardouin, *Memoirs or Chronicle of the Fourth Crusade and the Conquest of Constantinople*.

The new emperor proclaimed his intention to embark on a crusade to the Holy Land as soon as the empire was pacified and secured. Although the previous emperor, Mourtzouphlos, had been captured and executed, establishing control over the rest of the Byzantine Empire proved to be a challenging task.

Emperor Baldwin I received a quarter of the entire imperial territory, while half of the remaining three-quarters went to the Venetians. The other half was to be divided among the knights as imperial fiefs. Boniface of Montferrat was the most powerful among the knights as the king of Thessalonica. The greatest beneficiaries of this campaign were the Venetians, whose power was now based on possessing the most important ports and islands. The Venetians completely dominated the maritime route from their city to Constantinople, controlling even the entrance to Constantinople. Within the city, they had three-eighths of the urban territory, including Hagia Sophia.[i] The Frankish provincial princes had to swear an oath to the emperor of Constantinople, although Dandolo was exempt from this vassal obligation. Beyond the straits lay the remnants of Byzantine rule in Trebizond, Nicaea, and Epirus.

The Latin Empire could not survive politically, financially, or culturally. It was divided among too many larger and smaller rulers. A fragmented and complicated feudal system developed on the ruins of the Byzantine Empire. The Byzantine population hardly tolerated the Latin occupying power, mainly due to the arrogance of the conquerors and religious differences. The subordination of the Eastern Church to Roman authority was formally achieved but forcibly, not in the manner the pope had hoped for in terms of a union. According to Pope Innocent's plan, Byzantium was not to be subdued by arms but subordinated to the Holy See through a church union so that they could participate together in the Crusade. Foreign rule only deepened internal disunity.[ii]

On April 14th, 1205, exactly one year after the capture of Constantinople by the Fourth Crusade, Emperor Baldwin I was captured, and Louis of Blois was killed at the Battle of Adrianople. The Latin army was defeated by the forces of Tsar Kaloyan of Bulgaria, who had allied with local Byzantine insurgents opposing Latin rule. The battle was a devastating blow to the Latin Empire. Following this defeat, papal legate Peter of Capua recognized that the Crusade's original goal of reclaiming

---

[i] Nicolle and Hook, *The Fourth Crusade 1202-04*.
[ii] Bartlett, *The Making of Europe*.

the Holy Land had become unattainable. He formally absolved those fighting for the Latin cause in Greece of their crusading vows.

After 1205, disaster followed the Latin rule, including the death of Boniface of Montferrat in battle in 1207. His so-called Kingdom of Thessalonica was annexed by the Epirote Greeks in 1224. After the crisis of 1205-06, the Latin Empire was governed by a series of regents, minors, and guardians who held the imperial title: Henry of Flanders, Peter de Courtenay, Robert de Courtenay, Baldwin II, and John of Brienne.[i] Between 1204 and 1261, Constantinople ceased to be a center of bureaucracy and consumption. It no longer represented a functional capital except in name only.

The Restoration

The fall of Constantinople in 1204 was a turning point in Byzantine history, but it was not its end. While many Byzantine feudal lords submitted to the conqueror, joining the system of the new rule, and the common people, although dissatisfied, remained in their homeland, some Byzantine nobles left the occupied lands and moved to those provinces that were still unoccupied. Relying on the local Greek population, these refugees established new states in which Byzantium continued to live. In Asia Minor, Theodore Laskaris, the son-in-law of Alexios III, founded the Empire of Nicaea, and in the Balkans, Michael Angelos, the cousin of Isaac II and Alexios III, founded the Despotate of Epirus. A little earlier, independently of the fall of Constantinople, the Empire of Trebizond had been established on the southeastern coast of the Black Sea. It was founded by the grandsons of Andronikos I Komnenos, Alexios and David, who called themselves the Great Komnenoi, a name retained by later emperors of Trebizond.[ii]

The ruler of each of these states declared himself the true Byzantine emperor. They fought among themselves and against the Latins for control of the former lands of the Byzantine Empire. Although Epirus was initially the strongest of the three Greek states, the Nicaeans managed to take Constantinople from the Latins.[iii]

---

[i] Pears, *The Fall of Constantinople, Being the Story of the Fourth Crusade*.
[ii] Ostrogorsky, *History of the Byzantine State*.
[iii] Ibid.

Chapter 15: The Palaiologoi: The Last Stand

Restoration of the Empire

After the death of Emperor Theodore II Doukas Laskaris in 1258, his seven-year-old son, John IV, succeeded him. Due to the boy's age, Theodore appointed his trusted friend and court official, George Mouzalon, as regent. However, Mouzalon was assassinated shortly after Theodore's death—likely at the hands of aristocratic factions—and the regency passed to Michael Palaiologos, a powerful noble and military commander. Michael was soon proclaimed co-emperor and took control of the government.

During this period of political transition, neighboring powers took advantage of the weakened Byzantine position. While the Nicaean Empire remained intact, the earlier fragmentation of Byzantine authority had allowed both Bulgaria and Serbia to expand their influence. Although Bulgaria never fully regained its former golden age under Boris I and Simeon, it maintained a stable and sizable state. Serbia, under the rising Nemanjić dynasty, grew increasingly powerful and would pose a major threat to the Byzantine heartland in the 14th century.

The Latin Empire in Constantinople persisted for nearly sixty years following the Fourth Crusade. However, in 1261, General Alexios Strategopoulos exploited the absence of the Latin garrison and entered the city with a small force, reclaiming Constantinople for the Byzantines.

This marked the restoration of the Byzantine Empire under Michael VIII Palaiologos, but it also ushered in a final phase of slow decline from which Byzantium would never fully recover.[i]

Latin influence would never recover again. After the capture of the capital, Michael ordered the blinding of John IV in order to become the supreme emperor. Patriarch Arsenios excommunicated Michael for this, but Arsenios was soon deposed and replaced by Joseph I. With Joseph's support, Michael began restoring monasteries and various public buildings. Hagia Sophia was renovated, and the harbor and walls of the city were fortified. Several hospitals, markets, and public baths were constructed, and a new mosque was built to replace the one destroyed during the Fourth Crusade. Byzantine rule was once again established in its glorious capital.

Michael VIII made significant contributions to the intellectual and cultural life of Byzantium. He initiated a dynasty that supported scholars, artists, and theologians, leading to the restoration of Constantinople as a center of learning and artistic production. Beginning in 1272, he formally co-ruled with his son, Andronikos II. This joint rule lasted for ten years and was characterized by the controversial union with the papacy in 1274 after the Second Council of Lyon.

After the death of Michael in 1282, Andronikos faced economic difficulties and internal strife, including conflicts with the aristocracy and the Orthodox Church. The threat of attack from the rising Turks became a reality, resulting in the loss of significant territories in Asia Minor. Despite appearances, Andronikos was not a weak ruler, and the circumstances he was involved in couldn't suppress his interest in science and literacy.[ii] Just as he co-ruled with his father, his son Michael IX assisted him. The concept of having two leaders is a notable characteristic of the Palaiologos dynasty. However, the practice of dividing the states among family members sparked disputes and led to internal strife.

---

[i] After being imprisoned by Theodore II, Alexios sided with Michael and quickly rose to the rank of grand domestic (*megas domestikos*), or commander-in-chief. He was directly below the emperor.

[ii] Ostrogorsky, George, *History of the Byzantine State,* Rutgers University Press, 1969, p. 447.

Other Threats

Having faced continuous threats from the Latin states in Greece, the Ottoman Turks, and the Bulgarians and Serbs made Byzantines look for allies. Western European states provided alliances, but they were not always effective and often fragile.

The threat of invasion from the Turks in the east was not the main concern for Byzantium at that moment. The Serbian kingdom was gaining territories in the south, which was a major concern since the time of Serbian Grand Prince Stefan Nemanja (r. 1166-1196), reaching its peak during the reign of King Milutin II (r. 1282-1321). In 1282, Milutin captured Skopje, demonstrating his strength to the fallen Byzantium. Andronikos proposed to Milutin a marriage to his sister, Eudokia, but she stubbornly declined. To settle the situation and fearing Milutin's backlash, the Byzantine government proposed a marriage with Andronikos's five-year-old daughter, Simonida.[i] After their marriage in 1299, Byzantine influence rapidly grew in Serbia, although there would be numerous conflicts in the years to come.

Andronikos II lost his authority as he reached old age. Having less and less power, he became embroiled in a fight with his grandson Andronikos III, widening the gap between rivals. Various conflicts during Andronikos II's last three years of life in the First Palaiologian Civil War forced his inevitable abdication. Andronikos III attempted administrative and military reforms to strengthen the empire but faced internal opposition and losses to the Turks.

Despite the Byzantine Empire's decline, a new generation of aristocrats emerged, most notably John Kantakouzenos. As Serbia grew into a significant threat, Byzantium attempted to form an alliance with Bulgaria. However, the Serbian victory at the Battle of Velbazhd in 1330, where Tsar Michael Shishman was killed, thwarted these plans. The defeat weakened Bulgarian-Byzantine cooperation and marked the beginning of Serbian dominance in the central Balkans.

In the wake of this battle, political upheaval followed in both Bulgaria and Serbia. Ivan Alexander seized the Bulgarian throne, and Serbian nobles overthrew Stefan Uroš III and installed his son, Stefan Dušan. The alliance between these new rulers emboldened Dušan to campaign

---

[i] Laskaris, Mihailo, *Vizantijske princeze*, Pešić i sinovi, 1997, p. 58.

against Byzantium. Ongoing disputes among the Palaiologoi further undermined the empire, allowing Dušan to conquer much of Macedonia. Meanwhile, Andronikos III suffered defeats in Asia Minor at the hands of the Turks. Though he maintained relative control during his reign, his death in 1341 triggered a devastating civil war from which the Byzantine Empire never recovered.

Civil Wars

When Emperor Andronikos III died in 1341, his nine-year-old son, John V Palaiologos, was named his successor. John VI Kantakouzenos, a powerful noble and former grand domestic, was expected to serve as regent. Kantakouzenos envisioned a revival of Byzantine strength. However, opposition quickly formed around the queen mother, Anna of Savoy, and Patriarch John XIV Kalekas, creating a hostile political environment. Quarrels and mistrust escalated into a civil war, plunging the empire into further instability. During this time, the Ottomans gained a foothold in the Balkans, Serbian forces under Stefan Dušan advanced toward Thessalonica, and the Bulgarians posed an ongoing threat.

John VI Kantakouzenos presiding over a synod.[185]

During such a vulnerable time, the opportunity for the opposition to rise couldn't go unnoticed. Patriarch John took over as regent, and Kantakouzenos was proclaimed an enemy. Alexios Apokaukos became the chief minister and head of the navy, making him one of the most powerful men in the Byzantine Empire.

This event led to a major crisis in Byzantium. There was a year-long war between Alexios's supporters and aristocrats loyal to Kantakouzenos, resulting in the decrease of power of the nobles. Seeing an opportunity to intervene, Serbian King Dušan welcomed Kantakouzenos in 1342 and formed an alliance with him. Despite initial setbacks, Kantakouzenos eventually declared himself emperor in Thessaly with the help of John Angel, the despot of Thessaly.

This surprising "selfish" ascension of his ally prompted Dušan to move toward Constantinople. The Palaiologos family, who had previously tried to gain Dušan's trust, now had the chance to bring him over to their side, especially since Dušan's son, Uros V, was married to John Palaiologos's sister.

Alexios Apokaukos, a bitter enemy of John VI Kantakouzenos, remained influential during the civil war and continued to wield harsh administrative control. By the end of his life, he had clamped down on political opponents, ordering executions and building a prison for his enemies. In 1345, during a visit to this newly constructed prison, Apokaukos was unexpectedly lynched by the inmates. With his chief rival gone and the Palaiologos faction significantly weakened, Kantakouzenos, who was supported by Ottoman forces, entered Constantinople and was crowned emperor.

However, the main beneficiary of the Byzantine turmoil was Stefan Dušan of Serbia. He had already captured Macedonia and Thessalonica and, in 1346, took Serres, declaring himself emperor of the Serbs and Greeks. After the civil war, he further expanded his empire, incorporating Thessaly and Epirus. His realm stretched from the Danube to the Gulf of Corinth and from the Adriatic to the Aegean Sea, absorbing many former Byzantine territories.

By this time, the Byzantine Empire had been reduced to a shadow of its former self, holding only parts of Thrace and a few scattered islands. Internal fragmentation, exacerbated by the distribution of provinces among various members of the Palaiologos family, further contributed to the collapse of centralized authority. A plague emerged in 1348 and continued to spread all over Europe for years.

The empire was in an abysmal state, and Dušan could have swooped in to end it all, but he suddenly died in 1355. His son Uros wasn't fit to keep his father's weakly solidified empire together. Byzantium was in such a poor state that it couldn't even bother to retrieve some of the territories Dušan had taken.

The Battle of Kosovo

The rapid decline of Serbian power encouraged the Turks to occupy the Balkans. With no real power to fight back, the Turkish occupation of the Balkans reached its peak during the time of Sultan Murad I. The Serbian Empire was divided into many states, with the despotates of the nobles Ugljesa and Vukasin being the first in line to defend the Serbian Empire. The Battle of Maritza in 1371 saw both despots fall.

Andronikos IV conspired with others to start an uprising against his father, John V, but was stopped by Murad I. Andronikos was replaced by his brother Manuel II as co-emperor. Andronikos managed to escape imprisonment and, with the help of the Genoese, besieged Constantinople and breached the city. Alliances with the Ottomans helped them retake the Peloponnese from Kantakouzenos. Only the Serbs were able to offer some opposition to the impending Turkish occupation. The most powerful of the nobles, Prince Lazar, and his ally, King Tvrtko I, made an alliance with Byzantium.

The fateful battle took place on June 15th, 1389, in Kosovo. The forces of Prince Lazar and his allies stood in front of Sultan Murad's army. The battle ended in a stalemate, although both leaders were killed during the fighting. Despite the indecisive outcome, the battle is significant for its impact on Serbian identity and for marking the beginning of Ottoman dominance. This became a symbol of Serbian resistance and delayed a larger Ottoman campaign.

After a hard-fought battle at Kosovo, the Ottoman heir, Bayezid I, continued to attack Byzantine lands. He used John VII, son of Andronikos IV, to retake Constantinople. After John V's death, both Manuel II and his nephew John VII sought an alliance with various European leaders. Backed by some and opposed by others, they were intermittently on the throne.

Mongol Invasion and the Reduction of Ottoman Power

An even greater threat for the Turks, and subsequently everyone in the Balkans, came from the Far East: the Mongols, led by Timur. He founded the Timurid Empire in Persia and central Asia, claiming descent from Genghis Khan and seeking to restore the Mongol Empire. Timur's campaigns across central Asia, the Caucasus region, and parts of the Middle East were notorious for their brutality and massacres of civilians. Parts of Baghdad and Delhi were devastated to the point that they suffered a decline in urban life and economic activity for decades.

The Battle of Delhi in 1398, where Timur defeated Sultan Mahmud Tughlaq, was particularly brutal. After the passage of his hordes, "there couldn't be heard a dog barking ... or a kid crying."[i]

In 1402, Timur and Bayezid I clashed at the Battle of Ankara in central Anatolia. Although Bayezid had numerical superiority, Timur's tactical mastery—especially feigned retreats and encirclements—led to a decisive Ottoman defeat. Bayezid was captured, and the humiliation of the loss halted the Ottoman advance, triggering a decade-long civil war known as the Ottoman Interregnum.

Bayezid's defeat was later dramatized in European art, where he was often portrayed in an iron cage. However, contemporary sources suggest he was treated with relative respect. Timur died in 1405 while preparing to invade China. Despite his impressive conquests, his empire disintegrated shortly after his death and never rivaled the legacy of Genghis Khan.

The Ottoman Interregnum saw Bayezid's sons vying for control, a consequence of the harem-based succession system that bred internal rivalries. Ultimately, Mehmed I emerged victorious and reestablished unity by 1413, passing power smoothly to his son, Murad II. Despite an unsuccessful siege of Constantinople in 1422, the Ottomans gradually regained strength.

In the early 15th century, regional Christian leaders, including John Hunyadi of Hungary, Djuradj Branković of Serbia, and Skanderbeg of Albania, successfully resisted Ottoman incursions. While not connected to the Byzantine aristocracy, their efforts occasionally aligned with Byzantine interests and offered brief relief from Turkish pressure.

---

[i] Doukas 109, 20

The Council of Florence

In 1439, the Council of Florence was held. Emperor John VIII sought to reunite the Eastern and Western Churches in hopes of securing military aid against the Turks. Although a formal union was declared, it was widely rejected in the Byzantine world and failed to deliver meaningful Western support.

The rule of the Palaiologos dynasty during the late Byzantine period was marked by a controversial attempt to unite the churches during the 1430s and 1440s. A formal agreement was signed by representatives of both churches in 1439. Pope Eugene IV convened the Council of Florence, where intense theological discussions and negotiations took place. A papal bull called *Laetentur Caeli* was issued, proclaiming the union of the churches. This temporary union aimed to gain Western support against the Ottomans but was deeply unpopular among the Byzantine clergy and aristocrats.

Despite occasional successes, the Byzantine emperor failed to stop the inevitable Ottoman expansion. The failed union deepened the schism and highlighted the complexities of theological differences and cultural divisions that shaped relations between the East and the West. As the union proved unstable and most likely to fail, the pope began planning a crusade against the Ottomans.

The Battle of Varna

In 1444, a Christian alliance clashed with the Ottoman Turks near Varna on the Black Sea coast of present-day Bulgaria, where they suffered a significant defeat. The Christian coalition included Hungarian and Polish forces, with limited support from Wallachia, and was led by King Władysław III of Poland and Hungary. Military command was largely in the hands of John Hunyadi, a prominent Hungarian noble and general. This campaign was among the last major crusading efforts organized by Christian Europe with the intent of halting the advance of the Ottoman Empire and relieving pressure on Constantinople.

The alliance aimed to capitalize on internal instability within the Ottoman realm following Sultan Murad II's temporary abdication in favor of his son, Mehmed II. However, Murad returned to lead the Ottoman army in person. The arrival of a substantial Ottoman force near Lake Varna caught the Christian forces off guard, leading to internal disagreement over whether to retreat or attack. Ultimately, the decision was made to engage.

The battle initially favored the Christians, who managed to repel Ottoman attacks and pursued the retreating forces. However, the pursuit led to a breakdown in cohesion, and the Ottomans regrouped and counterattacked. In a decisive and ill-fated move, King Władysław led a charge with his personal guard against the Ottoman center in an attempt to break through to Murad's position. The charge failed, and Władysław was killed. His head was reportedly severed during the melee. His death triggered panic and a general rout among the Christian troops, leading to a devastating defeat.

The Battle of Varna marked a turning point in the struggle between Christian Europe and the expanding Ottoman Empire. It reinforced Ottoman dominance in the Balkans and underscored the declining capacity of European powers to coordinate effective military resistance during this period.

The Fall of Constantinople

In 1449, Constantine XI Palaiologos was crowned emperor of Byzantium, succeeding his brother John VIII. By this point, the empire had been reduced to Constantinople and a few outposts, so it was highly vulnerable. Constantine sought assistance from Western powers, particularly after the death of Ottoman Sultan Murad II and the accession of his son, Mehmed II, in 1451.

Mehmed II, later known as "the Conqueror," was determined to capture Constantinople and end the Byzantine Empire. He assembled a large, diverse army and initiated extensive preparations for siege warfare. Among the most significant strategic moves was the construction of Rumeli Hisarı, a fortress on the European side of the Bosphorus, directly opposite the earlier Anadolu Hisarı. This allowed the Ottomans to control naval traffic and block aid from reaching the city by sea.

Despite efforts at an ecclesiastical union between the Eastern Orthodox and Roman Catholic Churches, Western aid was minimal. Some reinforcements arrived, such as a Genoese contingent under Giovanni Giustiniani and a small group of Neapolitan troops, but no substantial military support came in time. Venice, while sympathetic, reacted too slowly.

As part of the city's defense, the Byzantines placed a massive chain across the entrance to the Golden Horn, a narrow inlet forming Constantinople's northern harbor. However, in a bold maneuver,

Mehmed ordered Ottoman ships to be transported overland on greased logs to bypass the chain, allowing entry into the Golden Horn.

The defending force numbered around seven thousand men, including foreigners. The city's population had dwindled to roughly fifty thousand, while the Ottoman army is estimated to have numbered between fifty thousand and eighty thousand. They were equipped with siege cannons, including the massive Basilic cannon, which was capable of firing giant stone projectiles.

The Ottomans also attempted to undermine the city's fortifications by digging tunnels, some of which were discovered and destroyed by the defenders. On May 21st, Mehmed offered terms of surrender to Constantinople, promising safe passage and preservation of property, but Emperor Constantine refused.

The final assault began after an extensive bombardment, which severely weakened the Theodosian Walls. On the morning of May 29th, 1453, Ottoman forces breached the city. Emperor Constantine XI is believed to have died fighting on the front lines. The city was subjected to looting in accordance with the Ottoman custom of granting soldiers limited plunder after a successful siege.

Mehmed II's conquest of Constantinople earned him the title Fatih ("the Conqueror"), and he subsequently transformed the city into the capital of the Ottoman Empire. This marked the end of the Byzantine Empire and a turning point in world history.

Mehmed II entering the city of Constantinople.[186]

Hagia Sophia was converted into a mosque, marking the end of the Byzantine Empire and the medieval period in Europe. The Ottoman threat spurred European powers to explore trade routes and contributed to the Age of Exploration.

The Successor States

After the fall of Constantinople in 1453, the Despotate of the Morea in the southern Peloponnese remained one of the last remnants of the Byzantine world. Its capital, Mystras, had long been a flourishing center of Byzantine culture, attracting scholars, artists, and theologians during the empire's final centuries. The despotate was ruled by Constantine XI's brothers, Thomas and Demetrios Palaiologos, who had governed the region since the 1440s.

Following Constantinople's fall, the Morea became a target of Ottoman expansion. Internal strife between Thomas and Demetrios weakened the region further. In 1460, Ottoman forces under Sultan Mehmed II conquered the despotate. Some local nobles surrendered and were integrated into the Ottoman system, while others fled to western Europe, particularly Italy.

Athens fell to the Ottomans in 1458. The Parthenon, which had served as a Christian church dedicated to the Virgin Mary since the 6th century, was converted into a mosque.

The other successor state was the Empire of Trebizond, located in northeastern Anatolia, with its capital at Trabzon. It was founded back in 1204 by Alexios I Komnenos following the Fourth Crusade. It flourished as a center of commerce and established relations with Georgia, uniting against the Ottomans. However, it ultimately fell under Ottoman rule in 1461, suffering a defeat from Mehmed II. The Ottoman Empire's superior forces forced the man in charge, David Komnenos, to surrender, ending the Empire of Trebizond. The nobles fled to Russia or Georgia.

Bonus Chapter: Byzantine Art, Architecture, and Society

The Byzantine culture blended a variety of influences. Founded on the vestiges of the ancient Roman Empire, the Byzantine Empire was also impacted by a variety of Eastern influences, which can be seen in the art, architecture, and society of the Byzantine Empire.

This was visible from the very early days of the Byzantine Empire. Hagia Sophia, for instance, uses arches and domes, a skill mastered by ancient Romans (one only has to see the Pantheon to know this), but it also introduces elements not familiar to ancient Romans, such as new ways to stylize columns and capitals.

The Byzantines also stopped fluting their columns, which gave classical columns their characteristic look, with long grooves running along the surface. The Byzantines were much freer in this respect, producing a whole variety of columns and capitals. This is visible in the many columns of Hagia Sophia. This church has become a model for many Byzantine churches and churches in other Orthodox Christian countries. The Church of Saint Sava in Belgrade, Saint Alexander Nevsky Cathedral in Sofia, and the Cathedral of Christ the Saviour in Moscow, to mention only a few of the grandest structures, still stand as evidence of the far-reaching influence of the Byzantine Empire.

Capital from Hagia Sophia.[187]

Due to the sheer extent of the Byzantine Empire, we have many examples of Byzantine architecture all across Europe. In Ravenna, Italy, the Basilica di Sant'Apollinare Nuovo still stands as a testament to Byzantine influence. This basilica was rebuilt by Justinian I, and it features beautiful gold mosaics depicting Jesus and the most important moments in his life.

The Byzantines took the art of mosaic from the Greeks and Romans and brought it to another level (see the Komnenos mosaic, the Empress Zoë mosaic, and, the most impressive of all, the Deesis mosaic, all of which are in the Hagia Sophia). These large churches needed a lot of decoration, so more and more lavish and impressive mosaics were commissioned. Although the empire saw iconoclastic conflicts, visual art in the Byzantine Empire thrived in the form of mosaics and frescoes, which were regularly used to adorn the interiors of the many churches the empire erected.

A photo of Hagia Sophia from the late 19ᵗʰ century. The four minarets that surround the church were added later by the Ottomans.[188]

Jesus Christ Pantocrator, a mosaic in Hagia Sophia.[189]

There are, of course, many other buildings worthy of mention. The Hippodrome of Constantinople, built by Constantine the Great, was immense and could hold up to 100,000 spectators. The building hosted numerous sculptures and works of art, as was the case with the Hippodrome in Rome. One notable artifact transferred to the Hippodrome of Constantinople was the Serpent Column, originally a dedication from the Greek city-states to the sanctuary at Delphi, commemorating their victory over the Persians at the Battle of Plataea. It was moved to Constantinople by Emperor Constantine I as part of his efforts to adorn the new imperial capital with prestigious relics of the classical world.

Conversely, some treasures were later removed from Constantinople, particularly during the Fourth Crusade in 1204, when Latin Crusaders looted the city. Among the most famous were the gilded bronze horses that once adorned the Hippodrome. These sculptures were taken to Venice and installed atop the façade of St. Mark's Basilica, where they became known as the Horses of Saint Mark.

An important influence on Byzantine culture was, needless to say, Christianity. Because of the church, a lot of individuals were able to access contemporary and classical knowledge, and a lot of church officials, monks, and priests went on to make high-quality historical, philosophical, and poetic works. Theodoret of Cyrus was an early Byzantine author remembered for his hagiographical work. He wrote down and commented on the lives of the most important ascetics who lived in the Middle East during this period. We also have the Cappadocian Fathers—Basil the Great, Gregory of Nyssa, and Gregory of Nazianzus—known for their work on the concept of the Holy Trinity, which is in use to this day by all Christian churches.

However, there were other, somewhat more secular minds, such as Theodore Metochites, who wrote poetic works, and the more classical-oriented thinkers, such as Michael Psellos and especially his pupil, John Italus, who was accused of heresy for reintroducing ancient ideas like metempsychosis (the migration of souls).

Byzantine intellectuals played a major role in the Renaissance and the rediscovery of ancient works. With the gradual dissolution of the Byzantine Empire, Byzantine intellectuals, who were well versed in classical literature, migrated to Italy, where they participated in the revival of classical ideas.

Byzantine Society

Byzantine society was very diverse, encompassing a wide range of ethnic, linguistic, and religious communities. The empire exerted significant and lasting cultural, political, and religious influence across several regions, including the Greek mainland, the broader Balkan Peninsula, the Middle East (notably Anatolia and parts of modern-day Syria), Egypt, and southern Italy.

The Byzantine society revolved around the imperial family and a number of wealthy, aristocratic families that vied for power. The power of these families came largely from the vast lands they owned, often for centuries. The lower classes were, themselves, a very diverse bunch. There were many highly educated and skilled workers, such as lawyers, clerks, teachers, bankers, and merchants, who sometimes could get very rich, although this did not automatically promote them to the aristocracy. The aristocracy was firmly entrenched in the bloodline, as well as land inheritance. What allowed skilled workers to move up a notch was their education, and education allowed at least some sort of class mobility in Byzantium, much as it does today.

Although craftsmen played a crucial economic role in Byzantine society—producing goods, supporting trade, and sustaining urban life— they were often regarded with a degree of condescension by the educated elite and aristocracy. This reflected the classical Greco-Roman ideal that manual labor, even when skilled, was inferior to intellectual or landowning pursuits. Social mobility decreased significantly in the lower tiers of society, with artisans and laborers typically having limited opportunities to rise in status. Craftsmen would usually pass their craft to their children, who were supposed to do the same job as their parents.

Then, there were free farmers who worked their own land, just enough to sustain themselves, and free farmers who owned no land and had to work other people's land in order to earn a living. The farmers' class was by far the most numerous (around 90 percent of the whole population).[i] Lastly were the slaves, who were below even the landless farmers. Slaves were bought and sold in the Byzantine Empire and procured through numerous conquests.

---

[i] Haldon, John F. The Byzantine Empire. The Dynamics of ancient empires: state power from Assyria to Byzantium, 2009, 205-254.

Although the Byzantine Empire is often mentioned as the first medieval state, slavery continued to be practiced.[i] In ancient Greece and Rome, the prevailing ideology condoned and justified the institution of slavery. The Christianity of the Byzantine Empire was, by definition, against slavery. However, the Byzantine Church managed to condone slavery.

Eunuchs were a very interesting subclass of the Byzantine Empire. They were employed in the royal palace as well as in state administration. The logic was the following: eunuchs were castrated, so they had no heirs and should have had no interest in organizing coups and assassinating emperors. Many slaves became state or aristocracy-owned eunuchs, and they were charged with a variety of jobs, such as serving and preparing food, keeping an eye on children, and doing household chores. The eunuchs could sometimes get very powerful, becoming generals or the emperor's personal advisors.

Byzantine society was deeply religious. The emperors were believed to be invested by God to rule. Natural catastrophes were interpreted as a sign from God that something was wrong with the state, and bold, successful usurpers were often seen as chosen by God to take the throne.

Administration

While the emperor stood at the apex of Byzantine society, effective governance required a complex administrative system. Assisting him were members of the imperial household, including his wife, close relatives, and influential court eunuchs. In the earlier centuries of the empire, especially during the transition from Roman to Byzantine rule, praetorian prefects played a central role in managing vast regions of the empire.

During the late Roman period, the empire was divided into four major praetorian prefectures: the East (Orientis), Illyricum, Italy, and Gaul. Each was overseen by a praetorian prefect who managed taxation, justice, and administration. However, by Justinian's reign in the 6th century, this system had begun to evolve. As Justinian reconquered lost western territories, he instituted new administrative structures, including the exarchates in Ravenna (Italy) and later Carthage (Africa), which combined civil and military authority in one office to better manage distant provinces.

---

[i] Slavery continued to be a thing in most medieval states, although it was less prominent in comparison to ancient times.

Below the prefecture level were dioceses. Usually, a prefecture consisted of several dioceses. A diocese, in turn, was divided into provinces, and a province was divided into poleis (cities) and their surrounding territories. Early on, the most important landlords in the cities were tasked with levying taxes, but as time moved on, the government was more in control of the tax system.

Let us briefly outline some of the most important titles in the Byzantine imperial hierarchy:

1. **Basileus (βασιλεύς)** - The official Greek title for the emperor, often paired with *autokratōr* (autocrat) to emphasize sole rule. The empress held significant ceremonial and sometimes political influence, often bearing titles such as Augusta or Autokratorissa. Imperial children born after their father's accession to the throne were called porphyrogenitus ("born in the purple"), referencing their birth in the Porphyra, a special chamber in the Great Palace decorated with purple stone.

2. **Despotes (δεσπότης)** - Literally meaning "lord," this was one of the highest court titles. It was often granted to the emperor's sons or sons-in-law. It signified a rank just below the emperor and was associated with ruling major provinces, such as the Despotate of the Morea, in later centuries.

3. **Sebastokrator (σεβαστοκράτωρ)** - A composite of *sebastos* ("venerable") and *kratōr* ("ruler"), this prestigious title ranked immediately after despotes and was typically given to close male relatives. It rarely applied to foreign rulers, who were more commonly styled as despotes.

4. **Kouropalates (κουροπαλάτης)** - Meaning "guardian of the palace," this title signified close proximity to the emperor and great courtly influence. Like many high court titles, it was often awarded to male relatives or distinguished allies. Also, certain palace roles—such as the *nipsistiarios*, a eunuch who assisted in imperial purification rituals—were of symbolic importance due to their ceremonial closeness to the emperor.

5. **Logothetes tou dromou (λογοθέτης τοῦ δρόμου)** - Head of the imperial postal and intelligence service, this official oversaw communication and foreign affairs. The office evolved from the *magister officiorum* of the late Roman bureaucracy and became one of the most powerful civilian roles in the empire.

6. **Military Titles** – The *megas domestikos* was the commander-in-chief of the Byzantine army, while the *megas doux* oversaw the imperial navy. Other notable ranks included the *stratopedarches*, a high-ranking general, and the *droungarios*, who commanded naval or cavalry units depending on the period. These roles formed the backbone of Byzantine military leadership, particularly in the empire's middle and late periods.

Conclusion

The Byzantine Empire owed a lot to its geographical position between Europe and Asia. "New Rome" became the cradle of a new and powerful society. However, its precious position made the Byzantine Empire alluring to numerous invading forces. In the end, the Byzantine Empire was exposed to numerous attacks from all sides. Bulgarians, Slavs, Crusaders, and numerous Muslim invaders from Asia weakened the empire so much that the only thing that was left was the highly prized city of Constantinople, which finally succumbed to the unrelenting siege of the Ottoman Turks in 1453.

Nevertheless, Byzantine society continued to exist. The Byzantines were to submit to Ottoman rule, but their society was never completely destroyed. In fact, the hardships that the Ottomans brought to the Byzantines only served to strengthen the Byzantine-Greek identity, which finally broke out of subjugation in the 19th century.

The Byzantine Empire is the second greatest Greek empire, coming centuries after the short-lived but illustrious Hellenistic empire of Alexander the Great. While Alexander's empire, in a way, lacked a decisive unifying factor, the Byzantine Empire found its unifying factor in the form of Christianity.

Crucially, the Byzantine Empire was able to spread its influence in Europe, shaping the cultures of countries such as Serbia, Bulgaria, North Macedonia, and Russia. Modern-day Greece, although proud of its ancient past, bears more evidence of the thousand years of the grand Byzantine Empire, which to this day fuels Greek national pride.

Today, there is a prospect of Greece having a conflict with Turkey, which continues to have a strong hold over Istanbul (or Constantinople as it was once called). Hagia Sophia functioned as a mosque for centuries and was made into a museum by the famous founder of the Turkish Republic, Ataturk. It has been recently converted back into a mosque, which was a symbolic act by the Turkish government that seeks to affirm its supremacy. Cyprus continues to be an island where Turkey and Greece quite literally clash. The animosity, rivalry, and conflict between the two countries spans around six hundred years. Will we see another European conflict, this time with the Greeks (possibly aided by a bigger power) facing the Turks?

It is important to note that the Byzantine Empire did not simply leave a sense of pride or a desire for revenge. It also brought cultural illumination to the Balkans and Russia. Millions and millions of Slavs today have to thank the Byzantine Empire since it brought not only religious and cultural influence but also very basic elements of society, such as the Cyrillic alphabet. Slavic peoples, such as Serbians, Russians, North Macedonians, and Bulgarians, in turn, continue to stay true to the Orthodox Christian faith of their ancestors. The influence of the Byzantine Empire is still very much felt today despite ceasing to exist around six hundred years ago.

Here's another book by Enthralling History that you might like

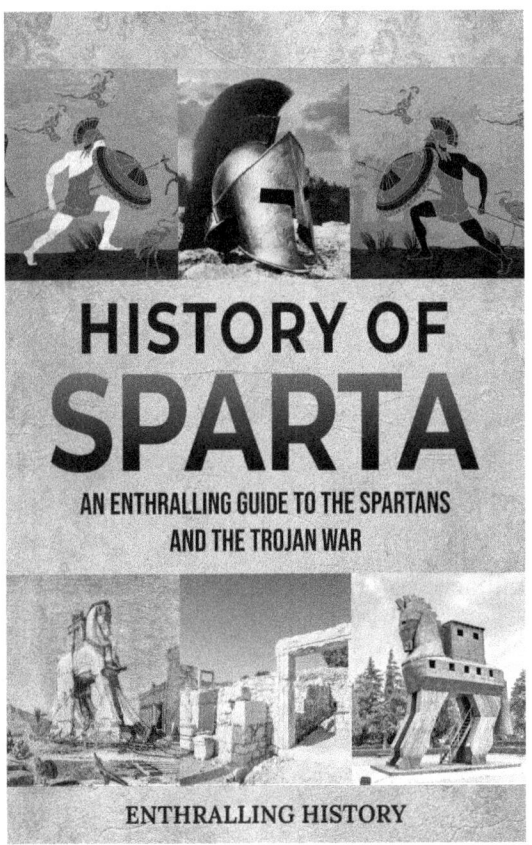

Free limited time bonus

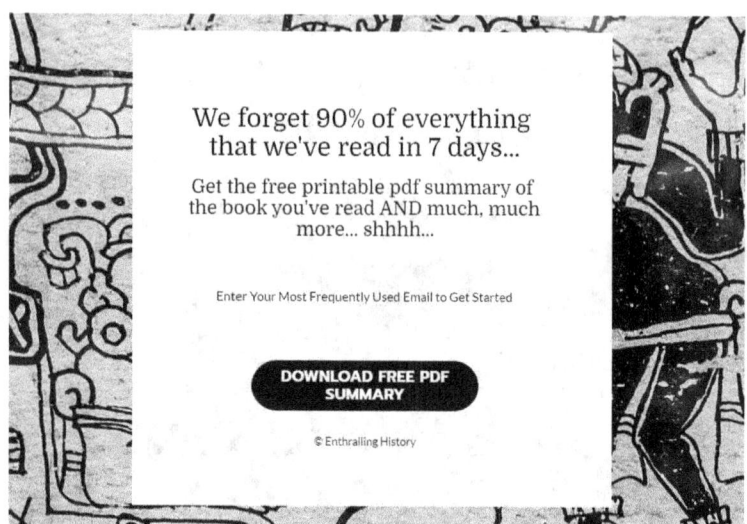

Stop for a moment. We have a free bonus set up for you. The problem is this: we forget 90% of everything that we read after 7 days. Crazy fact, right? Here's the solution: we've created a printable, 1-page pdf summary for this book that you're reading now. All you have to do to get your free pdf summary is to go to the following website: https://livetolearn.lpages.co/enthrallinghistory/

Or, Scan the QR code!

Once you do, it will be intuitive. Enjoy, and thank you!

References

Part 1

Abbe, Mark B. "Polychromy of Roman Marble Sculpture." In *Heilbrunn Timeline of Art History*. New York: The Metropolitan Museum of Art, 2007. http://www.metmuseum.org/toah/hd/prms/hd_prms.htm.

Appian. *Punic Wars*. http://www.perseus.tufts.edu/hopper/text?doc=Perseus%3Atext%3A1999.01.0230%3Atext%3DPun.%3Achapter%3D16%3Asection%3D111.

Arena, Valentina. "The Roman Republic of Jean-Jacques Rousseau." *History of Political Thought* 37 (2016): 8-31. http://www.jstor.org/stable/26228683.

Barchiesi, Alessandro and Walter Scheidel. *The Oxford Handbook of Roman Studies*. Oxford: Oxford University Press, 2010.

Boatwright, Mary T., Daniel J. Gargola, Noel Lenski, Richard J. A. Talbert. *The Romans: From Village to Empire: A History of Rome from Earliest Times to the End of the Western Empire*. Oxford: Oxford University Press, November 22, 2011.

Bono, P., and C. Boni. "Water Supply of Rome in Antiquity and Today." *Geo* 27, (1996), 126-134. https://doi.org/10.1007/BF01061685.

Bourne, Ella. "The Messianic Prophecy in Vergil's Fourth Eclogue." *The Classical Journal* Vol. 11, No. 7, (April 1916), 390-400. https://www.jstor.org/stable/pdf/3287925.pdf.

Caesar, Julius. *The Gallic Wars*. Translated by W. A. McDevitte and W. S. Bohn. The Internet Classics Archive. http://classics.mit.edu/Caesar/gallic.1.1.html.

Casson, Lionel. *Everyday Life in Ancient Rome*. Baltimore: Johns Hopkins University Press, 1998.

Cicero. *Pro Cluentio.* http://www.thelatinlibrary.com/cicero/cluentio.shtml.

Davies, Penelope J. E. *Architecture and Politics in Republican Rome.* Cambridge: Cambridge University Press, 2017.

DiBacco, Cory R. "The Position of Freedmen in Roman Society." *MAD-RUSH Undergraduate Research Conference*, (Spring 2017), JMU Scholarly Commons. https://commons.lib.jmu.edu/cgi/viewcontent.cgi?article=1069&context=madrush.

Dio, Cassius. *Roman History.* Translated by H. B. Foster. Published in Vol. I of the Loeb Classical Library edition, New York: Macmillan Publishers, 1914. https://penelope.uchicago.edu/Thayer/E/Roman/Texts/Cassius_Dio/1*.html.

Duncan, Michael. *The Storm Before the Storm: The Beginning of the End of the Roman Republic.* New York: PublicAffairs, 2017.

Eckstein, A. M. "The Pact Between the Kings, Polybius 15.20.6, and Polybius' View of the Outbreak of the Second Macedonian War." *Classical Philology* 100, no. 3 (2005): 228-42. Accessed July 22, 2021. doi:10.1086/497859. https://www.jstor.org/stable/10.1086/497859?seq=1#metadata_info_tab_contents.

Enthralling History. *Ancient Rome: An Enthralling Overview of Roman History, Starting from the Romulus and Remus Myth through the Republic to the Fall of the Roman Empire.* Las Vegas, 2021.

Farnsworth Gray, Harold. "Sewerage in Ancient and Mediaeval Times." *Sewage Works Journal* Vol.12.5 (1940): 939-46.

Gowers, Emily. "The Anatomy of Rome from Capitol to Cloaca." *The Journal of Roman Studies* Vol.85 (1995): 23-32.

Gwynn, David M. *The Roman Republic: A Very Short Introduction.* Oxford: Oxford University Press, 2012.

Hammond, N. G. L. "Which Ptolemy Gave Troops and Stood as Protector of Pyrrhus' Kingdom?" *Historia: Zeitschrift Für Alte Geschichte* 37, no. 4 (1988): 405-13. http://www.jstor.org/stable/4436071.

Josephus, Flavius. *The Jewish War.* http://penelope.uchicago.edu/josephus/war-3.html.

Kane, J. Robert. "The Third Punic War: An Intelligence Failure from Antiquity." *American Intelligence Journal* 36, no. 1 (2019): 161-66. https://www.jstor.org/stable/27066349.

Lintott, Andrew. "Political History, 146-95 BC." In *The Cambridge Ancient History*, edited by John Crook, Andrew Lintott, and Elizabeth Rawson, 92. Cambridge: Cambridge University Press, 1992.

Lintott, Andrew. *The Constitution of the Roman Republic.* Oxford: Oxford University Press, 2003.

Livius, Titus. *The History of Rome, Volumes I - V.* Translated by George Baker. New York: Peter A. Mesier et al., 10.
https://oll.libertyfund.org/title/baker-the-history-of-rome-vol-1.

Martin, Thomas R. *Ancient Rome: From Romulus to Justinian.* New Haven: Yale University Press, September 10, 2013.

Mitchell, Thomas N. "Roman Republicanism: The Underrated Legacy." *Proceedings of the American Philosophical Society* 145, no. 2 (2001): 127-37.
http://www.jstor.org/stable/1558267.

Myers, Richard. "Montesquieu on the Causes of Roman Greatness." *History of Political Thought* 16, no. 1 (1995): 37-47.
http://www.jstor.org/stable/26215859.

Nicolaus of Damascus. *Life of Augustus.* Translated by Clayton M. Hall.
https://web.archive.org/web/20070714144802/http://www.csun.edu/~hcfll004/nicolaus.html.

O'Connell, Robert L. *The Ghosts of Cannae: Hannibal and the Darkest Hour of the Roman Republic.* New York: Random House, 2011.

Osgood, Josiah. "The Pen and the Sword: Writing and Conquest in Caesar's Gaul." *Classical Antiquity* 28, no. 2 (2009): 328-58.
https://doi.org/10.1525/ca.2009.28.2.328.

Ovid. *The Art of Love (Ars Amatoria).* Translated by A. S. Kline. Poetry in Translation.
https://www.poetryintranslation.com/PITBR/Latin/ArtofLoveBkII.php.

Plutarch. *Fall of the Roman Republic.* London: Penguin Classics, April 25th, 2006. Internet Archives:
https://archive.org/stream/FallOfTheRomanRepublicPlutarch.rOpts/Fall%20Of TheRomanRepublic%20Plutarch.r-opts_djvu.txt.

Plutarch. *The Parallel Lives.* Loeb Classical Library edition, 1914.
https://penelope.uchicago.edu/Thayer/e/roman/texts/plutarch/lives/home.html.

Polybius. *The Histories.*
http://penelope.uchicago.edu/Thayer/E/Roman/Texts/Polybius/home.html.

Price, Sara. "The Roman Republic in Montesquieu and Rousseau." *Western Political Science Association* 2011 Annual Meeting Paper.
https://ssrn.com/abstract=1766947.

Sheridan, Paul. "The Sacred Chickens of Rome." *Anecdotes from Antiquity.* November 8th, 2015. http://www.anecdotesfromantiquity.net/the-sacred-chickens-of-rome/.

Storey, Glenn R. "Regionaries-Type Insulae 2: Architectural/Residential Units at Rome." *American Journal of Archaeology* 106, no. 3 (2002): 411–34.
https://doi.org/10.2307/4126281.

Virgil. *The Aeneid Book IV.* Translated by A. S. Kline. Poetry in Translation, 2002. https://www.poetryintranslation.com/PITBR/Latin/VirgilAeneidIV.php.

Part 2

Addis, F. (2020). *The Eternal City: A History of Rome* (Reprint ed.). Pegasus Books.

Ambler, J. L. (n.d.). Introduction to ancient Roman art (article). Khan Academy. https://www.khanacademy.org/humanities/ancient-art-civilizations/roman/beginners-guide-rome/a/introduction-to-ancient-roman-art

Andrews, E. (2022, July 21). 8 Ways Roads Helped Rome Rule the Ancient World. HISTORY. https://www.history.com/news/8-ways-roads-helped-rome-rule-the-ancient-world

Augustus Closes the Temple of Janus. (2019, October 10). History Today. https://www.historytoday.com/archive/foundations/augustus-closes-temple-janus

Bileta, V. (2021, July 9). Rome Halts the Huns: The Battle of Châlons (Catalaunian Plains). TheCollector. https://www.thecollector.com/the-decisive-battle-of-chalons-catalaunian-plains-an-in-depth-review/

Campbell, C. J. (2022, March 24). Peace & Prosperity: What Was the Pax Romana? TheCollector. https://www.thecollector.com/what-was-pax-romana/

Cartwright, M. (2022, July 30). Roman Roads. World History Encyclopedia. https://www.worldhistory.org/article/758/roman-roads/

Cartwright, M. (2022, July 31). Roman Baths. World History Encyclopedia. https://www.worldhistory.org/Roman_Baths/

Cartwright, M. (2022, July 31). Roman Siege Warfare. World History Encyclopedia. https://www.worldhistory.org/Roman_Siege_Warfare/

Cartwright, M. (2022, August 1). Circus Maximus. World History Encyclopedia. https://www.worldhistory.org/Circus_Maximus/

Cartwright, M. (2022, August 1). Praetorian Guard. World History Encyclopedia. https://www.worldhistory.org/Praetorian_Guard/

Cartwright, M. (2022, August 1). Roman Senate. World History Encyclopedia. https://www.worldhistory.org/Roman_Senate/

The Cursus publicus: The Courier Service of the Roman Empire: History of Information. (n.d.). History of Information. https://www.historyofinformation.com/detail.php?id=1394

Gill, N. S. (2018, March 17). What Was Life Like During the Pax Romana? ThoughtCo. https://www.thoughtco.com/what-was-the-pax-romana-120829

Jasiński, J. (2022, June 29). Scutum. IMPERIUM ROMANUM. https://imperiumromanum.pl/en/roman-army/equipment-of-roman-legionary/scutum/

Klein, C. (2022, July 21). How Ancient Rome Thrived During Pax Romana. HISTORY. https://www.history.com/news/pax-romana-roman-empire-peace-augustus

Land, G. (2018, August 9). Trade and Transport at the Height of the Roman Empire. History Hit. https://www.historyhit.com/trade-and-transport-at-the-height-of-the-roman-empire/

Mark, J. J. (2021, July 31). Ancient Roman Society. World History Encyclopedia. https://www.worldhistory.org/article/1463/ancient-roman-society/

Mark, J. J. (2022, August 1). Vestal Virgin. World History Encyclopedia. https://www.worldhistory.org/Vestal_Virgin/

PBS. (n.d.). The Roman Empire: in the First Century. The Roman Empire. Social Order. Slaves & Freemen | PBS. https://www.pbs.org/empires/romans/empire/slaves_freemen.html

Preskar, P. (2021, December 30). The Praetorian Guard —Power, Greed, and Terror | History of Yesterday. Medium.

Provincial Government of the Roman Empire | UNRV.com Roman History. (n.d.). UNRV History. https://www.unrv.com/government/provincialgovernment.php

Ricketts, C. (2018, July 25). 5 Important Roman Siege Engines. History Hit. https://www.historyhit.com/important-roman-siege-engines/

Ricketts, C. (2018, July 30). Divorce and Decline: The Division of East and West Roman Empires. History Hit. https://www.historyhit.com/divorce-and-decline-the-division-of-east-and-west-roman-empires/

Ricketts, C. (2018, August 9). The Growth of Christianity in the Roman Empire. History Hit. https://www.historyhit.com/the-growth-of-christianity-in-the-roman-empire/

Roman Carriages. (n.d.). Vita Romae. https://www.vita-romae.com/roman-carriages.html

The Roman Empire and Trade. (2015). History Learning. https://historylearning.com/a-history-of-ancient-rome/the-roman-empire-and-trade/

Roman Roads. (n.d.). Vita Romae. https://www.vita-romae.com/roman-roads.html

Severus: Rome's first African Emperor. (n.d.). Sky HISTORY TV Channel. https://www.history.co.uk/article/severus-rome%E2%80%99s-first-african-emperor

Warfare History Network. (2022, July 14). The Roman Gladius. https://warfarehistorynetwork.com/article/the-roman-gladius/

Wasson, D. L. (2022, July 30). Roman Emperor. World History Encyclopedia. https://www.worldhistory.org/Roman_Emperor/

Wasson, D. L. (2022, July 31). Constantine I. World History Encyclopedia. https://www.worldhistory.org/Constantine_I/

Wikipedia contributors. (2022, April 11). Temple of Janus (Roman Forum). Wikipedia. https://en.wikipedia.org/wiki/Temple_of_Janus_(Roman_Forum)

Wikipedia contributors. (2022, May 27). Peregrinus (Roman). Wikipedia. https://en.wikipedia.org/wiki/Peregrinus_(Roman)

Wikipedia contributors. (2022, June 25). Pax Romana. Wikipedia. https://en.wikipedia.org/wiki/Pax_Romana

Wikipedia contributors. (2022, July 19). Testudo formation. Wikipedia. https://en.wikipedia.org/wiki/Testudo_formation

Wikipedia contributors. (2022, July 27). Baths of Caracalla. Wikipedia. https://en.wikipedia.org/wiki/Baths_of_Caracalla

Wikipedia contributors. (2022, July 29). Roman Forum. Wikipedia. https://en.wikipedia.org/wiki/Roman_Forum

Wikipedia contributors. (2022, July 30). Marian reforms. Wikipedia. https://en.wikipedia.org/wiki/Marian_reforms#Marian_reforms

Williams, J. A. (2022, May 6). What life as a Roman emperor was really like. Grunge.Com. https://www.grunge.com/855148/what-life-as-a-roman-emperor-was-really-like/

Part 3

"Emperor Constantine's Edict against the Arians." *fourthcentury.com*. 23 January 2010. Archived from the original on 19 August 2011. Retrieved 20 August 2011.

"Online Chapel - Greek Orthodox Archdiocese of America." *www.goarch.org*.

"The Antiquities of the Jews (13.298)." *Lexundria*.

Angold, Michael. *The Byzantine Empire, 1025-1204*.

Bartlett, Robert. *The Making of Europe*.

Besançon, Alain. *The Forbidden Image*.

Brubaker, Leslie, and John Haldon. *Byzantium in the Iconoclast Era (ca. 680-850)*.

Bury, J.B. *A History of the Later Roman Empire*.

Bury, J.B. *The Invasion of Europe by the Barbarians*. W.W. Norton & Company, 2000, p. 42.

Carlan, C.U. "Life and Death in the Ancient World: The Tetrarchy and the Last Persecution of Christians (303-311)."

Cleenewerck, Laurent. *His Broken Body*.

Diehl, Charles. *History of the Byzantine Empire.*

Dimitrov, Ivan Zhelev. "Bulgarian Christianity." In *The Blackwell Companion to Eastern Christianity*, 2007, p. 47.

Dunstan, W.E. *Rome.* Lanham, MD: Rowman & Littlefield Publishers, 2010. ISBN 9780742568341.

Edmondo, Lupieri. "Friar of Ignatius of Jesus (Carlo Leonelli) and the First 'Scholarly' Book on Mandaeism (1652)." *ARAM Periodical* 16 (2004): 25-46.

Ehler, Sidney Zdeneck, and John B. Morrall. *Church and State Through the Centuries: A Collection of Historic Documents with Commentaries.* 1967.

Ehrman, Bart D. *Lost Christianities: The Battles for Scripture and the Faiths We Never Knew.* Oxford: Oxford University Press, 2005. pp. 95-112. ISBN 978-0-19-518249-1.

Fouracre, Paul, ed. *The New Cambridge Medieval History* Set.

Gonzalez, Justo. *The Story of Christianity*, Vol. 1. Harper Collins, 1984. p. 176. ISBN 0-06-063315-8.

Goodyear, Michael. "Compromised Defense - The Conquests of Basil II." *The Michigan Journal of History* 5.

Hamidovic, David. "About the Links Between the Dead Sea Scrolls and Mandaean Liturgy." *Aram Periodical* 22 (2010): 441-451.

Haldon, John. *Byzantium at War.*

Haldon, John F. "The Byzantine Empire." In *The Dynamics of Ancient Empires: State Power from Assyria to Byzantium*, 2009, pp. 205-254.

Handy, Lowell K. "The Appearance of Pantheon in Judah." In Diana Vikander Edelman (ed.), *The Triumph of Elohim: From Yahwism to Judaism.* Peeters Publishers, 1995.

Hitchcock, Susan Tyler, and John L. Esposito. *Geography of Religion: Where God Lives, Where Pilgrims Walk.* National Geographic Society, 2004. p. 281.

Holmes, Catherine. *Basil II and the Government of Empire (976-1025).* PhD Thesis, University of Oxford, 1999.

Holmes, Catherine. "Basil II (AD 976-1025)." *De Imperatoribus Romanis*, 2003.

Holmes, Catherine. "Political Elites in the Reign of Basil II." In *Byzantium in the Year 1000.* Brill, 2003. pp. 35-69.

Houben, Hubert. *Roger II of Sicily.*

Howard-Johnston, James. *East Rome, Sasanian Persia and the End of Antiquity.*

Hunt, E.D. *Eusebius of Caesarea, Life of Constantine.* Translated by Averil Cameron and Stuart G. Hall. *The Journal of Ecclesiastical History* 52, no. 2 (2001): 338-396.

Hupchick, Dennis P. "Simeon's Campaigns for Imperial Recognition, 894-927." In *The Bulgarian-Byzantine Wars for Early Medieval Balkan Hegemony: Silver-Lined Skulls and Blinded Armies*, 2017, pp. 149-219.

Ilić, Nikola. "Da li je srpski knez Višeslav bio Hrišćanin?" *Teološki Pogledi* 55, no. 1: 95-112.

Jeffreys, Elizabeth. "The Beginning of Byzantine Chronography: John Malalas." In *Greek and Roman Historiography in Late Antiquity*. Brill, 2003. pp. 497-527.

Jedin, Hubert, John Dolan, and Karl Holland. *History of the Church*.

Kaldellis, Anthony. *Streams of Gold, Rivers of Blood*.

Kantakouzenos, John. *The History of John Kantakouzenos*, vol. II. Catholic University of America, 1979, p. 80.

Kennedy, Hugh. *The Great Arab Conquests*.

Kolrud, Kristine, and Marina Prusac. *Iconoclasm from Antiquity to Modernity*.

Krsmanović, Bojana, and Dejan Dželebdžić. "John Tzimiskes and Nikephoros II Phokas: The Background and Motives of a Premeditated Murder." *Zbornik radova Vizantološkog instituta* 47 (2010): 83-120.

Laskaris, Mihailo. *Vizantijske princeze*. Pešić i sinovi, 1997, p. 58.

Layton, Bentley. "Prolegomena to the Study of Ancient Gnosticism." In L. Michael White and O. Larry Yarbrough (eds.), *The Social World of the First Christians: Essays in Honor of Wayne A. Meeks*. Minneapolis: Fortress Press, 1995.

Leszka, Mirosław J. "The Monk versus the Philosopher: From the History of the Bulgarian-Byzantine War 894-896." *Studia Ceranea* 1 (2011): 55-70.

Liddell, Henry George, and Robert Scott. *A Greek-English Lexicon*. The Perseus Project.

Maier, Paul L. *Eusebius: The Church History*. Grand Rapids: Kregel Publications, 1999, p. 374.

Mashkin, Nikolai. *A History of Ancient Rome*. Gospolitizdat, 1956, p. 406.

Miller, Patrick D. *The Religion of Ancient Israel*. Westminster John Knox Press, 2000. ISBN 978-0-664-22145-4.

Mitchell, Stephen. *A History of the Later Roman Empire AD 284-641*. Oxford: Blackwell, 2007, p. 198.

Nicolle, David. *The Great Islamic Conquests, AD 632-750*.

Nicolle, David, and Christa Hook. *The Fourth Crusade 1202-04*.

Nestor. *Primary Chronicle*, p. 64. https://www.mgh-bibliothek.de/dokumente/a/a011458.pdf

Orlandis, José. *A Short History of the Catholic Church*.

Ostrogorsky, George. *History of the Byzantine State*. Rutgers University Press, 1969.

Pagels, Elaine. *The Gnostic Gospels*. New York: Knopf Doubleday, 1989. ISBN 978-0-679-72453-7.

Painter, Sidney. *A History of the Middle Ages 284–1500*. London: MacMillan Press, 1973, p. 33.

Pears, Edwin. *The Fall of Constantinople, Being the Story of the Fourth Crusade*.

Procopius. *The Secret History*. Penguin Books, 1982, p. 38.

Riley-Smith, Jonathan. *The Crusades*.

Richardson, Ernest C., Philip Schaff, and Henry Wace. *The Life of Constantine*. In *A Select Library of the Nicene and Post-Nicene Fathers of the Christian Church*, Series 2, 1890, vol. 2: 481–540.

Rukavishnikov, Alexandr. "Tale of Bygone Years: The Russian Primary Chronicle as a Family Chronicle." *Early Medieval Europe* 12, no. 1 (2003): 53–74.

Runciman, Steven. *Byzantine Civilization*.

Smith, M.D. "The Religion of Constantius I." *Greek, Roman, and Byzantine Studies* 38, no. 2 (1997): 187–208.

Socrates of Constantinople. *Church History*, Book 1, Chapter 33. In Anthony F. Beavers, *Chronology of the Arian Controversy*.

Sordi, Marta. *The Christians and the Roman Empire*. Norman: University of Oklahoma Press, 1994, p. 134.

Thaler, Kai. "Iraqi Minority Group Needs U.S. Attention." *Yale Daily News*, 9 March 2007. Retrieved 4 November 2021.

Theodoret of Cyrus. *The Ecclesiastical History of Theodoret*, Book 3, Chapter 31.

Villehardouin, Geoffrey. *Memoirs or Chronicle of the Fourth Crusade and the Conquest of Constantinople*.

Waldron, Byron Lloyd. *Diocletian, Hereditary Succession and the Tetrarchic Dynasty*. PhD diss., 2018.

Wheeler, Joe L. *Saint Nicholas*. Thomas Nelson, 2010.

Zosimus. *Historia Nova*. Translated by R.T. Ridley. *Zosimus: New History*, Byzantina Australiensia 2. Canberra, 1982.

Image Sources

1. https://commons.wikimedia.org/wiki/File:Bardin_Tullia.jpg
2. Painting by Heinrich Friedrich Fuger. Photo modified: zoomed in. © José Luiz Bernardes Ribeiro; https://commons.wikimedia.org/wiki/File:Brutus_Sentences_his_Sons_to_Death_by_Heinrich_Friedrich_Fuger_-_Staatsgalerie_-_Stuttgart_-_Germany_2017.jpg
3. https://commons.wikimedia.org/wiki/File:The_Death_of_the_Consul_Papirius,_by_Philipp_Friedrich_Hetsch,_1795,_oil_on_canvas_-_Germanisches_Nationalmuseum_-_Nuremberg,_Germany_-_DSC03431.jpg
4. https://commons.wikimedia.org/wiki/File:Secessio_plebis.JPG
5. https://commons.wikimedia.org/wiki/File:Eugene_Guillaume_-_the_Gracchi.jpg
6. https://commons.wikimedia.org/wiki/File:OstianInsulae.JPG
7. https://commons.wikimedia.org/wiki/File:Roman_fresco_Villa_dei_Misteri_Pompeii_001.jpg
8. https://commons.wikimedia.org/wiki/File:Triclinium_-_Arch%C3%A4ologische_Staatssammlung_M%C3%Bcnchen.JPG
9. https://commons.wikimedia.org/wiki/File:Gladiators_from_the_Zliten_mosaic_3.JPG
10. https://commons.wikimedia.org/wiki/File:Pompeii_-_Casa_del_Poeta_Tragico_-_Theater_3.jpg
11. https://commons.wikimedia.org/wiki/File:Parco_della_Grotta_di_Posillipo5_(crop).jpg
12. Nick, CC BY 2.0 <https://creativecommons.org/licenses/by/2.0>, via Wikimedia Commons; https://commons.wikimedia.org/wiki/File:Roman_Aqueduct,_Spain1.jpg

13 Ra Boe / Wikipedia, CC BY-SA 3.0 DE <https://creativecommons.org/licenses/by-sa/3.0/de/deed.en>, via Wikimedia Commons; https://commons.wikimedia.org/wiki/File:Baia-Complesso_Termal_Romano_2010-by-RaBoe-018.jpg

14 Credit: Benjamín Núñez González, CC BY-SA 4.0 <https://creativecommons.org/licenses/by-sa/4.0>, via Wikimedia Commons; https://commons.wikimedia.org/wiki/File:Detalles_del_Templo_de_Portuno,_Roma,_2017_04.jpg

15 https://commons.wikimedia.org/wiki/File:Patrizio_Torlonia.jpg

16 Greg Willis from Denver, CO, usa, CC BY-SA 2.0 <https://creativecommons.org/licenses/by-sa/2.0>, via Wikimedia Commons; https://commons.wikimedia.org/wiki/File:Pompeii_-_Cave_Canem_(4786638740).jpg

17 Johny SYSEL, CC BY-SA 3.0 <https://creativecommons.org/licenses/by-sa/3.0>, via Wikimedia Commons; https://commons.wikimedia.org/wiki/File:AR_serrate_denarius_of_C._Sulpicius_C._f._Galba.jpg

18 https://commons.wikimedia.org/wiki/File:Bal_BBC1.jpg

19 Rijksmuseum, CC0, via Wikimedia Commons https://commons.wikimedia.org/wiki/File:Beleg_van_Jotapata_door_de_Romeinen_onder_Vespasianus,_RP-P-1896-A-19368-2321.jpg

20 User:MatthiasKabel, CC BY-SA 3.0 <http://creativecommons.org/licenses/by-sa/3.0/>, via Wikimedia Commons; https://commons.wikimedia.org/wiki/File:Helmet_typ_Montefortino_01.jpg

21 Classical Numismatic Group, Inc. http://www.cngcoins.com, CC BY-SA 2.5 <https://creativecommons.org/licenses/by-sa/2.5>, via Wikimedia Commons; https://commons.wikimedia.org/wiki/File:Pyrrhus_Kingdom_of_Epirus.JPG

22 Piom, translation by Pamela Butler, CC BY-SA 3.0 <http://creativecommons.org/licenses/by-sa/3.0/>, via Wikimedia Commons; https://commons.wikimedia.org/wiki/File:Pyrrhic_War_Italy_en.svg

23 https://commons.wikimedia.org/wiki/File:Macedonia_and_the_Aegean_World_c.200.png

24 https://commons.wikimedia.org/wiki/File:Stallaert-Dido.jpg

25 GalaxMaps, CC BY-SA 4.0 <https://creativecommons.org/licenses/by-sa/4.0>, via Wikimedia Commons; https://commons.wikimedia.org/wiki/File:First_Punic_War_237_BC.png

26 Maglorbd at English Wikipedia, CC BY-SA 3.0 <https://creativecommons.org/licenses/by-sa/3.0>, via Wikimedia Commons; https://commons.wikimedia.org/wiki/File:PW2_Rhone_218BC.PNG

27 PMRMaeyaert, CC BY-SA 4.0 <https://creativecommons.org/licenses/by-sa/4.0>, via Wikimedia Commons; https://commons.wikimedia.org/wiki/File:PM_110453_Liebig_Chromos.jpg

28 Goran tek-en, CC BY-SA 4.0 <https://creativecommons.org/licenses/by-sa/4.0>, via Wikimedia Commons; https://commons.wikimedia.org/wiki/File:Western_Mediterranean_territory,_150_BC.svg

29 Harrias, CC BY-SA 4.0 <https://creativecommons.org/licenses/by-sa/4.0>, via Wikimedia Commons; https://commons.wikimedia.org/wiki/File:City_of_Carthage_circa_149_BC.png

30 Damian Entwistle, CC BY-SA 2.0 <https://creativecommons.org/licenses/by-sa/2.0>, via Wikimedia Commons; https://commons.wikimedia.org/wiki/File:Carthage_National_Museum_representation_of_city.jpg

31 Metropolitan Museum of Art, CC0, via Wikimedia Commons; https://commons.wikimedia.org/wiki/File:Julius_Caesar_MET_267739.jpg

32 User:Feitscherg, CC BY-SA 3.0 <http://creativecommons.org/licenses/by-sa/3.0/>, via Wikimedia Commons; https://commons.wikimedia.org/wiki/File:Map_Gallia_Tribes_Towns.png

33 Diagram Lajard, CC0, via Wikimedia Commons; https://commons.wikimedia.org/wiki/File:Roman_bust_in_Ny_Carlsberg_Glyptotek,_crop.jpg

34 Alphanidon, CC BY-SA 4.0 <https://creativecommons.org/licenses/by-sa/4.0>, via Wikimedia Commons; https://commons.wikimedia.org/wiki/File:Pompey_the_Great.jpg

35 https://commons.wikimedia.org/wiki/File:Julius_Caesar_from_a_Cameo.jpg

36 С. И. Сосновский, CC BY-SA 4.0 <https://creativecommons.org/licenses/by-sa/4.0>, via Wikimedia Commons; https://commons.wikimedia.org/wiki/File:Statue_of_the_Emperor_Octavian_Augustus_as_Jupiter_(4).png

37 GingerJesusFMIRL, CC BY-SA 4.0 <https://creativecommons.org/licenses/by-sa/4.0>, via Wikimedia Commons; https://commons.wikimedia.org/wiki/File:Caesar-augustus1.jpg

38 Gary Todd from Xinzheng, China, PDM-owner, via Wikimedia Commons; https://commons.wikimedia.org/wiki/File:Claudius_as_Jupiter,_1st_C._AD,_Round_Hall_by_Michelangelo_Simonetti,_Vatican_Museum_(48465336326).jpg

39 User:Historicair, Ifly6, CC BY-SA 3.0 <https://creativecommons.org/licenses/by-sa/3.0>, via Wikimedia Commons; https://commons.wikimedia.org/wiki/File:Map_of_the_Ancient_Rome_at_Caesar_time_(with_conquests)-en.svg

40 Argentino, CC BY-SA 3.0 <https://creativecommons.org/licenses/by-sa/3.0>, via Wikimedia Commons; https://commons.wikimedia.org/wiki/File:Roman_Empire_borders_and_influence.gif

41 Pascal Reusch, CC BY-SA 3.0 <https://creativecommons.org/licenses/by-sa/3.0>, via Wikimedia Commons; https://commons.wikimedia.org/wiki/File:Ponte_Quattro_Capi.jpg

42 https://commons.wikimedia.org/wiki/File:Vincenzo_Camuccini_-_La_morte_di_Cesare.jpg

43 https://commons.wikimedia.org/wiki/File:The_Battle_of_Actium,_2_September_31BC_RMG_BHC0251.tiff

44 Jani Niemenmaa, CC BY-SA 3.0 <http://creativecommons.org/licenses/by-sa/3.0/>, via Wikimedia Commons: https://commons.wikimedia.org/wiki/File:Roman_Empire_Map.png

45 Miguel Hermoso Cuesta, CC BY-SA 4.0 <https://creativecommons.org/licenses/by-sa/4.0>, via Wikimedia Commons: https://commons.wikimedia.org/wiki/File:Livia_y_Tiberio_M.A.N._01.JPG

46 https://commons.wikimedia.org/wiki/File:The_Assassination_of_the_Emperor_Caligula.jpg

47 https://commons.wikimedia.org/wiki/File:Proclaiming_claudius_emperor.png

48 https://commons.wikimedia.org/wiki/File:Robert,_Hubert_-_Incendie_%C3%A0_Rome_-.jpg

49 Loudon dodd, CC BY-SA 3.0 <https://creativecommons.org/licenses/by-sa/3.0>, via Wikimedia Commons: https://commons.wikimedia.org/wiki/File:Janus1.JPG

50 https://commons.wikimedia.org/wiki/File:Turner_Ovid_Banished_from_Rome.jpg

51 https://commons.wikimedia.org/wiki/File:Traianus_Glyptothek_Munich_72.jpg

52 https://commons.wikimedia.org/wiki/File:Milecastle_39_on_Hadrian%27s_Wall.jpg

53 Jean-Pol GRANDMONT, CC BY-SA 3.0 <https://creativecommons.org/licenses/by-sa/3.0>, via Wikimedia Commons: https://commons.wikimedia.org/wiki/File:0_Antoninus_Pius_-_Museo_Chiaramonti_(Vatican).JPG

54 https://commons.wikimedia.org/wiki/File:Commodus_is_strangled_by_Narcissus.png

55 Attar-Aram syria, CC BY-SA 4.0 <https://creativecommons.org/licenses/by-sa/4.0>, via Wikimedia Commons: https://commons.wikimedia.org/wiki/File:Odaenathus_Kingdom.png

56 Blank map of South Europe and North Africa.svg: historicair 23:27, 8 August 2007 (UTC), CC BY-SA 2.5 <https://creativecommons.org/licenses/by-sa/2.5>, via Wikimedia Commons: https://commons.wikimedia.org/wiki/File:Map_of_Ancient_Rome_271_AD.svg

57 Coppermine Photo Gallery, CC BY-SA 3.0 <http://creativecommons.org/licenses/by-sa/3.0/>, via Wikimedia Commons: https://commons.wikimedia.org/wiki/File:Tetrarchy_map3.jpg

58 https://commons.wikimedia.org/wiki/File:Battle_of_the_Milvian_Bridge_by_Giulio_Romano,_1520-24.jpg

59 User:MapMaster, CC BY-SA 2.5 <https://creativecommons.org/licenses/by-sa/2.5>, via Wikimedia Commons: https://commons.wikimedia.org/wiki/File:Invasions_of_the_Roman_Empire_1.png

60 https://commons.wikimedia.org/wiki/File:Cole_Thomas_The_Course_of_Empire_Destruction_1836.jpg

61 https://commons.wikimedia.org/wiki/File:Antichina_piranese.jpg

62 https://commons.wikimedia.org/wiki/File:Minturno_Via-Appia.jpg

63 https://commons.wikimedia.org/wiki/File:Bige_Mus%C3%A9e_de_Laon_050208.jpg

64 https://commons.wikimedia.org/wiki/File:Carruca.jpg

65 https://commons.wikimedia.org/wiki/File:PSM_V18_D470_Ancient_roman_farm_kart_and_oxen.jpg

66 https://commons.wikimedia.org/wiki/File:Silk_route.jpg

67 https://commons.wikimedia.org/wiki/File:Cicer%C3%B3n_denuncia_a_Catilina,_por_Cesare_Maccari.jpg

68 Historien spécialiste du bassin minier du Nord-Pas-de-Calais JÄNNICK Jérémy / Wikimedia Commons & Louvre-Lens: https://commons.wikimedia.org/wiki/File:Lens_-_Inauguration_du_Louvre-Lens_le_4_d%C3%A9cembre_2012,_la_Galerie_du_Temps,_n%C2%B0_058.JPG

69 https://commons.wikimedia.org/wiki/File:Sejanus_is_arrested_and_condemned_to_death.jpg

70 No machine-readable author provided. MatthiasKabel assumed (based on copyright claims)., CC BY-SA 3.0 <http://creativecommons.org/licenses/by-sa/3.0/>, via Wikimedia Commons: https://commons.wikimedia.org/wiki/File:Scutum_1.jpg

71 CC BY-SA 3.0 <http://creativecommons.org/licenses/by-sa/3.0/>, via Wikimedia Commons: https://commons.wikimedia.org/wiki/File:Roman_gladius-transparent.png

72 Cassius Ahenobarbus, CC BY-SA 3.0 <https://creativecommons.org/licenses/by-sa/3.0/>, via Wikimedia Commons: https://commons.wikimedia.org/wiki/File:Colonne_trajane_1-57_(cropped).jpg

73 Walters Art Museum, Public domain, via Wikimedia Commons: https://commons.wikimedia.org/wiki/File:Roman_-_Pair_of_Snake_Bracelets_-_Walters_57528,_57529_-_Group_(cropped).jpg

74 Hartmann Linge, CC BY-SA 3.0 <https://creativecommons.org/licenses/by-sa/3.0/>, via Wikimedia Commons: https://commons.wikimedia.org/wiki/File:Lauersforter_Phalerae_Museum_Burg_Linn.jpg

75 https://commons.wikimedia.org/wiki/File:Jean-L%C3%A9on_G%C3%A9r%C3%B4me_004.jpg

76 Pascal Radigue, CC BY 3.0 <https://creativecommons.org/licenses/by/3.0/>, via Wikimedia Commons: https://commons.wikimedia.org/wiki/File:Mosaique_echansons_Bardo.jpg

77 https://commons.wikimedia.org/wiki/File:Alessandro_Marchesini_-_Dedication_of_a_New_Vestal_Virgin_-_WGA14054.jpg

78 https://commons.wikimedia.org/wiki/File:Platner-forum-republic-96_recontructed_color.jpg

79 BeBo86, CC BY-SA 3.0 <https://creativecommons.org/licenses/by-sa/3.0>, via Wikimedia Commons: https://commons.wikimedia.org/wiki/File:Forum_romanum_6k_(5760x2097).jpg

80 FeaturedPics, CC BY-SA 4.0 <https://creativecommons.org/licenses/by-sa/4.0>, via Wikimedia Commons: https://commons.wikimedia.org/wiki/File:Colosseo_2020.jpg

81 Gzen92, CC BY-SA 4.0 <https://creativecommons.org/licenses/by-sa/4.0>, via Wikimedia Commons https://commons.wikimedia.org/wiki/File:Thermes_de_Caracalla_-_Plan.jpg

82 Naples National Archaeological Museum, CC BY 2.5 <https://creativecommons.org/licenses/by/2.5>, via Wikimedia Commons: https://commons.wikimedia.org/wiki/File:Doryphoros_MAN_Napoli_Inv6011-2.jpg

83 https://commons.wikimedia.org/wiki/File:Statue-Augustus.jpg

84 Jean-Pol GRANDMONT, CC BY 4.0 <https://creativecommons.org/licenses/by/4.0>, via Wikimedia Commons: https://commons.wikimedia.org/wiki/File:0_Arc_de_Septime_S%C3%A9v%C3%A8re_-_Rome_(5).JPG

85 iessi, CC BY 2.0 <https://creativecommons.org/licenses/by/2.0>, via Wikimedia Commons: https://commons.wikimedia.org/wiki/File:Ostia_Antica-strada01-modified.jpg

86 https://commons.wikimedia.org/wiki/File:Atrium_interior.jpg

87 Domus_romana_Vector001.svg: *PureCorederivative work: PureCore (talk)derivative work: Papa Lima Whiskey 2, CC BY-SA 3.0 <http://creativecommons.org/licenses/by-sa/3.0/>, via Wikimedia Commons: https://commons.wikimedia.org/wiki/File:Domus_romana_Vector002.svg

88 https://commons.wikimedia.org/wiki/File:Jean_L%C3%A9on_G%C3%A9r%C3%B4me_-_Chariot_Race_-_1983.380_-_Art_Institute_of_Chicago.jpg

89 https://commons.wikimedia.org/wiki/File:Jean-Leon_Gerome_Pollice_Verso.jpg

90 https://commons.wikimedia.org/wiki/File:Mignard_-_The_Shepherd_Faustulus_Bringing_Romulus_and_Remus_to_His_Wife.jpg

91 Themadchopper, Antoine-François Callet, CC0, via Wikimedia Commons: https://commons.wikimedia.org/wiki/File:Saturnalia_by_Antoine_Callet.jpg

92 https://commons.wikimedia.org/wiki/File:Raphael_Baptism_Constantine.jpg

93 https://commons.wikimedia.org/w/index.php?curid=86235336

94 Capitoline Museums, CC BY-SA 3.0 <https://creativecommons.org/licenses/by-sa/3.0>, via Wikimedia Commons, https://commons.wikimedia.org/w/index.php?curid=25646964

95 Kunsthistorisches Museum, CC BY-SA 4.0 <https://creativecommons.org/licenses/by-sa/4.0>, via Wikimedia Commons, https://commons.wikimedia.org/w/index.php?curid=122518568)

96 Cplakidas, CC BY-SA 3.0 <https://creativecommons.org/licenses/by-sa/3.0>, via Wikimedia Commons, https://commons.wikimedia.org/w/index.php?curid=5084599)

97 https://commons.wikimedia.org/w/index.php?curid=117976

98 www.livius.org, CC BY-SA 4.0 <https://creativecommons.org/licenses/by-sa/4.0>, via Wikimedia Commons, https://commons.wikimedia.org/w/index.php?curid=92452046

99 User:MapMaster, CC BY-SA 2.5 <https://creativecommons.org/licenses/by-sa/2.5>, via Wikimedia Commons, https://commons.wikimedia.org/wiki/File:Invasions_of_the_Roman_Empire_1.png

100 https://commons.wikimedia.org/wiki/File:Sack_of_Rome_by_the_Visigoths_on_24_August_410_by_JN_Sylvestre_1890.jpg

101 No machine-readable author provided. Neuceu assumed (based on copyright claims)., CC BY-SA 2.5 <https://creativecommons.org/licenses/by-sa/2.5>, via Wikimedia Commons, https://commons.wikimedia.org/wiki/File:Justinien_527-565.svg

102 Petar Milošević, CC BY-SA 4.0 <https://creativecommons.org/licenses/by-sa/4.0>, via Wikimedia Commons, https://commons.wikimedia.org/wiki/File:Mosaic_of_Justinianus_I_-_Basilica_San_Vitale_(Ravenna).jpg

103 Cplakidas, CC BY-SA 3.0 <http://creativecommons.org/licenses/by-sa/3.0/>, via Wikimedia Commons, https://commons.wikimedia.org/wiki/File:Constantinople_imperial_district.png

104 Petar Milošević, CC BY-SA 4.0 <https://creativecommons.org/licenses/by-sa/4.0>, via Wikimedia Commons, https://commons.wikimedia.org/wiki/File:Empress_Theodora_mosaic_detail.png

105 Ghent University Library, CC BY-SA 4.0 <https://creativecommons.org/licenses/by-sa/4.0>, via Wikimedia Commons; https://commons.wikimedia.org/wiki/File:Archive-ugent-be-B96419FA-8AA4-11E3-9E68-C04DD43445F2_DS-441_(cropped).jpg

106 User Fphilibert from fr.wiki, CC BY-SA 3.0 <http://creativecommons.org/licenses/by-sa/3.0/>, via Wikimedia Commons, https://commons.wikimedia.org/w/index.php?curid=4577053)

107 Classical Numismatic Group, Inc. http://www.cngcoins.com, CC BY-SA 2.5 <https://creativecommons.org/licenses/by-sa/2.5>, via Wikimedia Commons, https://commons.wikimedia.org/w/index.php?curid=112987672)

108 Mohammad adil at the English-language Wikipedia, CC BY-SA 3.0 <http://creativecommons.org/licenses/by-sa/3.0/>, via Wikimedia Commons, https://commons.wikimedia.org/w/index.php?curid=5031572)

109 https://commons.wikimedia.org/w/index.php?curid=75718994

110 https://commons.wikimedia.org/w/index.php?curid=17019845

111 Ergovius, CC BY-SA 4.0 <https://creativecommons.org/licenses/by-sa/4.0>, via Wikimedia Commons, https://commons.wikimedia.org/wiki/File:Umayyad_Caliphate_720_AD_(orthographic_projection).svg

112 ByzantineEmpire717+extrainfo+themes.PNG: User:Amonixinatorderivative work: Hoodinski, CC BY-SA 3.0 <http://creativecommons.org/licenses/by-sa/3.0/>, via Wikimedia Commons, https://commons.wikimedia.org/w/index.php?curid=17633268)

113 https://commons.wikimedia.org/w/index.php?curid=3078150

114 https://commons.wikimedia.org/w/index.php?curid=114448071

115 https://commons.wikimedia.org/w/index.php?curid=4140266

116 https://commons.wikimedia.org/w/index.php?curid=42281965)

117 Own work, CC BY 4.0 <https://creativecommons.org/licenses/by/4.0>, via Wikimedia Commons, https://commons.wikimedia.org/w/index.php?curid=120098653

118 Ádám Kolláth, CC BY-SA 4.0 <https://creativecommons.org/licenses/by-sa/4.0>, via Wikimedia Commons, https://commons.wikimedia.org/w/index.php?curid=118846577)

119 https://commons.wikimedia.org/w/index.php?curid=2352102)

120 https://commons.wikimedia.org/w/index.php?curid=123642115

121 Wooofer, CC BY-SA 4.0 <https://creativecommons.org/licenses/by-sa/4.0>, via Wikimedia Commons, https://commons.wikimedia.org/w/index.php?curid=134238343

122 https://commons.wikimedia.org/w/index.php?curid=120420584

123 Unknown 10th-century artist, CC BY-SA 4.0 <https://creativecommons.org/licenses/by-sa/4.0>, via Wikimedia Commons, https://commons.wikimedia.org/w/index.php?curid=125448658

124 https://commons.wikimedia.org/w/index.php?curid=564187

125 https://commons.wikimedia.org/w/index.php?curid=11572784

126 Nécropotame (French version); Cplakidas (English translation), CC BY-SA 2.5 <https://creativecommons.org/licenses/by-sa/2.5>, via Wikimedia Commons, https://commons.wikimedia.org/w/index.php?curid=4078443

127 https://commons.wikimedia.org/w/index.php?curid=17017357

128 MapMaster, CC BY-SA 4.0 <https://creativecommons.org/licenses/by-sa/4.0>, via Wikimedia Commons, https://commons.wikimedia.org/w/index.php?curid=3692668

129 https://commons.wikimedia.org/w/index.php?curid=11349375

130 MapMaster, CC BY-SA 3.0 <http://creativecommons.org/licenses/by-sa/3.0/>, via Wikimedia Commons, https://commons.wikimedia.org/w/index.php?curid=1622291

131 https://commons.wikimedia.org/w/index.php?curid=23724829

132 https://commons.wikimedia.org/w/index.php?curid=5603413

133 https://commons.wikimedia.org/w/index.php?curid=111923528

134 https://commons.wikimedia.org/w/index.php?curid=3107592

135 https://commons.wikimedia.org/wiki/File:John_VI_Kantakouzenos.jpg

136 https://commons.wikimedia.org/wiki/File:Zonaro_GatesofConst.jpg

137 MM, CC BY-SA 4.0 <https://creativecommons.org/licenses/by-sa/4.0>, via Wikimedia Commons, https://commons.wikimedia.org/w/index.php?curid=45598631

138 https://commons.wikimedia.org/w/index.php?curid=11158906

139 Edal Anton Lefterov, CC BY-SA 3.0 <https://creativecommons.org/licenses/by-sa/3.0>, via Wikimedia Commons, https://commons.wikimedia.org/w/index.php?curid=15165689

www.ingramcontent.com/pod-product-compliance
Lightning Source LLC
Chambersburg PA
CBHW072103050526
44107CB00099B/396